Revenant Ecologies

Revenant Ecologies

Defying the Violence of Extinction and Conservation

AUDRA MITCHELL

UNIVERSITY OF MINNESOTA PRESS
MINNEAPOLIS • LONDON

Copyright 2023 by the Regents of the University of Minnesota

All rights reserved. No part of this publication may be reproduced, stored in a retrieval system, or transmitted, in any form or by any means, electronic, mechanical, photocopying, recording, or otherwise, without the prior written permission of the publisher.

Published by the University of Minnesota Press
111 Third Avenue South, Suite 290
Minneapolis, MN 55401-2520
http://www.upress.umn.edu

ISBN 978-1-5179-0680-1 (hc)
ISBN 978-1-5179-0681-8 (pb)

A Cataloging-in-Publication record for this book is available from the Library of Congress.

Printed on acid-free paper

The University of Minnesota is an equal-opportunity educator and employer.

Contents

Preface and Acknowledgments	vii
Introduction: Two Stories/Theories about "Extinction"	1
1. "Megadeath"? Questioning Concepts of "(Mass) Extinction"	33
2. (Bio)Plurality: Difference, Sameness, and the Violence of Biodiversity	59
3. Earth/Body Violence: The Systematic Destruction of (Bio)Plurality	95
4. Invasive States: Colonialism, Capitalism, and Narratives of Invasion	121
5. Genocide, Eliminative Violence, and Extinction	157
6. Apocalyptic Conservation: From "Human Extinction" to "Half-Earth"	197
7. Revenant Ecologies: Practices of Reversal and Return	241
Conclusion: Returning Futures	281
Notes	307
Bibliography	335
Index	361

Preface and Acknowledgments

One of the lessons I've received while writing this book is the importance of introducing oneself—that is, of locating oneself within lines of history, identity, relationships, community, and place. This is a practice that most of my Indigenous interlocutors carry out as a matter of course, yet it is generally ignored and/or frowned upon in Western scholarship. I've been taught that these introductions need to be offered not only to humans I meet but also to the land and water; to plants newly grown, withered, or returned; to animals born, migrating, and dying; to changes in the wind, rain, and weather patterns, in the seasons and years. As these beings, lands, and lifeforms constantly change and renew themselves, I cannot take for granted that they know me, or I them. Introductions make it possible to locate each other, to find shared connections, and to be honest about the nature of relationships so that we can keep each other safe, especially when dynamics of violence are at stake. Where I live, in the settler colonial state currently called Canada, it is important not only to recognize on whose lands one lives but also to acknowledge one's implication in ongoing histories of colonialism and broader social structures, to which my ancestors and I are no exceptions. So I want to take a moment to introduce myself here.

I am a white settler disabled person born in the mid-1980s in what is currently called Calgary, Canada. My mother's family were migrants from near Lviv, Ukraine, and the eastern parts of Poland, who arrived in Treaty 1 territory in the early twentieth century. My father's ancestors, from Scotland and the Isle of Man, benefited from a colonial land-grant program, acquiring lands in the Miramichi Valley (Mi'kmaq'i) in the mid-nineteenth century. Their descendants, working in agriculture and the rail industry, viii *Preface and Acknowledgments*

lived on the lands of Cree, Saulteaux, Métis, and Nakota Sioux people in Treaty 7 territory; the lands of the Niitsitapi, Nakota, and Tusuut'ina in Treaty 6 territory; and the Anishinaabeg, Cree, and Métis in Treaty 1 territory. I spent my first days on Niitsitapi land and was raised on Skwxwú7mesh and xʷməθkʷəẏəm lands. I have lived as part of dominant settler cultures in Northern Ireland, Scotland, Turrbal, and Yuggera Country, the ancestral and treaty lands of the Haudenosaunee, Attawandaron (Neutral), Anishinaabeg, and Huron-Wendat peoples. As a result of my ancestors' efforts to bequeath this future to me and other settlers (Whyte 2017b), I continue to live on stolen lands and to benefit from colonization. As such, it is my responsibility to create good relations with the land and its peoples, to act in solidarity with them, and to respect their laws, including but not limited to treaties. Indeed, this book was written on the Haldimand Tract, which are the ancestral and treaty lands of the Haudenosaunee and Anishinaabe peoples; the Dish with One Spoon Treaty, which are the ancestral and treaty lands of the Haudenosaunee and Anishinaabe peoples and a meeting place for many Indigenous peoples; and Tiohtià'ke/Mooniyang on unceded Kanien'kehà:ka and Anishinaabe lands. I want to offer my gratitude to the peoples who have co-created and cared for these places over millennia, and whose land it will always be.

WRITTEN WITH GRATITUDE . . .

. . . above all, to the lands and waters that have hosted me, whether for a few days or a decade, and to all the beings who co-constitute them. They have all nourished me, challenged me, and taught me different ways of being in different worlds. Most of this book was written on Haudenosaunee and Anishinaabe lands: in Tka:ronto (currently called Toronto), on parts of the Haldimand Tract, and later in Tiohtià'ke/Mooniyang (currently called Montreal). The idea for it germinated on Turrbal lands, in Mianjin (currently called Brisbane). Visits to other lands and countries have also nurtured and guided the work, including Gumbaynggirr and Gadigal Country, and Kānaka Maoli, Sápmi, Chumash, Cahuilla, and Ohlone lands. My understanding of ecologies will always be indebted to the Skwxwú7mesh, xʷməθkʷəẏəm, and Niitsitapi lands who gave me my first experiences of cohabitation and nurtured my love for (bio)plurality. I want to express deep gratitude to the people who take care of these lands, waters, and worlds. Throughout the book you will find the names and citations of the work of dozens of such people who put their lives, bodies, and minds on the line

Preface and Acknowledgments

every day to defend and (re-)create worlds—some of whom I know personally, and others whom I have never met. I want to thank them all from my heart, and my gut, for all that they do.

However, as the Introduction discusses, academic citation practices recognize only a small section of the people and other beings who nurture a piece of work—and only those whose contributions fit within Western knowledge frameworks. This book was also fed and cared for through land-based work and laughter, cooking and eating, crafting, planting, talking and logistics, friction, conflict and grief—that is, by *relationships*—that don't show up explicitly in its pages but without which it would not be possible. So, here, I want to thank a few people, groups, and communities who offered me the gift of relationships. For more than six years, Dr. Judy Da Silva and her family have shared with me not just knowledge but a whole way of being and flourishing with brilliance, empathy, and humor. I also want to thank the group of people who attended Judy's gathering at Slant Lake in 2017, who shared so much about the kinds of futures that are (still) possible. I want to thank the Bawaka Research Collective (especially Djawundil Maymaru, Ritjilili Ganambarr, and Lirrina Munungurr) and Aunty Shaa Smith for welcoming with generosity and care someone from such a different world—and of course, for teaching me to weave! I want to thank the team of gardeners and volunteers at Hoʻoulu ʻAina in the Kalihi Valley, Oʻahu, Hawaiʻi—although my visit with you was short, I will never forget the lessons on revenance I learned there or the feeling of that rich soil sinking into my skin. Thank you to Lorene Sisquoc for showing me what it means to keep knowledge, language, and practices alive across cultures and generations. Miigwech, niá:wen, marsi, and thank you to the community who formed to support the vigil for Indigenous children in midtown Tka:ronto from July 2017 to January 2018—especially to Sigrid, Sue Lynn, and Carrie but also to the elders, the neighbors, the visitors from afar, and the group of Two-Spirit youth who kept the fight going. Being together with you through those seasons altered me in ways I may never fully process. Thank you also to all the participants and community members who generously hosted and/or attended the intercommunity gatherings in Waterloo, Canada (2016), Cambridge, UK (2016), Gumbaynggirr Country, Australia (2017), Rovaniemi, Finland (2017), Ohsweken, Canada (2018), and Kirikiriroa, Aotearoa/New Zealand (2019), and the many online meetings that followed. Whatever grows from those connections, the chance to be together, in those times and places, was transformative.

x *Preface and Acknowledgments*

I also want to thank several groups of nonhumans who have dramatically changed how I understand what it means to cohabitate. Some of them appear in these pages: the gray-headed and black flying foxes of eastern Australia (see chapter 5); Gete Okosomin and her squash, corn, and bean siblings (see Conclusion); and the Black Oak savanna (see Introduction and chapter 1). I also want to thank the family of crows whose nest I was lucky to live next to for four years, who taught me about unconditional love, different formations of family, creating in and with loss and grief, and the creative power of iteration. I want to thank the turkey vultures who accompanied me on so many walks, unafraid to make a connection, letting their gentle presence be felt even as they navigate landscapes of hate and devastation. I want to thank the waters of Niigani-Gichigami, the Pacific Ocean (and its many waters, moana, gaagal, gapu, and other forms), and the Eramosa, Speed, and Kaniatarowanenneh / Gichigami-Ziibi, who held me when I most needed it and who taught me how to sense with my whole body. Thank you to the animals who are my daily companions: my resident cats and the more than thirty other foster animals who were part of my family during the writing of this book—including quite a lot of rabbits, a frog, and even a baby squirrel. And of course, I want to thank Liam, the large, bipedal, mostly furless primate who has been my closest companion for fifteen years.

Last but not least, thank you to the scholars, researchers, students, and colleagues who contributed to this work over the past seven years, in so many ways: through co-creation, coauthorship, and co-organization; through intellectual comradery; through input, response, feedback, or support; through opening up networks and connections and inviting me into your worlds; through emails, posts, and sporadic online chats stretched out across years; or through offering spaces and places to speak, which allowed these ideas to circulate and breathe. To name just a few of them (in alphabetical order): Michelle Bastian; Tony Burke; Aadita Chaudhury; everyone who took part in the Creatures Collective (in lots of different ways); Simon Dalby; Stefanie Fishel; Krisha Hernández; Tim Leduc; Cara Loft; Mko:mose Andrew Judge; Fikile Nxumalo, Veronica Pacini-Ketchabaw and other members of Common Worlds Collective; Corin Parsons; Ni Nok Cuma Gook Amanda Plain; June Rubis; Noah Theriault; Zoe Todd; Ames Val; and Kyle Powys Whyte. I am also grateful to everyone who invited me to and / or participated in the series of talks and events in which this work was shared, including at the University of California, Riverside (United

Preface and Acknowledgments xi

States), the University of New South Wales (Australia), Macquarie University (Australia), the University of Michigan (United States), the University of Western Ontario (Canada), the Second Colloquium on Peaceful Coexistence (Finland), Remembrance Day for Lost Species 2019 (UK; special thanks to Persephone Pearl and the ONCA team); the Volkenkunde Museum (Netherlands; special thanks to Wayne Modest and the Taking Care team); and at Oxford University, UK. Thanks to my current and former colleagues and students at the Balsillie School, the University of York, and elsewhere for bringing so much of yourselves into your work and the issues you care about. I am also deeply grateful to the Social Sciences and Humanities Research Council of Canada (Partnership Development Grant 890-2017-0046 PI Audra Mitchell and Connections Grant 611-2017-0443 PI Audra Mitchell) and the Canada Research Chairs Secretariat (Canada Research Chair 2018-01-01 PI Audra Mitchell) for funding much of the research that has shaped the ideas in this book and for providing me with the time to undertake it. Big thanks to the Independent Social Research Foundation, which has offered financial support but also collegiality, connection, and belief in my work at several pivotal stages.

I also want to thank the two anonymous readers of the manuscript, who offered such thoughtful, constructive, and nuanced feedback. Thanks also to Pieter Martin and the University of Minnesota Press team for a truly engaging and collaborative publishing process.

I am sure that I have forgotten to name many people—not to mention the many other colleagues and friends who have helped sustain me through these years, in other contexts, projects, and subject areas—but know that your contributions are reflected in these pages.

All errors in this work are mine alone.

To the marginalized writers, artists, creators, and knowledge keepers whose work is cited throughout this book: citation is not enough. What you share, and what it costs you to share it, matters more than I can say—and certainly more than I can cite. Thank you for your vital and world-creating labor.

This book is dedicated to the revenants, in all their forms, and to the worlds that are coming (back), which I am grateful to be able to help welcome.

Introduction

Two Stories/Theories about "Extinction"

A wave of erasures is moving across earth, shattering worlds in its wake.[1] It cuts through what Western science calls "species" and "life" but also through fragile membranes of kinship and thick histories that draw together lands, waters, air, and energy in the collaborative work of thriving. Driven by relentless rhythms of consumption, occupation, extraction, and violence, this rupture unfolds unevenly, forcing open the seams of some worlds as it reinforces the borders of others. How can this phenomenon be grasped, explained, and responded to? According to the dominant story/theory, promoted by Western scientists and policymakers, these changes mark the start of earth's "sixth mass extinction event."[2] Pointing to a rapid decrease in species and their populations over the past few decades, these thinkers predict that more than three-quarters of existing life-forms may be destroyed within as little as three centuries (Barnosky et al. 2011; Ceballos et al. 2015). Yet, despite its devastating effects and future implications, most Western scientists view the sixth mass extinction as the unintended consequence of desirable activities intended to improve "human life" or achieve what they regard as "progress" (Wilson 2002; Barnosky 2014). As a result, they call for strategies for *managing* destruction and preserving life-forms for the use and benefit of *humans*, making it possible to sustain existing global political, economic, social, and ecological orders. This approach, conservation, has inspired a global movement, harnessing the attention, resources, and influence of states, international organizations, NGOs, and millions of citizens, especially in the Global North. Since the late 1980s, conservation has focused on the need to protect biodiversity, or the variety of life-forms and the functions they play within ecosystems, as a stock of resources for human use, benefit, and enjoyment. Reflecting the imperatives of international politics, conservation is often presented as an ultimatum, or a zero-sum game. If it is not immediately and unreservedly adopted, expanded, and intensified, many scientists warn, we may be left to inhabit a planet stripped of "its most precious treasure . . . LIFE!" (Ceballos 2016, 285). Humans are not immune from this threat: indeed, emerging discourses on human extinction (see chapter 6) intensify fear and urgency, framing conservation as the only possible response and as a now-or-never bid to protect the survival of "humanity." In so doing, these discourses mask the profound forms of violence on which conservation is based, including colonialism, racism and white supremacy, extractive capitalism, anthropocentrism, heteronormativity, and ableism. Indeed, one of the main aims of this book is to show that extinction *and* conservation are manifestations of these global structures of interlocking, mutually magnifying violence. To uncritically pursue increasingly ambitious conservation plans—including late conservationist E. O. Wilson's plan to convert half the earth's surface to national parks or President Joe Biden's goal of preserving 30 percent of U.S. land, fresh water, and ocean by 2030—is to entrench rather than to transform these structures of violence.

However, extinction, conservation, and biodiversity are not the only frameworks that can describe, explain, and respond to the violent destruction of earths' plural worlds and life-forms. Many distinct knowledge systems, in particular those tended by Indigenous, BIPOC, and majority world thinkers, offer stories/theories of extinction that better describe the role of violence, law-breaking, and the failure or refusal to maintain good relations—often originating from sources outside an affected world.[3] Many of these stories/theories point to forms of violence that target and break down the relationships between particular communities and their other-than-human kin, including the structures of violence mentioned previously. As such, they often call for radically different modes of response: instead of seeking to sustain harmful structures, they demand the total *transformation* of dominant political, economic, and ecological orders. What's more, they provide alternative understandings of what is destroyed by what Western science calls "extinction": not just the resources or capital implied by terms like "species," "ecosystems," or "biodiversity" but irreplaceable relationships and the conditions of co-constitution that enable the thriving of *plural* life-forms.

Introduction 3

Foregrounding this latter set of stories/theories, this book aims to shift popular understandings of extinction, reframing it as an expression of global structures of violence. Instead of agreeing that conservation is the only possible response to extinction, it argues that multiple struggles against global structures of violence—including anti-colonization, anti-racism, land reclamation, BIPOC resurgences, the revitalization of BIPOC legal systems, and modes of governance—are vital and necessary in protecting earth's multiple possible futures. It also resists white apocalyptic future narratives (Mitchell and Chaudhury 2020) that leverage the threat of a sixth mass extinction to entrench existing power structures and close down imaginaries of alternative futures. Without diminishing the gravity and enormity of the harms in question, the book pays close attention to narratives that counter the all-or-nothing logics of mainstream conservation thinking and mainstream futurisms. Indeed, it ends by examining the idea of "revenance"—that is, the theory that this time of immense rupture and destruction is also shaped by currents of return, of tending and renewing life toward alternative futures. In so doing, it aims to support and foreground projects of global political transformation that work toward dissolving global structures of violence and seeding *multiple* futures of rich coexistence.

TWO STORIES/THEORIES OF "EXTINCTION"

To better understand this argument, it is useful to begin with two very different stories about extinction, each emerging from specific worlds, places, and cultural contexts and speaking to broader global or cosmological contexts.[4] These two stories/theories offer different accounts of what extinction is, who and what is responsible for causing and responding to it, and by what means it should be addressed. By comparing these stories/theories, we can begin to challenge the dominance of discourses of the sixth mass extinction and conservation and to see that there is more than one way of understanding and responding to the destruction of life-forms.

STORY/THEORY I: THE "SIXTH MASS EXTINCTION"

In the geological here and now, a wave of biological extinctions is taking place. Currently it is accelerating. . . . The rainforests . . . are inexorably being cut to ribbons. In less than a century most will be gone. Millions of species—lemurs, parrots, beetles, frogs, spiders, orchids, jaguars—are set to vanish. . . .

4 Introduction

> At current rates, another century or two should see us competing with the great extinction events of the past. . . . We [humans] are briefly in the golden age of our power, our dominance. But we are destined to extinction also. . . . Once a geological age or two has passed, there will be nothing but the odd bone or gold ring to show that we were ever here. (Zalasiewicz 2008, 2, 125, 131)

> An Armageddon is approaching at the beginning of the third millennium. But it is not the cosmic war and fiery collapse of mankind foretold in sacred [Judeo-Christian] scripture. It is the wreckage of the planet by an exuberantly plentiful and ingenious humanity . . . [that is] in a final struggle with the rest of life. . . . The race is now on between the techno-scientific forces that are destroying the living environment and those that can be harnessed to save it. (Wilson 2002, xxiii, 43)

These quotes embody the major themes of stories/theories of the sixth mass extinction and the global conservation movement: the rapid destruction of earthly life, the urgency of a comprehensive response, and the ultimate threat to human survival. These themes entwine as parts of a vast, epic, multivoiced story/theory centered on a common protagonist: humanity, who confronts a profound existential crisis. Brilliant but wayward, with an immense appetite for growth, exploration, and improvement, this subject is now forced to face the unintended consequences of its efforts to better itself and follow its natural urge toward development and progress (Wilson 2002; Barnosky 2014). As a result of its frenzied striving for progress, humanity has begun to undermine the basis of its own survival. As a result, it must now take on a hero's task: stopping the hemorrhaging of life-forms. To complete this task, humanity must defeat the fearsome four horsemen of extinction (Diamond 1984): habitat degradation, destruction, and overexploitation; coextinctions; the direct killing of plants and animals; and the transmission of invasive species across the planet. The stakes are almost indescribably high: "what happens here on Earth, in this century, could conceivably make the difference between a near eternity filled with ever more complex and subtle forms of life and one filled with nothing but base matter" (Rees 2003, 7). Locked into this cosmic battle, humanity must marshal its most powerful weapons—science, technology, and knowledge—to conserve what is left of life, manage its processes, increase its diversity, restore its systemic functioning, and perhaps even bring extinct beings back to life. In this story/theory, humanity's success will determine whether it is able to continue its growth, flourishing and evolving, or whether it, like 99 percent of the life-forms that have existed on earth, will lapse into extinction.

Fundamentally apocalyptic in its tone and content, this story/theory invokes Manichean struggles between cosmic forces of good and evil, darkness and light, emptiness and plenitude. Despite its grounding in the apparently secular Western sciences, it explicitly invokes images of reckoning, hell, cosmic punishment, and piety (in the form of conservation) that speak to the worldviews of the Euro-descendent peoples to whom it is primarily directed and whose origin stories it centers.[5] Indeed, echoing uncomfortably with millenarian discourses, this story describes the current historical juncture as cosmological crossroads embodied in a biological and geological event: a mass extinction. Defined as the elimination of 75 percent or more of existing species in a relatively short geological timespan, such phenomena have occurred five times previously in earth's history. Anthony Barnosky (2011) and his team contend that current extinction rates may in fact be higher than those that sparked the previous five mass extinction events, perhaps "severe enough to carry extinction magnitudes to the Big Five benchmark in as little as three centuries" (Barnosky et al. 2011, 60). Similarly, Gerardo Ceballos (2015) and his team find that the extinctions that have taken place between 1500 and 1900 would have taken several millennia to occur at the background or baseline rate of extinction (see chapter 1). According to these authors, "these estimates reveal an exceptionally rapid loss of biodiversity over the last few centuries, indicating that a sixth mass extinction is already under way" (Ceballos et al. 2015). Indeed, a 2016 report by the Worldwide Fund for Nature (WWF 2016) suggests that ecological changes in the past four decades have resulted in a 58 percent decrease in populations of the animal species it analyzes (see chapter 6). Yet despite overwhelming evidence of major changes to earth's ecosystems, future extinction scenarios are notoriously difficult to model accurately because of the absence—and indeed the impossibility—of directly observable evidence. Since the fossil record for life-forms that have gone extinct since the last mass extinction event is patchy (Plotnick, Smith, and Lyons 2016), analysts must extrapolate and infer from past extinction events, data on current extirpations, or representative samples, as in the WWF report.[6] This can produce distorted predictions, including the under- or overestimation of extinction rates, patterns, and trends (Régnier et al. 2015; Lamkin and Miller 2016). Nonetheless, discourses on extinction are shaped by an overarching narrative of declension (Heise 2010) that taps into fears of the apocalypse that are widespread within Euro-descendent cultures (see Colebrook 2014).

Central to this narrative is a tragic irony and fable: in its efforts for improvement and a better life, amid its greed and mastery of ignorance, humanity has caused the harms that threaten life on earth. Unlike the cyanobacterial blooms and asteroid collisions that put an end to millions of earlier life-forms, the current crisis is described as "something we are 'doing to ourselves'" (Barnosky 2014, loc. 574): as science writer Elizabeth Kolbert (2014, 3) puts it, "we [humans] are the asteroid." Crucially, the term "human" is used here in a universal sense, as if responsibility for the crisis could be equally attributed to all members of *Homo sapiens* across vast differences of time, space, and culture. By presenting current patterns of extinction as generically anthropogenic, or the results of *human* activity, this story/ theory obscures the vast inequalities of responsibility and suffering, along with immense differences in political and economic organization, that attend global patterns of extinction and other forms of ecological violence (see Malm and Hornberg 2014; Davis and Todd 2017; and chapter 6).[7]

The same figure, humanity, is also cast as the potential victim of ecological collapse and the predicted crises to follow, including massive disruptions to economic and food systems, mass deaths, authoritarian governance, and global warfare (Barnosky 2014; Oreskes and Conway 2014). Some commentators recognize how unevenly harm is distributed across human groups. For instance, the Convention on Biological Diversity (CBD 2010a, 5) argues that the poor, who "tend to be most immediately dependent on [ecosystems,] would suffer first and most severely." However, the dominant narrative presents these possibilities as threats to the survival of humanity as a whole. Indeed, the prospect of human extinction lurks menacingly behind narratives of the sixth mass extinction, as illustrated by Jan Zalasiewicz's (2008) story quoted in the first epigraph of this section. Zalasiewicz's book is just one example of a growing genre of speculative (non)fiction, often written by science journalists, that imagines the demise of *Homo sapiens* (see chapter 7) in a biological *and* figural or symbolic sense (see Colebrook 2014; Mitchell 2017b). Some queer, feminist, and anti-colonial theorists see this juncture as an opportunity for transcending entrenched inequalities rooted in race, gender, sexuality, disability, and species (see Braidotti 2013, 2022; Colebrook 2014; Mitchell and Chaudhury 2020; Piepzna-Samarasinha 2023; and chapter 7). However, most discussion of human extinction takes place in the context of existential risk, a discipline concerned largely with prolonging the survival, enhancement, and ongoing (posthuman) evolution of humanity at all costs, often in ways that perpetuate inequalities and harms (see Mitchell and Chaudhury 2020). As this book argues, such discourses frequently justify widespread and pervasive forms of violence and oppression as part of their zero-sum narrative, which pits considerations of multi-life-form justice against the posited existential threat of human extinction.

Not least among these efforts is the practice of conservation, which is presented in Western scientific stories/theories of extinction as the primary—if not the only—possible mode of response. Mainstreamed in the late twentieth century, the idea has become commonplace in much of the Global North and is generally presented as an unequivocally good practice; indeed, as this book illustrates, critiques of conservation emerging from Western scientific discourses tend to focus on whether particular projects meet their intended goals or targets, *not* on critically questioning the practice or its logics. However, decades of resistance by Indigenous, BIPOC, anti-colonial, and other groups affected by conservation projects originating in the Global North shed a different light on conservation's roots, legacy, and future goals, including its entwinement with colonialism, capitalism, land grabbing, and the destruction of Indigenous sovereignties.

Conservation in its dominant forms should be understood as an outgrowth of global colonialism. Indeed, as William Adams's (2004) work shows, the practice emerged from the efforts of colonial governors to protect stocks of wildlife for elite hunters in the face of heightening pressure on ecosystems from settlement, land clearing, and extermination by lower-class settlers; the displacement of Indigenous communities and resulting disruptions to ecosystems; and overhunting by elites themselves. Maintaining distinctions of class and race was also a major motivation of the formation of wildlife reserves, and eventually the global national parks movement in the late 1970s, starting with the creation of Yellowstone National Park in California in 1872. Promoting access for white middle-class people to "untouched" nature and recreation, the creation of national parks has frequently involved the violent displacement of the people who co-created and cared for these lands for millennia (see Brockington and Igoe 2006). In addition, it has helped create and sustain differences of race, class, and disability by creating spaces designed to reflect and foster white, wealthy, ruggedly masculine, and nondisabled forms of citizenship among visitors (D. Taylor 2016; Jaquette Ray and Sibara 2017).

Through the twentieth century, buoyed by increased public engagement with national and/or wildlife parks, international and global organizations such as the International Union for Conservation of Nature (IUCN) and the WWF gained significant international support and membership. Nonetheless, despite several failed attempts in the early twentieth century to create an overarching international governing body for conservation, it was not until the early 1990s that an international framework gained significant state recognition. Emerging during the Rio Earth Summit in 1992, the *Convention on Biological Diversity* fused increasingly influential discourses on biodiversity (see chapter 2) with state-centric notions of sovereignty and resource management. It begins by stating unequivocally that "states have sovereign rights over their own biological resources . . . [and] are responsible for conserving their biological diversity and for using *their* biological resources in a sustainable manner" (UN 1992, 1, emphasis mine). This wording reflects not only the extension of state sovereignty into the ecological sphere (see M. Smith 2011) but also Cold War–era anxieties over the integrity and strength of the nation-state in the aftermath of decolonization movements and Soviet expansionism. Importantly, in so doing, it entrenches claims to state-based sovereignty that also work to preclude other assertions of sovereignty, including those made by Indigenous peoples.[8] Working within this discourse of ownership, the CBD also devotes substantial attention to regulating the *ex situ* use and management of biodiversity, including genetic materials that may prove valuable in industries such as pharmaceuticals and foods.[9] As part of its effort to regulate such practices, including "bioprospecting" or "biopiracy" (Shiva 2002), in which private actors mine ecosystems for valuable genetic materials, and in line with its statist commitments, the CBD prioritizes *in situ* approaches to conservation such as the creation of reserves and parks. However, as chapter 1 discusses, *ex situ* conservation such as species survival plans, genetic libraries, and even plans to "de-extinct" life-forms have all become central to conservation practices and involve significant international cooperation. More recently, notably in the 2010 Nagoya protocol (CBD 2010b), the UN has acknowledged that bioprospecting and biopiracy also violate Indigenous rights by appropriating not only resources but also the intergenerational knowledge regarding them. However, this protocol continues to frame biodiversity in terms of Eurocentric and state-centric notions of property and intellectual property, which clashes with many Indigenous political and legal systems.

At the same time, since the late 1980s, international conservation efforts became entwined with two other powerful emerging doctrines: economic development and human rights. As the commercial and scientific value of biodiversity was rapidly extracted and exported to serve global markets, Indigenous, peasant, and rural communities were increasingly prevented from accessing ecosystems and economic benefits. As a result, many Indigenous and rural communities ignored and/or deliberately broke externally imposed conservation restrictions (for instance, constraints on hunting, gathering, or burning in national parks, or killing animals that harmed their crops) in order to survive in rapidly shifting economic contexts. As Paige West (2004) demonstrates, major conservation bodies such as the IUCN and the UN Environment Programme (UNEP) blamed poverty and traditional subsistence practices for the failure of their projects and worked more aggressively to integrate the offending communities within conservation economies. This argument became the basis for a wide-ranging set of conservation-as-development (West 2016) schemes, in which communities living in areas designated for conservation by international organizations would be induced (or compelled) to accept restrictions and actively participate in conservation in exchange for economic opportunities, education, infrastructure, medicine, and other goods. Although these programs were billed as win-win arrangements, West (2016, 35) contends that they were ultimately concerned with "changing the actions and practices of local people in order to meet the end goal of conservation." This involved shifting them from diverse subsistence practices to commodity-based systems of production "sanctioned by conservation biologists and development practitioners as environmentally appropriate" (West 2016, 35).[10] In other words, conservation-as-development constituted a widespread erasure of the very lifeways responsible for creating and maintaining the biodiverse ecosystems over which it sought control. Importantly, since the 1990s, this discourse has shifted from development and increasingly toward the seven dimensions of human security: physical, environmental, food, health, political, economic, and cultural security, which, together, are expected to provide a good standard of human life. The destruction of biodiversity is understood to threaten each of these forms of security—for instance, the extinction of important plant species might undermine food security, ecosystem integrity, and cultural knowledge and create physical insecurity through economic consequences. Just as it was previously presented as a form of development, contemporary conservation is often framed as a source of human security (see CBD 2010a; WWF 2016) and, more recently, as a way of meeting the UN Sustainable Development Goals (SDGs) (UN 2015).

The fusion of concepts of biodiversity with various forms of economic value has intensified since the early 2000s with the emergence of the financial conservation paradigm (see chapter 2). Within this framework, biodiversity is treated as a form of capital and conservation is increasingly framed as a matter of financial management, as reflected by the appointment of former private sector CEOs to top positions in major conservation organizations (see West 2016 and chapter 6). One of the prominent offshoots of this movement has been the effort to convince communities in the Global South to access global capital from which they are structurally excluded by using biodiversity as a banking system or insurance policy (Roe et al. 2010). Stressing the non-use value (MEA n.d.) of ecosystems, this strategy involves convincing Global South communities to abstain from traditional relations with ecosystems and to transform them to conform with international conservation standards so that their services remain available for use by citizens of the Global North. As such, Global South communities are incentivized to absorb the ecological harms created by high-consumption lifestyles in the Global North (see McAfee 1998; Sian Sullivan 2013).[11]

More recently, eco-modernist approaches have sought to merge financial and economic conservation strategies with concerns about human security, eschewing images of wild nature and fortress conservation (Brockington 2002) and seeking to steer the planet toward biodiverse futures through market-based innovation, intensive management, and interventions that include the design and engineering of entire ecosystems (Kareiva and Marvier 2012).[12] Arguing that "human activities" are "utterly pervasive" throughout the biosphere and have helped constitute biodiversity as it is experienced today, Peter Kareiva and Michelle Marvier embrace the explicit (re)design of ecosystems. The "human-centered landscapes" they envision are intended to center human needs, including rights, justice, fairness, and equality, with the aim of "jointly maximiz[ing] benefits to people and to biodiversity" (Kareiva and Marvier 2012, 962). Kareiva and Marvier insist that "conservationists must work with corporations" (2012, 967), including by designing conservation projects that accommodate extraction. So although they claim to champion the rights and needs of the global poor, theirs is ultimately an "environmentalism of the rich" (Dauvergne 2016) that hinges on and sustains existing, deeply unequal economic and power structures. At the same time, while it recognizes that ecosystems are co-constituted by and with humans, it problematically equates the violent and globally destructive world-forming powers of capitalism and colonialism with the long-term co-creation of ecosystems by Indigenous and BIPOC peoples.

This brief critique of the mainstream conservation movement shows that it is deeply embedded in colonial, capitalist, and racializing discourses. Of course, Western stories / theories about extinction are certainly not homogenous; many thinkers within these traditions have highlighted these connections (see, for instance, Barnosky 2014; Klein 2014; Haraway 2015; J. Moore 2015). However, they rarely center or theorize extinction in detail, often mentioning it briefly as part of a list of disruptions, treating it as part of a broader syndrome associated with climate change or the Anthropocene, or assuming that it is an (indirect) outcome, rather than a direct expression, of violence. What's more, these critical thinkers are often surprisingly uncritical in their use of terms such as "extinction," "species," "biodiversity," and "conservation."[13] Other scholars in the Western tradition address the political drivers and ethical implications of extinction from within more-than-human, postcolonial / decolonial, feminist, and other critical traditions arising from European knowledge systems, sometimes in conversation with diverse Indigenous knowledge systems (see, for instance, Rose 2011a; van Dooren 2014; Kirksey 2015; Heise 2016). However, these thinkers tend to focus on specific instances of extinction and / or on particular species or ecosystems (albeit in multiple settings) rather than centering the broad, global structures that drive them. Yet, despite this growing body of critical work, the mainstream discourses outlined here remain overwhelmingly dominant within international politics, policymaking, and public discussion of extinction, biodiversity, and conservation. Political support and funding have followed, making conservation a significant form of global governance in the twenty-first century and a hegemonic discourse to the point that critiquing it is often interpreted as a denial of the threats to earth's life-forms.[14] My aim in this book is not to vilify the scientists, policymakers, practitioners, and indeed community-based conservationists who have spent decades honing these approaches, nor to dismiss the important insights they can offer. Rather, my goal is to approach the extinction / conservation / biodiversity narrative as *one* powerful story / theory in a context of diverse others that overlap, confirm, and contest several of its elements and that challenge its logic of no alternatives. With this in mind, let's turn to a

12   Introduction

second, very different story/theory of extinction and possible modes of response.

STORY/THEORY 2: THE TREATY WITH THE HOOF CLAN

According to an Anishinaabe story/theory, a long time ago, the Waawasashkeshigook (deer), Moozoog (moose), and Adikwag (caribou)—the Hoof Clan—suddenly disappeared.[15] At first, none of the people noticed, but after a while, some changes became obvious: in the autumn, the hunters came back with no meat, and when the snow fell, not a single hoof print was seen in the snow. By Ziigwan (spring), no one in the community had seen a moose or caribou for nearly a year. Sad, guilty, and hungry, the Anishinaabeg and their relatives became irritable and fell out with each other—the dogs wagged their tails sharply, the eagles started to bite, the bears growled, and the skunks sprayed everywhere. Finally, the people decided to take action to restore harmony in their world. They rose before sunrise and lit a sacred fire, prayed, spoke their minds, sang, and offered semaa (tobacco). Together, they decided to send four runners—Ziigwaan, Niibin (summer), Dagwaagin (autumn), and Bboon (winter)—to search for the hoofed animals. The first three of these runners returned without news. But eventually, an exhausted Bboon returned from the far north, where he had met a young deer. The deer had informed Bboon that the Hoof Clan had left the territory permanently because the Anishinaabeg were wasting meat, not sharing food, and failing to treat the bodies of the hoofed animals with respect. The Anishinaabeg decided to send a delegation of diplomats, spiritual people, and mediators to negotiate with the Hoof Clan.

Through these negotiations, the delegation learned that the Hoof Clan, fed up with being bound to a treaty that the other partner (the people) did not uphold, had followed their allies the crows north as an act of resistance. The Anishinaabe delegation listened carefully and acknowledged the mistakes they had made. Then each party talked, reflected, and decided what they were willing to give up so that the others could thrive. Eventually, they arrived at an agreement: the Anishinaabeg would honor and respect the Hoof Clan in life and death. They would take only what they needed, use the flesh of the animals they killed carefully, offer semaa with the killing of each animal to acknowledge the suffering caused to the Hoof Clan, and seek other food sources when their four-footed relatives were struggling. What's more, the Anishinaabe delegation promised to protect the homes of the Hoof animals for *each of their respective* future generations,

Introduction 13

and those of the other life-forms who depended on them. In exchange, the Hoof Nation agreed to offer their bodies to the Anishinaabe so that the people could feed their families and continue to flourish. After this, the hoofed animals returned to Anishinaabeg territory, where they will stay—for as long as this agreement is honored.

The story of the Treaty with the Hoof Clan offers a distinct theory of what Western science calls "extinction": in response to *violence, disrespect,* or the *violation of agreements* and *relational commitments,* the animals exercise their agency to withdraw and renegotiate the conditions of coexistence. This relationship is reciprocal, based on mutual respect and the nuanced forms of compromise necessary to honor very different forms of life and their needs. In addition, this story / theory tells us that extinction is a matter of lively, dynamic political and ethical contestation—not simply a matter of management imposed on the basis of abstract frameworks, models, or predictions. As such, it suggests, responding to extinction needs to be *political and ethical*: to attend to the specificity of relations; to respect different forms of agency, interests, and futures; and to understand flourishing as a shared project carried out with myriad other beings and life-forms.

The Anishinaabeg peoples are not alone in framing extinction in such terms—distinct yet resonant stories / theories can be found in many other knowledge systems. For example, a story / theory shared across many Inuit communities concerns a being called Sedna, an indweller of the deep ocean who was formerly a young Inuit woman.[16] When in human form, Sedna resisted the pressure her father placed on her to marry. One night, a fulmar (in some versions of the narrative, an Inuit sled dog) snuck into her home and had sex with her, after which her father banished her to an island to live with the bird / man. Eventually tiring of life on the island, she summoned her father, who killed the fulmar man and reclaimed his kin. However, on the return journey, the other fulmars whipped up a powerful storm in retaliation for the death of their kinsman. To appease the wildly flapping birds, Sedna's father threw his daughter overboard. As she clung frantically to the side of the boat, her father chopped off her fingers, joints, hands, and forearms, which turned into seals, walruses, and whales and swam away. Sedna herself sank to the bottom of the sea, where she transformed into a powerful being responsible for taking care of all marine animals and capable of controlling their movements.[17] Since then, it has been the duty of Inuit people to uphold the protocols that keep Sedna happy, including offering songs, giving newly killed seals a drink of melted snow (not salt water), and gifting part of the liver of the first-killed sea mammal of the season to Sedna.[18] If Sedna is happy with the behavior of her Inuit kin, their hunts will be successful and the people will have enough to eat. However, if the people break the protocols, she may call the animals back to her and prevent them from moving by tangling them in her long hair. In order to eat again, the Inuit must restore the protocols and may also send a medicine man to the bottom of the sea to comb and braid Sedna's hair.

In recent years, Inuit knowledge keepers have drawn on this story to understand unusual animal behaviors—for instance, unseasonal hunting by polar bears, the northward migration of southern species, and the overall decline in Arctic char (Leduc 2010)—related to climate change. Far from contesting or denying the warming of the global climate, this interpretation demonstrates that it is a *harm* stemming from the breaking of protocols and deep-seated relationships. Some tellings of Sedna's story directly address complex forms of land-based sexual violence (see chapter 3). For instance, in one version, Sedna is a survivor of sexual abuse perpetrated by her father. She demands that shamans are sent to heal her and restore her ability to experience sexual pleasure in order that the animals can be released (Ipellie 1993). Here, the healing of gendered bodies, sexualities, and sensualities, including those of the land itself—not necessarily in the form of *reproduction,* the centerpiece of many conservation programs—is understood as crucial to ecological balance.

Kānaka Maoli knowledge-keeper Davianna Pōmaika`i McGregor (2007, 222) offers another resonant story/theory, in which the Akule stopped frequenting the ocean between Puko'o and Wailua on the island of Moloka'i for a period of nearly twenty years.[19] According to Kūpuna Waldemar Duvauchelle, the fish disappeared after an old man used a kuū'ula stone to pray for fish, who arrived in such numbers that they flooded the cove and, not being caught fast enough, began to die from lack of oxygen.[20] Although the fishers tried to chase the fish out of the pond, they all eventually perished, and since that day, no Akule returned to Puko'o. Another kūpuna, Daniel Naki, attributed the disappearance of the fish to problems between the fishermen.[21] According to him, the fishermen kept grumbling among themselves, wishing each other bad luck. Hearing their discord, the fish disappeared, refusing to return until more respectful relations were restored. In this story, the desire of human fishers to access more fish than they needed (what Western scientists working in the area often call overfishing) along with competition and ill will between humans not only altered

Introduction 15

the fishes' ecosystem and population dynamics but also disrupted the terms of the ancient relationship between humans and Akule.

While each of these stories/theories offers insights into sudden absences of life-forms, it is not helpful to look for exact analogues with what Western science describes as extinctions (or extirpations); instead, one should focus on the distinctness of each story/theory from Western ones (and from each other). Attempts to make direct comparisons between Western scientific stories/theories and Indigenous ones—including in the context of traditional ecological knowledge (TEK) initiatives—too often frame the former as a template against which the latter are measured for accuracy or used (selectively) as data to supplement or confirm Western theories (see Cruikshank 2004; D. McGregor 2005; Whyte 2017). But it is not simply the case that the phenomena called "extinction" in the Western sciences are *experienced* differently by different peoples (which they are) but also that diverse stories/theories describe *different phenomena*. Extinction is only one framework by which to address the disruption of life-forms across the planet. What's more, the fact that certain stories/theories may remain opaque or beyond the full grasp of outsiders (myself included) does not mean that these knowledge systems *lack* concepts or other means for understanding the phenomena in question.[22] In addition, the idea of extinction as it is articulated in Western scientific and policy discourses may not make sense within certain knowledge systems, ecosystems, and/or cosmovisions. For example, West (2004) shares that many Gimi people she worked with in the eastern highlands of Papua New Guinea only began to use the concept of extinction after working with international conservation organizations for several years. Doing so required overriding some key elements of their knowledge system, including the idea that nothing can be permanently lost or destroyed. According to West (2004, xvi), for some (especially older) Gimi, the idea of extinction is

> antithetical to the way that they see the world. For older Gimi, there is no such thing as the loss of something. All matter has been here for all eternity, and when things die or disappear, they are simply changing form. People's bodies and life forces go back to their ancestral forest, the reserve for matter, as do other things that seem to go away.

It is not the case that these members of the Gimi community do not *understand* the idea of extinction, lack frameworks for explaining changes in the ecosystem, or are mythical and unscientific in their beliefs. Instead, they *disagree with* or *diverge from* the beliefs of conservationists, hold *alternative* ideas about the sources of changes, and *pose distinct questions* regarding what is happening and how to respond. By learning from examples like these, in this book I aim to work respectfully across multiple stories/theories without presuming the primacy or superiority of any of them.

One of the major aims of this book is to challenge the dominance and homogeneity of the term "extinction." This is the reason why I place the term in scare quotes—certainly not to deny or cast doubt on the phenomena it seeks to explain. I continue to use the term "extinction" throughout the book for two main reasons. First, Western scientific and political stories/theories of extinctions offer valuable insights and frameworks; they are simply not the *only* frameworks available, nor necessarily the most desirable, effective, or just. Second, I want to address the *structures of extinction*—that is, the set of ideas, material assemblages, flows of power and resource, ideologies and social patterns, and subjectivities and discourses that the idea generates (see Mitchell 2017a). Just as concepts such as race and gender are socially constructed *and* have material, tangible manifestations and consequences, so does extinction, and it is my intention to critically engage these.

Further, I do not mean to dismiss or ignore the *convergences* and *resonances* across the multiple stories/theories discussed in this book. Indeed, all the stories/theories discussed so far identify the withdrawal, dislocation, or elimination of life-forms as a major disruption to ecosystems and multispecies worlds, and the different roles of (specific groups of) humans in causing this. However, the plural ways in which these issues are presented and interpreted have vastly different implications for response and action. For instance, the stories/theories of the Hoof Clan, Sedna, and the Akule point to the role of *particular groups* of humans and their relations with *specific* more-than-human kin, each linked to unique places and histories, and to precise responsibilities. This contrasts greatly from the generic universalism of the Western scientific story/theory in which an abstract figure of humanity is collectively, but in a general way, responsible for causing and responding to global ecological harm. Further complication arises in the meetings between these distinct worlds, including when the protocols or laws between a human community and other life-form(s) are disrupted by a third party (for instance, settlers or multinational companies). Such third parties are not embedded in orders that they disrupt and may not be held responsible under their own systems for harms caused to others. Indeed, while extinction is generally understood as a bad thing within Western scientific discourses and some of its drivers (e.g., poaching, extralegal logging) are illegal, others are considered benign or even desirable—and extinction itself is not illegal. Being locked into a dynamic of unequal responsibility (and sometimes impunity for the third party) dumps the full weight of healing ruptured relations onto the shoulders of directly affected communities.

Second, in the three stories/theories discussed here, the Hoof Clan, Sedna, and the Akule do not simply sit back and passively go extinct. On the contrary, they possess and assert agency by choosing the conditions of their relationships with their human kin by refusing to hold up their end of an agreement broken by the other party. These beings are not mere resources to be managed but rather partners in co-flourishing and governance (Watts 2013), participants in the bettering of their conditions (see S. Taylor 2017), interlocutors to be respected and with whom to be respectfully negotiated. What's more, the terms of their relationships with humans are not one-size-fits-all but rather specific to their needs, histories, and collective futures—for instance, one would not attempt to coax the Akule back to the cove by working to appease Sedna. Addressing their absence requires learning about their life-form, the lands and worlds it is part of, and what is needed to make amends. This includes awareness of other life-forms and their respective needs and futures and performing ceremonies and other actions specific to them. At the same time, these stories/theories are not narrowly local, as international discourses often imply; they each reflect comprehensive cosmovisions that are aware of broader worlds and spheres. Nor are these stories/theories merely repositories of empirical data; rather, they also offer what Euro-descendent thought categorizes as theoretical, abstract, or meta concepts (see Deloria 2003; Kuokkanen 2007). For example, as settler Australian scholar Margaret Somerville and Gumbayngirr thinker Tony Perkins (2011, 4–5) write, Gumbayngirr people understand Corindi beach as the "centre of a contemporary global world." Similarly, for Kānaka peoples, the piko (umbilical cord) embodies the idea that one is grounded in a particular place, which is nonetheless the center of a broad cosmos (Corntassel et al. 2018). What's more, some communities, such as the Sarayaku Kichwa community (Kichwa of Sarayaku 2018), explicitly articulate (and generously offer) their unique forms of inter-life-form relations as models for others—including the international community—to respectfully adopt. Although it is both unwise and harmful to uncritically transfer ideas from one context to another, it is not the case that Indigenous and BIPOC knowledges are narrowly "local" in their focus and concerns; this is a construct of colonial systems that engender these scales as forms of power.

Finally, in the Anishinaabeg, Inuit, and Kānaka stories/theories shared here, the absencing of life-forms is a grievous harm, but it is not necessarily final or irreversible (and its ethical weight does not depend on its irreversibility). *If* the ethical-legal wrongs that caused the withdrawal of life-forms are sufficiently and appropriately redressed, then it is *possible*—although not guaranteed—that these beings will return. One might protest what these stories refer to is not what Western science codes as "extinction" but rather something more akin to population decline, or perhaps to extirpation (the elimination of a life-form in a specific locale or bio-region). In addition, thinkers in the Western scientific tradition might warn that treating extinction as *potentially* reversible could lead to a slippery slope, in which even the *possibility* of reversibility is interpreted as license to continue harmful activities (an argument sometimes applied to de-extinction narratives; see Wilson 2016). However, these arguments are based on the troubling assumption that simply *replacing* (simulacra) of life-forms would restore *relations* with them and make reparations for harms. In contrast, the stories/theories detailed here prescribe precise codes of conduct and difficult transformations that require significant sacrifice and permanent, encompassing societal change. They offer no guarantees; nor do they foreclose on all future possibilities of restoring relations with the absent(ed) beings, as do narratives of total and irreversible destruction. The milieu of uncertainty—the conditional, contingent possibility of *revenance*—held in these stories/theories offers grounds for resisting totalizing apocalyptic narratives and holding open plural futures. It is in this space of possibilities, plural, that this book maneuvers.

THINKING WITH BIPOC KNOWLEDGES
AS A WHITE SETTLER SCHOLAR

Before beginning to delve deeper into these ideas, it is important to say a few words about the ethically ambivalent process of working with Indigenous knowledges and stories/theories as a white settler scholar. This reflection is offered not with the intention of absolving myself of guilt or responsibility but rather with the goal of acknowledging the violent dynamics in which

Introduction · 19

this work takes place and demonstrating a commitment to minimizing the harms that result from Western academic research. My approach is deeply shaped by the works of Indigenous thinkers and from continuing conversations with scholars and knowledge keepers from multiple communities. However, my thinking is not *of* or *from* these communities, and I do not have the blood memory, collective, embodied, or other capacities that enable understanding of the full nature of these knowledges. I am a *student* of these knowledge systems—*not* an expert in or of them, nor a keeper of them. As such, my analyses should never be used to replace, displace, or discredit those to whom the knowledge belongs and part of whom it is.

I want this book to critique pervasive logics of co-constitutive violence—including colonization, whiteness, genocide, extractive capitalism, racism, ableism, and anthropocentrism—that shape patterns of extinction.[23] However, as a person whose subjectivity has been formed, habituated (Shannon Sullivan 2019), structurally invested (Harris 1993; Moreton-Robinson 2015), and in crucial ways rewarded by this system, my efforts to critique such logics of violence will likely always reproduce aspects of them. In addition, my specific subjectivity means that it will always be difficult (if not impossible) for me to find fulcrums of critique outside whiteness and Eurocentric and colonial thought. What's more, while I may be able to access empathy and/or *analogous* or *resonant* (but not identical) modes of experience from lived experiences of ableism as well as gendered and heteronormative violence, there are forms of oppression such as racism and anti-Indigenous violence that I will never experience or fully understand. As such, I rely on and defer to the insights shared by members of Indigenous, racialized, and other marginalized communities that reflect generations and centuries of critique of the violences in question.

Several other issues arise from engaging with Indigenous and BIPOC knowledge as a white settler academic writer. First, given the integral role of universities and Western academia in colonialism, racism, and other systems of oppression, this dynamic raises thorny issues of appropriation, misinterpretation, entitlement, and "ontological expansion" (Shannon Sullivan 2019, 16). The latter term refers to the common belief among white people that we have a right to insert ourselves into others' spaces and worlds.[24] These problems are compounded by the common habit among white scholars of appropriating Indigenous knowledges in an effort to save or recuperate our own systems and power structures (Whyte 2016). I have sought to minimize these harms by citing with care and rigor, and through the careful and community-informed selection of sources, questions, and methods (discussed later in this section). Second, by writing about Indigenous knowledge systems in English and within colonial academic frameworks, I will inevitably reproduce problems associated with the (mis)translation of knowledge. I have tried to minimize the possible harms caused by this process by working only with materials written in English by members of the relevant communities. In addition, to challenge the exclusive, canonical conventions of Euro-descendent forms of academic writing, including citation practices that concentrate and compound power among a privileged few (see Ahmed 2013), I have sought to prioritize sources grounded in lived experience, intergenerational knowledge, and grounded normativity (Coulthard 2014; L. Simpson 2017); from established and rising scholars alike; and from academic *and* land- or community-based knowledge keepers. Of course, these strategies are inflected by my own assessments of these criteria, which are influenced by the educational and epistemic systems in which I am immersed.

Third, no matter how much I may support arguments, actions, and initiatives undertaken by BIPOC and other marginalized communities, I *cannot* and do not pretend to "do" resurgence (L. Simpson 2017), decolonization (Tuck and Yang 2012), or Indigenous research (L. Simpson 2011; Geniusz 2015).[25] Instead, I adopt an ethics of *anti*-colonialism that recognizes my implication in the structures I critique (Liboiron 2020) and an overarching framework of what Anishinaabekwe thinker Kathleen Absolon (2011, 000) calls wholistic research, both of which, Absolon states, non-Indigenous people can contribute to. The latter involves reflecting on one's engrained cosmological assumptions and relationships; recognizing that a broad community supports the research process and attending to its needs; participating in transformative, experiential forms of learning; and drawing on numerous methods and sources of knowledge (for instance, experiences, dreams, stories, and direct teachings from other beings such as the land and waters). In addition, when engaging with stories/theories from other knowledge systems, I have sought wherever possible to learn about and from the *methodologies, practices,* and *approaches* integral to the relevant knowledge system (see L. Smith 2008; Kovach 2009; Oliveira and Wright 2015), including elements such as language structure (Kimmerer 2013) or the role of sensory information (Oliveira 2014) in order to approach the knowledge with as much respect and care as possible.

A fourth issue relates to the way that Western academia extracts knowledge from its broader ecosystems, worlds, and relations, erasing the connections and forms of care through which it is kept alive and vibrant, and in which it grows. The knowledge engaged with directly in this book is not based on anthropological studies *of* communities or on interviews with members of communities but rather on the published work of members of relevant communities. This approach is intended to limit the colonial tendency of doing research "on" Indigenous peoples, instead citing research and knowledge created by them.[26] It is also intended to respect the cultural limits of my own knowledge and the boundaries of what can and cannot be shared outside of each community (see L. Simpson and Manitowabi 2013; A. Simpson 2014). Nonetheless, every aspect of the book—from the questions it asks to the sources I engage with and the metaphors I think with—is indebted to a much broader process of learning rooted in, and inseparable from, relations with specific people, communities, places, and other beings. I have been generously afforded many opportunities to engage with these worlds, including by spending time on the land and water across North America / Turtle Island, Australia, Sápmi, and the Pacific Islands; sitting and working alongside aunties and uncles, grandfathers and grandmothers from many communities; gardening, weaving, sewing, growing and picking foods and medicines; sitting in vigil, cooking, walking, water walking, and much more.[27] Many of these experiences did not happen in the context of research or work but rather in social relationships and political collaborations. Nonetheless, they enabled and nourished my thinking, along with my mind and body, and as such were the soil in which these ideas sprouted and grew. By acknowledging the broader worlds in which this book is grounded, my aim is not to make a claim to authenticity but to acknowledge the profound gift that is relational knowledge and its crucial role in thinking and writing (Kuokkanen 2007; Craft 2017).

Fifth, the way that non-Indigenous thinkers present and attribute Indigenous knowledge often reproduces colonial harms—for instance, the conflation of distinct knowledge systems or the fetishization of unique arguments and insights as representative of entire peoples. Each author cited in this book is an original thinker; however, the vast majority of Indigenous authors cited here *also* identify their knowledge as collective, often doing so through the practice of self-identification as a member of a particular Indigenous community (including, in some cases, place-names and titles). I reproduce

22   Introduction

this self-identification wherever possible when citing Indigenous authors. As Métis thinker Max Liboiron (2020) points out, white thinkers do not tend to do the same but rather assume that they are examples of a universal humanity. To address this problem, Liboiron uses the term "unmarked" when scholars do not self-identify, a practice that I adopt here—not to flatten the complexity of (self-)identity but to contest the white/colonial/Eurocentric claims to a universal humanity.[28]

Sixth, since the forms of violence with which this book engages straddle the planet, I draw from knowledge systems, stories, and cosmovisions from multiple communities. This practice does not imply the commensurability of knowledge systems nor their conflation into a generic category. It is crucial to note that the stories/theories I engage with are certainly not intended to represent entire knowledge systems—just as Euro-descendent philosophers might balk if the work of, say, Friedrich Nietzsche were treated as a representation of all Western philosophy. I treat these stories/theories as unique beings, shared by thinkers situated in particular places, times, material conditions, and ongoing histories. Any implicit emphasis on particular cosmovisions (such as those of the Great Lakes area, where I lived and worked during most of the period of writing this book) is not intended to impose hierarchies among knowledge systems but rather to highlight the emplaced and embodied ways in which I have come to interact with this knowledge.[29]

TERMS AND CONCEPTS USED IN THIS BOOK

One challenge of critiquing one's own knowledge system is finding ways to signal to existing discourses within that system without directly reproducing and entrenching it. As this book discusses, concepts like "extinction," "species," and "biodiversity"—terms originating from precise Western scientific contexts but often taken for granted in broader discourses—impose particular ways of knowing as if they were universal. Throughout the book, I continue to use these terms in order to speak to (and against) dominant discourses. I also use several terms that may be less familiar to most readers, either as meeting places where different knowledge systems partially overlap or as placeholders for future terminologies (including reclaimed knowledge and language). Their role is to partially suspend dominant paradigms while still learning from their perspectives, nuancing their claims, and fostering contestation. I want to briefly introduce some of these terms here, all of which will be elaborated in the chapters that follow.

Introduction

BEINGS, LIFE-FORMS, AND WORLDS

I often use the term "beings" to discuss all entities and forces that collaborate to compose worlds where other Western academic texts might, depending on context, employ "individuals," "people/persons," or categories such as "animals." Beings need not be discrete and autonomous, as the term "individual" suggests; they may or may not be human or recognized as "persons" within various knowledge systems; and they need not be "alive" in the Western scientific sense. They are not limited to human "agents" or models of agency nor are they dependent on anything like "consciousness," and they may contribute to the co-composition of worlds and events in various ways. Reflecting the knowledge systems discussed in this book, the term "being" may refer to entities that exist in different physical forms and/or multiple timescales—for instance, in Yolŋu knowledge systems, Guwak is simultaneously a bird, a constellation, a Dreaming (see chapter 2), and an active constituent of kinship structures (Bawaka Country et al. 2020). Another example of a being is a waterway, which cannot be disaggregated into "individuals," takes multiple physical forms (not only as ice and liquid but in flowing, splashing, evaporating, and burbling), traverses temporal scales and periods, and actively shapes landscapes and communities.

In a similar way, I use the term "life-forms" not as another word for species but rather to challenge, perforate, and blur the boundaries of the concepts of "species" and "life" while recognizing the collective nature in which beings organize themselves within ecosystems and worlds. Life-forms are continuities forged, transformed, and sustained through collaboration, conflict, and coexistence among beings that share core commonalities but are constantly changing and pluralizing (see chapter 2). They are composed of *at least some,* though not necessarily only, beings who convert energy and process matter in order to sustain, transform, and reproduce themselves. As such, and as the next chapter will discuss, at least some co-constituents of a life-form are subject to what the Western sciences call "death": the cessation of processes of energy conversion and the decay of material bodies. What's more, although many life-forms are composed largely of organisms, the term "life-form" cannot be *reduced* to them because beings themselves may take multiple forms. That is, a life-form may include organisms, inorganic beings and forces (e.g., water, climate), ancestors, histories, knowledge systems, and collective futures—which cannot be easily (or nonviolently) separated from the organisms in question. In addition, members of life-forms may take several forms across time: for instance, as organisms, as decomposing bodies, and ultimately as components of soils, minerals, or chemicals.

The term "life-form" is also temporal and durational: it speaks to the ways in which diverse beings collaborate to sustain continuity-with-change —that is, a sense of cohesion across time shaped by constant transformation. Life-forms sustain and transform their collective continuity in many ways, including but not limited to the formation of ecosystems, adaptations, migrations, evolution, sexual and other forms of biological reproduction (e.g., gene transfer; parthenogenesis), knowledge and cultural transmission, and interactions with other life-forms, such as the treaties and protocols discussed earlier in this chapter. In other words, the work of life form*ing* that life-forms carry out is not only what the Western sciences would call biological but also cultural and political (see Grosz 2004) in ways that may, but do not always, include any humans. Life-forms also culturally and politically reproduce themselves transformatively, including through shifts in morphology or habitat, the adoption of members of one life-form by another, and the formation of kinship across life-forms. For example, Nick X̱EMŦOLTW̱ Claxton (2018, 96) reflects on a W̱SÁNEĆ story/theory shared with him by elder YELḰÁTTE (Dr. Earl Claxton Sr.). In this story/theory, a young W̱SÁNEĆ woman marries a man who turns out to be a salmon and who teaches the people how to survive famine by weaving reef nets from the inner bark of the Pacific willow. Through biological, sexual, cultural, and political means, this marriage strengthened and sustained both life-forms while merging them in important ways. In some knowledge systems, multi-life-form reproduction can also occur through nonsexual relationships (see Grosz 2004) or relationships between beings of very different kinds (including nonliving beings). For instance, Anishinaabeg/Métis/ Norwegian scholar Melissa Nelson's work on Indigenous eco-eroticisms (2017) interprets stories in which women from various communities are impregnated by and reproduce with other kinds of beings: for instance, a Kootenai story about a woman who reproduces with a star, a Yurok woman who raises children with a stick, and an Anishinaabe woman who conceives children with a wind. According to these stories/theories, transformative ways of ensuring continuity across different beings and life-forms are integral to collective flourishing.

I use the term "world" to refer to the *conditions,* including the material, social, and spiritual structures, that plural beings and life-forms co-constitute

Introduction

in order to enable and sustain their collective flourishing with others. Contrary to its common uses in Euro-descendent discourses, the term "world" should not be conflated with the "planet" or "globe": myriad worlds coexist on and beyond earth (see de la Cadena and Blaser 2018). As several scholars in the field of critical international relations (IR) and global studies argue, the shifting relations between these worlds (re)shape more-than-human political formations and conditions at multiple scales and form a crucial part of "world(s) politics" (see, for example, Agathangelou and Ling 2009; Inoue and Tickner 2016; Kurki 2020). These approaches depart from assertions, common to Euro-descendent thought, that there is a single "world" that is interpreted and responded to in different ways by diverse "cultures" (see Viveiros de Castro 2012), a "common world" that forms the medium and common denominator for plural worlds (Arendt 1998), or an overarching "cosmopolitical" field (Stengers 2005) in which all possible worlds are contained. Instead, this book understands worlds as irreducible, partially overlapping, open-ended trajectories in which plural beings and life-forms (see chapter 2) create, modify, and conflict over specific conditions of coexistence, each from their own unique contexts and positions.

Worlds can take various shapes and sizes, exist on multiple physical-temporal scales, and vary greatly in structure, from tight-knit, place-based kinship relations to loosely connected, universalistic models of governance. They are bounded by the patterns of interaction and relations carried out by their co-constituents, but they are also porous and open to transformations (each to different degrees and extents across time). Beings and life-forms can exist simultaneously in multiple worlds or, in some cases, move across worlds. For instance, the sudden appearance of a new life-form as a result of climate change may prompt multiple changes in a world, including the embrace of this life-form and its induction into kinship systems, its rejection, or the subsumption of the existing world by the new life-form, among other possibilities. Each world is unique, yet not strictly divisible; worlds blend, interpenetrate, hybridize, conflict, and subsume others. However, this does not suggest all changes and disruptions to worlds are ethically neutral; on the contrary, many of the forms of violence discussed in this book work by deliberately and systematically destroying the bases of worlds they seek to dominate.

Indeed, although it does not necessarily constitute a normative position in itself, recognizing the plurality of worlds makes possible a particular ethics of worldly care. In its positive form, this ethics involves working to ensure the flourishing of other worlds, perhaps even if this involves relinquishing the dominance—or perhaps even the existence—of one's own. This ethics promotes the creation of, as Cree writer Billy-Ray Belcourt (2016, 22) puts it, "worlds that slip-slide into others without disavowing their hybrid alterities." However, even in its most minimal, negative form, this ethics involves ensuring that no single world expands to encompass all others. Belgian philosopher Luce Irigaray (2008) contends that care for one's own world *is* to care for those of others. Though deeply Euro- and anthropocentric, her vision makes an important ethical demand: to limit the horizons of each world so that none can subsume all others or foreclose the possibilities of their becoming.

Throughout this book, I also use some conventional terms in idiosyncratic ways. For instance, throughout, I refer to "earth" rather than "the earth" or "Earth," to recognize the singularity of this planet but also its multiple forms, states, and possible futures across deep time. Finally, the terms "humans" and "humanity" appear in scare quotes in the first pages of this book in order to highlight the constructed nature of this abstract, ethical-political term. Throughout the book, I also draw attention to the immense effort, resources, and forms of violence that continue to be invested in sustaining a specific and exclusive global idea of "humanity" (see Mitchell 2014a) that excludes many actual humans on the basis of race, disability, gender, sexuality, and other factors. By calling this term into question, this book does not seek to undermine or criticize the use of human rights frameworks by many communities as a strategic means of resisting violence and asserting their own forms of self-governance. However, it resists the tendency within academic and popular writing to speak of "humans" as if they constitute a generic group.

I would also like to offer a brief note on the style of writing used throughout the book. As an Autistic, Dyspraxic, and multiply disabled writer, I relate to language differently than many of my nondisabled and/or allistic colleagues. Elements such as the unconventional use of everyday words, iteration, "fractal" or nested concepts, complex sentences, emphasis on concrete imagery, distinct use of punctuation, and intricacy of structure are all associated with distinctly Autistic writing styles (see Yergeau 2017; Rodas 2018). These elements reflect the different ways that Autistic bodyminds encounter and process information, sensory data, and relationships; how we navigate our worlds; and how we connect with others. They are also routinely dismissed by mainstream knowledge systems, held up as evidence of "unintelligence" or "incapacity," and/or impugned as "bad" writing (often with the use of proxy terms such as "jargon" or "poor grammar"). In contrast, many Autistic writers and our supporters embrace these differences in language use as distinct styles—such as "Autistic long-form" (Piepzna-Samarasinha 2023)—but also as ways of queering language (Yergeau 2017; Walker 2021) or offering openings to distinct ecological relations (Mitchell 2022). Following this latter path, and in solidarity with all marginalized communication systems, I actively embrace Autistic writing throughout this book and invite readers to do the same.

OUTLINE OF THE BOOK

I like to think of this book in relation to one of the revenants that inspired it: the squash plant discussed in the Conclusion. It was written in a plantlike way, building from a set of key arguments, then branching and probing out in multiple directions to form a whole that is multiple in its meanings, implications, and possibilities for ongoing growth. As a result, each of the chapters is very different in its content and subject. Some readers may be more interested in some parts of the book than others, and that's perfectly fine! Most of the chapters can also be read on their own, or in any order (although the discussion of "(bio)plurality" in chapter 2 may help make sense of some of the arguments and language in the chapters that follow). For example, the first two chapters are more theoretical and abstract than those that follow and may be of most interest to readers who want to delve into the philosophical bases of ideas of extinction and biodiversity. Chapters 3 and 4 focus on specific logics of violence (earth/body violence and the invasive state), with a more practical focus on diagnosing the sources of extinction and plenty of detailed examples. They might be of most interest to readers who are concerned with the links between extinction, violence, and oppression and in ethical-political change, policy, or governance. Chapter 5 turns toward the legal, political, and ethical analysis of extinction and its relationship to genocide, including several case studies. It may be of interest to those concerned with legal and political remedies to eliminative violence (against nonhumans) or in the prevention of genocides. Chapter 6 continues in a more political vein, focusing on the convergence between powerful—and oppressive—futurist discourses in the fields of politics and conservation. Chapter 7 and the Conclusion get actively normative and transformative, engaging with Indigenous futurist stories/theories, alternative forms of leadership, and agendas for radical ecopolitical change. They may appeal most to readers who want to generate, imagine, and incubate alternative ecologies and modes of coexistence. (They are also the two chapters of the book that readers may find most hopeful.) Whichever elements of the book drew you here, I hope that you find something that helps you feel connected to the worlds that you care about and the futures you are working toward.

It is also important to note that most of the chapters of this book engage directly with profound acts and structures of violence, including genocide, racism, eugenics, ableism, homo- and transphobic violence, gendered violence, physical and sexual abuse and assault, police violence, police and/or state-sponsored violence, and more. Many readers who care about the themes of this book are disproportionately likely to be affected by these forms of violence, so please know that you are seen, heard, remembered, and cared for. There may be some parts of this book that you do not wish to read, or that you might want to take a break from, or to read when you have access to support networks. In general, the first two chapters of the book deal largely with the underlying logics of violence involved in discussions of extinction, conservation, and biodiversity, with some discussion of genocide, colonial violence, and (interspecies) eugenics. Chapters 3–4 include more detailed descriptions of various forms of violence, including gendered and sexual violence, police violence, colonial violence, ableism, and racism. Chapter 5 deals directly with kinds of eliminative violence, including genocides against several Indigenous communities and their nonhuman kin. In chapter 6, I analyze discourses and frameworks that include white supremacist, ableist, eugenicist, heteronormative, and colonial beliefs, along with imaginaries of large-scale death and harm. Chapter 7 and the Conclusion shift toward more positive discussions of possible futures but also engage with stories that include ongoing colonial violence, eugenics, and sexual violence.

The overall structure also takes its cues from our plant cohabitants (see chapter 3). Chapter 1 works to loosen the compacted soil of mainstream discourses on extinction, building from the insights offered by the different stories/theories discussed in this chapter. It dives more deeply into Western scientific discourses of extinction, showing how they conflate concepts of death, existence, and nonexistence and frame the issue as one of bio-, necro-, and thanato-political management. Chapter 1 also examines how the abstract quantitative and scalar thresholds embedded in the concept alienate ethical and political responsiveness, impose Eurocentric historical schemas, and negate relations beyond Western scientific notions of life, nonlife, extant, and extinct.

Chapter 2 questions the uncritical embrace of biodiversity as a universal way of understanding difference among life-forms, showing how the concept privileges forms of difference rooted in internal homogeneity, external difference, substitutability, and generic processes of difference making. This kind of difference expresses the logics of, and is aligned with, the managerial and extractive logics at the heart of mainstream conservation practices and the political-economic orders they support. Crucially, it argues that, when aggressively promoted through global conservation strategies, biodiversity often displaces and destroys other forms of difference. This includes a set of conditions that I call "(bio)plurality": the fundamental co-constitution of irreducibly different beings, life-forms, and worlds, which produces unique, irreplaceable constellations and forms of difference making, or (bio)pluralization. I argue that universalizing discourses and material manifestations of biodiversity not only fail to protect but also often displace and destroy (bio)plural relational structures and the conditions of (bio)plurality.

Spreading roots into deeper and wider forms of critique, the next few chapters work to show that extinction is in fact an expression of multiple forms of global structural violence that systematically target and destroy (bio)plurality. After framing extinction as an expression of multiple forms of intersecting, global, *structural* violence, chapter 3 focuses on earth/body violence. This form of violence involves the forceful dissolution of bodies, minds, and forms of affect that are distributed across (bio)plural bodies and cohabitats, and the suppression of the myriad forms of relation making (including intimacy, co-absorption, kinship, and eroticism) that sustain them. Channeling violence and harm along the lines of race, disability, gender and sexuality, and earth/body violence works to corrode forms of power generated and sustained through (bio)plural relations, converting relations of mutual nourishment into sites of trauma and harm.

Chapter 4 examines how the logics of invasive states and the logics of colonial capitalism that sustain them work to break down and aggressively replace existing (bio)plural relations with ones designed for the benefit of invaders (including, in many cases, conditions of biodiversity). Grounded in examples of the ongoing dispossession and transformation of BIPOC lands by invasive states and societies, the chapter moves to contemporary practices of biosecurity, colonial conservation, and their role in perpetuating structures of (dis)possession. It also examines logics of extraction and specifically the systematic dismemberment of (bio)plural bodies in order to release certain parts for commodification, circulation, and waste. Similarly, the forms of eliminative violence and genocide discussed in chapter 5 function by attacking the bonds that co-constitute unique more-than-human worlds and ways of being with the aim of eradicating them—and their ability to resist domination. That chapter examines attempts to destroy more-than-human ways of being, multi-life-form collectives, and groups of nonhumans who have status such as "persons" or "nations" within relevant legal orders. It argues that although "extinction" and "genocide" should not be elided conceptually, there are cases in which the former constitutes the latter. However, it also argues that there are forms of eliminative violence exceeding the boundaries of genocide (and ecocide) that drive the systematic destruction of (bio)plurality, which also require attention. From this perspective, responses to extinction based on managing and increasing stocks of biodiversity will not stop extinctions, let alone the systematic destruction of (bio)plurality, of which they are one expression. In fact, such strategies are likely to prolong and intensify the forms of destruction in question. Instead, the systemic destruction of (bio)plurality demands the amplification, proliferation, and strengthening of modes of *ethical-political action* aimed at dismantling complex formations of violence, repairing the worlds they harm and imagining new orders into being.

Sprouting from these critical roots, the last three chapters engage with normative stories/theories about possible futures shaped by extinction. Chapter 6 interrogates an emerging trend toward apocalyptic thought—specifically, human extinction or existential risk—within global politics and increasingly within conservation discourses. While claiming to hold the interests and future (singular) of humanity at its core, these discourses actually seek to protect and shore up existing forms of racial, colonial, economic, ableist, gendered, and other forms of power. They produce limiting models of "the future" (singular) and repertoires of response grounded in oppression and the intensification of the forms of violence that destroy (bio)plurality. Their prescriptions for saving humanity through conservation range from population control and massive-scale surveillance to the annexation of half the planet in the name of conservation projects led and shaped by billionaires. At the core of these apocalyptic stories/theories is a profound fear of reversal—a possibility that is, in contrast, centered and celebrated by the revenant ecologies foregrounded in chapter 7. Centering

Introduction

a range of BIPOC future visions, that chapter focuses on the possibility of revenance: the return of beings, life-forms, and worlds erased by global structural violence. It centers forms of agency and responsiveness rooted in co-embodiment, (bio)pluralization, the embrace of multiple temporalities, collaborative motion, and the proliferation of worlds—even if this marks the end of a currently dominant world. These revenant ecologies directly refute and refuse the narratives of extinction imposed by Western systems of power and knowledge production and the oppressive modes of governance that aim to control it, not least globalized conservation regimes. Building on these ideas, the conclusion follows the vines and tendrils of a particular revenant plant, gathering together the implications from each chapter and offering possible ways forward. These include attention toward addressing the violence and trauma associated with extinction; the large-scale, global return of land to BIPOC and land-based communities; forms of reparation that involve money but also active support for the reconstitution of communities and ecosystems; divestment from billionaire-led conservation and other strategies that ossify existing power structures; and the cultivation of desire for and unconditional love of difference, the conditions of (bio)plurality, and the possible worlds to come.

1 "Megadeath"?

Questioning Concepts of "(Mass) Extinction"

> 252 million years ago on Earth in late May on a Monday, the
> trilobites were going out for Starbucks before work. . . . [They] had
> limped through an extinction event only eight million years earlier,
> which had pruned off all but the hardiest and luckiest of their
> species. Nevertheless, they were alive and looking forward to
> another 200 million years. . . . But the Earth had a bad case of gas
> from a lot of undigested trees. Asteroids were due to boom through
> the atmosphere like falling angels, wings afire. The area that would
> one day be Siberia was going to hurl lava like a frat boy upchucking
> during rush week. Pangaea, the superest continent, was about to split
> like a tight pair of pants. The Permian Age was about to convulse,
> boil, then die, taking nine out of ten of all living species kicking and
> screaming into oblivion. The world would go dark. The ocean
> would become an airless acid bath. The clouds would rain death.
>
> The trilobites were blindsided by the end of their world. They
> were like, whoa, man. What the hell? What did we ever do to you?
> But no one answered and they had nowhere to hide. Nowhere
> was safe. Every last trilobite died. As the eons passed, they were
> pressed into fossils that would, one day, make lovely bookends and
> paperweights.
>
> Mass extinction sucks.
>
> —EDEN ROBINSON, *Son of a Trickster*

"Extinction is conceptually simple," write a trio of influential unmarked conservation biologists: "a species is extinct when its last member has died" (Purvis, Jones, and Mace 2000, 1124). With almost poetic brevity, this statement parses an immensely complex and multifaceted process into a crisp definition: "extinction" is the subtraction of lives that continues until all members of a species are dead. "Mass extinction" is defined with similar precision: the destruction of three-quarters or more of existing species within a relatively brief period of geological time. These definitions have garnered strong consensus within Western scientific discourses—while the specific numbers and parameters of thresholds are contested, the basic concepts and theories are rarely questioned, even when used by critical theorists.[1] Yet these terms and definitions embed an important and misleading set of assumptions into discussions about the destruction of earth's lifeforms. Not least, their focus on controlling death promotes bio- and necropolitical responses that leave untouched—and usually unrecognized—the forms of *violence* that drive it. At the same time, the numerical thresholds used to model and predict extinction and mass extinction distort and displace ethical responses. What's more, the use of thresholds to mark extinction events and / or geological epochs not only reflects a linear, progressive understanding of time but also places these disruptions in presents or futures in ways that ignore *continuing* histories of harm and disruption. Finally, mainstream Western scientific discourses present extinction and mass extinction in *ontological* terms: they impose a stark division between being and non-being that embodies particular forms of power (see Povinelli 2016) and models of relationality.

Haisla / Heiltsuk novelist Eden Robinson's (2017) darkly humorous story / theory of the Permian extinction, quoted at the beginning of this chapter, can help in thinking through this critique. Robinson's narrative could hardly contrast more with the bloodless precision of Western scientific definitions, and it is unlikely to be enshrined within those discourses as "traditional ecological knowledge" (TEK). On the contrary, it is precisely Robinson's subversive humor and nonconformity to such discourses that opens up different questions about the nature of extinction and mass extinction.[2] For instance, she portrays the trilobites in (satirical) social terms, as a collective connected by kinship and ancestry, with a long past and the expectation of a future. They have worked hard to regenerate after the previous extinction, and this new rupture constitutes not only their death in large numbers but also the obliteration of the world they have co-created and the severance of the connections they have struggled to nurture. When faced with the absurd inconvenience of mass extinction, this group does not passively go extinct but rather resists and protests, kicking and screaming into oblivion, a detail that undermines the depoliticizing tone of Western scientific definitions. The intentionally anachronistic device of sending the trilobites to Starbucks on a Monday and their (re)appearance as unwilling paperweights shows how extinction and mass extinction reach across and scramble Western registers of linear time. This, along with the satirically anthropomorphic descriptions of the pissed-off trilobites, also works to collapse the ethical distance between extinction and contemporary (Western) life created by abstract definitions, time frames, and numerical thresholds. And, although dead, these beings are not entirely gone: across immense temporal boundaries and the small matter of biological existence, they speak to contemporary interlocutors, maintaining presence, meaning, and relations despite being "extinct."

Reflecting on these differing accounts, this chapter examines how four patterns of thought—the conflation of extinction and death, threshold thinking, evental logics, and ontological approaches—work to constitute a cosmologically specific account of "(mass) extinction events" while presenting it as universal. I argue that these ways of thinking, in themselves and in combination, mobilize global public consciousness about extinction in specific ways, which often entrench existing structures of power and violence and cut off other possible modes of response. At the same time, by critiquing these ways of thinking, I highlight some of the alternative forms of thought and action that they erase. By questioning mainstream narratives in these ways, I hope to open up more space for addressing—and resisting—global extinction in *ethical-political* terms.

"MEGADEATH"?

On June 24, 2012, "Lonesome George," the last Pinta Island tortoise, died quietly in his enclosure in the Galápagos National Park. His body was found by the caretaker who had looked after him for forty years, during which time several unsuccessful attempts were made to mate him in order to secure the future of his subspecies. George's body was shipped to the United States to be taxidermized, then placed at the Charles Darwin Research Center (CDRC), where he became a permanent mascot for international conservation. George had already achieved worldwide fame as an "endling," a term coined to describe "the last surviving individual of a species of animal or plant" (Jørgensen 2017, 121). Like the deaths of other famous endlings such as Martha the passenger pigeon and Benjamin the thylacine, his passing was seen—and widely publicized—by international conservationists as monumental. Indeed, the collective emotion mobilized by endling narratives is intense: hundreds of thousands, even millions, of people all over the world mourn the loss of animals with whom they may never have interacted and raise of millions of dollars in donations to "save the last" of species they know only in the abstract (see Mitchell 2017a). Endlings stand in not only for their species but also for general fears of irreversible loss and threat. Popular endling narratives like George's create a sense of intimacy with extinction, of impossible witnessing. Indeed, on hearing of George's death, influential unmarked paleobiologist and scholar of extinction Anthony Barnosky (who was not present with the tortoise when he passed) commented that "extinction had happened before our eyes" (2014, loc. 129). Barnosky's comment embeds some complicated claims: that the death of an endling *is* extinction and that extinction is death writ large. Only through these logics could the death of a single animal be understood to enable millions of people to witness extinction, an event so widely distributed across time and space that, even at its current, vastly accelerated pace, it exceeds the longest of individual human lifetimes. In this narrative, extinction is a superlative for death—"a different, bigger kind of death" (Brand 2015) or a global process of "megadeath" (Wilson 2002, 96).

In contrast, I argue that what the Western sciences call "extinction" is *qualitatively different* from death. The late American-Australian settler scholar Deborah Bird Rose, who worked with the Aboriginal peoples of Yarralin, contends that extinction *cannot* be conflated with death for a simple reason: extinction negates both life *and* death as well as the relationships between them.[3] For the people of Yarralin, the lives and deaths of humans, animals, plants, and other beings sustain each other through the constant braiding, plaiting, or weaving of social and biological processes.[4] Through this work, life and death are dynamically entwined to produce continuity, novelty, repetition, new beginnings, and returns. The human members of the community play their role in the form of careful labor across generations—for instance, taking care of Country, performing rituals for the dead, "singing them back" home, and participating physically in cyclical processes, including birth and death. As Rose (2011b, loc. 2509) puts it, "life wants to live, wants to be embodied, and keeps finding its way back into life. Life is always in a state of metamorphosis, across death and into more life, crossing bodies, species and generations." Extinction, for Rose, is the force that cuts and severs this flow, destroying the possibilities of turning death back into life by eliminating many of the bodies and forms it could take. As she puts it, "as life itself collapses there is less and less toward which death can be turned" (Rose 2011b, loc. 1693).

"Megadeath"?

In contrast, mainstream discussions treat extinction as a magnification of Western secular scientific notions of death, understood as the permanent halting of an organism's *biological* functions, such as metabolism, homeostasis, and consciousness.[5] In Western secular cosmology, death is mutually exclusive of life and starkly opposed to it. It is absolute, final, irreversible, and total: there is no afterlife, no coexistence of the living and the dead, no possibility of (re)turning death into life. Much like Eurocentric conceptions of time, the transformation of life into death goes in only one direction. It is abject, feared, and despised: "death (alongside all other acts betraying the 'biological underside' of Homo *Sapiens*) [is viewed as] *indecent*—dirty and polluting" (Bauman 1992, 136). For this reason, German philosopher Zygmunt Bauman (1992) argues, Western societies have channeled immense energy into separating life from death and banishing death and the dead— for instance, by creating burial grounds that segregate the living from the dead, and a multibillion-dollar anti-aging industry and medical system that seeks to overcome death or "sur-vive" it (see Mitchell 2014a, 45). Rather than ensuring an even balance between life and death, this apparatus seeks to dominate and assume control of the processes of death to the point of its banishment—at least for some life-forms.

In pursuit of this power, contemporary societies dominated by Western secular cosmology mobilize complex bio-, necro-, and thanato-political forms of power, each of which work in different ways. Biopolitics "takes life as an object of direct intervention" (Esposito 2013, 14), seeking to manipulate not just specific organisms or life-forms but the processes of life, as if they were a generic substance (see chapter 2 and Helmreich 2009). In this framework, "the object of political action is no longer a 'life form,' its own specific way of being, but rather, life itself—all life and only life, in its mere biological reality" (Esposito 2013, 112). In this form, life is stripped of all other elements—its collective histories and futures, its creative and world-forming powers, its interactions with nonlife, and so on. It becomes a *quantity* to be managed, increased, and cultivated *against* the negation represented by death. Ironically, the practice of managing life often involves forms of killing and letting-die, including "thanato-politics" (Agamben 1995), which coerces the survival of some lives and mandates the destruction of others. Efforts to control life and death also frequently include "necropolitics" (Mbembe 2003, 11): calculations of "who may live and who *must* die" in order to privilege particular life-forms or segments of them. As Cameroonian philosopher Achille Mbembe (2017,

27) argues, this includes the construction of global structures to distribute intensities of death and killing, including along globalized racial and species lines.

Each of these logics plays an important role in mainstream efforts to govern extinction. Perhaps the most vivid example is found in *ex situ* conservation practices carried out in zoos and research institutions, which combine various bio-, thanato-, and necro-political techniques. As reflections of the Western secular disdain for death, zoos have become "biopolitical institutions devoted to the production and nurture of life [that] disturb and ignore the role of death," constructing eco-utopias "through the disavowal of mortality" (Chrulew 2011, 145). By hosting breeding programs—including those that subject animals to physical injury (see van Dooren 2014; Salazar Parreñas 2018) and/or long-distance transport—collecting and trading genetic materials, and trading animals, zoos play an important role in forcing *particular* forms of life to live. Since zoos rely heavily on revenues from the paying public, these choices are shaped by the pressures of global capitalism, including public discourses that make endlings such as Lonesome George into conservation celebrities. These pressures produce a disproportionate emphasis on large-bodied, charismatic animals that Western publics associate with endangerment and/or the exotic and whose perceived scarcity drives up demand for interaction "before they're gone" (Mitchell 2017a). In many cases, public demand for the existence—or indeed, the extinction—of these animals reflects legacies of colonial claims to ownership of particular life-forms and places (see Mitchell 2017a).

At the same time, many zoos engage in necropolitics in order to secure the thriving of life-forms made valuable by global discourses of conservation and endangerment. For instance, European zoos frequently allow animals to raise their young to the point where they would normally become independent, then euthanize the healthy juveniles in order to encourage "normal sexual behaviors" among the adults (van Dooren 2014, 119). Here, sexual reproduction is a tightly managed performance, in which animals are allowed to engage in the *processes* of reproduction but not to form intergenerational bonds or participate in the broader history or future continuity of their life-form. Instead, the work of ensuring the continuity of a life-form—and the potential futures opened by this—are controlled by the human staff of the zoo and its wider policy imperatives. This practice attracted international media attention in 2014 when the Copenhagen Zoo euthanized a healthy two-year-old giraffe called Marius, performing a public dissection and feeding parts of the giraffe's body to carnivorous zoo inmates.[6] Responding to international public outcry, a spokesperson for the European Association of Zoos and Aquaria (EAZA), of which Copenhagen Zoo is a member, justified the euthanasia on the basis that Marius was genetically redundant (see chapter 2). By EAZA's estimation, Marius's siblings provided the necessary genetic materials required for its programs, and he was taking up space better devoted to "more genetically valuable" animals (Rincon 2014).[7] In this case, necropolitics was used in service of a larger biopolitical goal: producing a gene pool that can enable European zoos to control the future conditions of giraffe reproduction to protect them from extinction.

Indeed, organisms are increasingly considered to be optional in these biopolitical efforts to fight extinction by managing the quantity and quality of life. A rising trend toward "genomics beyond organisms" treats genetic "manipulable bits of life" (Helmreich 2009, 56; Wilson 2016) that can be controlled and shaped without the mediation of bodies or life-*forms.* In this vein, a vast network of private, public, and university-owned gene banks is working to stockpile genetic materials as a kind of insurance policy against future extinctions. Prominent examples include (at the time of writing), the Frozen Zoo at the San Diego Zoo, the University of Nottingham's Frozen Ark project, the CryoBioBank at the Cincinnati Zoo and Botanical Garden, and the Global Seed Vault in Svalbard, Norway.[8] Although these genetic materials are primarily used as backup for more conventional breeding strategies or for research purposes, it is anticipated that they may eventually be used to revive dwindling populations of plant and animal species. They may also be integral to future projects of de-extinction: the creation of what we might call firstlings containing genetic materials from life-forms declared extinct—for instance, by splicing DNA recovered from fossilized woolly mammoths with African elephants or passenger pigeon genes with those of banded pigeons.[9] In "de-extinction" projects, the existence of *any* amount of DNA from the extinct life-form is used to classify it as a member of the extinct species in a way that eerily echoes the "one-drop rule," "blood quantum," and other racializing genetic laws (see TallBear 2015). This move erases the distinct genetic heritage, history and relational links, and coevolution with particular worlds of *all* the sources of DNA involved— and the unique potential futures of the hybrid being.

The concept of de-extinction raises interesting challenges to the Western secular concepts of life and death and the relationship between them.

At first glance, it may seem to promise possibilities of return, such as those enabled by the Yarralin peoples' "singing back," the reparation of treaties discussed in the Introduction, or the forms of revenance discussed in later chapters. But, upon taking a closer look, one can see that de-extinction does not offer forms of continuity in which the life-forms in question are actively engaged. On the contrary, the (quantities of) life to be brought back in the form of DNA is alienated and disembodied, temporally orphaned—sometimes by decades or even millions of years. This life is cut off from collective history, kinship, the intergenerational transmission of knowledge, and various processes of social and biological reproduction that make life-forms what they are. This certainly does not undermine or reduce the worthiness of the resulting forms of life to exist or the quality of life of potentially resulting organisms—or indeed, that of any being who is not robustly connected to its life-form in this sense.[10] However, it highlights and calls into question the idea that it is possible to directly *restore* what has been destroyed (see Brand 2013), a claim that can be used to obscure the harms and patterns of culpability that result in the total destruction of life-forms. Although most of its proponents recognize that de-extinction will not likely be able to be carried out on a scale large enough to replace extinct life-forms, it does promise a kind of absolution—a bio-genetic "do-over," in which investments in speculative techno-science are substituted for reckonings with ongoing histories of violence and large-scale political-ethical change. Indeed, as Dakota scholar Kim TallBear (2015) argues, contemporary biotechnological projects often express "Western desires to accumulate fragments of a world that is seen as suffering under the corrosive forces of modernity." From this perspective, de-extinction is an attempt to recover the shards of life blasted apart by centuries of colonial-capitalist violence *in order to shore up these structures* and ensure *their* continuity; the continuity of life-forms is only a means to this end.

The conflation of extinction with Western scientific definitions of death also limits its scope to those beings considered "living" or "biotic" within that knowledge system, erasing the distribution of harms across worlds (see Mitchell 2014b and chapter 2). What's more, the idea that every member of a species must die in order for extinction to take place creates an unhelpful binary. In many cases, ecological harms are so severe, complex, and/or extensive that they destroy the continuity and integrity of life-forms even when members of that species technically continue to exist. This is the case for many beings detained in zoos who are considered extinct in the wild, whose histories and kinship structures have been destroyed even though they are kept alive (see van Dooren 2014); and for species considered "functionally" or "ecologically" extinct—that is, still extant but no longer sufficiently abundant to play their former roles in ecosystems (McCauley et al. 2015).[11] Further, the narrow focus on "species" in mainstream narratives of extinction fails to capture harms to *worlds,* which may be destroyed even if their constitutive life-forms remain numerous. For instance, Toronto, the city where I lived while writing parts of this book, slouches around one of the last remaining fragments of Black Oak savanna. This is a unique prairie and oak landscape co-created by the Huron-Wendat, Anishinaabeg, and Haudenosaunee peoples and their nonhuman kin. Shaped and maintained through cyclical practices of burning, gathering, and hunting, this world was decimated by European colonization, displacement of Indigenous communities, rapid urban development, and regimes of fire suppression and chemical control that continue today. At the time of writing, approximately 1 percent of the original Black Oak savanna exists primarily in land maintained by Indigenous nations.[12] If the remaining fragments of Black Oak savanna were to be destroyed, this would mark the destruction of a unique *world*—even if members of *Quercus velutina* and other key life-forms that co-create this world grew plentifully elsewhere.

Finally, the tendency in mainstream Western scientific discourses to equate extinction with "megadeath" suggests a sense of passivity: it implies that life-forms simply "go extinct" or succumb to destruction. Extinction and conservation are framed as things that are *done to* species by humans, in ways that afford other life-forms little or no role in shaping their futures, including participating in the transcendence of their oppression (see S. Taylor 2017). Yet, in the Introduction, I discussed several examples of laws, practices, and adaptive arrangements in which animals, plants, and other beings exert various forms of agency—such as collective relocation, hiding, or deliberately reducing their populations—to protest ill treatment and negotiate their futures. These life-forms are active participants in their own continuities, using ingenious strategies in order to ensure their survival and future thriving, including finding ways to communicate and collaborate with beings very different from them. The conflation of extinction with passive death erases not only the *violence* threatening the integrity of these life-forms but also the immense labor and effort undertaken by plural life-forms to resist their elimination.

CROSSING A LINE: THRESHOLDS AND "MASS EXTINCTION"

If the deaths of endlings are used to mark the boundary between death and extinction, then what demarcates *"mass* extinction" from "extinction"? Again, the Western sciences offer a seemingly straightforward answer: "mass extinction" is defined as a situation in which 75 percent or more of currently existing species go extinct within a relatively short period of geological time.[13] These definitions anchor a recent wave of popular science books, news articles, and public discourse warning of an already-in-progress "sixth mass extinction" (see, for instance, Barnosky 2014; Kolbert 2014; Newitz 2013). Although these discourses refer to the Western scientific definition and the quantitative data on which it is based, they also tap into the broader cultural resonance of the term "mass" and its relationship to violence, using this emotional connection to amplify the sense of importance, enormity, and urgency. However, I argue that using the term "mass" in this way, and in the context of numerical thresholds, can *suppress* ethical-political responsiveness to extinction or channel it in counterproductive directions.

To construct such thresholds for "(mass) extinction," Western scientists rely on two main strategies, often used in combination. The first involves extrapolating patterns from data about past mass extinction events to explain present and probable future trends. The second strategy involves collecting contemporary data from extant life-forms to model future conditions. In the former strategy, the events in question can be analyzed in retrospect; however, since the fossil record is patchy (Plotnick, Smith, and Lyons 2016) and these events occurred millions of years in the past, accuracy and precision can be elusive. While the second approach is easier to replicate and verify since it focuses on extant life-forms, it confronts a different temporal challenge: "mass extinction" is too massive in timescale to be *observed* within the scope of (existing) Western scientific tools and institutions, and therefore it can *only* be modeled or predicted. Either way, Western scientific claims about "mass extinction" must always rely on always incomplete data and significant uncertainty—which, as we will soon discuss, introduces important ethical challenges.

In order to establish thresholds, Western scientists who study extinction posit "background rates": the average rates at which they calculate life-forms went extinct between the five previous "mass extinction events." For instance, Ceballos and his colleagues (2015) argue that the background

"Megadeath"? 43

rate of extinctions is generally assumed to be somewhere between 0.1 and 1 species per 10,000 species per 100 years (or 0.1 to 1 species extinction per million species per year). They calculate that, over the past century, the average rate of extinction of vertebrate species reached up to 114 times this background rate. As such, they contend, the extinctions that took place between 1500 and 1900 CE would have taken several thousand years if they had occurred at the background rate. Such calculations offer useful analogies for grasping the scope and speed of "(mass) extinction," and, at the same time, they shape how it is understood in ways that are not neutral. For instance, precisely because they are averaged, these rates smoothen out significant variations and unique events—for instance, earthquakes or large movements of animals, including people—that is, the *specificities* and *singularities* of earth's history. What's more, these rates generate and embed assumptions about what is normal or even natural when it comes to extinction and what is aberrant or worthy of urgent response. Depending on factors such as timescale, this can have important distortionary effects. For instance, if we took the time frame of Ceballos and his colleagues (1500–1900), then unique peaks of ecological destructiveness such as the European colonization of the Americas (see Cronon 1983; S. Lewis and Maslin 2015) and the Industrial Revolution would be flattened within the curve, while the disruptions of the twentieth and twenty-first centuries would not appear at all. In contrast, if we followed the WWF's (2016) time frame (1970–present), then most of this history of destruction would be similarly collapsed (and subtly naturalized) into the average rate preceding the period of interest, erasing the immensity and distinctness of each of these disruptions.

Thresholds for mass extinction also shape perceptions of and relationships with time in important ways. For one thing, they take for granted a temporal triptych of European secular cosmology: a vast, ever-receding past; a rapidly vanishing present; and an unknowable, uncertain, but path-dependent and unidirectional future. In the context of Western scientific discourses of extinction, this culturally specific temporality is presented as if it were a "natural fact" (see Wynter 2003) embedded in the fossil record and manifested in the population dynamics of extant life-forms. This sense of naturalness is accentuated further as rates of extinction are increasingly used to define global-cultural perceptions of time—for instance, a "time of extinction(s)" (see Heise 2010; Rose 2011b; Colebrook 2014; van Dooren 2014) or the sense of a rapidly diminishing future. At the same time, these schemes are overdetermined by colonial temporal regimes (Rifkin 2017) that project years, eras, and epochs over, for instance, the cyclical movements of the moon or the superpositional time of Dreamings (see chapter 2).[14] This imposed temporality also frames the phenomenon of mass extinction as something so enormous in physical and temporal scale that it encompasses and exceeds human perception, experience, and agency (see Morton 2013). Of course, this presumes that *all* humans perceive and inhabit time and space in the same way (as individuals with a life span that is dwarfed by Western geological time), erasing spatio-temporal differences in culture, cosmology, life form, and mode of minding (see Mitchell 2022).[15] As a result of this temporal framing, mass extinction is presented as a sublime excess into which it is almost impossible to intervene, which may suppress action oriented toward addressing the violence and healing the harms at stake, including restitution of broken laws and relationships (see Introduction).

In addition, the thresholds posited by Western scientists mark the temporal and numerical points at which rates of destruction and decline cross over from extinctions to a mass extinction event and, as a result, are afforded greater weight and urgency. The ways in which these cutoff points are defined have important implications for how "(mass) extinction" is approached in ethical and political terms. To flesh out this argument, it is useful to touch on legal and political responses to genocide, a concept to which I will return in more depth in the chapters that follow. As I argue, mass extinction should not be conflated with genocide, yet both involve forms of multiscale, eliminative violence that erases entire worlds from earth. For the moment, I focus on how these enormities are differently framed and what this can tell us about definitions of "mass extinction."

According to its legal definition, genocide involves the goal of eliminating distinct peoples in their entirety, efforts to prevent their restoration, and forms of violence that achieve these ends—usually, but not always (see chapter 5), with deliberate intent.[16] Crucially, genocide does not have to be "completed" in order to "count" as such—that is, genocidal actions and policies can and ought to be prosecuted if the group in question, through immense effort and labor, survives and reconstitutes itself in the face of its attempted elimination. Importantly, the numerical size of the population, the number of people killed, or the proportion of the population does not affect or modify the definition of genocide. That is, legally determining whether genocide has occurred or is occurring does not depend strictly on the crossing of defined numerical thresholds but primarily on ethical and legal determinations of the nature of the violence and its (intended)

"Megadeath"? 45

outcomes. In fact, the use of threshold-based thinking to inform political responses to genocide demonstrates the drawbacks and often horrific consequences of this approach. Notoriously, as genocide rapidly unfolded in Rwanda in 1994, Western states exploited not only conceptual uncertainty about whether the crimes "qualified" as genocide but also uncertainty about the numbers of deaths and the speed of killings in order to avoid intervention (see Barnett 2016). In other words, they used threshold thinking to (simultaneously and retroactively) justify their decisions to act in their own political and economic interests, standing by as mass killings took place with their explicit knowledge. The dire consequences of this approach contributed to the adoption of the precautionary principle in the (albeit inconsistently applied and arguably failed) norm of "Responsibility to Protect."[17] This principle works precisely by loosening or blurring the hard lines drawn around definitional thresholds, theoretically creating more space for response, including ones grounded in ethical and political arguments.

Importantly, the frameworks used to define these two expressions of eliminative violence have different sources and contexts. The definition of "genocide" was created and has been elaborated almost entirely by jurists, legal theorists, ethicists, and political thinkers and practitioners (the majority working in European or Euro-descendent traditions) and then elaborated by many other thinkers—including survivors of genocides. In contrast, the idea of "(mass) extinction" was generated and elaborated nearly exclusively by people working in the Western natural sciences. What would happen, then, if the phenomena that Western science defines as "extinction" were defined instead through diverse ethical, political, and legal contexts? The rest of this book will pose this question in various ways, and in the context of multiple cosmologies and worlds. For the moment, I focus on how this question affects the use of threshold thinking. If genocide were defined only in terms of quantitative thresholds, it would lose what is perhaps its most definitive claim: that there is something horrific, intolerable, and *morally* indefensible about the destruction of entire peoples (and their worlds). Throughout this book, I argue that the same thing can—and ought to—be said of what Western science calls "(mass) extinction." The fact that this phenomenon continues to be conceptualized and defined primarily by means of quantitative criteria creates numerous ethical problems and distortions.

First, it suggests (or at least introduces doubt) that anything *less* than the loss of 75 percent of species does not rise to the severity of a mass extinction event and therefore does not garner the higher level of severity and attention that this term confers. What, then, becomes of the centuries of harms to unique life-forms that have fragmented and decimated but not *eliminated* unique worlds or life-forms such as the example of the Black Oak savanna? Certainly, such examples are still treated as ecological "bads" in most mainstream discourses. Yet they are not afforded the more ethically and politically weighty title of "mass," "extinction," or "event," to which they are compared and against which their urgency is ranked or triaged. In a threshold-based framework, these harms remain (to lesser or greater degrees) data points in the curve of a background rate of normalized disruptions that, as mentioned earlier in this chapter, erases the concrete specifics of the beings harmed and worlds disrupted and naturalizes the harms they absorb. Second, thinking about "(mass) extinction" in relation to thresholds skews how the *type* of response is imagined. Specifically, it emphasizes the need to "reverse the curve" of extinctions by, for example, increasing populations of particular species or zoning areas with high proportions of biodiversity for conservation. Much as medical models of disability seek to solve the collective "problem" of different bodies/minds through "cure" instead of (also) addressing structural forms of ableism—and sometimes displacing and disincentivizing this work (see Kafer 2013; Clare 2017)—threshold approaches offload the labor of transformation onto the *subjects* of harm, failing to address structural causes.

An approach to "(mass) extinction"—and eliminative harms not captured by that term—rooted in the recognition of *violence, harm,* and *oppression* would dramatically change this conceptualization of and possibilities of response. It would shift attention to qualitative experiences of harm (and to measures that exceed the Euro-descendent division between qualitative and quantitative knowledge). This would make it possible to address deep-seated forms of structural violence that extend over large, plural temporalities and spaces, and that may take different forms throughout their trajectories. For instance, it would enable analysis of the ongoing effects of European colonization or the consequences of the "Columbian exchange" (see chapter 4). In a similar vein, a violence-informed approach would focus not just on deaths or extinctions—or on actions leading to these outcomes— but on any entities, events, or phenomena that move life-forms and worlds toward elimination. Again, the comparison with treatments of genocide— and particularly with recent critical elaborations of the concept—is instructive here. Critical discourses of genocide pay attention not only to what are often considered the effects, means, and/or evidence of the harm—killings, displacements, removal of children, and other forms of violence—but also to the *structures and cultures* that engender them and to "genocidal outcomes" such as the decimation of a population or the destruction of a language (see Barta 2000 and chapter 5). Discussions of genocide also often include detailed accounts of historical and temporal, often accelerating phases of violence (see Stanton 2016), which may not constitute genocide in themselves but that create contexts that support it. And, of course, assessments of genocide almost always include attention to political discourses and framings—such as the use of dehumanizing language, stereotypes, and social practices—that foster cultures and systems that support and/or promote genocide. If genocide were defined in the way that "(mass) extinction" currently is, in the absence of these features, it would be akin to aggregating statistics for murders and other specified harms in the relevant time and place and comparing it to the average rate of such crimes (for instance, homicide statistics). Certainly, these statistics would show the presence of violence and its accentuation at specific points, but the *eliminative* nature of the violence and the presence of *cultures and structures* that support it would be ignored. Along with "(mass) extinction," I would argue that this is precisely what is happening in global formations of (among other things) racism, sexual violence, and ableist violence. In these contexts, killings and other harms are individualized and aggregated as part of a naturalized background rather than recognized as intense expressions of collective, large-scale, structural (see chapter 3), and often eliminative violence.

In this vein, it is important to think carefully about how the term "mass" is mobilized in discussions of genocide and extinction, respectively. As mentioned, popular and Western scientific discourses of extinction use the term "mass" in a technical sense that refers to specific numerical thresholds. But they also tap into entrenched collective discourses and memory of "mass violence" and mass killing, emerging in particular from the wars and genocides of the twentieth century. In this context, the term "mass" often evokes the scale and totality of an act of violence. However, I focus on a different element of the term "mass": the process of *massification,* perhaps most famously outlined by German Jewish philosopher Hannah Arendt (1973). For Arendt, the creation of the "masses" required for totalitarian governance (and mass killing) involved the *systematic breaking of relations* to produce alienated, atomized individuals. Broken from their original contexts and recomposed as a homogeneous quantity of life (see the first sections of this chapter), these fragmented bits of worlds are vulnerable to totalizing forms of control, management, instrumentalization, and, indeed, elimination. In the chapters that follow, I show how global patterns of extinction entail a very similar process, involving the systematic dissolution of worlds by overlapping, structural forms of violence—including those involved in conservation efforts. Indeed, it is in this massified, homogenized form that life-forms and worlds become repackaged and valued as commodities, ecosystem services, endangered species, sources of genetic material, or biodiversity hotspots.

From this perspective, the use of the term "mass" in "mass extinction" is problematic in that it is used only descriptively (and sometimes metaphorically) and not *literally* enough. That is, it gestures toward and mobilizes an amorphous collective sense of severity and horror without making clear how and why this form of destruction occurs and recurs. What's more, it can be used to provoke urgent action but often toward processes that *support, increase, and rely on massification* instead of working to end it, including the bio-, necro-, and thanato-political forms of conservation discussed in this chapter and the extractive-capitalist ones I discuss in the chapters that follow. In a similar sense, the naturalizing language used in the Western sciences tends to treat life-forms as if they came in masses, obscuring or at least failing to explain how they have been transformed into this status by regimes of violence (including, and often leveraging, the Western sciences). I propose that, if the term "mass" is to be used in the context of "extinction," it should be placed in this broader context of "massification." Threshold thinking and arguments based on it can certainly be helpful in mobilizing public action. But if this action is not directed toward addressing the *violences* at the heart of "(mass) extinction," it might not only fail to address the escalating destruction of life-forms and worlds but in fact make it worse.

MASS EXTINCTION *EVENTS*

Within mainstream scientific discourses, mass extinctions are *events*—radical ruptures in time after which it is assumed that nothing will ever be the same. They mark monumental geo-historical changes, acting as bookends, boundary markers, or "golden spikes" to delineate the epochs (and epics) of Eurocentric time.[18] The converse is also true: Eurocentric measures of time are surveyed and mapped onto earth through the basic units of stratigraphy that organize Western scientific frames of geological time, engraving

"Megadeath"? 49

the deep history of the planet with Euro-American place-names.[19] This pattern of the naming and claiming of time periods continues today in the wildly influential movement among natural and social scientists to name a new Anthropocene epoch (see, for instance, Crutzen 2002; Zalasiewicz 2008; Steffen et al. 2011; S. Lewis and Maslin 2015).[20] As with the past five mass extinctions, the current, rapid destruction of life-forms is one of many indicators being used as evidence of a major break in time—or, more accurately, the universalizing meta-Time of Western scientific geological thought. And, as in discussions of the previous mass extinctions, Anthropocene discourses predict that this indelible change in Time will be inscribed directly onto the planet. Some Western scientists working in this context claim that mounting extinctions will "swe[ep] clean" the majority currently extant species—humans included—leaving only a new geological layer as evidence of our existence (Zalasiewicz 2008, 2). Even scholars critical of the Western scientific inscription of power onto place aver that the coming "sixth mass extinction event" is turning earth into a text of human excess (Szerzynksi 2012; Yusoff 2011) that will ultimately be overwritten by earth itself. In these discourses, the expected extinction event takes on a sense of the melancholic sublime (see Heise 2016), its scalar and moral enormity seeming to shatter Time itself, foreclosing all other futures and bringing history to a definitive end.[21]

Despite their pessimistic tones, counterfactual scenarios of "(human) extinction" are practically oriented: they encourage their audiences to "*imagine* the worst" with the hope of taking urgent action (while there is still time) to avoid it. That is, they hope to mobilize sufficient attention, resources, and efforts to ensure that the futures they imagine remain hypothetical. However, treating the predicted "(mass) extinction event" as a break in Time also has important implications for the formation and maintenance of contemporary subjectivities identified with, invested in, and recognized as examples of dominant norms of humanity (see Colebrook 2014; Mitchell 2017b; Mitchell and Theriault 2020). Specifically, it offers a binary horizon of existence/extinction against which imaginaries of the future of humanity can be projected in stark existential relation to their boundary conditions. As I have argued elsewhere (Mitchell 2017b; Mitchell and Chaudhury 2020) and discuss further in chapter 6, the sense of intensity and urgency generated by discourses of human extinction are powerful factors shaping imaginaries of hyper- and/or post-humans in whom currently dominant norms of race, ability, gender, and other factors are concentrated. At the same time, exposure to the sublimity of total destruction can, for such subjects, produce powerful somatic experiences of terror, sadness, stimulation, and pleasure (Mitchell and Theriault 2020). For instance, such subjects might experience the thrill of being alive to witness a break in Time, the comfort of knowing that one will die before the worst happens, the gloom that one may be part of the last generation to interact with particular life-forms, perhaps among the last humans, or, conversely, the hope that one will form part of an elite group of future survivors.

This subject-forming experience is based on an important paradox: that even as extinction is framed as inevitable, it remains unthinkable for most contemporary Western subjects who identify with dominant norms of humanity. More specifically, it is *made* unthinkable in at least two different ways. First, the temporal scales into which "(mass) extinction events" are projected are beyond the scope of Western secular time frames such as life spans, the time of governance, and so on (see Morton 2013). Second, contemplating the destruction of normatively defined humanity without immediately dismissing it as horrific and intolerable is considered anti-human, misanthropic, and even pathological (Colebrook 2014). In other words, within social, political, and ethical structures that seek to sustain existing norms of humanity, the acceptable response to the possibility of an extinction event is to bolster, sustain, or restore the systems that reproduce this norm (Mitchell 2017b). Yet, in a context in which humanity is overwhelmingly defined in terms of colonial-capitalist political and economic systems and by hierarchies of race, ability, gender, and species (see Wynter 2003; Ferreira da Silva 2007; Mitchell and Chaudhury 2020; Braidotti 2022), imagining the destruction of these systems may be a fruitful strategy for co-creating more inclusive futures.

Furthermore, the default position of *imagining* the total destruction of one's world as a *future possibility*, a horizon of subjectivity, and a *radical break* with existing conditions embodies immense existential privilege. This position is available only to those who have not experienced the ends (or near-ends) of their worlds or been told that this fate is inevitable and/or desirable. And, by positing itself as a universal experience—for instance, the common refrain that humanity faces an unprecedented existential threat—it erases the experiences of communities who live with and through this experience every day, often over centuries. Indeed, for many communities, the end of the world is not a feared future or a hypothetical event but a concrete part of their ongoing history. For example, Anishinaabe writer

Lawrence William Gross (2002) argues that his people long ago confronted world-ending violence with the advent of settler colonialism, which mandates the total destruction of Indigenous peoples (see Veracini 2010) and assumes that they will "disappear" into history (see Vizenor 1994). In this vein, Potawatomi philosopher Kyle Powys Whyte (2016, 207) argues that "some indigenous peoples already inhabit what our ancestors would have likely characterized as a dystopian future." As he explains:

> It would have been an act of imagining dystopia for our ancestors to consider the erasures we live through today, in which some Anishinaabek are finding it harder to obtain supplies of birch bark, or seeing algal blooms add to factors threatening whitefish populations, or fighting to ensure the legality in the eyes of the industrial settler state of protecting wild rice for harvest. Yet we do not give up by dwelling in a nostalgic past even though we live in our ancestors' dystopia. . . . We put dystopia in perspective as just a brief, yet highly disruptive, historical moment for us—at least so far. (Whyte 2016, 208)

As this quote suggests, current patterns of extinction (and indeed, the temporal claims of the Anthropocene) need to be understood in the context of centuries of *continuous* and *ongoing* colonial ecological destruction (Davis and Todd 2017), including the climatic effects of deforestation and other large-scale transformations of ecosystems (Cronon 1983; S. Lewis and Maslin 2015) but also ongoing genocides and forms of cultural domination—*not* as sudden deviations. From this perspective, world-destroying events do not necessarily mark final ends; they are part of *continuous* histories of ongoing violence experienced in the daily lives of the people and other beings doing the daily *and* intergenerational work of surviving them.

In a resonant sense, many disabled people are targeted for collective elimination through various ideologies of "cure," neo-eugenicist policies, and ableist popular attitudes in order to protect or enhance the future of humanity (see Clare 2017; S. Taylor 2017) in the face of its feared extinction.[22] As unmarked disabled thinker Alison Kafer (2013, 31, 2–3) puts it, in contemporary ableist societies, it is widely accepted that disabled people are a "threat to futurity" and that "a future with disability is a future no one wants. . . . A better future . . . is one that excludes disability and disabled bodies." Such attitudes are intensifying in contexts of fear surrounding ecological collapse, in which it is increasingly assumed that future humans need to be "fully" or even hyperabled in order to survive and rebuild societies and that "genetic flaws" may weaken the species when it is most vulnerable (see Mitchell 2022 and chapter 6). As such, for some disabled people, participating in societal structures means being forced to participate actively in structures that seek our collective elimination. For instance, Autistic people daily confront a multibillion-dollar global "war on autism" (A. McGuire 2016) supported by most states, the UN, and other key political actors and backed by medical-scientific establishments, whose aim is to eradicate the kinds of difference we embody as well as our collective identities and futures (see Mitchell 2022). Often starting in utero and continuing through lifelong behavioral interventions, surveillance, and structural violence (including abuse, high rates of murders, and incarcerations), the purpose of this war is to, in clinical terms, bring about the extinction of our ways of being (Mitchell 2022).[23] A future world without us is not a feared outcome but a goal fervently and explicitly pursued by the dominant cultures in which we live. What is made unthinkable in contemporary ableist societies is not the collective destruction of our ways of being human but rather their continued existence. As such, contemplating the eclipse of the currently dominant norm of humanity (distinct from humans in general) is *necessary* if we are to imagine futures that include diverse bodyminds.

Whether we are targeted for elimination on the basis of genocide, racism, ableism, or bodymind difference (see Clare 2017)—or by all the above and more—for those of us whose extinction is actively sought by the majority society, surviving the event of collective destruction is not just an abstract sublime, distant-future horizon against which our identity is sharpened or our adrenaline piqued. Nor is it merely a source of *anxiety*, which is defined by the absence or not-yet-presence of the feared thing; or a hypothetical scenario for fleshing out, testing, or supporting particular policy strategies. Rather, it is a painful, exhausting, sometimes exhilarating, everyday struggle that is *already well underway*, even as the dominant culture argues about whether or not an event is occurring or may occur.

The work done by communities actively surviving efforts to end their worlds is that of creating and foregrounding *continuities* in the face of proposed breaks in Western Time that seek to consign them to an exhausted, ossified, and impermeable past. The survivance (Vizenor 1994) of such communities by no means negates or reduces the severity of the violence it refuses.[24] Rather, it challenges the assumption of an event that constitutes

"Megadeath"? 53

a clean break between past and future and rejects the imposition of a final and irrefutable *discontinuity* in Western Time, which, as I argue in the chapters that follow, many currently dominant groups use to consolidate power. Continuity work cuts across the strata of Western Time, striating and scrambling ideas of neatly and irreversibly divided periods and historical phases. Crucially, it obstructs attempts to place certain worlds behind the temporal rifts inscribed by evental logics, trapping them in particular strata of the past and framing their ongoing presence as anachronistic or even antithetical to the future. Indeed, many communities who assert continuity into and beyond posited evental breaks are framed by dominant discourses as anachronisms or holdovers that may be instrumentalized to get to, but ultimately have no place in, the (post-evental) present and future (Whyte 2017b). Robinson's trilobites, mentioned in the chapter epigraph, satirically embody the work of traversing and muddling the neat stratification of Time. Although extinct, they appear in contemporary contexts, speaking twenty-first century colloquial English and sipping Starbucks coffee, refusing to stay buried in the geological strata to which they have been assigned by Western science. They chatter skeptically back at Western scientific narratives of (mass) extinction that refuse their continuity with the extant present or its many possible futures.

Finally, the idea of a mass extinction *event*—a momentous rupture in big Time—also shifts attention from the *experiential, embodied* elements of what Western science calls "(mass) extinction." As I mentioned in the previous section, threshold thinking about extinction uses timescales that are placed at odds with Western secular notions of everyday, mundane time (see Mitchell 2014a). This strategy distracts attention from the ways in which the harms in question are continuously embodied at multiple scales, including in the concrete lived experience of structural violence. Indeed, many of the concrete manifestations of what Western science calls "extinction" are more akin to "quasi-events" (Povinelli 2016): happenings that do *not* constitute a clear, clean break with history in the overarching, linear Western sense but that can nonetheless have profound, long-reaching legacies. For instance, the appearance of boreal fish, bears, and fungi in the Arctic regions (which some people report noticing over less than one lifetime; see Leduc 2010) may not constitute a sudden and total historical rupture of that ecosystem and world, let alone extinction itself. As such, they are not markers of Western Time in the grand, evental sense, but they are no less manifestations of extinction than the passage of geological epochs. In this

54   "Megadeath"?

book, I think about modes of comportment toward extinction that recognize its visceral, somatic, multitemporal, concrete, and *experiential* elements, which requires looking beyond the boundaries of Time and the horizon of the event.

TURNING AGAINST ONTOLOGY

"Extinction" signals the total, irreversible eradication of a life-form and possibly, in its total form, of life itself. When "life" is equated with "existence"— as it often is in contemporary Western scientific and philosophical contexts (see Meillassoux 2008; Povinelli 2016)—it is also assumed to mark a crossing from *being into nonbeing*. Indeed, despite the frequent conflation of extinction and death (see the first section of this chapter), the technical term most often used in the Western sciences to describe life-forms with living members is not "non-extinct" or even "living." Instead, it is "extant"—a word that means *in existence* (not specifically "alive"; and not related to "extinguishment," which is the source of the term "extinction"). The use of this term suggests that the idea of extinction marks a boundary not only between life and death but also between existence and nonexistence.

This way of thinking is distinctly *ontological*. That is, it presumes that there is a realm of "being" separate from (and also perhaps emergent from and supervening on) beings, life-forms, and worlds. In recent years, many academic fields, including anthropology, social theory, and international relations, have adopted what is often called an "ontological turn": a focus on conditions of being and nonbeing, or beliefs about them. I want to argue that this emphasis on ontology has been integral to Western scientific discourses on extinction since their inception in the nineteenth century and increasingly since the emergence of late twentieth-century discourses on "biodiversity" (see chapter 2). For instance, for unmarked environmental philosopher Holmes Rolston III (1985, 723, emphasis mine), extinction is more than "just" death in the sense that "it kills forms (species) *beyond* existences." Embedding the Platonic idea of abstract forms that undergird but are not reducible to earthly beings, Rolston treats "species" as categories that transcend the beings that compose them—as part of a higher plane of "existence."

Despite the universality attributed to it, the concept of "ontology"— and the particular notion of the relation between being and nonbeing described here—emerges from particular Euro-descendent cosmovisions.[25] Specifically, it draws from Parmenidean and Platonic Greek thought, the taxonomies of the European Middle Ages (Wilkins 2009), and, later, Heideggerian and other continental philosophies. Many practitioners of "ontological turns" want to dislodge or question universalist, Eurocentric ways of thinking and to center other cosmovisions.[26] Yet they do not often critically consider the colonial effects of presuming the universality of ontology itself (see Todd 2016)—for instance, by assuming that all cultures distinguish between being and nonbeing, beings and Being, extant and extinct. Such approaches ask in *which* ontology a being is embedded rather than critically questioning the assumption that all cosmovisions and worlds rest upon ontology. Put another way, this approach treats ontology as a universal, imposing it across other worlds.

Once we stop presuming that ontology is universal, we can easily detect several issues with ontological accounts of "extinction" and "mass extinction." One of them is the all-or-nothing dichotomy imposed by formal definitions of extinction, which distorts perceptions of what is lost, harmed, or at stake. We can find this logic at work in the example of the Black Oak savanna discussed earlier in this chapter. Western scientific discourses on extinction could account—in empirical and (particular) ethical terms—for the extinction of any of the "species" that co-compose it. However, these discourses provide no ontological category for the total destruction of this (or any) unique *world* if its constituent species still exist somewhere on earth. The term "extirpation" denotes the removal of a particular *life-form* from a world but not the destruction of the specific constellation of beings who co-compose it. Indeed, the destruction of a "species" is recognized as part of the Western scientific ontological framework, and death is understood as a means of transforming from extant to nonexistent. But the fragmentation of a living-and-nonliving, multispecies world, some of whose constituent beings still exist elsewhere, does not have a clear place in this framework because it does not disturb a Western scientific ontological category. This example demonstrates how ontological thinking in the context of "(mass) extinction" concentrates attention and concern on certain phenomena and directs it away from others, while imposing value judgments about their relative importance or gravity.

A second problem is that ontological approaches that rely on binaries between being and nonbeing, and/or being and Being, bracket out the various degrees and hybrids of existence, negation, possibility, virtuality, emergence, and (un)becoming that shape relations within and among plural worlds. Most importantly, they tend to rule out the possibility of relations between beings coded as "extant" or existent with two other categories: those declared to be "extinct" and those categorized as "nonexistent" (that is, never-existent or not-yet-existent) within Western science. Robinson's trilobites, for instance, do not exist in ontological terms: they are extinct, buried, crushed out of existence. Yet they still speak to us (or at least to Robinson) across the cordon of their "extinct" status, asserting their presence and expressing their anger at being converted into cheesy office paraphernalia. As fossils, they taunt us with the threat of our own mineralization, teasing us with material reminders of evolutionary ambush. They are not, according to Western science, extant—and yet here they are in spiky, contentious relation with scientific discourses, fossil records, school curricula, popular culture, a contemporary Indigenous novelist—and us as twenty-first-century readers.

Indeed, among diverse cosmologies, beings such as ancestors, future generations (human and otherwise), and possible worlds are not always relegated to the realm of nonbeing imposed by ontological thinking. In many cosmovisions, it is possible to have rich, co-constitutive relationships with beings that Western science codes as "extinct"—or never extant (for example, "mythical," "fictional," or "magical," all of which deny the status of being). For instance, Australian settler scholar Elizabeth Povinelli (2016, 68) describes a visit to the Queensland Gallery of Modern Art in Brisbane, Australia, during which she was accompanied by some of her Indigenous collaborators in the Karrabing film collective.[27] At the museum, the group encountered the preserved fossils of what Western scientists categorize as plesiosaurs and a pliosaurus. On encountering these fossils, a member of the Collective, Gracie Binbin, remarked that the former was the patrilineal Dreaming of her late husband and children, called a durlg ("sea monster") in their language (Povinelli 2016, 61). Plesiosaurs and pliosaurs, as animals, have been extinct—that is, have not existed—for tens of millions of years, according to Western science. Yet the *durlg-as-Dreaming* continues to exist and to sustain kinship structures, responsibilities, along with connections to Country and living relatives. For this reason, Povinelli clarifies, what the Karrabing group encountered in the art gallery were not simply "fossils *of*" durlgs but actually "two kinds of durlgs": the one named "plesiosaurus" and "pliosaurus" by Western science; and the vital, lively durlg Dreaming that remains (and always will remain) an active participant in the world that Binbin co-composes. In fact, several decades earlier, Povinelli had entered a small cave with a fossil that the then-middle-aged

Binbin had first encountered as a young woman. The cave contained a durlgmö—the fossil of a plesiosaur—which Binbin read as a sign that she and her kin, who were forcefully transferred from the saltwater region in which the durlg of her husband rests, now belonged to their new lands. In emerging from the sand, the durlgmö also demanded care from Binbin and her family, including the work of discussing its appearance and interpreting its possible meanings. The family was also made responsible for visiting the durlg regularly and protecting it from white people who might remove it and turn it into the kind of "fossils" the group met in the art gallery. As an animal recognized by Western science, it no longer lives and reproduces, but as a Dreaming, the durlg continues actively to co-create Country and the kinship structures that sustain it (see chapter 2). This example scrambles the tidy distinction between "extant" and "extinct," "Being" and "non-Being," on which ontological accounts of extinction and mass extinction hinge. By placing beings they count as "extinct" on the "other side" of existence, mainstream accounts of "(mass) extinction" cannot account for, and actively erase, the role of "extinct" beings in relational structures.

Another issue with ontological accounts of "(mass) extinction" is that they tend to treat "non-Being" as nothingness, and nothingness as empty. Being is understood as the locus and medium of all modes of existence, difference, and possibility. Non-Being, in contrast, is framed as a void, a pure vacuum with no potential for creativity, generativity, or, indeed, life. This distinction carries heavily ethical weight in Euro-descendent frameworks: since "Being" is associated with the flourishing of "life"—"humans" in particular—"non-Being" is framed as the enemy, the antithesis of creativity. This approach brackets the dynamic potential and significance of what ontology codes as "non-Being" within many other cosmologies. For instance, the Kumulipo chant, one of the most fundamental Kānaka Maoli moʻelelo (oral histories), locates the origin of the universe in what Western science might label as "nothingness." This cosmogony, or origin story, draws its name from "kumu" (source, origin, foundation) and "lipo" (dark, night, chaos) (Oliveira 2014), or the "slime that establishes the earth" (Kameʻeleihiwa 1992, loc. 310). From this void emerges the entire Kānaka Maoli cosmos, starting with coral polyps and proceeding through numerous periods in which deities, plants, humans, and islands form (see chapter 2). However, these beings and their becomings do not banish or eliminate the original state; it continues to exist as "Pō", a realm to which Kānaka return through death (Goldberg-Hiller and Silva 2011). Within this cosmovision, non-Being is an—perhaps *the* most—important source of the ongoing creative emergence of beings and life-forms. Far from a sterile antithesis to life and being, non-Being can be understood as a permanent source of creative energy and generative potential. Some Western philosophical and scientific narratives embrace a similar understanding of non-Being as the virtual (Deleuze 1994; Badiou 2009)—that is, a field of possibilities that are real but have not yet, and may never be, realized. From these perspectives, "the void" may be understood as a wellspring of radical material, social and political change, and transformation (see Badiou 2009). All these possibilities are precluded by ontological frameworks that understand "being/existence" as the realm of creativity, life, and flourishing and "nonbeing/nonexistence/ extinction" as a black hole—and that draw sharp lines between them. The durlgs discussed in this section, the "extinct" trilobites that air their grievances to Eden Robinson's (2017) characters, the saber-toothed tigers that cry out to Joe Sheridan and Roronhiakewen "He Clears the Sky" Dan Longboat (2006; see also chapter 2), the revenant buffalo herds described by Tasha Hubbard (2014; see also chapter 6), and many other beings all bite back sharply against this binary.

∼

The arguments in this chapter show that "extinction" and "mass extinction" are not as "conceptually simple" (Purvis, Jones, and Mace 2000, 1124) as many Western scientists suggest. On the contrary, each of these terms embody specific assumptions about cosmology, politics, ethics, and possibilities of response to global patterns of ecological destruction. In particular, I have shown how several dominant ways of thinking about "(mass) extinction events"—the conflation of extinction with (mega-)death, threshold thinking, evental logics, and ontological approaches—produce particular relationships with this phenomenon while displacing or erasing others. They also constrain forms of ethical-political response and, as the following chapters will demonstrate, channel it in ways that often support and entrench structures of power and violence. Having demonstrated how Western scientific discourses of extinction open up certain kinds of knowledge and action while shutting down others, I now look more closely at what they consider to be at stake in "(mass) extinction": "biodiversity."

2 (Bio)Plurality

Difference, Sameness, and the Violence of Biodiversity

> We are in the season of Wolmamirri. . . . [We] know it's
> Wolmamirri because the stringy bark is in flower. . . . [so] we know
> it is time to hunt stingray. . . . We feel these messages in our body,
> and our body sends messages to the fruits and the animals. . . . The
> wind may tell the miyapunu, the turtle, that it is time to leave the
> shore and head out to open sea. That wind would also tell us, if
> we listen, that it is no longer the right time to hunt miyapunu. We
> only hunt at certain times of year, at the right time. We only take a
> certain amount, the right amount. And it is not us who decide those
> times and those amounts, it is the animals, and it is Country. . . . [If]
> we do not attend to the messages, [if] we fail to harvest yam or hunt
> fish, that is disrespectful. . . . You see, all animals have their own law,
> their own tribes, their own songs, their own knowledge. . . . This is
> *diversity beyond measure,* beyond comprehension.
>
> —BAWAKA COUNTRY ET AL.,
> "Co-becoming Bawaka" (emphasis mine)

Reading these words, co-composed by members of the Bawaka Country research collective, one can sense the density of connection that enlivens and sustains Country.[1] As the Bawaka Research Collective stresses, these beings are related externally "to" each other not (only) as discrete objects but also as integral parts *of* each other. They are co-respondent, reflexive, and co-constitutive, furnishing and shaping the conditions of each other's existence. As the Collective puts it, they exist in a state of dynamic "inter-being." The forms of difference embodied by these conditions are, as the Collective states, "beyond measure" or even beyond "comprehension" by Western scientific modes of thought. In contrast, proponents of mainstream conservation are almost entirely concerned with kinds of difference that can be measured, managed, optimized, reproduced, and capitalized on by Western scientific knowledge systems. In this chapter, I argue that the kind of difference they seek to protect—and to *produce*—is different in kind (not degree) from what the Bawaka Collective describes. Indeed, the global-scale promotion of "biodiversity" may do substantial damage to the *plurality* that is nurtured by and integral to Country and other unique worlds.

Since the late 1980s, Western conservationists have created globally influential institutions, normative frameworks, and popular movements to protect what they call "biodiversity." This term was coined in order to shift the focus of conservation from particular species to the quality of *difference itself* as a property of ecosystems. Indeed, just as conservation draws on notions of "life" as a property of biological organisms (see chapter 1), the biodiversity framework treats difference as a quality or property that can vary in amount, degree, and quality and that is produced and embodied by ecosystems. Yet not all forms of difference are the same, and the way that difference is understood, produced, and sustained has important implications for life-forms and worlds, and the kinds of relations that make them.

The framework of biodiversity produces, records, and organizes difference by contrasting the *similarities* of beings within taxonomic categories with their *dissimilarities* to beings in other categories—most often, between species. For clarity, I refer to these distinctions as "internal sameness" and "external difference." However, these distinctions are not indisputable facts but rather reflections of how the Western sciences organize expressions of difference, and they introduce significant distortions to how we understand and relate to it. For instance, the strong emphasis on internal sameness within species imposes an unrealistic degree of homogeneity by erasing the singularity of particular beings and the unique histories of life-forms and multi-life-form communities. Further, while they claim to describe and preserve already existing forms of difference, many mainstream biodiversity and conservation initiatives actively entrain life-forms and worlds to conform to abstract ideals of difference. For instance, they may work to increase redundancy or substitutability in order to make ecosystems "work (better) for humans," whether in economic (see Sukhdev et al. 2010, 12) or cultural (Díaz et al. 2018) terms.[2] In other contexts, the biodiversity paradigm seeks to protect what it regards as universal processes, such as those related to evolution, above and sometimes to the exclusion of particular life-forms and worlds. In so doing, strategies aimed at preserving biodiversity often have deeply homogenizing effects. Specifically, they impose the *same kinds of difference* onto singular worlds across the planet, displacing unique modes of difference, differentiation, and the relations that nurture them. At the same time, the forms of difference they produce often align with, and may support, highly destructive processes such as extraction and commodification.

In this chapter, I pivot toward another kind of difference: (bio)plurality. This term gestures to, without claiming to encompass, the dynamic intersections among unique beings who create the grounds for each other's distinct modes of existence. I place the prefix "bio" in parentheses because plurality need not always be dominated by (or even include) beings that Western science classes as "living." It may also encompass rich relations among living beings, beings that are no longer living, those that never were living, those that are extinct, and those that may come to be (see chapter 1 and the Conclusion). Further, in contrast with the generic, universalized, linear processes central to discourses of biodiversity, (bio)plurality is embodied in multiple kinds of mobilities and generative "transmotions" (Vizenor 1994, 2015) of life-forms across multiple temporal and spatial scales, each exuding its own unique history.

My aim in foregrounding (bio)plurality is not to reject the concept of biodiversity wholesale or to substitute the former for the latter. Indeed, the ideas of "biodiversity" and "(bio)plurality" overlap in some respects and (radically) diverge in others but nonetheless coexist—both as conceptual tools and as modes of relating to contemporary ecosystems. I also use the term "(bio)plurality" as a bridge to highlight points of convergence and resonance between multiple knowledge systems. However, it should never be used to replace concepts distinct or inherent to specific knowledge systems, to conflate them, or to posit a universal claim to truth. Instead, the term "(bio)plurality" is a temporary, flexible tool intended to critique existing systems through which difference is projected upon life-forms and worlds by dominant knowledge systems. Having harnessed billions of dollars, global social support, and financing from the world's most powerful states, international organizations, nongovernmental organizations (NGOs), and, increasingly, powerful private-sector actors (see Dauvergne 2016), the biodiversity framework possesses powerful world-forming and world-transforming capacities. My goal here is to understand what kinds of worlds it works to create and protect—and what kinds of worlds it excludes and even destroys.

HOW "BIODIVERSITY" DISCOURSES MAKE DIFFERENCE

Organizations concerned with protecting biodiversity tend to present their work in terms of *protecting* difference as an already existing property of ecological systems. Much less attention is given to how these discourses and strategies *make* difference conceptually and concretely—that is, how they frame relations of difference between life-forms or how they implement them through practices and interventions ranging from legal protection to forced breeding. To better understand how the biodiversity framework makes difference, I examine several of the key distinctions it posits.

LIFE / NONLIFE

Perhaps the most fundamental marker of difference promoted by the "biodiversity" framework—and more broadly, by the Western sciences—is the one between "life" and "nonlife." This distinction shapes boundaries of concern and attention, underpins ethical and legal attitudes, and defines the stakes of conservation discourses. Indeed, seminal documents related to conservation, not least the *Convention on Biological Diversity* (UN 1992), make hard and explicit distinctions between "living organisms" and the other processes, elements, and materials that they consider to be part of biodiversity but not among its core components. Within the Western sciences, "life" is usually understood as the set of processes through which organisms convert energy to sustain and reproduce themselves. According to Western biochemistry, it is these capacities that differentiate the life processes of biotic beings from the redox (reduction-oxidation) processes that are also carried out by many abiotic beings (Povinelli 2016).[3]

In mainstream discourses on biodiversity, the broad category of life is segmented in subtle but important ways. For instance, conservation programs and databases such as the IUCN's Red List demonstrate a strong bias toward multicellular and especially vertebrate organisms. There is also a well-recorded bias toward "charismatic" animals such as mammals and/or animals and plants deemed valuable within current economic and cultural systems.[4] Popular discourses on mass extinction and conservation also tend to underplay the inequalities of threats to different life-forms and worlds. For instance, far from facing annihilation, many forms of bacteria, algae, and jellyfish are flourishing in contemporary conditions of climate change. This argument is by no means intended to deny or discount the severe threats and harms faced by so many of earth's life-forms. Rather, the point is that conservation programs based on biodiversity seek to protect not life in general but rather *certain forms of life* that reflect the commitments and values, narratives (see Heise 2010), and relational models preferred by its framers (Mitchell 2017a).

Meanwhile, in mainstream discussions of biodiversity, the term "abiotic" groups together a plethora of beings as radically different as water, soil, earthquakes, wind, fire, sunlight, oxygen, and the biochemical remains of dead organisms (see Noss 1990; Delong 1996). Within early discussions about the concept of "biodiversity," there was debate as to whether these entities should be categorized as "ecological" elements and subjects of conservation in themselves, and many conservation projects involve some degree of protection for "habitat" (see Swingland 2001). In practice, however, "abiotic" beings tend to be treated as mere factors in the production and protection of biodiversity, whose primary role is to support life. This approach reflects a hierarchy common to Western scientific knowledge, in which life is understood to be more complex and therefore "higher" than nonlife. Povinelli (2016) identifies this hierarchy as the key expression of what she calls "geontopower": an apparatus of control that enables the bio-, necro-, and thanato-political modes of governance discussed in chapter 1 by dividing governable life from less-governable nonlife.[5] Within geontological frameworks such as conservation, beings that qualify as forms of "life" may achieve relatively greater ethical status and legal-political consideration than those deemed to be "nonlife." However, they may also be subject to intensive interventions into their lives, processes, and relational structures. At the same time, within geontological frameworks, those beings considered to be "nonlife" are often neglected and their roles in co-constituting life-forms and worlds is too often disregarded.

External Difference / Internal Homogeneity

Another strategy of differentiation in biodiversity discourses involves framing species as internally homogeneous but different to each other. Difference, from this perspective, lies in the external relationship between groups of internally similar beings. Individuals of a species are deemed to be similar enough to be interchangeable in ways that matter for conservation—for instance, in terms of their reproductive compatibility. Even differences in the genetic makeup of each individual are valued primarily insofar as they can contribute to reproducing the patterns of sameness by which the species is defined. It is under this logic that Marius the giraffe and others

64 (Bio)Plurality

like him are euthanized by zoos (see chapter 1): they are considered redundant because they are understood to be genetically interchangeable with other individuals of their species. We could call this kind of distinction horizontal because it refers to differences at the same taxonomic level. Species are also differentiated vertically from other taxonomic categories—for instance, amphibians are demarcated from mammals at the level of class. Indeed, the nested hierarchies or "trees" of Western scientific taxonomy use processes of abstraction to create larger, less exclusive categories of internal similarity as we move "up" their levels. For example, the movement from species to genus, genus to class, and so forth groups life-forms together on the basis of increasingly broad similarities such as shared reproductive organs or the possession of a backbone. That is, this system generates, records, and organizes difference by abstracting similarities from singular, specific, and concrete difference.

DISSIMILARITY AND VARIATION

The biodiversity paradigm also marks and designates difference in the form of *dissimilarity* and *variation*. This way of thinking emphasizes a shared starting point or horizon of comparison (Angermeier 1994) against which differences are compared. Philosophically speaking, this means that the idea of "biodiversity" starts from sameness, understanding it as ontologically primary and originary, while framing difference as a secondary property of categories such as species.[6] We can see this logic at work in the abstractive thinking discussed in the previous section: as one moves "down" the levels of the tree, say, from class to order, more subtle differentiations are carved out against the horizon of sameness produced by the higher category.

This logic is derived from the taxonomic theories of Aristotle, which were taken up and elaborated by Carl Linnaeus (1758). Aristotle's goal was to classify life-forms by what he regarded as their "nature"—that is, by their "true" or "essential" form—rather than what he regarded as the superficial similarities and variations that could be observed in their everyday lives and interactions (see Cain n.d.).[7] Aristotle's framing produced a basic taxonomic structure composed of a genus and a differentia, which was elaborated by Linnaeus as more life-forms were cataloged by European scientists. Although taxonomic practice has been modified and developed significantly since (for instance, with the addition of the category of "domain" in 1990), its basic logic and structure remains intact. We can observe it today

(Bio)Plurality

in the system of binomial nomenclature still used in the Western sciences, which treats the "lower" and more specific category (species) as a modifier of the "higher" or more general one (genus). For instance, the Black Oak discussed in chapter 1 is named *Quercus velutina* in this system, where *Quercus* includes the whole genus of oaks, and *velutina* the species. Understood in its broader historical context, binomial nomenclature works as a difference-making machine in which specificity is produced against a presumed horizon of ontological sameness. Within this machine's rubric, sameness is understood as more basic, fundamental, or definitive of a life-form than its singular, concrete, or specific features.

In the same vein, the biodiversity paradigm emphasizes *variations* (see Swingland 2001; CBD 2010a)—that is, marginal differences between beings. Indeed, seminal definitions of biodiversity frame it as "the range of *variation or variety* or differences among some set of attributes" (Swingland 2001, 377, emphasis mine). "Variety" suggests a group of beings that are *versions* of each other, or more precisely, versions of an ideal model of their life-form. In other words, they differ in terms of a range or spectrum of marginal changes or deviations measured against a common horizon or ideal type. In this way, the paradigm reflects the logic described in the previous paragraph, in which sameness is treated as more fundamental or originary than difference.

My aim in highlighting this feature of the biodiversity framework is not to contest the importance of shared characteristics, common origins, or lines of descent within life-forms. Rather, it is to point out that the dominant strategy for making and organizing difference in the Western sciences starts with sameness, giving it ontological priority in the production of difference (see chapter 1). In short, the biodiversity framework promotes processes that generate *marginal*—versus radical, singular, or irrepeatable—difference, while reproducing patterns of sameness. This, in turn, shapes how practitioners of biodiversity recognize and (de)value various kinds of difference, and the forms of difference making that they recognize as desirable. As the following sections of this chapter will show, this is not the only way to understand difference among and between life-forms and worlds. On the contrary, there are *also* many forms of difference that are radical, originary, and irreducible to shared horizons or ideal models and that deserve protection, nurturing, and respect.

Nor is it my intention to suggest that all sameness is bad and all difference is good or that similarity does not play a role in producing difference.

66 (Bio)Plurality

On the contrary, dissimilarity, variation, and marginal difference all produce complex, generative repetitions that enable beings and life-forms to co-exist, thrive, and become "other than themselves" (Grosz 2011, 51). My concern is that the privileging of Western scientific ways of making difference has become so dominant as to erase or crowd out other forms of difference that are integral to life-forms and worlds. I am also concerned with how the emphasis on producing sameness and marginal difference promotes practices and relational models that benefit from the homogenization of life-forms and worlds, such as colonial-capitalist systems.

Logics of Substitution and "Redundancy"

Why do proponents of "biodiversity" pay so much attention to forms of difference rooted in sameness? One major reason is that repetition plays an important role in stabilizing and maintaining the kinds of relational systems that they wish to protect and increase. Indeed, many conservationists understand "diversity"—the main subject of their concern—as "an aggregate measure . . . [meaning that] the components may change without changing the level of diversity" (Norberg et al. 2008, 54). In short, it matters little which specific beings make up an ecosystem as long as the overall quantity of diversity within it remains stable.

The idea of ecological redundancy, central to mainstream Western ecological discourses, illustrates this point. Jon Norberg and his colleagues (2008) describe redundancy as follows: Suppose there are two groups of units, each of which has ten attributes. If all units have the same value for each attribute, then there is true redundancy—that is, the two groups are identical. However, if even a single value in one group differs or varies from the set of values expressed in the others, then this counts as diversity. Diversity of this kind is understood to make ecosystems more resilient, or resistant to disasters. Resilient ecosystems, defined in this manner, contain enough life-forms that are similar enough to perform the same function (e.g., apex predation or nitrogen fixing) but different enough that they are not vulnerable to the same threats (e.g., a pathogen that targets a particular species). These life-forms relate to each other as a kind of ecosystemic backup plan or insurance policy. If one is eradicated or severely reduced, the other can fill its niche without significantly interrupting the flow of ecosystem functions (UN 2003, 63).

The idea of redundancy also performs an important function in the global calculus of conservation and destruction. Specifically, it is reasoned that if services—for instance, carbon sinking—are measured against the total global ecosphere, then the disruption of these services in one region can be rectified by offsetting them in another. This strategy often involves installing *similar* ecosystems and life-forms—which are assumed to be *substitutable*—in place of those that are destroyed. This approach may appear to offer hope for resilience in the face of extinction cascades, but the logic of redundancy and substitution masks the large-scale destruction of unique worlds. For instance, it enables eco-modernists such as Peter Kareiva and his colleagues (Kareiva, Marvier, and Lalasz 2012) to argue that the extinction of the American chestnut, passenger pigeon, and "countless other species from the Steller's sea cow to the dodo" had "no catastrophic or even measurable effects."[8] These authors contend that the ecosystems of which these life-forms were part contained enough substitutes— that is, enough similar life-forms providing the same services and functions—to render the chestnuts, passenger pigeons, and dodos redundant.

As Whyte's (2017) work suggests, this kind of argument considers only the *functional* value of life-forms within Western scientific understandings of ecosystems. It ignores their integral, *co-constitutive* role within singular worlds that cannot exist without them. For instance, Whyte (2017) points out that "in the case of many of these species [the American chestnut], Indigenous peoples used them for canoe-building, food, and medicine." In other words, the fact that the perceived and privileged ecological "function" (in Western scientific terms) of the American chestnut could be carried out by (an)other life-form(s) misses the point. Many Indigenous peoples forged and nurtured relationships, kinship, forms of flourishing, and unique worlds not only with this species but also in many cases with *particular* trees or groups of them—not with abstract services or functions whose value is calculated at regional or global scales of analysis.[9] The logic of redundancy, and its framing as an unquestionably positive feature, masks the violence involved in rendering any life-form or world replaceable and therefore expendable. Within the calculus of redundancy and offsetting, as life-forms are moved across the balance sheet of global conservation, world-wrecking violence and the loss of irreplaceable life-forms and worlds are often made to appear ethically neutral.

It is important to note that the principle of redundancy is integral to the resilience not only of ecosystems but also of capitalist markets—and indeed, much mainstream ecological thinking of the late 1980s (when the idea of biodiversity was popularized) has its sources in market logics. For

68 (Bio)Plurality

instance, *variety* among species that can be used for the same purposes (e.g., hardwoods used as building materials) makes it possible to create hierarchies of value and corresponding opportunities for profit. At the same time, variety provides alternatives that protect the relevant industries if supply collapses, for instance through shifting focus to different species or changing the region of provenance. What's more, the logic of substitutability helps create the "masses" discussed in chapter 1, breaking down unique relations in order to create fungible stocks of desired qualities (e.g., the durability or aesthetic features of hardwood). The massification of life-forms is integral to their commodification, in which aspects of unique life-forms and worlds are severed from their contexts and invested with fungible financial value (Castree 2003; Kosoy and Corbera 2010). In the example discussed here, the inner wood of a tree is stripped of its outer bark, leaves, and roots, thereby disconnecting it from the soil, water, and other plants and animals with whom it forms a world. Through this process, one alienated feature of the tree can be used in financially profitable ways. This is true not only of the physical features of beings commodified in this way but also of the labor they provide in the form of ecosystem services (J. Moore 2015). As Mbembe (2017) shows, it is this same logic that has enabled the ongoing dissection of Black bodies in order to extract commodified labor.

The more abstracted these calculations become, the more they make equivalences between unique life-forms and worlds, and the more they frame them as expendable. For instance, the influential idea of "total economic value" (TEV; see Costanza et al. 1997) suggests that the value of all of earth's biodiversity can—and *should*—be assigned a dollar value on capitalist markets. Unmarked economist Robert Costanza and colleagues (1997) famously sought to calculate the value of ecosystem services provided across the planet by estimating the values of ecosystem services in biomes, multiplying the area of each biome and summing the subtotals. At the time of their study, this number was US$16 to 54 trillion (approximately $23.4 to 95 trillion in 2022 dollars). To put this number into perspective, in 2023, technology company Apple was valued at US$2.82 trillion. Not only does this line of reasoning create massive distortions within its own terms—the relative value of commodities—and expose the value of earth's life-forms to tumultuous market conditions such as inflation, market crashes, and price fluctuations. It also encourages people to relate to earth's ecosystems as if they were just another form of consumer item (such as a social media site) that can be easily exchanged for others rather than co-constituents of unique and irreplaceable worlds.

The logics of substitution and redundancy are increasingly influential within conservation-oriented policymaking, in particular strategies that include corporate and state actors, whose interests are traditionally seen to conflict with those of conservationists. A key example of this approach is the strategy "no net loss" (NNL) or "net positive impact" (NPI), which has been adopted by major organizations ranging from the European Union (2013) to the Australian–British mining giant Rio Tinto (Kareiva and Marvier 2012). According to the IUCN, which has partnered with major corporations and other conservation NGOs on NNL and NPI projects, the term "net"

> acknowledges that some biodiversity losses at [a] development site are *inevitable*, and that biodiversity gains may not be perfectly balanced in regards to the time, space, or type of biodiversity impacted. (IUCN 2015, 7, emphasis mine)

Instead, the restoration of damaged ecosystems is expected to replenish the amount of diversity at a particular site. This "amount" is measured in terms of the numbers of species and vegetation *types*, their long-term viability, their ecological function, and their contribution to evolutionary processes. Importantly, the restored or replaced biodiversity must meet the criterion of equivalency—that is, it must be "similar in *type* to biodiversity losses incurred by the project" (IUCN 2015, 12, emphasis mine). The idea of "equivalency" or of "types" erases the uniqueness of particular plants, animals, microbes, soils, and waters destroyed by such development projects, including their distinct histories in that place and relationships with other beings. In some cases, NNL and NPI arrangements involve compensation in the form of financial payments to humans affected by the project. However, there is no effort to restore or compensate for the harms caused by disrupting and destroying ecological relations forged over millennia or even for causing the extinction or extirpation of a species. As far as this account of biodiversity is concerned, the replacement of any *similarly* functioning biota constitutes full compensation for the destruction of the original ecosystem.

What's more, the IUCN report quoted here suggests that ecologically destructive development requiring compensation is "inevitable" and therefore must be mitigated (not prevented). Within such an approach, mainstream conservation naturalizes, concedes to, and ultimately props up ecologically destructive industries and actors, protecting them against future risks. In addition, destructive industries often use NPI projects to generate public support by claiming to leave eocsystems better than they found them. Beyond the erasure of the uniqueness of ecosystems, these claims reflect deep histories of racialized and colonial narratives claiming that lands not dominated by Western systems of management are polluted, degraded, or poorly stewarded and awaiting improvement (see Voyles 2015). It is also important to remember that, within the Lockean principles that undergird nation-states and the global system of states, "improvement" in the form of physical alteration is a primary means of possession or seizure of land, including by colonial powers.

Another expression of this logic is found in "biodiversity offsetting" or "biodiversity banking" schemes. Much like carbon-trading systems, these instruments allow developers to purchase fungible "credits"—or "standard noncontroversial units"—that entitle them to destroy particular species or types of ecosystems (Pawliczek and Sullivan 2011). The funds generated through the purchase of the credits support biodiversity banks: areas of privately owned land set aside for the conservation of endangered species or ecosystems *similar* to those being destroyed. This is possible only when biodiversity is imagined globally as a quantity of a generic substance that can be redistributed across the planet, transferring burdens and compensation to the places where they are most easily and profitably accessed. The global bartering of biodiversity, like the movement of investment capital, often involves large-scale transformations in certain regions to ensure the flow of benefits to other regions. This is evident in the report *Banking on Biodiversity: A Natural Way Out of Poverty* (Roe et al. 2010). It suggests that "biodiversity rich" regions in the Global South can develop ecologically responsible income streams by acting as stewards of banked biodiversity (Roe et al. 2010). In practice, this means converting much of their ancestral lands to "protected" spaces that are ultimately controlled by foreign investors (see Introduction and chapter 6). Not only does this practice solidify global structures of inequality and expropriation, but it also frames the predominantly Black and Brown inhabitants of the Global South as providers of services and capital for the Global North (Sian Sullivan 2013).

Protecting Processes

"Evolution is good," asserts the unmarked American conservation ecologist Michael Soulé (1985, 731), who is widely credited as a founder of conservation biology and co-originator of the concept of "biodiversity." This statement may seem like common sense to a contemporary reader raised within Eurocentric knowledge systems: evolution has produced all existing life-forms, including *Homo sapiens,* so members of our species are undoubtedly its beneficiaries. Yet it reflects a more complex normative commitment to protecting perceived progress toward greater levels of complexity and diversity. This perceived progress is valued not only because it increases the resiliency of ecosystems by enhancing redundancies or because it generates novelty and increases aesthetic pleasure or scientific interest (see UN 2003). It also carries the moral connotation of progressing toward more sophisticated, fit, efficient—in a word, more perfect—beings, which is a key value of Western modernity. As Brazilian political theorist Denise Ferreira da Silva (2007) argues, within eighteenth- and nineteenth-century European biological discourses, evolution was framed as the movement of a universal spirit toward greater perfection. Within this cosmovision, "evolution completes the formulation of productive *nomos* . . . by producing increasingly differentiated, specialized and complex living things" (Ferreira da Silva 2007, 108), the culmination of which is "Man" (see also Wynter 2003). Although in Darwin's writings, "Man" is often depicted as the sole species to transcend natural selection, some contemporary "posthumanists" or "transhumanists" are working ardently to ensure that "man" continues to improve through technologically mediated and expedited forms of evolution (see chapter 6). Interruptions to or reversals of this movement toward greater perfection—including the existence of beings who seem to threaten it, such as racialized and/or disabled humans (see S. Taylor 2017; Mitchell 2022), or indeed, the severance of evolutionary processes through extinction—are framed as threats to "Man."

A preoccupation with protecting evolution (as a way of protecting humanity) has been present in discourses on biodiversity from their inception. As David Takacs (1996) shows, this shift was part of the broader movement among conservation biologists in the late 1980s away from approaches geared toward individual species and toward (eco)systemic approaches. One of the most vocal proponents of this turn, unmarked American environmental philosopher Holmes Rolston III (1985, 722, emphasis mine in first line), states that what humans *ought to respect* are dynamic life forms preserved in historical lines, vital informational processes that persist genetically over millions of years, overleaping short-lived individuals. It is not the *form* (species) as mere morphology, but the *formative* (speciating) process that humans ought to preserve.

Normative terms such as "respect" and "ought to preserve" frame formative processes such as mutation and the transmission of genes as subjects of *ethical* status (there are ways that we "ought" to treat them) and *moral* concern (it is *right* to protect them). This argument echoes Soulé's (1985, 731, emphasis mine) contention that "there is an *ethical imperative* to provide for the continuation of evolutionary processes in as many undisturbed natural habitats as possible." We can also observe this normative commitment reflected in contemporary conservation policy. For instance, the guiding principles of Parks Canada (the federal agency that oversees the creation, management, and regulation of the country's national parks) defines wilderness spaces as those in which "little or no persistent evidence of human intrusion is permitted *so that ecosystems may continue to evolve*" (Parks Canada n.d., emphasis mine).

For some conservation biologists, evolution—rather than species or ecosystems per se—is the primary object of protection: life-forms and ecosystems are simply the necessary physical containers for the processes that drive it. For Rolston, Soulé, and others, the ethical status and moral importance of life-forms is contingent on their role in evolution; these beings are merely "process, product, and instrument in the larger drama" (Rolston 1985, 725) and not its heroes. Or, conversely, as Soulé (1985, 733) suggests, life-forms and worlds are merely the outcomes of the more fundamental good of evolution: "life itself owes its existence and present diversity to the evolutionary process. Evolution is the machine, and life is its product." More recently, ecologists have criticized the CBD for its focus on what they regard as the products of evolution rather than biological processes, which they see as "critical elements of existing biodiversity and the earth's ability to generate biodiversity" (Bohn and Amundsen 2008, 804).

Beyond the ethical, political, and social implications mentioned here, the focus on evolutionary processes requires critical attention because it privileges certain kinds of making difference while working to control or suppress others. Indeed, the focus on process in itself constrains which modes of change and transformation are considered desirable. In modern

(Bio)Plurality

Western thought, the concept of "process" is often taken for granted as a universal mechanism of change in systems, whether natural, economic, social, or political (Mitchell 2010; see also Arendt 1998). However, it is actually a very specific way of interpreting and noticing change, which emphasizes three major elements: abstraction, productivity, and continuity.

Processes are *abstract* in three different senses. First, they are seen as separate from, and therefore able to "work on"—for instance, to transform or consume—materials such as plants, minerals, or water. From this perspective, beings and life-forms that are subject to processes have limited agency in regard to the changes made to them: they may be able to intervene in processes (often with unintended consequences) but rarely to control them (Arendt 1998). Second, processes in Western thought are understood to be generic—that is, they are the same wherever and whenever they are found, although the materials they work on, the conditions in which they unfold, and their products vary dramatically. This is true for mainstream accounts of evolutionary processes, which are assumed to function in universal ways, at predictable rates and speeds, across all life-forms in all temporal and spatial locations. Another example can be found in the Western scientific notion of the water cycle, which imposes a universal definition of water as H_2O—a generic substance that is chemically identical and behaves predictably wherever it is found (see Linton 2009). This story obscures and negates unique waters such as the moana (deep sea), the po'ina kai (place where the waves break), and the 'ae kai (place where the waves wash up on the beach) (D. P. McGregor 2007; Oliveira 2014; Puniwai et al. 2016), cocreated by Hawaiian fishers, limu (seaweed) gatherers, surfers, navigators, fish, sands, and other beings. Similarly, it obscures the distinctness of the two layers of gapu (water) found in the bay at Bawaka in east Arnhemland, the upper level of which is of the Yirritja moiety and the lower layer of which is of the Dhuwa moiety (Burarrwanga et al. 2013), whose human members, respectively, must care for these different waters. By reducing these unique waters into H_2O and a universal water cycle, ecosystem services approaches efface the deep and enduring relations through which these worlds are sustained. Third, in many cases, including in the ecosystem services approach, processes are also abstract in the Marxian sense—that is, they are converted into abstract entities such as value, prices, and currency that are treated as commensurable (Castree 2003; Kosoy and Corbera 2010).

Second, most of the processes discussed in Western discourses of biodiversity are assumed to be *productive,* working on materials in order to

74 (Bio)Plurality

produce value, difference, or change. We can see this line of thinking at work in Soulé's claim that life is the product of evolutionary processes, which constantly work on the physical material of life-forms to generate higher levels complexity and degrees of perfection. Third, in order to maintain the forward motion of evolution, these processes must be *continuous,* functioning smoothly and consistently enough to allow for recuperation after disruptions. For instance, as discussed in chapter 1, the rate of speciation must, on average, be equal to or greater than that of extinction in order to produce gains or increases in biodiversity. Even following significant ruptures such as saltation (abrupt mutational change from one generation to the next) or mass extinction events, these processes are expected to recover their more gradual and predictable movement toward increased complexity and diversity.

To understand the importance of these assumptions in shaping biodiversity strategies and the ecosystems they target, it is useful to examine in more detail the ecosystems services paradigm, which has been actively mainstreamed by major conservation organizations since the early 2000s. The influential *Millennium Ecosystem Assessment* (UN 2003) considers "ecosystem services" in four categories of use that it defines as universal human needs. *Provisioning services* provide food, fuel, fiber, water, genetic materials, and other resources used to sustain societies and economies. *Supporting services*—for instance, the formation of soil and the water cycle—enable all other biotic processes, which in turn support provisioning services. *Regulating services* include the maintenance of a stable climate, carbon sinking, and the control of erosion. *Cultural services* refer to the role that nonhuman beings and processes play in constituting and sustaining human cultures over time. It is important to note that these services are defined in ways that reflect a specific understanding not only of human needs but also of their relationships to other beings and life-forms. For instance, these categories assume that *all* humans understand other life-forms as provisions or resources and that most abiotic beings are subjugated to the production of life (in supporting or regulating roles). What's more, the overall approach embeds the Western secular assumption (derived from Judeo-Christian theology and scripture; see Waldau 2001) that the fundamental role of ecosystems is to *serve* (provide services to) humanity.

Ecosystems services approaches aim to secure the continuity of biological processes, not only or primarily in order to safeguard evolution but also to ensure the stability of global economic and political systems. Their

(Bio)Plurality

basic premise is that ecosystems provide a number of services that are treated as free by governments, economies, and societies and are therefore not included in economic calculations or policymaking (de Groot et al. 2012). As a result, proponents of the paradigm claim, these services are taken for granted, used inefficiently, managed nonoptimally, and ultimately over-exploited. In order to create incentives for protecting these vital processes, they argue, it is necessary to enfold them within the structures of financial value (see J. Moore 2015). With this goal in mind, conservation economists work to calculate the total value of each service based on its replacement value: that is, the cost that one would have to pay if it were not provided for free. So, for instance, to calculate a service such as pollination, one might tally the financial cost of losing crops due to lack of pollination and the potential cost of carrying out pollination by hand or machine. In the case of a service such as water filtration, provided by groundwater and springs, one would need to consider the cost not only of carrying out the task but also of developing technologies to carry it out efficiently, along with the energy needed to fuel that work. By adding up the financial cost of these free services and converting them into market terms, proponents of the ecosystem services approach hope to convince governments and private companies that the cost of losing them is greater than that of protecting them. Some market-based approaches also promise to make ecological processes more efficient and/or productive in the future, as economies of scale are generated and technologies improve (Igoe, Neves, and Brockington 2010; Sian Sullivan 2013).

However, as I've already suggested, this move to flatten earth's life-forms and worlds into just one metric of value (that determined by capitalist markets) raises several problems. For instance, when integrated into markets, value is usually communicated in prices, which can fluctuate according to demand. In this case, scarcity of resources would actually be desirable for those speculating in ecosystem services markets. This issue has already been identified in the context of "biodiversity derivatives" (Mandel, Donlan, and Armstrong 2010), in which the near extinction of a species may raise its value as a commodity to be banked or traded. In a related sense, by framing these processes as economic goods, the ecosystem services approach creates favorable conditions for the privatization of these services, possibly on a global scale, which could severely restrict access for the world's most marginalized people—including those who have co-constituted and cared for these ecosystems for millennia. In short, mainstream and particularly financial discourses on biodiversity center processes that create value in markets and stability for states, with a view to preserving existing global structures of power—with all their inequalities and violences intact.

(BIO)PLURALITY

I now want to pivot toward another way of making difference. At its heart is irreducible, internal plurality based on the co-constitution of beings and on nonlinear, unique plural*izations*. Consider the words in the chapter epigraph, which are coauthored by Country—not only by the human writers who committed them to words but also by the sands, winds, Dreamings, waters, yams, fish, rocks, trucks, kangaroos, and myriad other beings who compose Country *and* each other (Bawaka Country et al. 2016). Indeed, within Yolŋu cosmovisions, relationality reaches far beyond the coexistence of discrete beings or groups thereof. Beings are literally made and remade by each other in each moment and are inseparably connected. This form of difference does not emphasize internal homogeneity or redundance; on the contrary, each being, let alone each group, is necessarily internally plural because it is conditioned by so many other beings, each of which is essential. Nor does difference emerge only in the relation between bounded groups, because, indeed, no group is bounded in the way suggested by the idea of biodiversity. Instead, difference is with/in, internal to every being, and all the beings that compose Country are to some degree internal to each other.

This experience of difference epitomizes what I provisionally call "(bio)plurality."[10] Crucially, plurality is not a synonym for diversity but a radically different way of experiencing and participating in difference. It emerges from and refers to distinct relational structures of interbeing (see the introduction to this chapter) that coexist with and are not reducible to diversity. Plurality should not be confused with theories of political *pluralism* within Euro-American thought and international theory, which focus on the interactions of multiple internally similar and externally differentiated groups sharing a field of action. This falls into the category that I have defined here as "diversity."[11] "Plurality," as I use the term, refers to a *condition of being (internally) plural*.

One way of teasing out the distinction between these concepts is to ask where they locate difference in relational terms. As discussed in this chapter, the concept of "diversity" focuses on *external differences* between internally similar groups, such that difference is located outside and between each discrete group. In contrast, from the perspective of (bio)plurality, difference exists in the *manyness* of *each* being—that is, its co-constitution, co-conditioning, and interbeing with myriad other beings.[12] Thinking about (bio)plurality entails paying attention to how beings, life-forms, and worlds co-create, co-disrupt, and navigate the conditions for their interbeing. It involves reciprocal difference making, although of course difference is distributed and experienced unequally across worlds (see Mitchell 2014b). At the same time, (bio)plurality is reflexive: to do something that affects one's self or world is to affect the others with whom one is co-constituted and vice versa. For this reason, it is important not to romanticize (bio)plurality; harmful, violent, or disruptive actions within conditions of co-constitution can create cascades of harm and violence across worlds.

In addition, (bio)diversity requires a separate, external horizon of comparison in which groups are differentiated in terms of identity and negative identity (e.g., a being is categorized as being "A" or "not-A"). In contrast, (bio)plurality is self-substantiating, positive difference-in-itself that requires no comparison or repetition, or "difference without identity" (Grosz 2011, 90). Plurality is singular difference that does not always survive abstraction beyond its concrete embodiments and manifestations. Although it certainly produces patterns, regularities, and repetitions—for instance, the flowering of the stringy bark plants mentioned in the epigraph, and the changing of seasons—each repetition has its own unique place in history. Even writing about (bio)plurality in the abstract, as I am doing, distorts this form of difference, since it attempts to translate an embodied condition into a system of abstraction designed to sublimate singularities. Put another way, within Euro-descendent thought, plurality works in practice but not in theory: those of us living within this knowledge system are immersed in plurality daily and our coexistence depends on it, but our knowledge systems struggle to reflect it without destroying or obscuring it. Yet (bio)plurality does not need to be abstracted in order to be sensible: it can be felt, observed, intuited, recorded (for instance, in bodies, songs, and land), related to, and cared for without the need for extensive abstraction.

To feel the pulse of plurality, it helps to attend to beings who embody it in intense ways. Among these are Dreamings, the multidimensional, intertemporal beings who continuously create, shape, and sustain landscapes, life-forms, kinship structures, and other aspects of Country across Australia. Before engaging with specific Dreamings, however, it is important to acknowledge the problems associated with this concept and its use in English. "(The) Dreaming" is a "grossly inadequate" (Nicholls 2014) umbrella term that originated in the work of white settler anthropologists such as Baldwin Spencer and F. J. Gillen ([1899] 1968) and A. P. Elkin (1943). In many cases, these scholars' work was aligned with the goals of the settler state— for instance, Elkin was a proponent of the forced assimilation of Indigenous peoples by white settler society. However, in the decades since its popularization, many Aboriginal and Torres Strait Islander peoples have worked to reclaim the concept of Dreaming(s) as a tool for enhancing solidarities and sharing certain aspects of their worlds with non-Indigenous people.

White settler anthropologists and their readers used the word "Dreaming" as an abstract category to group together numerous practices, words, and ideas that they extrapolated from specific communities and applied in a generalizing manner. In this way, their work reflects the forms of difference making described in the previous section—namely, the privileging of abstract similarity over concrete specificity. Specifically, the term "Dreaming" is believed to be a translation into English of the word Altyerrenge or Altyerr, used by Arrerntic peoples to discuss their origin stories. The origin stories and daily lives of Aboriginal and Torres Strait Islander peoples across Australia include similar beings, and each community refers to them with concepts rooted in their own traditions and laws (see Fletcher 2003).[13] Indeed, in the words of Warlpiri teacher Jeannie Herbert Nungarrayi (quoted in Nicholls 2014), Dreamings constitute and manifest Law, sets of "rules for living, a moral code, as well as rules for interacting with the natural environment" that are specific to and inseparable from each people and place.

Another issue is that early settler anthropological accounts of *the* "Dreaming" (and many contemporary popular culture accounts) framed it as a specific, completed time period consigned to the past by the advent of modernity and civilization.[14] The popular concept of the "everywhen," a term intended to contest this linear temporality, originates in British philosopher J. H. Muirhead's description of a "universal spirit" (see Nicholls 2014). It imports a distinctly Euro-centric and totalizing temporality rooted in monotheism that clashes with the plural, simultaneous temporalities of many Aboriginal and Torres Strait Islander worlds. In contrast, the beings referred to as Dreamings are multitemporal, traversing the periods and breaks carved out by the Western sciences (see chapter 1). They are also multiscalar, in that they simultaneously exist within what Western thought calls "deep time," in the temporality of biological processes (heartbeats, breaths, deaths), and in time frames that exceed and are not legible to Eurocentric knowledge systems.

Dreamings embody plurality prismatically: they are multidimensional, creatively ambiguous, and constantly transforming while existing in states of radical permanence. They are topographies and histories, embodying themselves in Country and its creatures as they change forms, move, rest, disappear, reappear, and intervene in the lives of their relatives (Rose 1992). One such being is often called the Rainbow Serpent in English, although they have many other names.[15] This Dreaming creates and sustains Country across several parts of Australia. According to Lardil artist and writer Goobalathaldin (1988), this serpent, whom his people call Goorialla, first emerged at a time when there was nothing on earth except the few humans who had come from the stars (see Bawaka Country et al. 2020). Suddenly, the earth was rocked by cataclysmic events—floods, volcanoes, droughts, and earthquakes. To protect themselves from these threats, many human ancestors transformed themselves into animals, birds, plants, insects, and rocks. These transformations marked a period of intensive creativity and change that white settler anthropologists would later call "the Dreaming" and generated the "multitude of life forms" that exist today (Goobalathaldin 1988). In the midst of all this tumult, Goorialla went searching for his people across what is now known to settlers as Cape York. As he slithered across the landscape, the movements of his massive body carved out a deep gorge, rivers and creeks, mountains, and a lagoon (Goobalathaldin 1988). However, shortly after he found his human relatives, Goorialla swallowed two of their children in a moment of irritation. Fearing the peoples' response, he fled to Bona-Bunaru, the only mountain already existing in that part of Country. Several other Dreaming beings—Emu, Brush Turkey, Brolga, Tortoise, Possum, and Barramundi—tried to climb the mountain in order to cut open Goorialla and free the boys, but they all failed. Finally, two tree-goanna brothers climbed the mountain with knives made of quartz crystal, opening his belly and releasing its contents. To their surprise, out flew a flock of rainbow lorikeets bearing all the serpent's colors. Angered by this intrusion, Goorialla thrashed about and hurled lightning, taking pieces of the mountain and throwing it around Country, leaving hills and mountains in his wake. Then he ran to the sea, where he has remained ever since. According to Goobalathaldin (1988), while Goorialla expressed his rage, some of the people were killed by the lightning and flying pieces of earth, while others transformed themselves into birds, insects, plants, and animals. Those who remained in their original forms became responsible for taking care of the creatures who had formerly been humans (Goobalathaldin 1988).

In another variation of this story written by Goobalathaldin with children in mind, Rainbow Serpent emerged from the ground, making large marks in the land as she traveled north. As she moved, she called out to the frogs and tickled their bellies until they released all the water they carried inside them. This water ran into the grooves made by the Serpent, forming the rivers and lakes and giving rise to trees and grasses. Then Rainbow Serpent gave the animals laws, turning those who break them into humans, and assigned them to totems that they should never hunt, so that everyone would always have enough to eat.[16] The coexistence of these two different but resonant stories about the Rainbow Serpent, told by the same person, is not a mistake or a contradiction. Instead, it demonstrates the multiplicity of this being, his distinct relationships with different groups of people and other beings, and his various roles in co-constituting worlds.

Rainbow Serpent is also an important co-constituent of Country in the southwest of Australia. Noongar man Everett Kickett (1995), from the Ballardong region, tells of a great explosion that released a number of giant, rainbow-colored serpents or wagyls, who called out to the sky, prompting a chorus of frogs. They moved in all directions, carving out rivers such as the Derbarl Yerrigan (Swan River) and creating hills and valleys—including one with deep grooves down its side where the serpents slid. According to Kickett (1995), these beings only traveled during the night for safety; meanwhile, other Dreaming beings created swamps where they could rest peacefully during the day. Now, Kickett says, wherever the serpents rest at night, or wherever their bodies pass, you can find fresh water. Notably, in a short film dramatizing this story and showing the places Kickett describes (Habedank 2012), a young boy points out that all the rivers and lakes are salty. Kickett replies that they were fresh before settlers came and cleared all the land and bush, washing salt content from the trees into the rivers.

Rainbow Serpent, in their many forms, exudes plurality. They are simultaneously multiple, co-constituted and co-constitutive beings: at once ancestor and spirit; the mountains, swamps, and rivers they create; their human kin; and the other animals they become. Appearing in multiple stories/theories, they are in many places and relations at once. They embody aspects of what the Western sciences call "living" and "abiotic" alike, and they often manifest as a geological force—for instance, by creating mountains and canyons, stopping the rain, creating a halo around the moon (to signal coming rain), or regulating human menstrual cycles by way of the moon and water (Northern Land Council 2018). Rainbow Serpent has many genders: in some cultures, he is male, in others, she is female, and in others they are ambiguous, nonbinary, or intersex (Northern Land Council 2018). What's more, they do not conform to the sexual norms of Western science, let alone the biological species concept: they give birth, lay eggs, suckle allies such as flying fox and budgerigar, walk around "chucking rain" in a "phallic manner" (Rose 1992) and gestate new species (e.g., rainbow lorikeets) in their belly. Rainbow Serpent is also many different animals at once, sometimes embodying snakes, scorpions, bats, birds, crocodiles, dingoes, or lizards (Northern Land Council 2018), and may appear as one being or many. They are also in relation with many other spirit beings, including the Bunyip, a fearful crocodile-sized water-dwelling marsupial (Northern Land Council 2018), as well as kin to many groups of humans.[17] Just like Sedna and the Akule (see Introduction), Rainbow Serpent relates in unique ways to different human groups and areas of Country, as reflected in the many different stories about them. For instance, the Australian Bureau of Meteorology (2014) notes that Aboriginal and Torres Strait Islander nations in monsoonal areas associate Rainbow Serpent with epic interactions of sun and wind, whereas central desert communities, who experience less drastic seasonal shifts, offer calmer stories of the Serpent's movements. Rainbow Serpent and their stories respond to changes felt across Country— for instance, the violent process of colonial deforestation that released the salt deposits into the river system in Kickett's story—while remaining permanent. Indeed, Rainbow Serpent exists in—and generates, through their actions and motions—multiple times, including ancestral, biological, and evolutionary and seasonal cycles.

Rainbow Serpent shows how plurality can be *originary*: according to these accounts, the proliferation of beings and life-forms that exist today do so *by virtue of* their co-constitution and transit across multiple forms, facilitated by the Serpent and other Dreamings. Within kinship structures related to Dreamings, these conditions are expressed in complex ways. For instance, in the community with whom Rose (1992) lived and worked at Yarralin, kinship and identity are cross-cut by generational distinctions that determine parentage and rules for intermarriage, and each person is related to more than one other life-form (for instance, flying fox and rainbow, or catfish and brolga). Each of these kin life-forms, in turn, has its own special relations with other beings—for instance, emu with Earth and brolga with Sky Country. In one regard, these kinship structures govern external forms of difference: they distribute responsibility across groups that reproduce socially and biologically, and they create bonds among beings that are shaped by internal similarities (for instance, body plan or genealogy). Yet each of the beings in question, including moieties (kinship groups), are recognized as internally plural *and* co-constitutive of one another. They are not simply humans who have "turned into" brolgas and catfish (or vice versa) or people who are *related to* catfish and brolgas; rather, they are always already human *and* catfish *and* brolga. As Rose (1992, 224) puts it, within this world "everything is, at the same time, a singularity, a multiplicity, and a whole." Yet this is not a unitary or homogenous whole that generalizes or sublimates difference like the taxonomic categories discussed in the previous section. Instead, it is a whole that nurtures, and cannot exist without, the difference of those who co-compose it. This point is crucial: whereas the kinds of difference (and sameness) identified by (bio)*diversity* are understood to be generic, the kind of difference engendered by Dreamings, by Country, and by their (human and nonhuman) kin is *singular*. Indeed, this kind of difference is "singular plural" (Nancy 2000)—a "we" that is always composing itself and therefore is, in every moment and instantiation, unique.

Despite their contrasting uses in everyday English, plurality and singularity are not opposites—in fact, they are indispensable to one another. Each being, life-form, or world is singular because of the unique constellation of beings that renders it plural; and it is plural because of the unrepeatable singularity of the beings that collaborate in its existence. For this reason, even cloned beings are singular plural: despite identical genetic structures, they each inhabit unique conditions, spatio-temporal coordinates, nodes in relational webs, and concrete experiences. From the perspective of plurality, then, each being life-form and world is incommensurable, and therefore nonsubstitutable. One cannot talk about the net loss of plurality or redundancy of beings in conditions of (bio)plurality—it is simply not possible to replace, compensate for, or make substitutions for singular-plural beings.

PLURALITY BEYOND "LIFE"

Plurality is not exclusively a condition or property of what the Western sciences call "life"; it is distributed across multiple beings and the relations

(Bio)Plurality 83

among them. Indeed, I bracket the prefix "bio" in "(bio)plurality" precisely to signal the complex metabolisms, exchanges, and relations that exist among biotic and abiotic beings, embodied and spirit beings, and other kinds of beings that exceed these categories. Of course, what Western science understands as "life" is a powerful contributor to (bio)plurality—its energies, forms of motion, and creative, purposeful tendencies help proliferate modes of being and generate bonds between beings. Yet other beings also make crucial contributions—for instance, those labeled as "geological" by Western science; ancestors, spirits, and deities; and beings deemed extinct by Western science (see chapter 1). With their disproportionate focus on "life," mainstream accounts of biodiversity radically undervalue the integral connections between these beings—ironically missing much of the complex difference nourished by worlds.

As discussed in the first section of this chapter, Western scientific discourses draw rigid boundaries between "biological" processes (those interactions that produce the "sovereign self-organization" of organisms) and inanimate or "geological" processes, which are understood to unfold in a more or less mechanical way and to function largely as resources for life.[18] In many cosmovisions, however, what Western science frames as "life" and "nonlife," as well as ancestors and other spiritual forces rarely discussed by Western scientists (except sometimes as elements of culture), nourish and co-constitute each other. This is especially clear in cosmovisions that embrace more-than-life cycles in their stories/theories of creation, origin, and (re)generation. In these stories, life and nonlife conceive, create, gestate, bear, take care of, and return to one another. In every stage and phase of being, they pluralize each other; none is a mere resource for the other. Anishinaabe-Mohawk scholar Vanessa Watts (2016, 151) reflects on this relationship among her communities and the land they care for:

> She [earth] is our history and our material, biological mother. Therefore we are of her. Our materiality, spirits, minds, and emotions are all interconnected and share a material connection to land. In this birth, we (and other beings) inherit throughout our lifetime . . . stories, histories, meaning, territory (land, waters, rocks, air), humans, non-humans, the spirit world, protocols, and governance systems.

Reflecting on this relation, Watts emphasizes the importance in her community of burying the placenta after the birth of each new baby, introducing the new being to the land that co-constitutes it.[19] Similarly, the burial of bodies in the earth after death enables them to return to the land and participate in the process through which future generations inherit responsibility for it. In the worlds that Watts inhabits, people are born and made of land, which is part of the processes of reproduction—and of continuity (see chapter 1).

Similar relations between earth, sea, and body resonate through the work of Kānaka Maoli thinkers and the cosmovisions from which they write. For instance, the Kumulipo (see chapter 1) offers a complex genealogical moʻolelo in which different modes of existence give rise and / or birth to each other (Kameʻeleihiwa 1992). As Kānaka scholar Katrina-Ann R. Kapāʻanaokalāokeola Nākoa Oliveira (2014) interprets the chant, being starts with a state of darkness and chaos that embodies itself in male and female forms. These forms give rise to sea creatures, the first of which is a coral polyp (see D. P. McGregor 2007), followed by fishes and shrubs, insects, birds, reptiles, pigs, rats, and dogs. In the eighth wā (a period of creation, comprising several generations) the first woman, Laʻiliʻi, and first man, Kiʻi, arise, along with the gods Kāne and Kanaloa. In the following wā, honua (earth) is born, along with several gods and humans. In the twelfth wā, the sky god Wākea procreates with a kino lau (manifestation) of the earth goddess Papa, giving birth to the ancestors of the Kānaka. In this wā, too, arrives a stillborn fetus, which, when planted, sprouts the first kalo (taro) plant, the staple food of the Kānaka. Following this, Papa gives birth to several of the islands of the Hawaiian archipelago. In this cosmic more-than-life, multibeing cycle, deities give birth to other deities and to plants and animals, which in turn give birth to humans, who beget islands and ʻāina. Beings cast by Western science as biotic and abiotic, or bracketed by the Western sciences as purely spiritual, participate actively in each other's creation and continuity. In a manner resonant with that described by Watts, these relations are sustained in part by depositing the piko (umbilical cord) in pohaku (sacred rocks) and planting the ʻiēwe (placenta) after the birth of a human (Aluli and McGregor n.d., 5). Traditionally, ʻiēwe were planted in the soil, along with a specially selected tree, on the relevant family's land, which permanently connected the child to ʻāina and ʻohana (extended family, including ʻāina) but also to its ancestors and to the future (D. P. McGregor et al. 2003).[20] These practices sustain the plurality and co-constitution among living and nonliving bodies, endowing human children with the māna (power) of earth and other beings and strengthening the intergenerational capacity to mālama ʻaina (take care of the land). Crucially, this moʻolelo not only highlights the co-(re)production and plurality of living and abiotic beings but also challenges the Western scientific notion that abiotic beings are mere resources for "life" by showing that the reverse can also be true. In addition, these accounts of descent offer exuberantly queer understandings of how life-forms and worlds pursue their collective continuity, eschewing narrow, heteronormative frameworks that limit it to biological reproduction (within species). In these stories, worlds are birthed—or hatched, or extruded, or transitioned to, or decomposed into—by the relations of myriad, often radically different beings, all engaged in the erotic (see Nelson 2017) work of coexistence.

Plurality is also expressed in the myriad forms of co-consciousness that Leanne Betasamosake Simpson (2017) refers to as "Indigenous intelligence[s]." These forms of collaborative cognition and meaning making have enabled many peoples and their nonhuman kin to co-create, survive, and flourish across times within their distinct worlds. They diverge from modern "naturalistic" ontologies (Descola 2005), in which agency and intelligence are understood as exclusive features of individual subjects that transcend and impose themselves upon the inert matter of the universe (see Bennett 2010). In this vein, several Western anthropologists who draw on Indigenous knowledge systems argue that the Western concepts of "intelligence," "mind," and the capacity for meaning making are in fact distributed *across* environments (see Bateson 1972; Ingold 2002). For instance, Eduardo Kohn's (2013) *How Forests Think* asserts that semiosis and meaning making are features of living worlds. Working with the Runa community of Avila, Amazonian Ecuador, he comes to understand that signs are not things but living relational processes.[21] These signs respond to the worlds they inhabit as they anticipate, imagine, and extend themselves into possible futures. For example, Kohn argues, by embodying its elongated snout, the giant anteater selectively remembers its genetic ancestors but also "stand[s] to a future anteater . . . [to] the possibility that there will be ant tunnels into the environment into which the snouted anteater will come to live." This particular mode of intelligence and communication is not "in" human (or anteater) minds or bodies, nor is it projected "onto" other beings by them. Rather, it is *distributed across* different kinds of bodies, structures, forces, and rhythms, and it emerges in their relations.

Indeed, within many cosmovisions, humans and other life-forms think, act, and adapt *through* and *as* land, air, water, and other beings, in a form of

86 (Bio)Plurality

practical co-intelligence that Watts (2013) calls "place-thought." A resonant concept can be found in the practice of ᕐᓚᐅᓂᖅ or silatuniq, an integral principle of ᐃᓄᐃᑦ ᖃᐅᔨᒪᔭᑐᖃᖕᒋᑦ (Inuit Qaujimajatuqangit, or Inuit knowledge, institutions, and technology). Silatuniq, which Inuit scholar Betsy Annahatak (2014) translates as "respectful state of being in the world," involves lifelong and intergenerational embodied attunement to a forceful being that the Inuit know as Sila. Inuit philosopher and knowledge-keeper Jaypeetee Arnakak describes Sila as "an ever-moving and immanent force that surrounds and permeates Inuit life, with it most often being experienced in the weather" (quoted in Leduc 2016, 3). Indeed, Leduc (2016) notes that Western academics have interpreted Sila to mean either "weather" (for instance, in the context of TEK) or an "air spirit" (in anthropologies). Instead, Leduc argues, Sila is a sentient being *with whom* Inuit must think and act practically, and wisely, in order to negotiate survival. For Arnakak, Sila exists in a state of constant flux and change: "everything is mutable— only [Sila's] sentience, order and change are constant" (Arnakak, quoted in Leduc 2010, 12). Many Inuit interpret and navigate changes by attuning themselves to Sila—not only cognitively but also physically, kinetically, affectively, and spiritually. Inuit writer Sheila Watt-Cloutier (2015) describes how this form of wisdom is embodied through experiential modes, such as hunting, sewing, or preparing food—skills that are transmitted, refined, and adapted across generations. This way of knowing can emerge only from living and working *with/in* Sila. Indeed, as Annahatak (2014, 28) states, reaching maturity in an Inuit community means practicing silatuniq until one becomes wise, or silattutuq, which she translates as "one who has a big world . . . [that] includes the interconnections of all beings in it" and is able to avoid doing them harm. In these worlds, wisdom is not simply a tool for survival imposed on the land but rather a state of literally sharing (a) mind.

Co-intelligence is also embodied in the rich account of imagination articulated by Haudenosaunee thinkers Joe Sheridan and Roronhiakewen Dan Longboat (2006). For these authors, imagination—the basis of creating and caring for worlds and their futures—is inherently ecological. It is

> the cognitive and spiritual condition of entwining with local and cosmological intelligences . . . the spiritual medium of those powers that engage humans without humans being the prime movers of the act. (Sheridan and Longboat 2006, 371)

(Bio)Plurality

It is this capacity that has allowed "old-growth cultures," including that of the Onkwehonwe, to sustain mutually nurturing modes of coexistence with specific places and relations.[22] According to Sheridan and Longboat (2006, 367), the Haudenosaunee tradition respects "sentience that is manifest in the consciousness of that territory." Land participates in this collaborative mode of consciousness just as much as coyotes, wolves, Onkwehonwe, or even extinct beings such as saber-toothed tigers do. By violently breaking these relations, colonization and other modes of systemic violence destroy shared minds and distinct forms of land-based intelligence, along with the unique bodies of collective knowledge they hold. These forms of violence actively undermine the "capacity for thinking with nature and beyond species-specific consciousness" and "auge[r] against the continued capacity to know how to think with everything" (Sheridan and Longboat 2006, 370–71).

These insights show that two of the key elements that the Western sciences associate with ("higher" forms of) life—intelligence and consciousness—are properties of *worlds*, not solely of individuals or of those beings classified as living in that system. This has crucial implications for the concept of "extinction." Specifically, mainstream Western scientific discourses of extinction presume that, insofar as it is a harm, it affects only living beings whose sentience and purposefulness enables them to experience harm, have interests and futures of which they are aware, and so on. Although conservation discourses increasingly integrate some aspects of Indigenous knowledge systems, they do not take literally (see Povinelli 1995) the possibility that nonliving beings are *harmed* by the destruction of life-forms. In contrast, the arguments discussed in this chapter suggest that if properties like intelligence, consciousness, and sentience are distributed across worlds, then so is the capacity to experience harm (see also Mitchell 2014b). My argument is not necessarily that rocks, waters, or spirits can be harmed in isolation from the co-constituents of their worlds or in the *same* way that animals or humans can (this is beyond the scope of my knowledge—and my knowledge system). Instead, my argument is that harms are not localizable to any one (kind of) member of the relational structures that compose worlds, nor are they neatly compartmentalized within one group of their co-constituents. For this reason, as I argue in the chapters that follow, efforts to understand the forms of harm and violence associated with extinction should focus not on specific life-forms but rather on the destruction of the relations that engender worlds.

PLURALIZATIONS

Plurality is not a static property, object, or substance. It is kinetic, a condition produced by intersecting *pluralizations* that stitch and loop themselves across multiple times, places, and modes of experience. Its movements may be linear and nonlinear; backward, forward, or multidirectional; traversing multiple dimensions, ranges, and scales. Plurality is thick with patterns and repetitions but also with novelties, changes, surprises, and sudden disjunctures. What's more, it cannot necessarily be traced to a single moment of origin, and it may ramify in multiple directions at the same time. Consider the stories/theories about Rainbow Serpent(s). Although they are certainly origin stories, there is no single, definite moment of origin to which all others are traced: different beings, worlds, and relations spring forth at various points in the stories/theories like plants propagating from leaves. Their narratives are not entirely path-dependent but rather are rich with contingency. Although there are moments of acute or dramatic change, *every* moment and interaction in these stories/theories is originary, making the worlds anew in each moment. As stated by Aunty Shaa Smith, "the power and strength of Gumbayngirr Country is very much alive and active in its eternal becoming" (quoted in Morelli, Williams, and Walker 2016, iii).

Stories/theories like the ones shared in this section, with their attention to detail, specifics, and multiplicity, tune attention to pluralizations and their exuberant mobilities. Western scientific theories tend to impose a sense of stasis or gradual consistent progress in their assessment of patterns and consistencies across time and space—recall the smoothened curves of the processes discussed in the first part of this chapter or of the background rates of extinction discussed in chapter 1. In contrast, stories/theories of pluralization move with the changes and singularities hiding in these patterns: the dramatic spikes, sudden plunges, jagged edges, and other forms of movement that cannot be charted in two dimensions. For instance, Anishinaabe legal scholar John Borrows (2010) emphasizes the power of unresolved stories/theories that leave room for the contingency and unique interpretation of the listener or reader, for whom each telling of a story/theory is mediated through their unique relations, experiences, and knowledge at various life stages. For Borrows, some stories/theories are living beings, who change each time they are heard or read, just as they transform the listener or reader and reconstitute her or his world. They invite storiers and their audiences to participate actively in pluralization by making different the meaning of a story each time it is told and received (L. Simpson 2017).

Similarly, Anishinaabe philosopher and storier Gerald Vizenor asserts that Native stories privilege movement where Western discourses tend to arrest it, especially in their attempts to isolate what they see as distinct elements of "nature" (e.g., species or living and abiotic beings).[23] He argues, for instance:

> The learned botanical name *cypripedium acaule* . . . inadvertently denatures the exquisite poetic blush of a moccasin flower in the moist shadows, and other more common names and comparative similes lessen the motion of images, such as the heavy breath of bears, the marvelous shimmer of early morning dew, twilight favors on a spider web, ravens tease of hunters in camouflage, stray shadows leaning over the fence, or the perfect dive of a water ouzel in a mountain stream. (Vizenor 2015)

Vizenor argues that the conventions and grammatical structures of writing in English and other European languages tend to dull receptivity to movement and the lively interplay of temporalities because they are primarily oriented toward nouns and objects. As such, they encourage speakers and readers to understand and interact with their worlds as though they were composed mostly of objects onto which movement is projected by subjects or forces. Meanwhile, many BIPOC languages place significantly more emphasis on verbs and gerunds (Darug Country et al. 2017), which frame beings as components of collective motions at various scales. For instance, in the southern dialect of Gumbayngirr, the addition of an -*a* verbalizer turns a thing not only into an action but into a *transformation*— for instance, bigurr, "tree," becomes bigurrra, "turning into trees." This centering of motion and transformation enables speakers of this dialect not only to notice, move with, and learn from transformations in their worlds but also to participate in and care for these collective changes. A similar facility for motion is embedded within Anishinaabemowin and related languages. As Potawatomi scholar Robin Wall Kimmerer (2013) points out, 70 percent of words in the Potawatomi language and related tongues are verbs, compared to only 30 percent in English. The preponderance of verbs in languages offers a "grammar of animacy" (Kimmerer 2013, 55) that reflects the dynamism of beings, including many that are viewed as inanimate due to their classification in Western science. For instance,

90 (Bio)Plurality

she reflects on the Anishinaabemowin verb "wiikwegma"—"to be a bay." According to Kimmerer (2013, 55, emphasis mine), this term tells us that,

> *for this moment,* the living water has decided to shelter itself between these shores, conversing with cedar roots and a flock of baby mergansers. Because *it could do otherwise*—become a stream or an ocean or a waterfall, and there are verbs for that, too. . . . A bay is a noun only if water is *dead.* When *bay* is a noun, it is defined by humans, trapped between its shores and contained by the word.

From this perspective, trapping difference and the *capacity to be different* in the constraints of nouns and objects polices their fundamental contingency—their ever-present capacity to be otherwise—curtailing their future potential for movement and change. Just as the restriction of BIPOC mobilities has been used by colonial states to foreclose upon resistance (see the chapters that follow), the imposition of nouns exerts power in the form of arrest. This is not a purely semantic argument, since, as discussed in this chapter, concepts such as "biodiversity," with all their connotations, become the basis for powerful world-forming, world-altering, and sometimes world-destroying structures and discourses. In the context of "biodiversity," reifications—from Rolston's (1985) framing of evolution as an object of protection to Rachel Carson's (2022) treatment of nature as a thing that can be lost to the commodification of ecosystem services—form the basis of practices that arrest and constrain pluralizations.

In contrast, Vizenor (2015) argues that Indigenous stories embody "transmotion": the unpredictable, nonlinear, tricky convolutions of open-ended becoming across times and spaces. In stories of transmotion, creation does not unfold only through consistent, gradual, exclusively repetitive processes. Instead, it creates itself through the singular interactions, maneuvers, and reversals that interrupt or simply texture processes and continuities. For instance, it is expressed in "a heartbeat, ravens on the wing, the rise of thunderclouds and the mysterious weight of whales . . . the migration of birds, traces of the seasons, shadows in the snow" and the movements of totemic beings across space, time, and stories (Vizenor 2015). The cocreativity of these beings is punctual, improvisational, and responsive; it emerges in and as the singular meetings of beings. As Australian settler writer Elizabeth Grosz's (2011) work suggests, these evolutionary encounters are not always oriented toward (re)production: they also produce intensity,

(Bio)Plurality

91

beauty, and spectacle, stimulating life into new forms, directions, and dimensions *for their own sake* and in non-instrumental ways.[24] Pluralization exceeds the imperatives of reproduction and perhaps even of survival in the Western scientific sense of maintaining individual lives (see chapter 1).

Indeed, pluralizations can be playful, frustrating, deceptive, and risky, as the fates and futures of entire life-forms and worlds are endlessly improvised (Heise 2010). Trickster transmotions (Vizenor 1998)—such as teasing, sleight of hand, shape shifting, cooperation, betrayal, irony, play, and surprise—play a crucial role, appearing in pluralizations and their stories as "transmutations of time, gender, water, myths, ironic figures and the many mutations of tricksters" (Vizenor 2015).[25] For Vizenor (1998), earth itself is a "trickster creation" that "teases" animals, plants, places, and worlds into being through unpredictable events, as well as sly and sometimes violent or painful interactions. As Vizenor hints, it is possible to understand the entire sweep of evolutionary change as a form of trickster transmotion, in which beings employ combinations of cleverness, deception, resourcefulness, adaptation, shape-shifting, chance, and circumstance to navigate their survival and flourishing. Humor is also an important feature of this epic story/theory of pluralizations. For example, unmarked theorist Ursula Heise (2010) detects moments of tragicomedy in stories of extinction and speciation, as life-forms adopt outlandish shapes or try unusual genetic experiments in their attempts to survive. Sensing humor within pluralizations may have a weighty role in maintaining continuity: as Gross (2002; see also chapter 1) narrates, his Anishinaabe kin have continually used humor to address, and overcome, world-destroying violence. In a similar sense, playful forms of co-creation—for instance, hiding, moving among or blending genders, changing bodily features or habitat over millions of years, even going extinct and continuing to haunt and taunt the extant (recall Robinson's trilobites in chapter 1)—are crucial to continuity. These transmotions allow beings to evade, withdraw, and cheat their own destruction across huge spans of time and space.

These tricky maneuvers also directly trouble the totalizing narratives of extinction promoted by mainstream conservation regimes. One example of this is the regular reports of sightings of thylacines in Tasmania (Hunt 2016). This marsupial was declared extinct in 1936, upon the death from neglect of the last individual known to Western science in the Hobart Zoo. Yet since the death of this apparent "endling" (see chapter 1), reports of sightings appear in the Australian media at least yearly. Indeed, one enthusiast, who claims to have sighted a thylacine in September 2017, has devoted twenty-six years to gaining proof of their continued existence (ABC News 2017). These apparent sightings continue to tease settler Australian imaginations, appearing not only in the news but also in pop culture formats such as Julia Leigh's (2001) book *The Hunter* and its film adaptation. In each of these appearances, the ghostly thylacine tricks, confuses, casts doubt, taunts, and even tortures the European settler agents of its (apparent) destruction. In so doing, it resists the totalizing logics and pronouncements of Western scientific extinction discourses, refusing to allow the matter of its extinction—and the causes of this erasure—to be laid to rest in the settler collective conscience. Indeed, even when they are manifested as (apparent) withdrawal and (incomplete) disappearance, transmotions cross the extant/extinct boundary (see chapter 1), expanding and enriching pluralizations.

The improvisational, sometimes humorous or playful dimensions of pluralizations, however, should not detract from their status as deeply purposeful forms of *labor*. Indeed, the contingency and unpredictability described in stories/theories of pluralization attest to the immense work carried out by life-forms and worlds in adapting to often cataclysmic change. As Australian settler scholar Thom van Dooren (2014, 16) argues, the "flightways" through which life-forms emerge and transform themselves through their own unique histories are not accidental outcomes or the product of impersonal processes but rather "incredible *achievements*." Van Dooren stresses that this work does not require the kind of "intentionality" often associated with human subjects in Euro-descendent knowledge systems. Even if beings are not conscious of these goals in a Western subjective sense, he contends "it is their striving for continuity that achieves [them] nonetheless" (van Dooren 2014, 38). This striving is expressed not only in their biological survival but also in their kinship structures, their relationships with other life-forms and beings as co-constituents of worlds, the unique stories and histories that they pass through generations in various forms (learning, genetics, modes of communication), and other facets of their collective existence. As such, van Dooren (2014, 7) argues, just as there is no universal history of a life-form, there is "no single 'extinction' phenomenon." As he puts it,

> what is lost in extinction is not "just" the current manifestations of a flight-way—a fixed population of organisms—but all that this species has been, as

(Bio)Plurality

well as all that its past and present might have enabled it to one day become. (van Dooren 2014, 38–39)

In other words, the destruction of whole life-forms and worlds destroys not only particular manifestations of (bio)plurality but also pluralizations and their potential to create open-ended futures.

(BIO)PLURALITY: REFRAMING EXTINCTION

Having been mainstreamed over the past few decades with remarkable success, the idea of "biodiversity" is all but taken for granted when the topics of "extinction" and conservation are raised. The other forms of difference that it marginalizes, displaces, or even helps erode are almost never discussed. This problem is accentuated by the tone of urgency that infuses conservation discourses. Having settled on a consensus for understanding what is at risk—and what is worth conserving—conservationists and their supporters are eager to move as quickly as possible to protect it. Although many Western scientists are aware of alternative accounts of difference, they "want to be able to treat this diversity efficiently" (Adams 2004, 234) in order to address the urgency of the threat. As a result, they tend to generalize about other kinds of difference or to include them as subsets of biodiversity—for instance, by creating a generic and homogenizing system of Indigenous, traditional, and cultural knowledge (or TEK) that generalizes across myriad distinct and irreducible knowledge systems.

Yet, as this chapter has shown, biodiversity and (bio)plurality reflect radically different forms of difference, each rooted in distinct cosmovisions, models of relationality, and ways of understanding, making, experiencing, and embodying difference. I am not suggesting that either concept is more "correct" or even that (bio)plurality should replace (bio)diversity in responses to escalating ecological harms. Rather, my point is that focusing on just one mode of difference to the exclusion—and destruction—of all others is to make specific ethical-political choices about which beings, life-forms, and worlds deserve to exist and which do not. The overwhelming dominance of biodiversity and the logics associated with it, mediated by global formations and discourses of conservation, are creating a profound imbalance. They are privileging and producing biodiversity at the cost of, and sometimes through direct violence toward, (bio)plurality. As a result, they often converge—whether or not intentionally—with forms of structural violence that deliberately target (bio)plurality, as the next few chapters argue.

What's more, this chapter has shown that, by emphasizing internal difference and external dissimilarity against an assumed background of sameness, discourses of biodiversity exert a *homogenizing* effect on the life-forms and worlds they aim to protect. This chapter has also argued that extinction is not experienced by life-forms or worlds in isolation. Rather, it is distributed across a multiplicity of life-forms, other-than-life-forms, and the worlds they co-compose, and across lands, climates, Sila, Country, and ancestors, who do not and cannot "go extinct" in the Western scientific sense. Indeed, it is the *relations* between these beings and the life-forms and worlds they co-constitute, the *conditions* of (bio)plurality that they co-create, and the *pluralizations* in which they participate that are systematically destroyed by global extinction.

These arguments suggest a radically different account of what is threatened and destroyed by global patterns of extinction. With this in mind, the next section of this book offers a different account of what Western science calls "extinction," reframed as the systematic destruction of (bio)plurality. Discourses of biodiversity have made significant contributions to protecting *certain* life-forms and drawing attention to global forms of ecological destruction. However, by failing or refusing to examine how their underlying logics amplify global structures of violence, proponents of biodiversity and conservation often actively participate in them.

3 Earth / Body Violence

The Systematic Destruction of (Bio)Plurality

> Breathe in. With each inhalation, the extensive relations of finance capital are pulled into your lungs, passing through membranes, attaching to receptors, rearranging metabolism, altering gene expression. Breathe out. With each exhalation, you are reconnecting to the greater fulsomeness of our relations.
>
> —MICHELLE MURPHY, "Alterlife and Decolonial Chemical Relations"

As the previous chapters have argued, the concepts of "extinction" or "biodiversity loss" cannot do justice—either figuratively or literally—to the systematic destruction of beings, life-forms, and worlds. With this in mind, I now shift focus from Western scientific accounts of extinction toward the *systematic destruction of (bio)plurality* by means of interlocking, global structures of violence. "Systematic," in these contexts, does not always or necessarily mean "planned," "premeditated," "intentional," or centralized (see chapter 5). Rather, it refers to forms of violence and harm that follow, express, and elaborate particular logics and that circulate through *systems,* including those on which life-forms and worlds rely for survival and collective continuity. Métis thinker Michelle Murphy (2017; see chapter epigraph) shows how this kind of violence converts relations of co-constitution into conduits of pervasive harm. This kind of violence is *ecological* (see Dhillon 2017) and atmospheric (Simmons 2017) in that it encompasses and infiltrates multiple aspects of worlds, including but not limited to bodies, temporalities, possibilities of movement, relation and interaction, and sources of sustenance, from eating to breathing. It is also material and embodied in landscapes, architecture, language, aesthetics, social norms, and many other factors that shape everyday possibilities of coexistence. Systemic violence is continuous but often changes speed, form, and intensity across space and time. It can be local or nonlocalized, and it often emerges from multiple sources, making it difficult to trace or attribute to any single actor (a feature often required by Western/ized legal structures to hold an aggressor formally responsible; see chapter 5).

Systemic violence is rooted in shared logics that leave their distinct signatures on radically different worlds across earth. In this chapter, I focus on one of these logics: earth/body violence, or the breaking of connections and long-standing relationships between bodies and earth (including water, air, other inorganic elements, and other entities). This kind of violence does more than simply destroy or fragment habitat: it undermines the fundamental relations of coexistence. Indeed, the term "habitat destruction" depicts ecosystems as the environment "for" or "of" internally homogeneous species and groups of them: that is, as a shifting store of resources; an external shelter; and a dynamic, interactive stage on which patterns of conflict and cooperation are played out. In contrast, rather than focusing on the *inhabitation of* ecosystems, this chapter turns attention toward the practices of *cohabitation as* ecosystems. In other words, rather than assuming an external ground against which life processes take place, this approach highlights the emergent negotiations, conflicts, adaptations, and dynamics through which life-forms and other beings actively create and constrain the conditions of each other's existence. It also foregrounds how these dynamics forge, sustain, and transform emergent modes of coexistence that cannot be disaggregated or reduced to specific life-forms, or their fates, needs, or interactions. This approach is distinct from the mainstream focus on individual species or cascades of threat and risk amongst discrete but linked species. Instead of focusing on the effects of the destruction of co*habitat* (used as a noun), it attends to interruptions of the currents and flows of cohabit*ation* (used as a verb; see chapter 3), including relations, practices, and processes of exchange and sharing. From this perspective, systematic violence that targets conditions of (bio)plurality does not simply damage external habitats on which life-forms rely instrumentally. It also disrupts the modes of cohabitation through which multiple life-forms have negotiated and maintained conditions of coexistence over millennia or even many millions of years.

Earth/body violence is one of several interlocking and mutually magnifying logics and *cultures* of violence that target the conditions of (bio)plurality, more of which are discussed in the next three chapters. These forms of systematic violence, and the structures they sustain, are just as important in driving global patterns of extinction as the factors most frequently cited in conservation discourses: habitat destruction, fragmentation, direct killing and overexploitation, the global movement of invasive species and pathogens, and, increasingly, climate change and pollution (see WWF 2018). In this chapter, I argue that the goal of managing habitat destruction is an inadequate and often inappropriate response to the wide-reaching infiltration and weaponization of the conditions of (bio)plurality. Specifically, it ignores, fails to address, and sometimes exacerbates specific modes of violence—including environmental racism, environmental ableism, gendered and sexual earth/body violence, and conditions of unconsent—that work to dissolve (bio)plurality and propel patterns of extinction. Shifting emphasis toward systematic violence has important implications for how extinction is conceptualized and responded to. It suggests that instead of (only) attending to the ecological, biological, and managerial elements of habitat destruction, it is necessary to restore and (re-)create (bio)plural relations rooted in elements such as intimacy, trust, pleasure, and love. It is also important to attend to the different forms of consent that each lifeform, being, and world may give *or refuse* and to nurture conditions for cohabitation.

EXTINCTION AS VIOLENCE

Few people concerned with conservation, biodiversity, or ecological issues would disagree that extinction is a "bad thing" but in what precise way? For instance, should it be understood as a harm, a crime, or a violation of international norms? Currently, the mainstream concept of "extinction" exists in an uncomfortable limbo between the depoliticizing descriptors of the Western sciences and the ethical, political, and legal frameworks used by states and in the international legal system to address other harms, bads, and wrongs. For sure, the term "extinction" is often mobilized in overtly political, ethical, and legal ways. The potential consequences of extinction are highlighted in order to shape conservation and resource management policies and to mobilize global public sentiment to support conservation projects. Meanwhile, *some* activities that drive extinction are illegal under national and international laws (e.g., poaching and illegal deforestation); however, others are legal and even directly subsidized by states. Unlike, say, genocide or human rights violations, extinction in itself is not a defined crime in international law, nor is there a specific international norm prohibiting it. As a result, extinction cannot be directly addressed within the political, ethical, and legal orders that dominate international politics in the way that other forms of violence are.[1]

This is because extinction is rarely understood as a form of violence *in itself*. Images of violence are often used as *metaphors* in conservation discourses, but they are rarely accompanied by thoroughgoing analyses of extinction *as* an expression of violence. For instance, unmarked American entomologist E. O. Wilson (2002, 57–58, 94) refers to extinction as a "sniper shot," the destruction of a habitat as "a war against nature," and *Homo sapiens* as "the serial killer of the biosphere" (see also chapter 1). Yet these phrases are purely rhetorical: they have no specific legal or ethical consequences. Wilson is neither suggesting that *Homo sapiens* could or should be tried for mass murder (whether in international courts or the legal mechanisms of an affected community), nor that this "war" should be subject to the Geneva Conventions (although some proponents of "ecocide" legislation make this argument; see chapter 5). At the same time, metaphors of war and arms races are often deployed to support conservation strategies that demonize and physically target global majority communities, replicating entrenched structures of geopolitical violence. For instance, efforts to halt "poaching" in parks and nature reserves often ignore traditional hunting practices and structural conditions of poverty while implementing indiscriminate shoot-to-kill policies against those perceived to be poachers (Duffy 2014). Even studies of the direct effects of human physical conflict on species and ecosystems (McNeely 2003; Hanson et al. 2009; Milburn 2015) tend to focus only on the *effects* on ecosystems of physical and material violence among humans. None of these discourses adequately addresses systematic and structural violence or examines how extinction can, in itself, constitute a form of violence.

Part of the reason why existing discourses make it so difficult to think about extinction in terms of systemic violence is because they tend to frame extinction only in terms of negation (see Brook and Alroy 2017)—that is, the loss, destruction, or absencing of life-forms. They do not consider the formations, structures, and subjectivities that produce and sustain conditions of extinction (Mitchell 2016). Purely negative accounts of extinction also create the impression of passivity—for instance, of species being lost, disappearing, or "going extinct" rather than *being* actively destroyed or extinguished. At the same time, mainstream discourses on extinction tend to ignore the enduring, repeated *structural* patterns in which it is manifested, to which concepts of "structural violence" (Galtung 1996; Farmer et al. 2006) usefully point. This concept was developed to move beyond accounts of direct, usually physical, violence exerted on a specific object by a specific subject. Instead, it emphasizes how violence is distributed, wielded, and imposed through a huge variety of linked social, economic, legal, political, spiritual, and cultural structures, often going unnoticed and taken for granted by those who most benefit from it. Structural violence cements and increases the power of dominant actors by permeating every aspect of the existence of marginalized groups. In so doing, it comprehensively constrains the life chances, experiences, capabilities, and freedoms of different groups who have been stratified along the lines of race, ethnicity, disability, gender, sexuality, class, sect, or other categories.

The concept of structural violence is a good starting point for engaging with the systematic destruction of (bio)plurality, but it does not address all the dimensions of systemic violence. First, while original accounts of structural violence are limited to harms affecting humans, the systemic violence of extinction includes many other beings, life-forms, and co-constituents of worlds (see chapter 2). What's more, the forms of structural violence that destroy (bio)plurality disproportionately target certain *relational structures* and *ways of relating* (not only ascriptive categories such as gender or religion). In addition, discourses of structural violence can benefit from discussions of how violence moves across and manipulates time. For instance, they should account for "slow violence" (Nixon 2011), which shifts focus from acute, immediate acts to ones that stretch and unfold over years, generations, or even centuries—a point also stressed by theories of settler colonialism (see Wolfe 1999; Veracini 2010). In addition, as Murphy (2017) points out, some forms of structural and/or systematic violence may be interrupted yet continuous—for instance, they may go dormant for periods only to be reanimated by unexpected events or conditions. What's more, the kinds of systematic violence that target (bio)plurality move across and through multiple temporalities (see Rifkin 2017) simultaneously. For instance, a mining company's destruction of a Dreaming being embodied in rock form (see Povinelli 2016) moves in the immediate time of the interaction between bulldozer and stone, in the longer duration of global extractive capitalism, and in the always time of Dreamings. For this reason, the concept of systematic violence invoked here is related (and indebted) to structural violence but not reducible to it. With all this in mind, I now shift toward several of the key logics that define systematic violence, starting with one of its most elemental forms: earth/body violence.

EARTH/BODY VIOLENCE

> They [colonizers] did not realize that body and homeland cannot be separated, that they are not distinct entities, that no matter where our bodies are we can feel our homelands in the night, can hear our ancestors murmuring and humming under our skin, can feel the lakes and rivers that we come from slowly trickle over rock. . . . The knowledge, teachings and ancestors that dance through rock and water, forest and sky, also dance within our own bodies. . . . Body is homeland. (Christie-Peters 2018)

In her vibrant works of painting and writing, Anishinaabekwe artist, curator, and arts programmer Quill Christie-Peters connects to the visceral, erotic, "radical relationality" through which she, her (bio)plural kin, and the lands they all share *love* each other. In her paintings, the continuity between land and other bodies, organic and otherwise, is electric: flesh, fluid, and stone bodies entwine, give birth, and reabsorb each other in a pulsating interchange of energy, life, and death. Christie-Peters (2018) "chuckles deeply" at the profound misunderstanding of these relationships by European colonizers past and present, who insist on treating land, water, plants, and animals as mere environments or resources for humans and for singling out organisms as the only (relevant) kinds of bodies. Eurocentric knowledge systems, she points out, lack a clear or nuanced understanding of these relationships or their true generative and nurturing power. However, perhaps instinctively, subconsciously, or stemming from a general resentment of difference, these forms of violence sense and systematically attack the connections between queerly co-constituting bodies and the libidinal tides through which they nourish and (re-)create each other. I refer to this logic of destruction as "earth/body violence."

Earth/body violence functions by breaking fundamental relations of co-constitution that are vital to the emergence and sustenance of worlds and to the many forms of (bio)pluralization that produce radical difference (see chapter 2). It is an expression of the ongoing compulsion, integral to post-Enlightenment Eurocentric world building, to sever "humanity" from "nature" (see Merchant 1983; Plumwood 2001; Povinelli 2016), not least by implementing heteronormative ideals of reproduction and reproductivity, eroticism, and love (see A. Simpson 2014). The slash in the term "earth/body" signals the continuity of earth and the multiple bodies it constitutes but also the violent cuts through which they are separated. Although it attacks the relations between human bodies and land in general, this kind of violence more intensely targets those bodies that form *intimate, erotic, loving,* and/or *familial* connections to land, water, air, and other nonhuman bodies. Earth/body violence works through and combines vectors of race, gender, disability, body type, and sexuality, disproportionately targeting bodies whose potentialities for (bio)pluralization (see chapter 2) most disrupt the sexual and erotic politics of the state (see A. Simpson 2014). By damaging relational systems, these cuts prepare the way for further forms of systemic violence—for instance, they may be used to erase land relations to expedite colonial land grabbing or to prevent the regeneration of (bio)plural communities as a strategy of genocide.

One way of understanding how earth/body violence systematically attacks (bio)plurality is to reconsider the concept of "habitat destruction," widely considered to be the primary driver of extinction (see WWF 2016). In mainstream Western scientific discourses, "habitat" usually refers to an external, supporting environment, resource base, or substrate from which life-forms draw sustenance and shelter. From this perspective, habitat destruction is undesirable if it harms the life-forms in question. In contrast, in the relations of exuberant co-constitution reflected in Christie-Peters's work, radically different bodies *act as each other's habitats.* That is, a multitude of different bodies provide (partial) homes for each other and negotiate the conditions for each other's flourishing or harm. Bodies are not *in* environments or habitats but always in and part of other, often profoundly different bodies. For instance, animal bodies are simultaneously immersed in water bodies and the micro-bodies of minerals; as they are eaten or absorbed into earth or fire, or as they nourish micro-biota; as they give birth, breathe, decompose, erode, erupt, and exchange energy. It is not only the case that certain bodies provide a "first environment" for gestated beings (an argument often made regarding pregnancy and childbearing; see NYSHN 2016). Rather, *all* bodies are always already within specific constellations of other bodies. Crucially, this relationship is not always positive, healthy, or nourishing. As Black American scholar Tiffany Lethabo King (2018) puts it, bodies engaged in intimate co-constitution are "porous" to each other: open to multidirectional exchanges of energy, substances, and effects that can nourish or be exploited through structures of violence (King 2018; see also Tuana 2008). Indeed, while porosity can create conditions for mutual flourishing, it can also facilitate the flow of harms, ranging from the bioaccumulation of heavy metals to intergenerational trauma.

In such dynamics, relations shaped by greater degrees of porosity, intimacy, and co-constitution are more vulnerable to conversion into conduits of systemic violence. It is by exploiting and instrumentalizing such systems that the forms of violence discussed in this book convert relations of cohabitation into structural, targeted sources of harm.

ENVIRONMENTAL RACISM AND EXTINCTION

In order to reshape and possess worlds, earth/body violence mobilizes and amplifies other vectors of violence, including those related to race, gender/sexuality, and disability/body difference. Key examples of these violent synergies are found in formations of environmental racism, environmental ableism, and land-based gendered and sexual violence.

Environmental racism "targets for demise" (Pellow 2016, 3) racialized bodies (and their cohabitats), framing them as dumping sites for pollution and other externalities seeping from the production of white supremacist cultures. Racialized American scholar David N. Pellow (2016, 3) describes how

> people of color, people of lower socioeconomic status, [I]ndigenous and immigrant populations, and other marginalized communities are disproportionately affected by ecologically harmful infrastructures, such as landfills, mines, incinerators, polluting factories, and destructive transportation systems, as well as by the negative consequences of ecologically harmful practices, such as climate change/disruption and pesticide exposure.

As Chicana scholar Laura Pulido (2000, 2017) argues, environmental racism performs a triple function: segregating racialized bodies from white ones; distancing white communities from the harms they produce; and using racialized bodies to sink, and therefore obscure, harms and culpability for causing them, often by framing states and companies as neutral actors. Jamaican American writer Dorceta Taylor's (2014) seminal work on environmental racism shows how these practices create and deepen patterns of social segregation by reserving natural and healthy spaces for white middle-class and elite communities. For instance, the mostly Latinx and Mexican American community of Manchester, Texas, next to the Houston Ship Channel, has been progressively surrounded by oil refineries, petrochemical and fertilizer plants, a metal shredding facility, a wastewater treatment plant, a tire plant, and an interstate highway, all of which saturate the land, air, and water with heavy pollutants (Foytlin et al. 2014, 185). Similarly,

Earth / Body Violence

the Anishinaabe community of Aamjiwnaang, near Sarnia, Ontario, has been deliberately engulfed over several decades by the industrial installations of the "Chemical Valley" (which process, among other chemical products, crude oil from the Alberta Tar Sands). This community copes with regular uncontrolled leaks of benzene into the air from nearby factories—often without any warning—along with the pollution of the river system with solvents and crude oil, and constant noise and light pollution (Wiebe 2016). Large-scale projects of extraction and the policies (or lack of regulations) that facilitate them have "wastelanded" (Voyles 2015) entire regions—that is, treated them as empty repositories for waste, following and deepening preexisting racist spatial logics. For instance, in the Bakken oil fields, which traverse the ancestral lands of multiple Indigenous nations across so-called North Dakota, Montana, Alberta, and Saskatchewan, an estimated three hundred spills of untreated petrochemicals went unreported between 2012 and 2013 alone. The rupture of a single pipeline owned by Summit Midstream Partners LLC in North Dakota in January 2015 dumped three million gallons of saltwater-drilling waste, including radioactive materials, into the watershed (Garcia Cano 2015). Similarly, countries such as Ghana and Côte d'Ivoire (Besser 2021), the Philippines, and Bangladesh (Liboiron 2020) are treated by Northern states as dumping grounds for textile (including textile production), plastic, chemical, electronic, and other forms of waste. As these materials break down and infiltrate water, soil, and air and enter the food chain, they toxify entire communities, cementing the geopolitical power structures that enable and manifest ongoing structures of colonization (Liboiron 2020).

In the examples discussed here, environmental racism involves the zoning of certain places as dumps for pollution. This practice is known as "siting": the decision to concentrate known or predictable ecological harms in some places and, crucially, away from others. In some cases, the perceived remoteness of a place—constructed in relation to centers of power such as major cities or capitals, or the seat of imperial power—is used to justify such decisions. For instance, this logic is reflected in the siting of nuclear testing by the United States, Australia, and several European states in the South Pacific and desert areas in North America and North Africa. Often, the perceived sparseness of the human population—often an artifact of colonial projections of emptiness on Indigenous societies and/or the displacement of Indigenous and other marginalized peoples by the majority population—is cited as justification for the siting of ecologically harmful projects. Still other siting decisions reflect the locations of influential political and economic actors who lobby to be protected from environmental harms. All these factors are evident in the rerouting of the Dakota Access Pipeline away from white-dominated urban areas such as Bismarck, North Dakota, and toward the lands of the Standing Rock Sioux tribe (Thorbecke 2016).

Environmental racism can also take the form of structural indifference or apathy toward existing, often long-standing risks and threats, often in the form of infrastructural or environmental degradation. Examples of such harms include the more than forty thousand superfund sites across the United States, where major ecological harms have occurred (see LaDuke 1994; NYSHN 2016).[2] They are also found in the prevalence of contaminated water supplies in areas such as the majority Black city of Flint, Michigan, and the (at the time of writing) at least fifty-six Indigenous nations in Canada that have not had access to clean drinking water for a year or more.[3] Indeed, in the United States, as of 2019, fifty-eight out of every one thousand Indigenous people lack access to clean drinking water, while only three out of one thousand white people do (U.S. Water Alliance 2019). Meanwhile, in Australia, many Indigenous communities deemed to be remote (from large cities) have access to water for only nine hours per day during one season (Beal 2017; N. Hall et al. 2017). What's more, as Murphy (2017) argues, even ecological harms that affect all organic bodies accrue unequally in racialized bodies. She recounts how the greasy film covering modern office towers in cities like Toronto or Chicago attracts airborne polychlorinated biphenyls (PCBs) that dissolve with rainfall and enter water systems such as the Great Lakes. Murphy points out that although all people alive today contain PCBs in their bodily fluids, people engaged in traditional activities that involve direct contact with these water systems—for example, through fishing, rice gathering, or travel by boat— are more heavily exposed to these pollutants. In this manner, the logic of earth/body violence turns activities that are integral to particular communities' thriving, continuity, and healing into conduits of harm. Although this violence is structural and diffused over time and space, it nonetheless targets particular bodies and relationships.

Targeting of certain worlds, bodies, and cohabitats for earth/body violence involves not only damaging their structures of sustenance but also *substituting* the forms of order preferred by the colonial-capitalist state. In this way, environmental violence is used as a means of appropriating and dominating land and altering earth/body relations. By framing lands as uninhabitable, damaged, or otherwise violable, and by marking them in material and physical ways (e.g., through pollution or physical disruption), states and corporations actively exert their ability to annex and control territory (see Serres 2011). This practice modifies the Lockean notion of "mixing labour with land," instead laying claim to land by permeating it with racist forms of power (Ferreira da Silva 2007) or ecological damage (Serres 2011). At the same time, the harms inflicted through these forms of systemic violence are used as further justification for state interventions, through which the power of colonial actors is consolidated. Paiute anthropologist Kristen Simmons (2017) describes these conditions as "settler atmospherics," conditions in which colonial violence and modes of control become the encompassing *medium* through which necessities such as breathing, eating, and drinking must be met. As Christie-Peters (2018) puts it, "much like the weather, settler colonialism is immersive, generating an environment that I must necessarily interact with." In this way, environmental racism does not simply destroy existing worlds but also weaponizes relations (see Todd 2022) such that they harm rather than sustain their co-constituents.

ENVIRONMENTAL ABLEISM

The logic of dumping ecological harms into bodies and cohabitats framed as damaged, degraded, or impure (Voyles 2015), or whose elimination is actively desired (see Kafter 2013; Mitchell 2022), also underpins what I call "environmental ableism."[4] Disability is often marginalized in discussions of environmental justice, including efforts to address environmental racism (Jaquette Ray and Sibara 2017). Yet it disproportionately affects racialized and/or colonized communities on a global scale and is frequently an *expression of,* and/or compounded by, environmental racism and other kinds of structural violence (and vice versa).[5] Just as the depiction of racialized bodies as already polluted (see King 2018) is frequently used to mask environmental racism, the assumption that disabled bodies are already damaged (beyond repair or redemption) often obscures ecological ableism. These violent logics converge in communities like Aamjiwnaang, where high rates of cancer are regularly attributed by government and corporate actors to "lifestyle." That is, high cancer rates are blamed on the combination of genetic predisposition and life choices made by individuals in the community rather than its politically and economically driven engulfment by highly polluting chemical processing plants (see Wiebe 2016). The individualization of disability—that is, its framing as a matter of individual genetics and/or choice rather than social, economic, and political exclusion, violence, and oppression—is a common feature of the dominant medical model of disability (see Kafer 2013; Silberman 2015; Jaquette Ray and Sibara 2017).[6] As disability activists have long argued, public discourses frequently assume that our quality of life (as if there is one agreed standard of "quality"; see Kafer 2013) is inherently lower than that of able-bodied people. These assumptions underpin political decisions that discount or dilute entitlements to live, die, flourish, suffer, be protected, or collectively exist, especially when our needs are placed in competition with communities deemed to be "natural," "healthy," or "pure" (Tuana 2008; Shotwell 2016; Clare 2017; S. Taylor 2017). For instance, the labeling of communities with high rates of disability (and issues such as drug use, poverty, and domestic abuse) as "at risk" is often used to naturalize the dumping of ecological and social harms into them (Tuck and Yang 2012; Murphy 2017) *instead of* in places where quality of life is perceived to be higher. As a result, places targeted for ecological racism often face positive feedback loops in which layers of multiplying harms are used by states and corporations to justify additional siting of harms within them. For instance, Indigenous communities affected by centuries of economic and political oppression *and* the ecological harms of extraction often experience heightened rates of reproductive health issues; cancer, heart and lung disease, effects on the brain and brain development, diabetes, lead and other heavy-metal poisoning, viral and bacterial infections, and metabolic and endocrine disruptions (NYSHN 2016). At the same time, they are disproportionately affected by chronic social stressors that are compounded or magnified by environmental ableism. These include sexual, domestic, and family violence; the ongoing epidemic of Missing and Murdered Indigenous Women and Girls; trafficking for both labor and sexual exploitation; increased rates of HIV and other sexually transmitted diseases; increased violent crime and rates of incarceration of BIPOC people; increased drug and alcohol use; alcohol-related traffic fatalities; suicide; land trauma and dispossession; loss of culture and self-determination; divisions in family and communities; removal of children by the state; mental health crises; and intensified conditions of poverty (NYSHN 2016, 13). As a result,

Earth/Body Violence 107

this dangerous intersection of extractive industry, the violence that accompanies it, and a population of women and young people who are already targets of systemic violence and generational trauma, sets the stage for increased violence on the land leading to increased violence on Indigenous people. (NYSHN 2016, 9)

Similar harms are experienced by entire cohabitats that, after sustaining and surviving repeated violence, become less able to resist or withstand additional, and often intensifying, harms. We can understand these cohabitats and the bodies that create them as being disabled by colonization, racism, and capitalism and subjected to environmental ableism. For instance, the fragile Arctic tundra, disturbed through centuries of mining and climate change, now has less capacity to absorb and break down chemicals or sequester CO_2 as a result of reduced vegetation. This change reduces its perceived ecological value (see chapter 2), making the land more amenable to mining. This arbitrage of harm follows the capitalist logic of sunk costs: harm to bodies assumed to be already damaged is considered less bad than it would be to normative bodies, because the former are simply expected to live shorter, less pleasurable and/or productive lives, and are valued less (S. Taylor 2017). This way of thinking helps influence decisions about the allocation of ecological and other harms, including the siting decisions discussed in the previous section.

Disabled bodies also tend to be more deeply and immediately affected by ecological harms than nondisabled ones. For example, we are more likely to be economically marginalized and/or dependent on public housing and therefore less able to relocate from places that become polluted (Piepzna-Samarasinha 2018). We are also three to four times more likely to die in natural disasters due to noninclusive emergency practices (Fuji 2012); and we frequently face disbelief and discrimination when reporting the bodily effects of toxins and other environmental harms (Chen 2012; Alaimo 2017). What's more, in order to get our needs met or engage with our worlds, disabled bodies often exist in intense and intimate relations of cohabitation—including with human carers who assist with bodily needs but also other beings such as animals, plants, water, and ecosystems—that are often deemed excessive by dominant social standards (see Clare 2017; Judge 2017; Piepzna-Samarasinha 2018; Mitchell 2022). Indeed, these relations are often framed as inappropriate forms of dependence (see Montgomery 2012), and/or a drain on resources and social systems.[7] As such, they are

108 Earth/Body Violence

labeled as "unproductive" or "inefficient" by structures of ableism and targeted for elimination or assimilation—even as they offer alternatives to the individualizing tendencies within colonial-capitalist societies (see Kafer 2013; Piepzna-Samarasinha 2023).

LAND-BASED SEXUAL AND GENDERED VIOLENCE

A similar logic propels forms of systemic violence that target specific genders, sexualities, and relations of cohabitation. These forms of earth/body violence not only distort existing constellations of (bio)plurality but also disrupt (bio)pluralizations in the form of love, pleasure, intimacy, and eroticism—crucial elements of collective power. Gender and gendering are hallmark (although not exclusively) Eurocentric modes of structural violence that intensively shape the relations imposed on bodies through colonial-capitalist relations (see chapter 4). Perhaps most famously, Eurocentric discourses on gender and sexuality have focused on entrenched images of earth as a woman who can be repeatedly violated (Merchant 1983; Plumwood 2001), as a failing, victimized "Gaia" (see Latour 2016), or as a vengeful, erratic "Medea" (Lovelock and Margulis [1974] 2010; Ward 2009). While pointing to deep-seated structures of sexism and misogyny, such critical imagery also reproduces heteronormative gender binaries and relational patterns, effacing the multiplicity of genders, sexualities, and relations that sustain (bio)plural worlds (see Grosz 2004). In fact, this austere gender and sexual binary is far from natural: in order to install it over and against worlds of prolific difference, settler colonial states must deny, outlaw, and attack expressions of gender, sexuality, and eroticism that exceed and challenge them (see A. Simpson 2014). As Christie-Peters (2018) puts it,

> The settler state has recognized how Indigenous women, Two-spirit, queer, trans, and non-binary relatives . . . so beautifully weave our bodies within our homelands, seamlessly connecting our communities to all of creation. The state has watched these people—the ways they tended to the waters, articulated power, and upheld our communities—and has responded by explicitly targeting these community members.

In other words, the (bio)plurality of genders and sexualities within Indigenous communities is targeted by settler colonial states precisely because

Earth/Body Violence

it is so integral to the co-creation and sustenance of worlds and their resistance to domination.

This logic is exemplified by the cultures of major colonial-capitalist actors, including mining companies such as the Canadian-owned mining giant Barrick Gold and its peers (see Mining Watch 2017). Operating mines in at least eighteen countries—in Turtle Island and Abya-Yala (South America), Australia, Southeast Asia, west Asia, sub-Saharan Africa, and South America—and financially supported by the Canadian settler state and other governments, Barrick works to assert de facto sovereignty over the lands it mines. Crucially, it does so not only by dissolving ecosystems and dissolving Indigenous systems of governance but also through systematic forms of land-based gendered and sexual violence, including hundreds of reports of gendered and sexual assaults. For example, the communities surrounding Barrick's Porgera Joint Venture Gold Mine in Papua New Guinea (on Ipili lands) have survived the repeated burning of villages, extrajudicial killings of people perceived to oppose the operation, the widespread dumping of mining tailings into the river and soil systems, and the destruction of local food production systems based on subsistence farming and animal husbandry, along with reports of at least 253 rapes of women.[8] In this case, Barrick's predecessor Placer Dome admitted to eight killings on the part of its security staff, and Barrick acknowledged the credibility of reports of sexual violence. However, Barrick's response was to create a "Non-judicial Remedy" framework that offered no independent legal counsel for survivors, demanded that they surrender legal rights in exchange for one-time financial payouts, and did not address sexual or physical violence or detention by Barrick employees (Mining Watch 2017, 19–20).[9] Similarly, in its North Mara mine in Tanzania, Barrick and its partners' security staff engaged in 229 documented killings and 69 injuries (as of 2017) of members of the Kurya herding community; there were also many reports of rape and gang rape (often followed by the abandonment of survivors by their husbands) and severe beatings of women. Once again, Barrick's response to this campaign of violence was nonjudicial, and most rape survivors received less than C\$8,000 and were compelled to surrender their rights to sue Barrick and its partner Acacia. Similar cultures of gendered, sexualized, and racialized violence surround the notorious "man camps" that support mining operations across North America. For instance, in the Bakken oil fields, Indigenous women were 2.5 times more

likely than other women to be assaulted, while 86 percent of their assault-
ers were non-Indigenous men working in man camps created to support
the mining industry (NYSHN 2016, 8). Similarly, Ginger Gibson et al. (2017)
report that the hypermasculine culture in work camps near Lake Babine
First Nation in northern British Columbia has resulted in increased sexual
harassment, sexual assault, and demands for sex work; pay inequity; and
heightened vulnerability of women as they seek transport to access social
and health services.[10] These examples show how the targeting of gendered
and sexualized bodies is integral to the cultures and operational strategies
of companies seeking to remove obstacles to extraction.

Similar dynamics and cultures of gendered and sexualized violence
also thrive in the context of global conservation organizations. As Dorceta
Taylor (2016) shows, the American environmental movement is overwhelmingly dominated by white, male, middle-class norms that continue
to be reflected in its leadership structure (see also chapter 6), militaristic
organizational culture, and hostility toward 2SLGBTQIA+ people (Gilpin
2016).[11] For example, a report conducted in 2000 found that more than half
of female employees of the U.S. National Park Service had reported incidents of sexual harassment, sexual assault, discrimination, hostile work environments, and a culture of retaliation, among other issues (Gilpin 2016).
Entrenched cultures of gendered and sexualized oppression have been
recently reported in two of the world's largest conservation organizations,
Conservation International (CI) and the Nature Conservancy (NC) (Belmaker 2018). Indeed, in 2019 NC's then-president Brian McPeek resigned
in the wake of an investigation into the organization's culture of sexual
harassment (Colman 2019). What's more, studies suggest that a culture of
gender- and sexuality-based discrimination, homophobia, harassment, and
assault permeates the wider fields of conservation biology (see Tulloch
2020) and conservation leadership (Jones and Solomon 2019) in both academic and field settings (Clancy et al. 2014). Most of these incidents affect
the relatively privileged staff working at the headquarters or home countries of these organizations, who may have access to legal supports. However, they are part of a broader institutional culture that also permeates their
field operations, where—much like the employees of mining companies—
conservationists generally hold positions of social, economic, and political
power in relation to the communities with whom they work. In some cases,
conservation organizations also work directly with police and/or military
actors, law enforcement, regulators, employers, and policymakers. As such,

their organizational cultures can significantly influence social dynamics and social outcomes in the communities where they carry out their work. Although there is little specific research on the subject, the presence in conservation organizations of cultures of systemic violence, militaristic organizational models (Duffy 2014), substantial power differentials between staff and locals, and, often, the presence of armed force engender significant risk of sexualized violence. Indeed, this has historically been the case in the context of peace-keeping and peace-building interventions operating under similar structural conditions and objectives.

Conservation organizations may also promote explicit cultures of gendered and sexualized violence through the relational conditions they enforce upon other life-forms. For example, Filipina anthropologist Juno Salazar Parreñas (2018, 85) documents the conditions of "forced copulation" and "compulsory heterosexuality" to which female orangutans are subjected at the Lundu wildlife center in Sarawak, Malaysian Borneo, as a result of global breeding imperatives (see chapter 1).[12] Salazar Parreñas (2018, 85, emphasis mine) argues that, through their practices, discourses, and culture, such organizations engender "a *system of sexual violence*" that encompasses orangutans and their human kin alike. For instance, she describes several incidents in which young female orangutans were locked into cages with larger males who beat, dragged, and forcibly penetrated them, causing substantial injuries and at least one death. Described by the center as "natural," these incidents ignore the conditions of captivity in which these encounters took place. These include the decimation of the primates' ecosystem, which would previously have provided enough space for the females to escape unwanted sexual advances by males; and the imperative for breeding, which prevents the neutering of males and increases the likelihood of aggressive behavior (Salazar Parreñas 2018). What's more, Salazar Parreñas describes how the culture of sexual violence at the Center is further reflected in references to rape between humans. For instance, she documents keepers and tourists claiming that the female orangutans were subjected to violence because they were "beautiful" or "forcing themselves to get raped" and laughing at the females' explicitly expressed fear (2018, 124). While eschewing simplistic definitions that elide rape and the natural behavior of male mammals, Parreñas's work draws attention to how conservation installations can become conduits and multipliers for broader cultures of gendered and sexualized earth/body violence that cross life-forms.

EARTH/BODY VIOLENCE, (UN)CONSENT, AND THE DESTRUCTION OF (BIO)PLURALITY

Earth/body violence and other forms of systemic violence corrode (bio) plurality by attacking relations of intimacy, bonding, connection, pleasure, comfort, eroticism, and reproduction, all of which are integral to the work of continuity (see chapter 1). They do so by breaking relations based on consent and/or creating conditions of unconsent: dynamics in which consent is not accessible to all involved is not considered relevant. Conditions of unconsent are created in several ways: by denying or disregarding the need to obtain consent; by framing certain beings as unable to give and withhold it, by virtue of racist, ableist, gendered, or sexual stereotypes; or by ignoring existing laws, rules, norms, and practices of consent within specific worlds, and only counting forms of consent that reflect the norms of the aggressor (i.e., demanding that consent be written instead of verbal).[13] For instance, the logic of unconsent is reflected in the assumption that nonhumans cannot give consent and therefore do not need to be accounted for in negotiations related to ecologically disruptive projects.[14] Even when carried out with the guidance of international norms such as the UN Declaration on the Rights of Indigenous Peoples, formal attempts to obtain consent are generally motivated by the desire to gain permission to do something that is likely to harm a community. In addition, since UNDRIP is not binding in international law, consent is often treated as a means of expediting or legitimating actions that have already been decided rather than a genuine prerequisite. In the absence of meaningful and enforceable opportunities to withhold consent, these dynamics can produce conditions of unconsent.

Earth/body violence is often an important contributor to conditions of unconsent. Specifically, existing (often nonconsensual) harms to bodies, cohabitats, and worlds are frequently used by states, corporations, and other actors as evidence that consent to do more harm is not required. They argue that the harms would only be marginal given the extent of existing damage; or that, since these bodies or cohabitats are already harmed, consent must have already been given/taken at some point in the past, or was never deemed to be necessary. In such situations, further harm is framed not as violence, since beings in question are assumed to have already been dehumanized or stripped of ethical status (see Mitchell 2014b). Instead, additional harm is framed as a natural state of at-risk or damaged bodies (see

Murphy 2017). In this circular manner, earth/body violence and other forms of systematic violence compound, magnify, and facilitate each other.

What's more, through this logic, a community's achievement of surviving repeated violence is often misrepresented as consent for further violation. Indeed, Australian settler scholar Lorenzo Veracini (2010, 12) describes how early European colonizers leveraged their anger at finding their promised "virgin territory" to be "already married to another man"—that is, inhabited by Indigenous peoples—as justification for violence against those peoples and the land. In so doing, they reversed the direction of harm, creating narratives in which their violent and often genocidal actions were understood as justified, retaliatory, or even rooted in sexual injury to *them*. As Mohawk thinker Audra Simpson (2014) demonstrates, this ethos of resentment and sexual vengeance, channeled through white settler masculinities, remains integral to settler states' consolidation of power through the murder of Indigenous women and 2SLGBTQIA+ people *and* large-scale ecological harm. By framing certain bodies as endlessly and justifiably violable, this logic, ironically, frames them as *in*violable: that is, it denies these bodies the status of violability.

In a similar sense, within the anthropocentric Western scientific and social frameworks that distinguish between living and nonliving (see chapter 2), or sentient and nonsentient (see S. Taylor 2017), most of the co-constituents of (bio)plural worlds and cohabitats are construed as fundamentally unable to give or withhold consent and are thus stranded in conditions of perpetual unconsent. Instead of moral patients able to experience *harm* or *violation* in themselves, let alone moral agents whose actions are themselves subject to ethical analysis, they are treated as if they are only capable of sustaining *damage*. In Western philosophical thought, this term applies to nonsentient objects and can be rectified through replacement, repair, or compensation (to their human "owners") rather than, for instance, restitution, apology, diplomacy, or political transformation.

This problem is illustrated by states', corporations', and international organizations' attitudes toward nonhumans in formal processes of consent, including the principle of free, prior, and informed consent (FPIC) entrenched in the UN Declaration on the Rights of Indigenous Peoples (UNDRIP 2007).[15] While I certainly do not wish to undermine the decades of struggle by Indigenous peoples that led to UNDRIP, largely as a result of the opposition and interventions of states in its language and terms, this document offers a highly constrained account of consent. For instance, it only requires consultation (not robust forms of consent) for activities undertaken on Indigenous land and it requires only that relevant communities be *informed* of these activities. In addition, it encourages states and corporations to reverse-engineer consent, offering communities limited opportunities to modify plans substantively (Amnesty International 2016). Consent processes under UNDRIP also rely on colonial systems of governance and decision-making (e.g., the "chief and council" system installed by the Canadian settler state, or town hall meetings) or majority rule (instead of, for instance, deliberative, consensus-based forms of decision-making used in many Indigenous communities; see Borrows 2010; Umeek 2012). By virtue of its anthropocentrism, this model of consent excludes *all* non-human co-constituents of worlds from processes of consent and frames them as not being capable of giving or withholding it except indirectly (e.g., through human representatives).

In contrast, in many Indigenous and BIPOC forms of governance, non-human beings participate in decision-making (Umeek 2012) and in giving and withholding consent in ways *appropriate to their mode of being and place in relational structures* (see chapter 1). For example, Anishinaabekwe elder and botanist Keewaydinoquay (quoted in Geniusz 2009, 58–61) describes how plants give and withhold consent and how to ensure that one has obtained consent before gathering them. She explains that one should

> never take a plant for healing without first talking to the species and then to the particular plants, asking for their permission, and asking that they please give healing. . . . Then you promise that you won't take so much of it that its grandchildren won't live after it.

In addition, offering asemaa (tobacco) as a respectful greeting and in recognition that one is asking for something is necessary, but not sufficient if the plant does not consent. One cannot rely on Eurocentric methods, such as verbal or written responses, to tell whether consent has been given. Instead, Keewaydinoquay offers, one must pay attention to how the plant communicates in its *own terms*: for instance, does it come away freely from the ground when one pulls or does it resist? Is it, or the desired part (say a flower or fruit), growing within easy reach, or does it require substantial and possibly risky maneuvers to reach it? Does an insect sting you when you try to reach for it? All these impediments to the picking of the plant may signal that consent has not been given and that to force its removal or alteration may be a violation. Crucially, it is the responsibility of the one who wishes to pick the plant—or to alter, enter, use, or otherwise affect any other body—to understand the ways that it gives or withholds consent. It is *not* the responsibility of the plant or other body to conform to the picker's norms and practices.

A resonant perspective is reflected in the Secwepemc Women's Declaration, which was created in opposition to the construction of pipelines and other infrastructure, including man camps. The declaration stated unequivocally:

> We, as Secwepemc women, declare that we do not consent! We do not consent to the desecration of our sacred land; we do not consent to the transgressions on our sacred bodies! (Secwepemc Assembly 2017)

From this perspective, the violation of earth is *necessarily* a violation of gendered BIPOC bodies. Sacred lands and sacred bodies are understood to be continuous, and violence against either of these entities is recognized as the violation of their relations of co-constitution. This framework rejects the colonial distinction that presumes that (some) humans are capable of giving consent and that nonhumans are inherently incapable. What's more, by rejecting consent to extractive processes *in perpetuity* on the basis of Secwepemc law, the declaration contested colonial processes of consent. In other words, from the perspective of the Declaration, any efforts by governments and corporations to gain consent to disrupt the land and water would necessarily take place in conditions of unconsent.

SYSTEMIC VIOLENCE, EARTH/BODY VIOLENCE, AND THE DESTRUCTION OF (BIO)PLURALITY

So far, I have argued that the violent disruption of earth's ecosystems (and efforts to conserve them) are inseparable from systemic—including racialized, ableist, gendered, and sexualized—violence against particular bodies, cohabitats, and the relationships that sustain them. Within these formations of violence, myriad forms of connection, intimacy, and coproduction across (bio)plural worlds are forcefully replaced by monocultures (see Shiva 1993) of masculine, heteronormative relations and modes of domination.[16] Pervasive contamination of cohabiting bodies, including water, air, and soil, makes sensual, erotic, reproductive, and other relationships fraught with risk, while, at the same time, enforcing established patterns of domination. From cellular to global scales (Pellow 2016), these forms of racialized, ableist, gendered, and sexualized violation are sustained through a culture that promotes and normalizes the violation and conditions of unconsent. All of this contributes to the erosion of (bio)plurality, which, unlike biodiversity, relies not only on *biological* production but also on the sustenance and proliferation of singular difference. This kind of difference emerges from relational structures, laws, agreements, kinship structures, erotic and pleasureful encounters, love, and other modes of generative connection. Earth/body violence attacks these processes, and the worlds they generate, in a number of devastating ways.

First, it is used deliberately to injure, attenuate, or break strong relations between human and other bodies—especially those of racialized, disabled, female, 2SLGBTQIA+ people—in order to open up resources and land for exploitation. This can lead to the withdrawal of particular bodies from conditions of mutually nurturing exchange. It also imposes homogenous relations of heteronormativity that, while promoting hetero(sexual) reproduction, may halt or sever processes of socially reproductive or nonreproductive (see Grosz 2004; TallBear 2015) relationality that are integral to the social, cultural, aesthetic, and other elements of the continuity of worlds. Earth/body violence also distorts intimate relationships between bodies, turning them from nourishing and pleasureful to traumatic, painful, and harmful—for instance, by turning a place for gathering food into a site of penetration by toxins or a trigger for memories of sexual violence. Similarly, the siting of ecologically harmful activities on certain lands can transform them into "white places" (Pulido 2017)—and/or nondisabled (Kafer 2017) or masculine places. This may render these places inaccessible to the BIPOC, disabled, and women or 2SLGBTQIA+ communities who have long been in relations of cohabitation with them. As a result, specific groups of humans may lose the ability to carry out their responsibilities in caring for other beings and life-forms, often resulting in the degradation of ecosystems.

At the same time, systematic forms of violence such as earth/body violence saturate (bio)plural worlds with multiple layers of physical, social, economic, and psychological harms, fundamentally altering relational models. For instance, they may lead to the engulfment of survivors of violence within state systems of healthcare, policing and carceral institutions, childcare, and infrastructure. For instance, Pellow (2016) shows how the penetration of BIPOC communities by pollutants and climate change is often attended by the increased presence of police forces, producing the combined corrosion of social and physical safety and of ecological stability and access. Similarly, the harms generated by earth/body violence are used to open communities to increased surveillance by governmental and corporate bodies, including testing of lands, water, air, and flesh (human, plant, and animal) by government or university-based researchers or corporations involved in pollution (see Wiebe 2016). As Murphy (2017, 496) argues, Western techno-scientific research purporting to track damage and offer remedies to harmed communities often

> surveils and pathologizes already dispossessed communities. Despite often antiracist intentions, this damage-based research has pernicious effects. . . . [It] tends to resuscitate racist, misogynist, and homophobic portraits of poor, Black, Indigenous, female, and queer lives and communities as damaged and doomed, as inhabiting irreparable states that are not just unwanted but less than fully human.

Once violenced cohabitats are pathologized in this way, their ability to generate alternative futures is encumbered by increasingly invasive forms of discipline and control. However, it is crucial to resist the assumption that such bodies are permanently and irreversibly destroyed or neutralized. In her discussion of "alterlife"—the forms of life altered through the confluence of chemical, genetic, racial, colonial, and other forms of violence— Murphy (2017) rejects dichotomies between "pure" (see Shotwell 2016) and "damaged" life. Instead, she understands chemically altered life as part of relational systems that may embody and sometimes extend patterns of harm but nonetheless persist and foster distinct forms of thriving. In the section on environmental ableism in this chapter, I discussed how disability activists and thinkers reject the notion that our lives are less valuable and perhaps irredeemable because of their perceived dysfunctionality, nonproductivity, or devaluation when indexed against ableist norms. In a resonant way, Murphy (2017, 500) counsels that instead of rejecting "alterlife" as lost or destroyed, we should "embrac[e] impure and damaged forms of life, pessimistically acknowledging ongoing violence," and recognize "alterlife [as] resurgent life, which asserts and continues nonetheless." In other words, alterlife—a dimension of racialized, disabled, gendered, and queer cohabitats—plays a crucial role in the work of the continuity of life-forms and worlds, and it is integral to (bio)plurality.

For all these reasons, simply focusing on "habitat destruction" or the physical and material alteration of ecosystems cannot come close to adequately recognizing or addressing the systematic targeting of (bio)plurality through earth/body violence. From this perspective, attempts to reverse harms to ecosystems must involve not (only) managing or replacing damaged habitat but also supporting processes of healing and enabling the (self-)restoration of the relations of *cohabitation*. Addressing conditions of unconsent and engendering conditions of consent would not involve simply negotiating permission to harm targeted bodies and cohabitats but instead restoring and/or creating relations of consensual intimacy, pleasure, and embodied exchange within relations of cohabitation. Indeed, pleasure activists (brown 2019) and trauma specialists (van der Kolk 2015) alike agree that visceral, embodied, sensual experiences of pleasure, comfort, and joy are integral to healing trauma, including that arising from racial, ableist, and gendered or sexualized violence. In this vein, efforts to address earth/body violence might focus on revitalizing sensual relations deemed immoral or subversive by colonial, imperial, capitalist, and other power structures. For example, it might involve the work of communities to restore consensual relationships with and between other beings and life-forms, such as those between humans, beavers, sticks, and stars described by Anishinaabe/Métis/Norwegian scholar Melissa Nelson. To honor and destigmatize these relationships, Nelson (2017, 232) argues, is "to truly feel [that] the sensuous gravity of the life that surrounds us and is within us is an act of profound intimacy, vulnerability and courage." Similarly, returning to the story/theory of Sedna (see Introduction and chapter 2), Inuk scholar Alootook Ipellie (1993) shares a telling in which the sea goddess is a survivor of sexual abuse and intimate family violence, who will only release the animals she keeps once she is able to achieve orgasm on her own terms. Inuk artist and author Tanya Tagaq (2018) mirrors this story in her protagonist's sensual and ultimately reproductive relationship with the land, sky, and an arctic fox ancestor, through which she is able to survive and heal from sexual trauma. These stories/theories suggest that earth/body violence cannot be healed by transforming isolated aspects of harmed bodies—in this case, nonhuman ecosystems—while leaving their relations with their humans severed, toxic, unsafe, or painful. Instead, relations of consensual intimacy, trust, mutual nourishment, pleasure, and love need to be reestablished. As Christie-Peters (2018) declares, her Indigenous "body is the muskrat that keeps building its worlds so that one day we may live, full and whole. Falling in love with my body is falling in love with all of the elements of creation that I come from."[17] It is relations like these—of consensual intimacy and, indeed, love—that can help restore (bio)plurality and resist the systematic destruction of life-forms and worlds.

4 Invasive States

Colonialism, Capitalism,
and Narratives of Invasion

As I write the first draft of this chapter (in February 2020), the Canadian state is engaged in an armed campaign on the unceded lands of the Wet'suwet'en nation in the northern part of what is currently known as British Columbia.[1] The state's aim is to enable a private corporation (Coastal GasLink, or CGL), financed by one of Canada's largest banks (RBC), to complete work on a pipeline carrying liquified natural gas (LNG) from the Alberta Tar Sands to ports along the Pacific Coast. As construction proceeds, the Unis'tot'en camp and healing center, villages, and camps set up to obstruct the movement of heavy machinery have weathered multiple raids by tactical teams of the Royal Canadian Mounted Police (RCMP).[2] These teams are often armed with heavy weaponry, riot gear, and canine units. Many of the people arrested are elders, hereditary chiefs, and their supporters. These actions are the most recent escalations of a long series of physical, legal, and political incursions by the federal and provincial governments that have been actively resisted by key members of the Wet'suwet'en community and leadership since 2007. Importantly, Canada, the province of British Columbia, CGL, and RBC do not have legal jurisdiction over or ownership of these lands. Instead, from the perspective of international law (and within relevant provincial and federal law), the actions of these entities constitute an act of aggression against an independent nation in contravention of the rule of law—in other words, war.

In solidarity, more than seventy Indigenous nations and political allies across Canada, the United States, Northern Europe, and Aotearoa/New Zealand have engaged in actions designed to block infrastructure—including roads, rail lines, and banks—on which the respective states depend economically and materially. At the time of writing, the longest-running action was a blockade carried out by the Mohawks of Tyendinaga, approximately halfway between Toronto and Montreal, on one of North America's most important freight and transport routes. A letter sent by the Sha'tekarihwate family of the Turtle Clan, Mohawk Nation, to the nation's treaty partner, (the former) Queen Elizabeth II, points out that the state's right to run roads and rail through their territories depends on two treaties between the Mohawks and the British Crown, which were violated by the Canadian state's attack on their ally (the Wet'suwet'en nation).[3] So, under the terms of the relevant treaties, the Tyendinaga blockade constituted a fully legal and proportional response to the actions of the Canadian state. Yet it was treated by the state as a criminal act and met with heavily armed police presence, surveillance, and multiple arrests.

These dynamics epitomize the interlinking of two crucial logics of violence that systematically target (bio)plurality: settler colonialism and extraction. They highlight the enormous effort, labor, and violence required to create and maintain relations of colonial domination and extraction (Moreton-Robinson 2015). At the same time, these examples show how settler colonialism and extractivism are both utterly reliant on the fracturing of (bio)plural relations—whether these relations exist between bitumen, sand, water, muskeg, and caribou; between Indigenous communities and their lands; or between long-standing treaty partners. In all cases, the breaking of co-constitutive relations is necessary to create and sustain invasive polities and the extractive economies on which they are grounded.

In this chapter, I examine how these interwoven logics contribute to the systematic destruction of (bio)plurality. First, I examine how logics of invasion pervade contemporary settler colonial states and, more broadly, global political, economic, and ecological discourses. I critically revisit discourses of invasive species, which are widely accepted in Western conservation biology as the second-leading global cause of extinction (Bellard, Cassey, and Blackburn 2016). Specifically, I shift attention from the targeting of particular species that are labeled as "invasive" and "exogenous" toward states, including laws and discourses of biosecurity. Instead, I focus on broader patterns and structures of sustained *political and economic invasion* that are foundational to contemporary states, and settler colonial polities in particular. I also highlight the deliberate and often involuntary movement of many life-forms—including humans—as part of large-scale processes of colonial terraforming intended to make land amenable to permanent invasion and carry out much of the labor it requires.

Next, I discuss how logics of extraction combine with patterns of permanent invasion to implement and sustain systems that target and destroy (bio)plurality. Converging with and magnifying patterns of earth/body violence (see chapter 3), logics of extraction benefit from and assist in the growth of settler colonial states *and* the assertion of sovereignty. Physical-mechanical processes of extraction literally fracture complex (bio)plural worlds in order to release the elements they value and to consign what is not valued to the status of waste. Simultaneously, homogenizing social-political *relations* of extraction are used to displace and replace existing (bio)plural relations and to prevent their regeneration. In so doing, they work to channel all interactions and collective energy toward a single horizon: extraction to the point of exhaustion—or, indeed, extinction. Within colonial-extractive polities, the saturation of all social, political, physical, and ecological systems with these logics (see J. Moore 2015) ensures their seamless reproduction and prevents disruptions to the global flow of capital. If and when this flow is disrupted, various forms of violence are deployed to enforce the resumption of extractive relations. The aggressions of the Canadian state against the Wet'suwet'en described here offers a clear example of these logics.

Logics of permanent invasion and extraction rely on systematic, comprehensive, and unceasing efforts to break down (bio)plural relations and dissolve conditions of (bio)plurality—whether to fuel their expansion or remove obstacles to it. If extinction is, as I have argued, an expression of the destruction of (bio)plurality, then addressing this harm requires a nuanced understanding of how invasive states and extractive relations work together to dissolve (bio)plural relations and the unique worlds they sustain.

INVASIVE STATES

Since 1500 CE, invasive species are believed to have caused 126 species extinctions and contributed to the extinction of around 300 more (Blackburn, Bellard, and Ricciardi 2019), earning them the dubious title of the second-most-important driver of contemporary extinctions (after habitat destruction; see chapter 3). Their global movements are tracked by powerful cultural narratives, including moral panics over "alien" and "exotic" species, which are often depicted as feral (Low 2002) and rapaciously destructive

(Subramaniam 2001). Although these narratives respond to real changes in ecosystems brought about (at least in part) by the global movement of life-forms, they focus blame, fear, and quite often hatred on specific life-forms while ignoring causes and conditions of their movement: global political and economic *structures of invasion,* including what I describe as invasive states. Indeed, the starting point of the studies cited here—1500 CE—is not coincidental. It marks an acceleration of European settler colonization, which did and continues to include the movement of tens of millions of bodies, including enslaved peoples, unfree and/or (super)exploited laborers, displaced peoples, and invaders themselves—along with billions of other nonhuman beings. Western scientific discourses on invasive species focus largely on the *unintentional* displacement of life-forms, for instance, through transit in the bilge water of ships, packing materials, or food products. However, global colonial-capitalist worlding has been fueled by the *deliberate* transfer and mass reproduction of billions of animals, plants, and other life-forms. Crucially, these life-forms are instrumentalized, often violently, by colonial-capitalist systems to dissolve existing (bio)plural worlds, creating conditions amenable to permanent invasion and the installation of extractive relations. In particular, settler colonialism, in which invaders seek to *permanently* replace existing worlds with their own social, political, economic, relational, and ecological models, instrumentalizes life-forms as one of its primary techniques of worlding.

To understand how the logic of settler colonial invasion systematically targets (bio)plurality, it is helpful to focus on four of its elements in particular: dispossession, elimination, replacement, and enforcement. *Dispossession* is the set of linked processes through which invaders take possession of a place and/or a set of beings *from* another community. It also includes the techniques through which they expand control, and, crucially, the apparatuses (narratives, laws, practices, norms, punishments, and more) used to maintain possession on a permanent basis (see Coulthard 2014; A. Simpson 2014; West 2016). Dispossession necessarily involves denying, erasing, or undermining existing relations of belonging and responsibility vis-à-vis lands or worlds.[4] As Quandamooka thinker Aileen Moreton-Robinson (2015, loc. 360) describes it,

> the sense of belonging, home, and place enjoyed by the non-Indigenous subject . . . is based on the dispossession of the original owners of the land and the denial of our rights under international customary law. Against this

stands the Indigenous sense of belonging, home, and place in its incommensurable difference.

As Moreton-Robinson argues, within her people's (and many other) cosmovisions, *people* belong to *lands* and must follow the laws embodied in the lands (not the other way around). In contrast, Eurocentric understandings of property involve individual assertions of ownership by *people over lands* and the submission of the land to *their* laws and prerogatives of use. Sometimes this process involves forms of relation making as superficial one-time verbal or written claims to ownership. Indeed, as the late Secwepemc political leader Arthur Manuel (2017, 5) explains,

> according to the tenets of the doctrine of discovery, all that Europeans had to do to expropriate the lands in a region was to sail past a river mouth and make a claim to all of the lands in its watershed. Our lands, given to us by our Creator and inhabited for thousands of years, were transformed into a British "possession," not only without our consent and without our knowledge, but also without a single European setting foot on our territory.

In such contexts, thousands of years (or more) of complex relations were evidently erased with a simple verbal or written declaration. However, as Australian settler scholar Patrick Wolfe (1999) has famously argued, such moments are often treated as constitutive of settler colonialism, which is in fact an ongoing *process* and an enduring set of *structures*.[5] Moreton-Robinson (2015, loc. 193) describes this work of entrenching settler colonial states as a "process of perpetual Indigenous dispossession." In other words, dispossession is not a single act that is completed in the moment of invasion but rather a set of relations that is engendered and *reenacted* every day within every structure of the invading polity. It is also an act that settlers or members of the invasive society (myself included) daily engage in by living on colonized land and benefiting from the continuing dispossession of Indigenous peoples.[6] As Moreton-Robinson (2015) points out, this process of continuous dispossession is also one of capitalization in the form of property. It converts Indigenous and other bodies of color, their lands, and nonhuman relations into commodifiable *possessions* from which value can be extracted and (re)invested into whiteness as a kind of capital from which power and privilege are derived (see Harris 1993), exploited, and increased over time.

126   Invasive States

In order to make such processes of dispossession square with their *own* legal and ethical systems, invaders have relied on several forms of eliminative logics and forms of violence. Perhaps the most fundamental example is the positing of desired lands as terra nullius, in which evidence of existing worlds is ignored, denied, and/or materially and socially destroyed in order to create an apparently empty space. As Australian settler scholar Lorenzo Veracini (2010, 17) describes it, the settler colonial process of *elimination* involves

> extermination, expulsion, incarceration, containment, and assimilation for [I]ndigenous peoples (or a combination of all these elements), restriction and selective assimilation for subaltern exogenous Others, and an ultimate affirmation of settler control against exogenous metropolitan interference.

The systematic destruction of (bio)plural relations—including the eco- and legal-political structures discussed in previous chapters—is integral to this process. As Audra Simpson (2016, emphasis mine) argues, the settler colonial state has "a *death drive to eliminate, contain, hide and in other ways 'disappear'* what fundamentally challenges its legitimacy: Indigenous political orders." Indeed, in the eliminative logic of settler colonial invasion, "only the settler body politic in its ultimate sovereign assertion against metropolitan interference and against indigenous residues or other insurgencies is *expected to survive*" (Veracini 2010, 17, emphasis mine). Importantly, such processes also align with the *desired extinction* of life-forms and worlds that obstruct invaders (see chapter 5).

Audra Simpson (2014, 2016) goes on to argue that the settler colonial impulse to destroy difference underpins extremely high and sustained rates of collective violence against Indigenous girls, women, trans, and Two-Spirit people. As she contends, this violence is often treated by police as an aggregation of linked but indirectly related individual acts while it actually constitutes a systematic attack against Indigenous ways of embodying gender and sexuality that confound Eurocentric norms (see chapter 5). This pattern of violence mirrors efforts by states to erode Indigenous land claims, titles, treaties, and laws. While they take place separately and over time, these efforts are not isolated but rather reflect a broader effort to extinguish legal orders and forms of power that challenge, limit, and rebuff the invasive state. Moreton-Robinson (2015) describes in detail how such processes functioned in the frameworks of the *Mabo* decision and the Native

Title Act of 1993, both in Australia. These two legal tools established criteria for determining native title, or the legal ability of Indigenous peoples to use and assert claims over their lands. However, far from straightforwardly recognizing existing claims, the Australian state used the act to place the burden to *prove* title onto the Indigenous communities seeking to make these claims. In this way, the rights for which generations of Aboriginal and Torres Strait Islander communities had fought were used by the state (against the spirit of the law) to *extinguish* their claims, effectively rendering them trespassers on their own lands unless and until they could prove otherwise. In a related sense, Dene scholar Glen Sean Coulthard (2014) argues that processes in which the colonial state is given the power to determine land rights force Indigenous communities to articulate and assert their rights within the terms and norms of invading states. Through these processes, settler colonial states, societies, and economies actively target existing (bio)plural forms of legal, ethical, and political order with the goal of clearing space for their own worlding projects.

Eliminative processes also enable another fundamental element of settler colonialism: *replacement*. Indeed, as Wolfe (2006, 389) puts it, "settler colonialism destroys to replace"—specifically, to install encompassing systems of order, governance, and power designed to nourish and reproduce invaders' ways of life and desired futures. This impulse to eradicate and replace is integral to the ecopolitical and world-forming actions of invaders, much of whose subjectivity is focused on "transforming the environment to suit the colonizing project and . . . renewing the settler in order to suit the environment" (Veracini 2010, 22). Indeed, one of the major hallmarks of global settler colonialism has been the wholesale transformation of existing ecosystems to create ecopolitical orders that resemble the places of origin of invaders and/or instill forms of order and power demanded by the invasive state (such as sovereignty and extraction). Such processes often proceed gradually, are distributed across large swathes of time and space, and are subject to substantial scope creep. For instance, American settler scholar William Cronon (1983) has shown how the unregulated resource grabbing of European mercantilists on the East Coast of what is currently called North America morphed into a process that would instrumentalize huge areas of land and Indigenous knowledges to widen access to the continent and its resources. The progressive destruction of these systems would also inaugurate changes in the (bio)plural exchange of oxygen and carbon dioxide that would play a pivotal role in contemporary *global* patterns of

128   Invasive States

climate change (S. Lewis and Maslin 2015). Similarly, the seventeenth-century demand for beaver furs in Europe nearly eradicated this life-form and is thus often discussed in terms of species extinction. However, its effects ramified far beyond one life-form, since beavers play a crucial role in co-constituting the (bio)plural relational orders of the continent, and on a scale greater than is recognized by most non-Indigenous people. As Anishinaabe scholar Nicholas Reo and Mandan/Hidatsa/Cree scholar Angela K. Parker (2013, 678) argue,

> the near-eradication of beaver transformed the ecology of the northeastern forest. Beaver dams create habitat for fish, waterfowl, and mammals that gather to use the collected water . . . so beaver population crashes impacted entire ecosystems and associated biota. These changes also meant a loss of wild game and food plants important in traditional diets of Algonquian peoples. In this way, overharvesting beaver reduced the availability of traditional foods, amplifying rapid changes in Algonquian food systems. Further, as beaver dam impoundments receded, colonizing Europeans easily converted newly exposed, nutrient rich meadows to agricultural fields [which] further reinforced colonial Dominance [sic].

Farther west, networks of beaver dams had helped form extensive irrigation systems that buffered inland and prairie Indigenous communities from sudden droughts and allowed for the seasonal growing of food (Daschuk 2013, xvi). This unique hydroscape was comaintained by the Indigenous communities who relied on it through careful restrictions on hunting and water use among and across communities. Its destruction, and that of the (bio)plural systems reliant on it, not only rendered inland Indigenous communities more economically dependent on trade with European invaders but also caused pathogens (often zoonotic) to be spread by the latter. This included tularemia, a pathogen that emerged and spread across beaver populations as water levels in the plains decreased due to the overhunting of beaver (Daschuk 2013, 49), further threatening the continuity of this life-form and the worlds it co-constituted. Notably, intensively targeted buffalo communities faced similar threats with the spread of anthrax, Texas tick fever, brucellosis, and bovine tuberculosis when millions of cattle and horses were moved north across the Great Plains following the American Civil War (Daschuk 2013, 102–3; see also chapter 6). In such ways, the targeting of (bio)plural life-forms and worlds by invaders—for elimination, profit, or both—spread across intricate ecological, political, and economic systems, attacking bodies, ecosystems, and relational orders alike; driving elimination; and expediting processes of dispossession.

In such contexts, invaders also target processes of (bio)pluralization (see chapter 2), including the practices through which multi-life-form worlds are co-created and regenerated. For instance, settler colonial polities regularly outlaw or strictly constrain practices such as controlled burning, which helps renew plant life, allows for movement of life-forms, and increases soil nutrient cycling (see Rose et al. 2011; Reo and Parker 2013). They also tend to crowd out, devalue, or illegalize low-intensity agriculture and food forest or swidden farming techniques (see West 2004; Salazar Parreñas 2018); seasonally regulated and/or seminomadic patterns of hunting, fishing, and gathering; the creation of fish and shellfish banks; and many other techniques of cohabitation.

Outlawing such practices is an important technique for asserting sovereign legal power and for establishing an invasive social order. It assists in the *enforcement* of the distanced, instrumental relations with nonhumans that are deemed correct or appropriate within Eurocentric cosmovisions (see chapter 3). Further, it enables the importation and expansion of large-scale systems of relations with nonhumans that provide the invasive polity with resources, power, and profit. For instance, starting in the sixteenth century, European civilizing processes on colonized lands have worked to replace intensive subsistence-based agriculture and/or hunting and gathering food systems with extensive European-style agriculture (Cronon 1983). The former frequently includes small-scale, seasonally variable, multi-life-form, subsistence-oriented practices governed by kinship structures (including usufruct or the staggered use of communal fields, rotation, and/or companion planting techniques).[7] In contrast, extensive agriculture requires huge tracts of land that are almost continually planted with monocultures or genetically similar crops, usually privately owned, and produced largely for trade and profit. Extensive agriculture also involves continual disruption of the land through practices such as permanent deforestation, plowing, overgrazing, irrigation, and heavy fertilization (Crosby 1986). Unmarked American scholar John W. Head (2017) calls this model "extractive agriculture" because it continuously draws enormous amounts of nutrients and water from soils over large areas to the point of exhaustion. It is also extractive in the sense that it uses the bodies of specific plants and animals as instruments for extracting value from lands and waters in order to produce commodities. In addition, extensive agriculture physically clears space for invaders' worlding efforts by removing existing worlds and replacing them with the ecopolitical and relational models of the invading polity.

Importantly, extensive agriculture involves the deliberate transportation, reproduction, and consumption of billions of animals, plants, and other life-forms, along with nonliving beings such as fertilizers, metals, and equipment. Some of these beings are endemic to the homelands of invaders (e.g., sheep), while others were absorbed into invader cultures via global networks of trade and colonization (e.g., chickens). The transferal of these life-forms allowed settlers to reproduce simulacra of their home cultures, or select features thereof, including ways of dividing, organizing, altering, and managing land; harvesting and preparing particular life-forms as food; and caring for, killing, and eating certain animals and plants. The combined effects of the large-scale implementation of these practices and the direct effects of the life processes of transported life-forms (for instance, eating, movement, and reproduction) have driven the massive-scale terra-forming of colonized lands and ecosystems. Because of the tendency of large farmed animals to change the vegetation, soil quality, and even geophysical characteristics of lands on which they are bred, livestock agriculture in particular has been an important driver of the "Columbian exchange." This term refers to the multicentury process in which large numbers of bodies—humans and other animals, plants, fungi, bacteria, and other beings—were, and continue to be, moved between worlds, often over long distances and between radically different ecosystems as part of processes of European colonization. Over five centuries, this process has led to an unprecedented movement of life-forms affecting all continents almost simultaneously (in geological-temporal terms) (Ricciardi and Cohen 2007). Before discussing this phenomenon, it is important to note the deeply problematic nature of the work from which this term arose (Alfred Crosby's 1972 *The Columbian Exchange*), including the author's heavy reliance on pseudo-scientific race thinking.[8] I cite it here with extreme reservation and qualifications (see the preceding endnote) and only because it remains among the few, and certainly the most seminal, attempts to describe the phenomenon of the large-scale, coercive movement of nonhumans as a central strategy of European colonization. Multiple rewritings of this history and more nuanced, critical, evidence-based work on this subject—not least reflecting BIPOC, land-based, and marginalized knowledge systems and histories—are sorely needed.

The importation of domesticated animals from Europe and its colonies —including pigs, dogs, cattle, chickens, sheep, and horses—dramatically changed each ecosystem with which these life-forms interacted. For instance, from the late fifteenth to mid-sixteenth century, the Caribbean islands were, in effect, used as laboratories for European invaders to experiment with the cultivation of these life-forms in different ecological and geological conditions (see Stannard 1994). Facing few predators or competition for food, these creatures rapidly diminished Indigenous plant life and Indigenous food systems. This, in turn, caused collapses of endemic animal populations, further expediting the reproduction of those brought by invaders. At the same time, the need for large plots of land to graze and provide range for animals such as cows and sheep aligned with invaders' desire to progressively annex land, while the physical impact of the animals' mouths, hooves, and excretions altered soil content and chemistry, landscapes, and vegetation. With this process of agricultural expansion came invasive infrastructure of the kind described by Moreton-Robinson (2015), including fences, signs, and other markings to designate enclosed agricultural and urban spaces (see also Cronon 1983). At the same time, grazing animals transferred from Europe brought with them biota to which endemic life-forms, such as llamas and alpacas in the Andean region, were not adapted, leading to large-scale disease, sickness, and death among the latter (Crosby 1972). In the case of these highland camelids, wholesale slaughter by early Spanish invaders—intended to bring about the starvation of Indigenous communities—severely disrupted the continuity of this life-form, their mountain cohabitats, and the multi-life-form cultures sustained by both (Stannard 1994).

It is important to note that the animals transferred across the planet as part of this process were not only used as instruments of domination but also experienced the fragmentation of their own worlds and the trauma of being forced into violent relations with others. In other words, they experienced their own distinct forms of earth/body violence (see chapter 3). Their relational orders were entirely assimilated within the colonial process: their bodies and labor were transformed in such ways that they became bearers and enforcers of colonial property rights, while their survival and reproduction in new environments became a linchpin of invasive states. As mentioned earlier in this chapter, many such animals (including chickens, donkeys, and cats) had already been displaced from their worlds of origin by trade and/or colonization and now became subject to new relational orders, including the forms of extreme exploitation found in extensive agriculture and, eventually, factory farms or other large-scale production models. At the same time, some of these life-forms—for instance, the swans associated with the British sovereign—gained elevated status among the dominant invasive culture, while others were reclassified as feral, weeds, pests, or trash animals (see Nagy and Johnson 2013; Ginn, Beisel, and Barua 2014; van Dooren and Rose 2016) and targeted for elimination.[9] What's more, as part of the same process, millions of animals per year came to be imported as "companion commodities" (Collard 2014) in the exotic pet trade. Today, this multibillion-dollar trade flows almost entirely unidirectionally, from biodiversity-rich areas of the Global South to the United States, Canada, other European settler states, and northern Asia. Many animals experience multiple forms of trauma and disconnection before arriving at their ultimate destinations. For instance, unmarked Canadian scholar Rosemary-Claire Collard (2014) notes that in Mexico and Guatemala, most macaw chicks are removed from nests, while many baby monkeys are collected from the dead bodies of parents shot by trappers, before being transferred multiple times to reach international markets. The relatively few animals who survive the process of being trapped and transported are placed in situations of extreme dependence and must conform to an unfamiliar relational context (usually of direct and intense dependence on humans) for which they have no inherited knowledge, preparation, or communal connections.

Plants, too, were and continue to be used by invaders as instruments for large-scale land acquisition and transformation. These include cereals such as wheat and certain varieties of rice traded as food commodities, as well as cellulose fibers used in global textile industries. Among the most impactful of these plants is cotton, a shrub endemic to many subtropical regions and grown in small-scale pluri-cultures by numerous land-based communities across the planet. The commencement of the European trade in cotton sparked a multicentury global assault on largely subsistence-based traditions of growing, spinning, and weaving and the violent transition to plantation growing and factory production in India, West Africa, Brazil, Turkey, Central Asia, and many other regions (see Beckert 2015). This was also the case in the Caribbean islands and later the southern United States, where the scramble to meet European demands for cotton was used to justify the enslavement of millions of Black people from Africa and the mass displacement of Indigenous communities (the latter to give invaders access to land and waterways) (Beckert 2015). Similar patterns persist today in the form of monocultural agriculture or factory farming, including in the production of beef, chicken, and palm oil. To create space for such large enterprises, enormous amounts of cohabitat are transformed into farmland: for instance, at the time of writing, 12 million hectares in Indonesia is devoted to palm oil monoculture; 107 million acres in the Brazilian Amazon basin is planted with soy; the average U.S. factory farm contains tens of thousands of pigs, cows, and sheep; and monocrop cotton farming occupies 35 million hectares of land globally. The intensive infiltration of soils and water systems by animal wastes, pesticides, fertilizers, and other agriculture by-products further extends the territorial reach of these installations through the logics of malfeasance and waste (see Serres 2011).

Each of these examples shows that invasion was a multispecies process, although by no means a mutually voluntary one. Instead, European human invaders weaponized a range of *deliberately* displaced and reproduced nonhumans in the project of eliminating existing formations of (bio)plurality and building worlds to accommodate themselves. Of course, along with the intentional and strategic movement of organisms came the unintended transit of other life-forms, to which the term "invasive species" is now routinely applied. These life-forms may compete with, predate on, or crowd out not only native species, perhaps even causing "invasional meltdowns" (Simberloff and Von Holle 1999; Ricciardi and Cohen 2007; Montgomery 2012).[10] They may also threaten life-forms that are *desired, valued, and deliberately cultivated* by invaders. It is in this context that efforts to *enforce* the boundaries and norms of invasive ecopolitical orders have come to the fore.

Many contemporary conservation strategies prioritize controlling and, often, eliminating so-called invasive species. Routinely couched in terms of care for native species and/or for biodiversity in general, the regulation of invasive species is, in fact, essential to securing the ecological conditions on which *invasive polities* rely. Indeed, contemporary biosecurity strategies do not seek to protect *all* native species; in fact, they often target endemic life-forms that threaten invaders' assets such as livestock or farmland. For instance, in a single year, the U.S. Wildlife Service culled more than forty million animals—including native species such as bobcats, wolves, and cougars—in order to protect farmland and farmed animals (Collard and Dempsey 2017). Meanwhile, biosecurity measures do not seek to eliminate *all* exogenous species; in fact, they actively protect and seek to ensure the tenure of many such life-forms on colonized lands. Indeed, biosecurity policies are generally designed to protect two categories of life-forms: species (usually introduced by invaders) deemed necessary to the economic survival and strength of the settler colonial polity; and native and/or endangered species or ecosystems that hold value for tourism, identity, as resources, or for other economic functions. In seeking to protect and shore up the ecosystems forged by invaders, biosecurity strategies work to indigenize them: that is, to posit them as the threatened natural state of the lands in question, further overwriting pre-invasion worlds (see Veracini 2010; Tuck and Yang 2012). Importantly, this often means that efforts to "restore" such ecosystems after periods of intense disruption (e.g., resource extraction) actually involves altering them to resemble particular *post-invasion* states.

At the same time, biosecurity strategies designate between pre-invasion ecosystems, which they frame as wild or untouched by human or nonhuman invaders, and synthetic or (hu)man-made areas (see Brown and Sax 2004), cordoning the former from the latter. This categorization erases the conditions of co-constitution by specific and nonhuman groups that sustained pre-invasion worlds, while grafting Eurocentric civilizational norms (e.g., the "made" versus the "natural") onto the lands in question. At the same time, biosecurity discourses often ignore or punish the ways in which Indigenous, BIPOC, and other marginalized communities continue to transform and (bio)pluralize their worlds by forging relations with life-forms deemed to be "invasive." One example is the integration of Norwegian brown rats (initially brought from Europe by traders) into Malagasy legal systems and kinship orders— in direct contravention of conservation rules and regulations (Sodikoff 2012). Another example is found in the Kānaka practice of adopting certain, potentially damaging foreign plants or animals such as pigs (Goldberg-Hiller and Silva 2015) by integrating them into food and fiber practices and "teaching them how to get along" with endemic life-forms.[11] Similarly, many Anishinaabe communities have responded to the cross-continental movement of plantains and dandelions by interweaving them with ancestral food and medicine systems (Geniusz 2015).[12] By ignoring, discouraging, and even penalizing such practices (Sodikoff 2012), biosecurity enforcers continue to monopolize the right to determine belonging, kinship, and citizenship. What's more, as Moreton-Robinson (2015) points out, adaptation to the alterations wrought by invasion is often used against Indigenous communities, not least in legal processes that demand

Invasive States 135

evidence of unchanged or continuous cultural practices. In such situations, Indigenous communities may be denied access to and control over their lands because they have adapted in creative and empathetic ways to invasive violence, (bio)pluralizing in ways that include forcibly displaced bodies rather than seeking to eliminate them.

At the same time, by dividing economically and politically exploitable migrant life-forms from those considered destabilizing or threatening, contemporary biosecurity practices strengthen the borders of invasive states and, by extension, the international order of states. Indeed, many biosecurity campaigns tap into widespread moral panics over the presence of foreign bodies within national spaces—that is, into fears of the intrusion of difference into bounded spaces constructed to be internally homogeneous (see chapter 2). Indian American scholar Banu Subramaniam's (2001, 28) seminal work on media and popular culture representations of invasive species in the United States shows how "the xenophobic [and racialized] rhetoric that surrounds immigrants is extended to plants and animals" and vice versa. Mirroring anti-immigration discourses and racialized representations of nonwhite immigrants, these narratives foreground imagery of dangerous foreign species arriving illegally via long journeys stowed away in ships, burrowed in food products, or clinging to the shoes of travelers. These organisms are accused of crowding, spreading disease, damaging crops, and threatening supplies of resources. Gender takes an important place in such narratives (Subramaniam 2001): female members of endemic life-forms tend to be framed as passive, helpless victims without agency and needing protection by colonial forces, echoing gendered colonial discourses of dependency (see Spivak 2003). At the same time, females of exogenous species are associated with overbreeding and superfertility, while males are often depicted as hypersexual and (sexually) aggressive. In many cases, heteronormative gender norms are interwoven with racial stereotypes in biosecurity narratives. For instance, Anna Lowenhaupt Tsing's (1995) analysis of media treatments of "Africanized killer bees" in the United States shows how their imagery maps white projections onto Black bodies of hypersexuality, aggression, and miscegenation. In 2022, yet another life-form labeled as "African"—the "giant African land snail"—has made headlines for forcing a Florida county into quarantine (Czachor 2022). This terminology clearly telegraphs racialized and partisan conflict concerning efforts to curtail the spread of Covid-19 *and* deeply racialized discourses of biosecurity surrounding the pandemic.[13]

Aided by biosecurity discourses, these attitudes have been mainstreamed within everyday practices such as a gardening, landscape design, and, indeed, conservation (Simberloff 2003). Some conservation scientists reject the social and racial analysis of invasive species discourses on the basis that it is political, insisting that these life-forms involve real threats to "livelihoods, way of life and life itself" (Cassey et al. 2005, 478). Of course, this is itself a political argument that promotes particular livelihoods, ways of life, and the value of a specific conception of life itself (see chapter 2) as inherently good and worthy of protection. It is certainly true that the global movement of life-forms creates tangible ecological harms; and it is *also* true that biosecurity efforts are shaped by political currents such as xenophobia, racism, and the survival imperatives of invasive states.[14]

An important example of this approach can be found in the historical and contemporary biosecurity policies of Aotearoa/New Zealand, which are among the strictest and most complex of any contemporary nation-state. Crucially, this country's culture of treating biosecurity as a public health measure also applies to humans. In addition to consistently erecting significant barriers to nonwhite immigrants, prospective newcomers whose disabilities are expected to impose a high cost on the health system, whether because they are Autistic, diabetic, have multiple sclerosis or cancer, or are deemed to be overweight, are routinely denied the right to residency and/or deported (Caplan 2013; T. McGuire 2022). This practice reflects the interlinking of ableism, Eurocentric body norms, racism, and ideas of ecological fitness in biosecurity policies and environmental movements (see Jaquette Ray and Sibara 2017; S. Taylor 2017). Such norms take on a particular intensity within settler colonial identities and subjectivities, which prize traits such as ruggedness and independence deemed necessary to survive in environments that are considered hostile (to invaders).

In Aotearoa/New Zealand, the term "biosecurity" first entered mainstream environmentalist discourses in the mid-1980s, when the Scientific Committee on Problems of the Environment of the International Council of Scientific Unions established a series of symposia to investigate the issue. Its importance grew in 1992, when the issue of invasive species was formally listed as a priority item (article 8h) in the 1992 Rio Convention. Following these actions, Aotearoa/New Zealand adopted its first formal biosecurity policy in 1993. However, this apparently new policy was based on established attitudes, norms, and practices that had played important roles throughout the founding, expansion, and development of the settler colonial state and which only latterly became associated with environmentalist goals. Frequently, these norms have been used to naturalize invasive state institutions, relational models, and ecopolitical frameworks while framing Indigenous ones as exogenous and/or ecologically disruptive.

We can see this logic at work in the state's history of its biosecurity framework. According to the Ministry for Culture and Heritage (MCH n.d.), pre-invasion Māori worlds were shaped by waves of ecologically destructive invasions (see also Crosby 1986), first by "Polynesian voyagers" (a term that denotes both foreignness and temporary tenure) and eventually by Māori "colonists" (a naming that equates Māori with European invaders). This narrative argues that, through their patterns of navigation and worlding, Polynesian peoples brought to the islands invasive species such as kūmara, yams, taro, gourds, rats, and kurī (dogs), "deforesting around 30 per cent of the landscape and hunting many bird species to extinction" (MCH n.d.). According to this story, preexisting patterns of ecological destruction were merely *augmented* by the large-scale importation and cultivation of pigs, goats, sheep, other livestock, British trees, grasses, birds, rabbits, deer, and fish by invaders, along with the rats, slugs, and insects brought to the islands "by mistake" by benignly described "European *visitors*" (MCH n.d., emphasis mine). What's more, the MCH story implies that the enthusiastic cultivation of potatoes and herding of pigs by Māori communities was a *substantial* or even *leading* factor in the destruction of native ecosystems in the nineteenth and twentieth centuries (MCH n.d.). These agricultural practices—along with histories of transit, interaction, exchange, and hybridization across Polynesia—are directly contrasted with invaders' images of Aotearoa/New Zealand as one of the "most isolated" places on earth, pure and safe from incursions of all sorts. In short, the MCH's story seems to retroactively accuse Māori communities—including those living on the lands long before European invasion—of corrupting the (entirely fictional) pure, unaltered lands of invaders' fantasies. This framing, which is another example of the use of DARVO by colonizers, criminalizes and delegitimates Indigenous land relations while all but erasing the immense ecological violence wrought by European settlers.

As the invasive state developed in Aotearoa/New Zealand, biosecurity policies mirrored its goal of achieving economic strength and regional power within a context of increased trade and immigration. During the late nineteenth and early twentieth centuries, settlers became concerned that pests arriving through trading ships could "cripple the nascent agricultural

138 Invasive States

and horticultural industries" integral to the development of their state (MCH n.d.).[15] In addition, the development of international markets for meat, enabled by refrigerated shipping containers, sparked the creation of agricultural standards. This led to a series of acts, including the Orchard and Garden Pests Act (1896), the Stock Act (1893), and the Noxious Weeds Act (1900), designed to block the entry of unwanted biota at ports. To enforce these policies, facilities at ports were equipped with specialized fumigation chambers, and agents were empowered to destroy any plants or livestock deemed to be infected. Many such facilities were initially created to quarantine "human 'clients'" (MCH n.d.) brought to British colonies as prisoners, indentured laborers, or in other categories of exploitation. In the crowded, carceral conditions of quarantine, many migrants died or experienced illness and violence, as evidenced by detainees' messages to family members, and records of illness and death that can still be seen scrawled on the walls of quarantine centers in the region.[16]

Indeed, the history of biosecurity is inseparable from the development of policies designed to control human migrants to invasive states on the basis of race, class, and ethnicity, as reflected by the post–World War II history of biosecurity in Aotearoa/New Zealand. During this period, the advent of air travel (which provided quicker and warmer transport for insects) and the movement of U.S. military ships across the Pacific brought additional life-forms to the islands. Although the MCH history sidesteps this point, the post–World War II period also brought significant increases in immigration to British colonies, including from Southern Europe and Asia, who were subjected to social discourses that associated them with infection or contagion. At this time, it became standard practice to fumigate passengers arriving on airplanes—a process called "disinsection"—until new chemicals were developed that enabled spraying during routine maintenance.

It was only as trade with Britain tapered and was replaced by relationships with North America, Australia, and Asian countries, and as global concern over biodiversity (see chapter 2) became widespread, that Aotearoa/New Zealand linked biosecurity to environmental goals. In this context, the Biosecurity Act (1993)

> extended the purpose of *border protection* from the old preoccupation with agriculture, horticulture and exotic forestry to protecting the country's natural environment. Organisms that would harm New Zealand's "biodiversity"

would be *resisted as strongly as those which could threaten access to international markets*. (MCH n.d., emphasis mine)

This passage emphasizes that the *primary* goal of biosecurity is to protect the state and its economic bases; conservation and environmental protection are regarded as means to this end. At the same time, the installation of biosecurity systems has expanded settler colonial states and created lucrative new industries. For instance, after several "outbreaks" of snakes and insects from major harbors, the government of Aotearoa/New Zealand employed twelve thousand people at five thousand facilities by 2004 to inspect shipping containers (MCH n.d.), allocating tens of millions of dollars to this sector.[17] In 2019, responding in part to new challenges brought by climate change, the Ministry for Primary Industries (MPI) began a major overhaul intended to enhance the Biosecurity Act (1993) on the basis that

it keeps our incredible country safe from pests and diseases. . . . It protects our taonga species and many of the things that are unique to *our Maori* and *national* cultural identity. . . . It protects *our way of life* so we can enjoy our unique environment. . . . It helps protect our primary industries from pests and diseases . . . which in turn protects their business, boosts productivity and *enhances their way of life*. . . . So New Zealanders, our plants and animals, and our unique natural resources, are kept *safe and secure from potential harmful pests and diseases from other countries*. . . . To ensure our primary industry export products meet export requirements and are fit for their intended use. . . . To provide New Zealand exporters with *access to international markets*. (MPI 2019, 1, emphasis mine)

These rationales position biosecurity as a feature of invader subjectivities and, indeed, as important tools and rituals for the performance of citizenship within the invasive state. The subtle but telling rhetorical separation between *"our* Maori" and the more seemingly neutral "national" identity reasserts the ongoing claims to possession (Moreton-Robinson 2015) of Māori communities, their kin, and their culture by the invasive state, while using them as a foil to affirm settler "national" identity.[18] Meanwhile, the MPI has invoked broader goals of nationalist mobilization in which "every New Zealander becomes a biosecurity risk manager" by monitoring and killing pests, collectively organizing against invaders, and pursuing careers in professional biosecurity (MPI 2016, 10). This mainstreaming of biosecurity practices is intended to create "a biosecurity team of 4.7 million" and "at least 150,000 people with identified skills [who] can be quickly drawn on to provide support during biosecurity incursions" (MPI 2016, 21)—effectively, a standing army and reserve for enforcing biosecurity. The MPI also identifies key subjects for protection, stating that "if you're a farmer, grower, gardener, tramper, or nature lover—you all have something at stake in our biosecurity" (MPI 2016, 2). This snapshot of a society defined by farmers, growers, gardeners, trampers and nature lovers—all traditionally European ways of understanding relations with land and life-forms—is seamlessly fused with the idea of good (bio)citizenship. Although "partnership" with Māori communities and the inclusion of their "culture" are mentioned many times, the specific roles allocated to them by the settler government are limited to implementing biosecurity within marae (extended household/community structures), building government-defined biosecurity measures into their land management programs, and "operating biosecurity management hubs" at takiwā (tribal district) levels. As such, biosecurity is framed as yet another way in which Indigenous communities and forms of governance are expected—and often required—to work within and *for* the imperatives of settler sovereignty. Indeed, it is intended that biosecurity logics become a unifying "reflex reaction" across the whole society, and that they become naturalized as "part of the social norm, culture and attitudes . . . an essential part of the New Zealand story" (MPI 2016, 11).

While they are often state led, biosecurity initiatives do not always emerge from governmental programs. In some cases, they are created and promoted by nonstate actors whose interests align with those of the invasive state, including settlers engaged in its primary industries. A clear example of this is found in contemporary efforts to revive markets for possum fur. These small marsupials, endemic to what is currently called Australia, were initially imported and released in 1837 by settlers interested in participating in an international market for possum fur and fiber. While this first attempt was unsuccessful, a second, government-supported wave of possum releases was carried out from the late 1850s until 1921, and "acclimatisation societies" worked to embed the animals into local ecosystems (Hutching 2015). From 1921 onward, during which period government regulations limited hunting, the possum population grew until they became so numerous that they were reclassified as pests, and all restrictions on hunting them were lifted in 1946. While the possum fur and fiber market remained a marginal sector of the economy (Guthrie 2016), the ecological transformations created by possums began to encroach on more lucrative and foundational industries propping up the settler state. These effects include significant forest dieback, especially among canopy species such as rātā and kamahi, which, in some areas, experienced more than 50 percent decreases within fifteen to twenty years of possum predation; and within conifer-broadleaf forests in which possums gradually eradicated their preferred species (Hutching 2015). In addition, possums have been identified as a major risk to the cattle industry—one of the country's most important primary industries—due to their capacity to carry bovine tuberculosis. In response, the government launched a major program of eradication, carried out in large part through the use of aerial cyanide-based poisons. The most common chemical used for this purpose, 1080, applied on the islands since the 1950s, is lethal to mammals but also kills birds, amphibians, and insects and, when added to cereal, carrot, or gel baits, can also leach into water systems. Some government programs involve the use of vaccines intended to lower fertility rates among possums to prevent their reproduction, mirroring the forced sterilizations often carried out on BIPOC and/or disabled people within invasive states (see Clare 2017; Mitchell 2022). At the same time, the desire to eradicate invasive possums has also mobilized (mostly white) hunters—including Predator Free 2050, a self-described "crown-owned charitable company" tasked with cofunding the extirpation of possums, rats, and stoats—who argue that the fur industry would not be lucrative enough to ensure "conservation" goals (Ministry for Primary Industries 2016). In the words of one trapper, possums should "fund their own demise" (Carey 2003) by incentivizing hunting, all while upholding the cultural and political importance of biosecurity.[19] The intensive targeting of possums as a biosecurity threat in many ways encapsulates the history of this strategy in Aotearoa/New Zealand. This life-form—kin to many Indigenous communities and protected as a native species in Australia (although *treated* as a pest by many settlers in that country; see Rose and Tsumura 2010)—was torn from its cohabitat, brought forcefully to the islands as an experiment in agricultural land annexation, and, when it failed to boost and eventually threatened the settler colonial economy, was slated for violent elimination. What's more, the rekindling of the fur industry and its efforts to align itself with conservation and biosecurity goals signals the flaring of a powerful settler frontier impulse concerned with the coercive protection of borders. Both logics embed the desire to consolidate, protect, and bolster settler ways of life, their permanence, and their prosperity, aligning with the values of mainstream conservation even as they systematically attack existing and emergent conditions of (bio)plurality. The entwinement of political and economic imperatives within these processes draws attention to a closely linked logic on which invasive states rely: extraction.

COLONIAL EXTRACTION AND THE
SYSTEMATIC DESTRUCTION OF (BIO)PLURALITY

> Extraction is a cornerstone of capitalism, colonialism, and settler colonialism. . . . It's taking something, whether it's a process, an object, a gift or a person, out of the relationships that give it meaning, and placing it in a nonrelational context for the purposes of accumulation. (L. Simpson 2017, 202)

Extraction is, at its core, the process of dismembering (bio)plural bodies and the cohabitats they form. Whether tearing a life-form from the other bodies it partially shares (see chapter 3), separating specific minerals from composite formations, or coercing physical labor from bodyminds, the fundamental function of extraction is to break co-constituted bodies into entities or substances that can be commodified. It should not be assumed that these entities existed *as* parts prior to being framed in this way within particular models of thought. Indeed, the idea that bodies (living or otherwise) are composed of alienable parts is an artifact of mechanistic post-Enlightenment European thought, which uses logics of abstraction to divide complex wholes into components on the basis of their perceived functions or values (see Foucault 1995; Merchant 1983). Mirroring the forms of difference making discussed in chapter 2, these "parts" are imagined as homogeneous in relation to their broader context, and then *produced* as such through material interventions. For instance, in the mining and refining process, metals such as gold are separated from the other substances with which they are alloyed in order to produce "pure"—that is, chemically homogenous—substances. In other words, the logics of extraction and of biodiversity both make difference (and value) by producing homogeneity and eliminating (bio)plural relations. It is also thanks to this logic that invaders could imagine and then physically divide the lively, complexly co-constituted bodies and cohabitats of the beavers discussed earlier in this chapter into two parts: a commodity (fur) and waste (the rest of the beavers' bodies, along with their extended social, kinship, ecological networks, and ecosystems).

As a logic of dismemberment, extraction is inherently *traumatic.* Just like the effect of trauma on human bodyminds, extractive relations inflict physical, somatic, psychological, and spiritual harms that are absorbed, ramified, and embodied in different forms and intensities across multi-life-form worlds (see Mitchell and Todd 2016). They also scramble and break connections and pathways through which beings and worlds are able to coordinate as plural wholes (see van der Kolk 2015). For example, a forest from which a particular type of tree has been extirpated may continue to exist for years or decades but is likely to experience negative feedback loops that cause fundamental symbiotic processes to break down and ultimately collapse (Cronon 1986). Similarly, primates forced into carceral social relations and forced breeding as a result of global conservation imperatives may reproduce biologically. However, they may also develop violent social and sexual dynamics whose physical, psychological, and cultural effects cascade across generations (Salazar Parreñas 2018). These forms of harm may fragment or dilute (bio)plural relations and modes of organization, which can facilitate the deeper extension of colonial and extractive power into targeted communities, cohabitats, and bodyminds. Indeed, as discussed in chapter 3, the manifestations of trauma are exploited by invaders to depict entire lands, peoples, and ecosystems as though they were already damaged and therefore infinitely violable.

Like earth/body violence (and often working in combination with it), extractive logics most intensely target bodies and cohabitats that directly resist or confound its logics and processes. These include racialized, disabled, gendered, queer, fat, young or old, poor, and nonhuman bodies or bodies in which many of these identities reside (see Wynter 2003; Ferreira da Silva 2007; Belcourt 2016; A. Simpson 2014; Mbembe 2017; Mitchell 2022). For instance, Mbembe (2017, 40) argues that global logics of slavery frame Black bodies as inherently recalcitrant containers in which the labor valued by invaders as a resource is trapped. Within this logic, Black bodies have been consistently depicted as "bodies of extraction . . . living *ore* from which *metal* is extracted" instead of vibrant cohabitants of complex worlds. Following this line of thinking, and applying the methods of Western scientific disciplines such as geology, geography, and economics (see Yusoff 2018), the violent extraction of Black bodies and worlds became naturalized as necessary in order to release the value of their labor in the form of slavery. The "ore" to which Mbembe refers encompasses not only physical labor but also energy, emotional and social labor, social and biological reproductivity, creativity, knowledge, and much more. It was and continues to be literally converted into metal in the form of money and, ultimately, the oil, rails, roads, factories, crops, rare earth metals, and other paraphernalia of capitalist production (see also King 2018; Yusoff 2018) through which other forms of value are transmitted globally. As Mbembe (2017, 40) contends, this entire process relies on the fundamental "separation of human beings from their origins and birthplaces"—that is, the destruction of conditions of (bio)plurality.

At the same time, bodies targeted for extraction are forced to (at least partially) internalize and reproduce relations that render them open to further extraction. This imperative applies not only to human bodies but also to the ecosystems discussed in chapter 2, which, when framed and managed in terms of biodiversity, must embody and conform to logics of capital in order to be legible to those systems and hold value within them. As Dutch ecologist Bram Büscher (2013, 22) puts it,

> Nature-to-be-conserved functions . . . as a peculiar kind of *fixed capital* whose value circulates through the capital embodied in and implied by its environmental services. This, I refer to as liquid nature—nature made fit to circulate in capitalist commodity markets.

In other words, logics of extraction fundamentally change the nature and mode of ecological relations, in this case into "liquid" modalities amenable to exchange on global markets.

Juno Salazar Parreñas (2018) and Collard (2014) show how a similar logic is at work within wildlife rehabilitation centers in Malaysian Borneo and Guatemala, both of which are embedded within international conservation and ecotourism networks. Such centers extract value from endangered species by altering their relationships with a range of human actors—scientists, tourists, volunteers, policymakers, and others—so that the animals in question become consistently and instantly available to these actors.[20] This access is converted into capital in the form of fees, grants, funding, governmental support, and other forms of value. In contrast to the more time-limited extraction of value from animal bodies associated with hunting or the pet trade, this process of extraction can continue throughout the lifetime of an animal, and intergenerationally if they are involved in breeding programs. To achieve this, the animals must be kept at least partially separated from their worlds of origin. That is, while an element of "wildness" (e.g., naturalistic enclosures) may be valued as a marker of the authenticity desired by tourists, these animals must be prevented from fully reintegrating (into) their worlds so that they are constantly available for further extraction.

What happens to worlds after the desired value or commodity has been extracted? When desired or valued elements are torn from their relational structures, the remainders are most often discarded as waste. Indeed, Mbembe (2017) argues that, following the extraction of labor and value, the Black bodyminds transformed by colonial capitalism are treated as discardable, reinforcing white systems of power. In other words, extractive relations are defined not only by the power to produce and exploit but also by the power to waste.

Although it is often discussed as an *outcome* of extraction, the practice and logic of waste are present throughout every stage of an extractive process, not least the conceptual and abstract work through which resources are identified and sectioned into parts. This process of dividing beings and worlds into valued and nonvalued elements involves complex taxonomic work. Unmarked Canadian settler scholars Rosemary-Claire Collard and Jessica Dempsey (2017) point to several distinct categories of value into which natural beings are divided within extractive economies. These include: "officially valued" beings that provide free and unfree labor, or property; the "reserve army," valued for its future exploitability; the "underground" value of labor that is productive but *not* formally valued (including care work, to which I would add the work of caring for land, water, and other life-forms); and the "commons," including regulated and protected lands and bodies. Crucially, their categories also include the "outcast surplus," discarded waste produced by capitalism (for instance, male chicks in factory chicken farms or industrial effluent); and "threats" to the extractive process, including human land defenders and organisms designated as "invasive."

One indicator of the importance of waste to extractive logics and processes is the wide range of specialized, often euphemistic, terminology and metaphors that have been developed to describe it and/or obscure it. For example, in the global mining industry, the term "overburden" encompasses the layers of rock and soil (which is often rich, ecologically crucial, and can take decades or even centuries to replenish itself) that impede access to valued minerals and gases. Meanwhile, the seemingly innocuous term "tailings" is used to describe mineral and chemical by-products of mining— that is, all the other intermixed mineral components blasted away in order

146   Invasive States

to access fossil fuels. A salient example of these terms and their physical expression is found in the Alberta "Tar Sands" (itself a euphemistic and colonial term), an area of about 55,300 square kilometers (at the time of writing) across which surface mining has been used to remove bitumen residing relatively close to the soil's surface.[21] This process has involved the wholesale removal of boreal forest and the mass draining of wetlands in order to ease the movement of equipment and expose the sandy deposits within which valued deposits are combined. Indeed, it is precisely because the oil deposits are so thoroughly intermixed with sand—and with the region's unique vegetation, water systems, and other (bio)plural networks— that the process has been so energy and labor intensive (and is thus often referred to as "extreme" extraction). As South Asian Canadian organizer Harsha Walia (2014) argues, the logic of waste and discardability is applied to the land and workers alike as well as to Indigenous communities whose land is affected. As Walia shows, many tar sands workers are undocumented international laborers who enjoy no formal rights, healthcare, or other support; work for less than minimum wage; and may be vulnerable to indenture and superexploitation (Walia 2014). As such, mining corporations are able to use and discard these workers without incurring any long-term financial or legal responsibilities (M. Wright 2006). And, as discussed in chapter 3, Indigenous communities on whose land the "Tar Sands" has been constructed are routinely treated by industry and the invasive state as obstacles to be removed and/or as dumping grounds for the social, political, physical, emotional, and cultural "tailings" of extraction.

Similar terms and logics of extraction-by-waste are also employed in other industries. For instance, the term "by-catch" is used in the commercial fishing industry to encompass the myriad fish, mammals, turtles, and birds caught and discarded in the wake of vessels (usually dead or fatally injured). In tropical forestry, the term "forest simplification" is used to describe the transformation of (bio)plural forests into monocultures designed to facilitate logging; all other species are considered discardable (Tsing 2015). Cronon (1986) describes how sixteenth-century British mercantilists burned large tracts of forest—including smaller members of the white pine species they valued—in order to access the especially tall trees they valued as masts for ships. Similarly, in extensive agriculture, forest is often labeled as "cover" that obstructs access to soil and land desired for agriculture or ranching and subsequently clear-cut to make way for these activities (Head 2017).

These euphemistic terms obscure or deflect attention from how much is destroyed or wasted by the extractive industries in order to gain access to desired entities. Indeed, unlike its use in medical or military contexts, the term "extraction" does not entail the clean and precise removal of a discrete item from its surroundings. On the contrary, it frequently involves the wholesale destruction of the beings, connections, and relations that surround and co-constitute a valued entity in order to "release" it for use in other worlds and processes. In this way, extraction-as-waste compounds—and actively supports—the eliminative impulse through which settler colonial states clear land for acquisition, while providing financial and material support for the expansion of colonial polities.

Unmarked American scholar Traci Brynne Voyles's (2015) account of the large-scale "wastelanding" carried out on ancestral Diné (and other communities') lands astutely captures this convergence of waste, extraction, and colonial power. She demonstrates how the naming practices of Spanish and English colonizers designated desert landscapes as already wasted or violable (for instance, by naming mountains after female genitalia or imposing the term "Navajo"—meaning "flat," "waste," or "useless" in Spanish—on a region and a people).[22] At the same time, invaders actively laid waste to food systems in order to not only promote the expansion of the U.S. state but also gain access to subterranean minerals, in particular uranium deposits. Having already designated the land as "wasteland," government agents and private prospectors had few qualms about using it to conduct highly polluting and physically destructive open-pit mining operations and, later, nuclear tests (the latter also serving to promote broader U.S. global imperial goals).

Voyles's history of the Rio Puerco, a tributary of the Rio Grande, encapsulates this multistage construction of waste-as-extraction. Named for the Spanish term for "pork" or "pig"—a term that, for its Catholic users, carried connotations of dirtiness or impurity—this river was marked from the early days of invasion as already polluted due to its high sediment content. On this basis, it was deemed a suitable dump for effluent from sheep farming, then further altered through the construction of corduroys, dams, and irrigation diversions—all of which increased its silt content. The river was further polluted by twentieth-century uranium mining processes, which withdrew enormous amounts of water from regional riparian systems to use for extraction and as "wastewater"—sometimes "dewatering" at the rate

148 Invasive States

of five thousand gallons per minute (Voyles 2015). Absorbing these nearly unregulated flows of waste, the smaller branch of the Rio Puerco was transformed from a seasonal stream to a perennial river with a high burden of toxic wastewater, including carcinogens such as barium, manganese, molybdenum, lead, selenium, and radium that accumulated in its clay bed. Even with the collapse of the uranium industry in the late twentieth century, many companies simply abandoned their installations, creating "zombie mines" that continue to leak radioactive and other contaminants into the river system, groundwater, and soil. Throughout these changes, the linked bodies of multiple Indigenous peoples and their nonhuman kin have been continuously "wastelanded"—that is, treated as repositories for the harms produced by these processes, even as these harms have been used to justify the expropriation of their lands (Voyles 2015). "Like tailings ponds," Voyles (2015, 217) asserts, "the discursive technologies of race and class purport to hold highly dangerous waste in the wastelands."

As discussed in chapter 3, the waste(land)ing of specific bodies and cohabitats along racist, ableist, gendered, and other lines renders them vulnerable to multiple processes of intervention, including restoration, reclamation, and remediation. Often, such processes become vehicles through which invasive/extractive forms of power further penetrate and encompass worlds. For instance, most mainstream projects of environmental reclamation do not involve the literal reclamation of lands by their original peoples or the restoration of their condition and relational orders *before* invasion commenced. More often, they focus on returning damaged ecosystems to a condition that existed *post-invasion* but prior to an acute act of damage. Quite often, these processes also involve the reassertion of private or state property claims and/or the search for new sources of value and profit. For instance, Jesse Cardinal (2014, 128), Métis co-organizer of the Tar Sands Healing Walk, argues that the "reclaimed" land along the path of this walk "now grows almost nothing," while it used to be home to verdant blueberry patches on which his people relied for food and medicine. Meanwhile, the presence of false gunshots, intended to frighten away waterfowl from toxic tailings ponds (Cardinal 2014, 129) in the area, sonically mark the land as being reclaimed for, and by, ongoing extractive processes.[23] In the context of the massive-scale dismemberment of a world, simply replacing soil and vegetation or reopening the paths of waterways constitutes not its restoration but the forms of *substitution* discussed in chapter 2. A robust sense of restoration would, at the very least, involve not only the return of the land to its original peoples but also concerted efforts to heal and reunify fragmented and traumatized bodyminds (along with their broader cohabitats or worlds), reconnecting severed links and re-creating strong, complex, dense connections and relational structures (see chapter 3).

In contrast, as in processes of gentrification, mainstream strategies of recovery in the context of the Tar Sands have involved the injection of additional capital into sites where devaluation caused by previous damage has created new opportunities for profit. In this region, mainstream conservation efforts designed to protect large ungulates such as moose and caribou from the effects of mining (such as habitat loss, lack of clean water, and pathogen exposure; see Laboucan-Massimo 2014) follow a similar model. Under the federal Species at Risk Act (SARA), measures to protect and/or restore their populations constitute part of the environmental impact assessment processes with which mining companies must comply. Indeed, these life-forms fit within the category of the "commons" described by Collard and Dempsey (2017): their survival holds financial value insofar as the continued operation and profit of mining operations are linked to it. Responding to declining numbers of large ungulates—and to the threat this raised for the profitability of Tar Sands operations—in 2005 the government of Alberta took the controversial decision to target the province's remaining wolf populations. In short, instead of curbing the activities and effects of mining companies, the government worked to eliminate a traditional predator of caribou. These wolves had already been nearly extirpated from their full range, yet they enjoy no formal protection in Canada (see Lameman-Massimo 2014)—not least because of the deep-seated hostility to wolves of settler colonial states in North America (see Stannard 1994; Mazis 2008; and chapter 5). Over fifteen years, the government of Alberta culled more than 2,100 wolves by means of strychnine poisoning, aerial shooting, and the encouragement of hunting in key habitats (Weber 2019). Mining companies were also able to include efforts to exterminate wolves in their environmental impact plans: for instance, CGL paid C$171,000 in 2019 for the killing of wolves to offset the effects on caribou of its destruction of critical habitat for a multitude of life-forms (S. Cox 2020). Meanwhile, the ongoing construction of roads to support Tar Sands operations actually *increased* the vulnerability of caribou to the few remaining wolf packs (Weber 2019), undermining the efficacy of this strategy. In this process, through the combined logics of extraction and colonial practices rooted in the policies of the colonial state, an entire life-form was consigned to waste. Despite its association with state-led conservation goals, this strategy was mobilized *not* primarily to protect the commons (large ungulates) but to ensure the smooth and uninterrupted process of extraction. This example mirrors the use of biosecurity policies to protect and enhance the industries relied on by the invasive state (discussed earlier in this chapter).

Extractive logics are also key features of increasingly influential financial modes of conservation, which seek to squeeze value from ecosystems and life-forms that are regarded as damaged or degraded. They do so through techniques such as global arbitrage, revaluation, the creation of new markets, and the investment of capital through the processes of restoration or reclamation.[24] For instance, unmarked American settler scholar Kelly Kay (2018) describes the increasingly common incidence of "hostile takeover" of "distressed" or "damaged" forests and ranchlands bought under special arrangements by environmental trusts such as the Nature Conservancy (which alone holds more than two million acres of land in the United States). Usually, these arrangements include a time-limited horizon in which the land can be held and restoration projects carried out before the land is sold to other (often net worth) buyers for profit. This creates incentives for conservation NGOs—acting as *property investors*—to prospect for lands with high conservation value (for instance, the presence of forests, wetlands, or other markers of biodiversity) that are significantly undervalued as a result of ecological damage (Kay 2018). Leveraging access to instruments such as subsidies, tax breaks, grants from multiple levels of government, and revenue sources (e.g., holiday rentals, sales of hunting rights or water, selling off of equipment or buildings), conservation investors draw on multiple modes of financing to extract value from these lands. In some cases, conservation criteria are met minimally, for instance through the removal of species designated as "invasive" by relevant jurisdictions, or simply by using the land commercially in ways that conform to local standards of sustainability. Land restored or conserved in this fashion remains in the hands of wealthy individuals (including those driving rural gentrification by purchasing multiple homes or developing tourist infrastructure). As Kay (2018) demonstrates, these actors have become skilled at capturing public funds and using the language and legal-political frameworks of conservation to increase their profit and concentrate control and ownership of land.

Dempsey and unmarked Canadian scholar Patrick Bigger (2019, 518) find a similar "waste-to-value conversion" approach at work in the Grazing-Works initiative funded by NatureVest (the conservation investing unit of the Nature Conservancy and the Northern Rangeland Trust, or NRT, in Kenya).[25] Framing overgrazing of cattle by pastoralists as the primary source of grassland degradation, the initiative charges a premium to collect cattle from pastoralist villages and grazing fields owned primarily by white elites. Cattle are then sold at market, and profits are reinvested in the purchase of more cattle, with small amounts allocated to local development projects. This service is available only to villages that, as a whole, enforce NRT's conservation standards and goals—the main element that differentiates the initiative from a traditional micro-finance arrangement (Dempsey and Bigger 2019). Indeed, the goal of this scheme—backed by a US$7 million private investment, half of which is intended to return 1 percent profit—is to transform a model in which pastoralists are paid to *not* graze their cattle to one driven by the incentive of profit and future equity (that is, participation in capitalist markets; see Introduction). Like the conservation-gentrification model employed by the Nature Conservancy, this approach leverages multiple sources of funds—global charitable donations, governmental and international NGO grants, infrastructure, and technical knowledge—to release value from lands, animals, and peoples defined as "degraded." In so doing, they also leverage and benefit from political systems rooted in racialized and colonial structures of governance, including the use of private white-owned land to regulate the activities of Black pastoralists and encourage their absorption in market systems. Such processes are not only financial in nature; they also involve the installation of comprehensive *relations of extraction*—that is, models of interaction and connection that ensure that particular bodies and cohabitats remain permanently available for extraction.

Just like (and often in collaboration with) settler colonialism's imperative of destroying existing relational systems to replace them with its own, logics of extraction generate their own relational orders and subjectivities. In so doing, they disrupt or erase existing worlds, reordering not only economic interactions but also spatial, temporal, somatic, sensory, spiritual, and other elements in ways that promote, stabilize, and sustain extractive processes. The creation of extensive agricultural systems by invasive polities reveals how these two logics are fused. Namely, intricate (bio)plural systems of cohabitation are replaced by relational orders that simultaneously enhance the sovereign power of the state *and* ensure the long-term extractability of the land, soil, and life-forms associated with it. In this transformation, multiple ecopolitical systems are replaced with a single, monocultural relational order, in which the majority of social, political, and ecological life are reoriented toward the extraction of one or more highly valued resources (Tsing 2005). At the same time, the (bio)pluralizations of life-forms and worlds are constrained from disrupting imposed colonial-extractive orders through a number of means, from physical barriers (e.g., fences, private property laws) and regulatory violence (e.g., policing) to the creation of sacrifice zones so polluted that entering them threatens the health or survival of many life-forms (see LaDuke 1994).

Within such zones, the protection of isolated fragments of previously existing worlds often takes the form of genocidal archiving (see chapter 5), in which relics of destroyed cultures are maintained as foils against which dominant invader subjectivities are honed and maintained (see also Moreton-Robinson 2015). For instance, Povinelli (2016) shares how the mining company OM Manganese treated the Dreaming beings Two Women Sitting Down, a female rat and bandicoot (respectively) who were embodied in a rock formation in the Northern Territories where the company was mining. As a result of OM's mining operations, the rock formation was shattered, and surrounding Country (including its physical features, vegetation, water systems, and more) was thoroughly altered. In a narrow interpretation of its legal responsibility to protect Indigenous culture, OM ensured that the immediate part of the rock formation in which the Dreamings were embodied remained physically intact. However, this notion of intactness treats the land as an assemblage of discrete objects rather than as a co-constituted world or cohabitat (for instance, it implies that a continuous rock formation has firm boundaries). Through this framing, a fragment of rock intended to *represent* the Two Women was severed from the remainder of the rock formation, soil, water, vegetation, and other elements of Country. At the same time, these two Dreamings were forcibly assimilated into a new set of relations designed to facilitate and justify ongoing extraction. Notably, this was the first context in which a legal suit for the destruction of a sacred site was successfully pursued in Australia—albeit for a comparatively small award in relation to the penalties for destroying the sacred sites of invaders.[26] Yet the relational order damaged by OM's acts was not restored by the company, nor were its traditional caretakers enabled to reclaim and heal Country in ways they saw fit. On the contrary, the strategy used by the legal system and OM—trading the destruction of the Dreamings for a financial award—entrenched relations of extraction.[27] Specifically, it assigned a financial value to the Two Women and to their destruction and, through the logic of substitution (see chapter 2), enabled OM to continue its extractive activities by simply paying this penalty. Such strategies change the fundamental nature of relationships in order to enable extraction, converting kinship or other forms of ecopolitical relations into financial forms. As the late Yolŋu knowledge-keeper Dr. Laklak Burarrwanga says of mining processes carried out on her land:

> Every tree that might be cut down, every lizard that might be killed, every rock that might be ground up and taken away, *these were all our mothers and our children*. They are all Dhuwa or Yirritja, just like us.[28] We are of our land, and it is of us. Nabalco [the mining company operating in the area] started mining, and it took part of us, killed our family. (Burarrwanga et al. 2013, 76–77)

Meanwhile, Nabalco understood this relationship as one in which not only money but also development (in the form of further investment in wage labor and capitalist systems of exchange) were traded with the caretakers of Country for ongoing access to resources. Far from being a one-off interaction, the implementation of this relational order involves the permanent marking of such lands as resources rather than kin—that is, the attempt to permanently replace (bio)plural relations with ones oriented to the alienation of value.

Extractive relations also exert a totalizing effect on relational orders. A key example of this is the idea of global reserves of substance such as fossil fuels, which require the totalizing and mapping of earth as an enclosed globe (see Sloterdijk 2016) and its subsequent dissection into the categories of resources and waste. Importantly, mainstream discourses of extinction and conservation mobilize this logic when they speak of percentage decreases across planetary populations of species, or indeed, extinction as the total, *global* elimination of a life-form. In this manner, extractive relations assign value to certain resources by imposing a temporal horizon of finality, finitude, or, indeed, extinction toward which all extractive processes drive. In other words, the (increasing) value of commodities is indexed against expected future scarcity or total exhaustion, and all possible relations with these entities are aligned against this horizon.

We can see this kind of thinking at work in mainstream conservation discourses that focus on valuing biodiversity in financial terms. For example, the WWF's *Living Planet Report 2018* (Grooten and Almond 2018, 15) asserts that "as climate change intensifies, nature's value is only increasing," not only as a source of financial value but also as a means of bolstering global security regimes (which it identifies with the agendas of "NATO and the Pentagon"). In short, "nature" is presented as a commodity whose value will rise precisely *because* of the threat of extinction and other dynamics that threaten its survival. What's more, the WWF adopts a distinctly speculative position in relation to "the incalculable potential future value of benefits we might derive from further discoveries [of species and their commercial uses]" (Grooten and Almond 2018, 15). Here, the potential value of existing life-forms and worlds is directly linked to the likelihood and timing of their destruction or extinction, which the *Living Planet Report* seeks to mathematically model (see chapter 6).

Whyte (2019) finds a similar logic at work in some versions of climate change activism. Specifically, he refers to the temporal horizon invoked by U.S. Congresswoman Alexandria Ocasio-Cortez's widely publicized 2018 comment that younger people fear that "the world is going to end in twelve years" (Cummings 2019). The projection of this temporal framework, he contends, creates an ultimatum that ignores and erases the more expansive and open-ended (possibly but not always or necessarily slower) "time of relationship" through which his ancestors have historically addressed crises of all kinds. By enclosing all possible futures within a homogeneous, totalizing temporality of finitude, such political discourses literally work to force into place particular forms—and *speeds*—of relationality, replicating the temporality of extraction and colonization.

While totalizing extractive relations are often associated with the "speed[ing] up" of processes, including ecological ones (J. Moore 2015), they also impose restrictions that impede, distort, slow down, arrest, and halt processes of (bio)pluralization. Examples include the previously discussed enclosure of racialized, disabled, and nonhuman bodies within "wastelanded" spaces and of toxins within these bodies (see Voyles 2015). They also encompass the damming or blocking of rivers, the severing of migration paths for animals and people, and the slowing of processes such as soil regeneration through toxification or the abandonment of mining infrastructure. Extractive logics work by fragmenting and individualizing *collective* movement, divorcing it from communal rhythms and breaking its connection to stimuli and reciprocal feedback from plural worlds. This can be observed in *ex situ* breeding programs in which complex relations of biological *and* social reproduction are homogenized within the extractive imperatives of (re)production (see van Dooren 2014; Salazar Parreñas 2018). For instance, as Salazar Parreñas (2018) describes, the complex and nuanced patterns of reproduction through which orangutans have traditionally pursued their collective continuity are reduced to carceral, often violent, conditions of forced breeding. At the same time, many of the Iban, Bidayuh, and other Indigenous workers who live and labor at the center share conditions of involuntary migration and displacement with the animals for whom they care. Their lives—including their living conditions, mobility, work hours, financial security, and the safety risks they must endure—are dominated by the imperatives of "breeding," which is itself linked to valuations based on the global scarcity of orangutans and their expected extinction. In this manner, conservation processes may be driving forces in the installation of extractive relations and the enclosure of entire worlds within them.

～

As this chapter has shown, the logics of settler colonialism and extraction work in similar ways—and often together—to systematically target conditions of (bio)plurality and break the resistance of (bio)plural worlds to their incursions. This process is essential to their imperatives of staking sovereignty over land and generating new sources of profit. Both logics are also tightly linked to elimination: invasive states lay claim to territories, peoples, and worlds by attempting to erase their existing relational orders; and the value derived from extraction is indexed against a horizon of exhaustion or extinction. Both, in turn, maintain intimate relationships with the logics and structure of genocide and other forms of eliminative violence, to which the next chapter turns.

5 Genocide, Eliminative Violence, and Extinction

When one speaks of genocide in the Americas, it cannot be understood in relation to the European holocaust, for example . . . which is focused on humans alone. Our genocide in the Americas included and continues to include our other-than-human relatives.

—KIM TALLBEAR, "Failed Settler Kinship, Truth and Reconciliation, and Science"

To dismiss the current extinction wave on the grounds that extinctions are normal events is like *ignoring a genocidal massacre* on the grounds that every human is bound to die at some time anyway.

—J. M. DIAMOND, "The Present, Past and Future of Human-Caused Extinctions" (emphasis mine)

She didn't intend to survive.[1] She had quarantined herself, banished her own body from the protective webbing of her kin, following her community's Law even in this paved-over place. Hanging from a low limb, she dipped close enough to the ground to be snapped up by passing cats. The webbing of her wing was torn, hanging bloodless from exposed bone and wrinkled against her russet belly fur like a popped balloon. Her wound telegraphed a sheet of barbed wire hugging the side of a brick-walled utility building right behind the roosting tree. This kind of fencing is deadly to the large, wide-winged flying fox. Mother bats are often snagged on these fences, starving to death on the rusted fangs of metal while their babies helplessly cling to their chests or wither in trees, waiting for the return of now-dead parents. Other adults and adolescents are trapped in plastic nets that are set out during the summer to protect fruit trees in suburban gardens. Still others are poisoned or attacked by dogs, cats, or other pets.

158   Genocide, Eliminative Violence, and Extinction

These bats' fates are among the many simultaneous slow-motion massacres carried out by the invasive state (see chapter 4) across the continent. Sometimes the killings are written into policy or law and centrally organized, while other times they are a form of vigilante justice meted out by citizens—some of whom even claim to find their targets "beautiful" but simply too smelly and noisy to coexist with humans (Skjonnemand 2011). Seeming to miss the irony, members of the invasive society refer to these extended bat families as "colonies" and panic over their perceived power to swarm, invade, and spread disease. Bats are favorite scapegoats for narratives of zoonotic doom, associated with vampires in Euro-descendent cultures and in Western medical discourses with rabies, the Ebola virus, and, more recently, the global Covid-19 pandemic.[2] When I encountered this little bat in 2014, the primary fear was lyssavirus: recent news programs were dominated by reports of an (unvaccinated) teenage boy who had died from that pathogen after handling an injured bat. Such diseases are extremely rare, and overwhelmingly kill bats rather than humans: in recent studies, only 5.4 percent of flying foxes and blossom bats—just 7 out of 187 tested—tested positive for the virus. Since 1996 and the time of writing (2022), the transmission of this virus has led to a total of only three human deaths. Still, based on fear of these pathogens, many Australians demand the total eradication of urban flying fox communities in order to protect "public health."

I asked around in the neighborhood and found out that this particular flying fox community were refugees who had been forced out of their previous roost (in a slightly more wealthy area of town) a few years prior, finding temporary shelter in this small islet of eucalypts in a corner of a busy public park. It was believed that they had previously been evicted—in technical terms, "dispersed"—many times in response to changes in city and state policies regarding their "protection" and "management." As massive bushfires and summer temperatures nearing 50°C are rapidly becoming the norm in eastern Australia, some flying fox communities have become permanent refugees (T. Moore 2016), fleeing across regions in search of pockets of shade, water, and accessible food, their numbers decimated by heat waves. In 2018–19, one-third of the remaining community of spectacled flying foxes was annihilated in a two-day period, while 2,000 gray-headed flying foxes died of heat stress in a single day at the southernmost (and coolest)

Genocide, Eliminative Violence, and Extinction

tip of their range (L. Cox 2019; Almond, Grooten and Petersen 2020). It is still not clear how many flying foxes were killed in the enormous bush fires that engulfed New South Wales and Victoria in the summer of 2019–20, which devoured more than 1 billion animals (not even counting the insects on which flying foxes and so many other animals feed) along with countless plants, consuming at least 30 percent of remaining flying fox habitat. In these conditions, panicked bats die en masse as they crowd together in a desperate attempt to flee the heat (Mao 2019), while some are forced to drop their pups midflight or abandon them at nesting sites. In the midst of this crisis, alarmist media outlets warned Brisbane residents of a "bat INVASION" that might "cause chaos in the city" (Mazzoni 2020) as flying fox communities sought urban-grown food sources. Meanwhile, the Rescue Collective, a Brisbane-based wildlife rehabilitation organization, shared reports of flying foxes being caught in fruit netting, brutally beaten to death by gardeners, and discarded in city-provided rubbish bins injured but alive. Even in conditions of extreme and increasing vulnerability and threats to their collective existence, these creatures—kin to many peoples and integral to Eastern Australian ecosystems, in particular eucalypt forests—continue to be targeted for elimination.

How can we best understand and analyze the kinds of violence discussed in this excerpt, which is based on my interaction with a particular flying fox in Brisbane in 2014? It reflects several clear elements of eliminative violence.[3] First, there is the intentional, planned, systematic, and centrally organized displacement and killing of a demonized group (flying foxes) by a dominant party (the invasive polity). Second, this is accompanied by a decentralized, unofficial but nonetheless systematic, form of auxiliary violence expanding and amplifying the effects of the first category (the actions of gardeners and homeowners). Third, we can observe the creation of structural conditions, including forced movements and the siting of barbed-wire fences near nesting spots that inflict injury, encourage starvation, engender immense collective stress and insecurity, and disrupt reproduction (biological and social). Fourth, and underpinning each of these forms of violence, there is the creation and propagation of narratives that demonize the targeted group, explicitly call for and reward acts that harm them, and normalize violence that could predictably lead to their elimination. There is also clear evidence here of systematic attempts to destroy

160 Genocide, Eliminative Violence, and Extinction

(bio)plurality, in the form of targeted attempts to break relations among flying fox communities, and between these bats and other life-forms, Country, and other beings. If flying foxes were humans, we would be discussing this violence—and perhaps extinction itself—in terms of genocide. So, should we be?

Some scholars, including Western scientists (Diamond 1989), critical environmental thinkers (Rose 1992; 2011a), and Indigenous scholars (Hubbard 2014; TallBear 2016), explicitly highlight the connections between genocide and extinction, in different senses and to varying degrees. Yet there is little clarity in these discourses about how the various phenomena associated with extinction relate to the international legal definition of genocide and therefore to the ways it might be applied to address, prevent, or make reparations for extinction. Some scholars, activists, and policymakers suggest that, since the concept of genocide was designed to apply to human groups, it is too anthropocentric to be applied to nonhumans and/or that doing so would dilute the concept beyond its intended uses. For this reason, many of them have sought to create distinct concepts that address large-scale violence but include nonhumans as objects. Among these approaches, the concept of "ecocide" has gained popularity in recent years. However, I argue that it entrenches many of the issues of colonialism, anthropocentrism, and the affirmation of structures (including the Westphalian state system and international law) that drive the systematic destruction of (bio)plurality.

Several other knowledge systems and legal-political orders provide alternatives, such as attending to violence that targets the co-constitutive relations between specific groups of humans and certain nonhumans; formally acknowledging violence against beings and relations that do not fit within the Eurocentric definition of "human"; and recognizing *some* other beings or life-forms as nations subject to collective violence. In this chapter, I examine how Inuit, Kānaka, and Nêhiyaw knowledge systems and political/legal orders provide distinct ways of accounting for harms targeted on their (bio)plural worlds, including acts of eliminative violence against Qimmit (sled dogs), manō (sharks), and buffalo.[4] Paying attention to these accounts requires foregrounding "how destruction is experienced and made sense of by targeted collectivities . . . within culturally specific meaning systems" (Woolford 2009, 84) rather than the universalizing, and often homogenizing, abstract concepts used routinely in international law.

However, this argument does not imply that extinction as such should be conflated with genocide, ecocide, or any other concept specific to a single

Genocide, Eliminative Violence, and Extinction 161

world. All these approaches may be useful in addressing particular *aspects* of an eliminative harm experienced by a life-form or world and may be more or less relevant and/or appropriate in specific cases. In addition, *some* of the frameworks emerging from Indigenous knowledge systems and legal-political orders *may* be applicable beyond their worlds, but this should not be automatically assumed to be true by outsiders, including states, NGOs, or international organizations. Instead, I argue that along with a plurality of legal remedies, it is also necessary to nurture forms of collective social, political, economic, and cultural transformations that address not only genocide, ecocide, or other concepts of eliminative harm but also the broader structures through which conditions of (bio)plurality are targeted.

WHAT IS THE RELATIONSHIP BETWEEN "EXTINCTION" AND GENOCIDE?

Genocide and extinction have a great deal in common. Both are defined by their extreme moral and ethical gravity, which radically exceed the limits of Euro-descendent philosophical systems, and the legal and political remedies they offer. In addition, both forms of violence are eliminative: they work (with varying degrees of intentionality or directness) toward the complete annihilation of a (human) group, life-form, and/or world. Rose (2011b, loc. 1588) describes this logic of "eliminative ideation" as a matter of "imagining a world without them [the targeted group], then setting out to create it." She goes on to argue that the violence experienced by flying foxes in Australia reflects

> a stunning convergence between speciocide . . . and genocide. It seems that eradicating a species, or group of species, is *not unlike* eradicating a clan or a tribe, or undertaking ethnic cleansing. Speciocide, *like* genocide, may in many cases be primarily about destroying the possibility of the enemy's on-going existence in the area you've defined as yours. (Rose 2011a, 131, emphasis mine)

Here, Rose compares the destruction of life-forms to genocides carried out against peoples but does not go so far as to argue that the two phenomena are the same. Nonetheless, her framing raises an interesting question: just how alike are genocide, extinction, and the targeted destruction of particular life-forms?

The Convention on the Prevention and Punishment of the Crime of Genocide (UNGC) defines the crime as follows:

162 Genocide, Eliminative Violence, and Extinction

acts committed with intent to destroy, in whole or in part, a national, ethnical, racial or religious group, as such:

(a) Killing members of the group;
(b) Causing serious bodily or mental harm to members of the group;
(c) Deliberately inflicting on the group conditions of life calculated to bring about its physical destruction in whole or in part;
(d) Imposing measures intended to prevent births within the group;
(e) Forcibly transferring children of the group to another group. (UN 1948)

Rose's work shows that dingoes, flying foxes, and other ancestral animals of Australia are subjected to all these techniques, often in combination. Indeed, for decades, the Australian federal and state governments have invested immense effort and resources in targeting dingoes, including efforts to extirpate them in particular regions and the erection of thousands of kilometers of wire fencing to cut the canines off from food and water sources, causing them to die of heat stress and forcing them to prey on livestock (prompting further killing by farmers). Rose contends that these actions create a pervasive atmosphere of terror, the aim of which is not only to kill but also to prevent flourishing and to eradicate a specific mode of collective existence.

Mainstream discourses on extinction focus on generalized and relatively indiscriminate (although unequal) threats to multiple life-forms, which arise as the unintentional effects of nonviolent actions. In contrast, the forms of eliminative violence described by Rose are carried out deliberately and in a targeted way against life-forms that are framed as "pest[s] requiring eradication . . . whose *extinction is sought*" (Rose 2011b, loc. 79, emphasis mine). Unmarked American scholar Glen Mazis (2008, 76) uses the term "speciocide" to describe this way of thinking, in which an *"entire animal species [is seen] as deserving to be annihilated."*[5] In such cases, even if the strong Cartesian meaning of intentionality that shapes the UNGC cannot be proven, there is ample evidence of a collective desire to eradicate these life-forms, and of the creation of genocidal *relations* and *outcomes* (Barta 2000; Short 2010).[6] "Genocidal relations" refers to social structures, norms, collective practices, and habits that work to eliminate particular groups through the logics they embody—for instance, those of white supremacy or eugenics (Short 2010). Such structures often become so deeply entrenched in a society that the majority of the population participates in them even if they

Genocide, Eliminative Violence, and Extinction   163

abhor genocide, let alone the idea of contributing to it (this is often the case in settler colonial societies; see chapter 4). Meanwhile, "genocidal outcomes" refers to circumstances in which genocidal conditions emerge even in the absence of a formal, centralized, "coordinated plan" (UN 1948). These outcomes are often the result of multiple, decentralized acts and processes governed by (partially) shared norms and goals (Powell 2007; Woolford 2009), collective tendencies, or "structures of domination and oppression" (Theriault 2010, 504).[7] Indeed, in the examples discussed so far in this chapter, eliminative outcomes arose from the actions of many different people (wildlife officers, farmers, homeowners, policymakers), acting without a single, centralized source of coordination, and responding in various ways to changing social norms (e.g., public discourses, social attitudes, formal policies, and bylaws). Even in cases where there does not appear to be a strong desire to destroy a *particular* life-form, eliminative relations and outcomes often emerge. From this perspective, it could be argued that the interlocking structures of violence described in these last four chapters produce and sustain *genocidal relations* on a global scale, which contribute toward the *outcome* of erasure for *many* life-forms.

However, Rose, Mazis, and other critical theorists who stress the links between genocide and extinction do so only in a conceptual, comparative, or metaphorical sense. They do not go so far as to call for the legal prosecution of eliminative harms against nonhuman life-forms as acts of genocide. Instead, they offer different concepts such as "speciocide" or "biocide," which tap into the rhetorical power of the concept of "genocide" but do not have formal legal force. These framings seem to accept that the concept of genocide is restricted to human peoples. However, I would argue that, in many cases, the systematic destruction of worlds, life-forms, and conditions of (bio)plurality fit within the already existing definition of genocide (UN 1948)—but not within the culturally specific understanding of the "genos" (Wynter 2003) it enshrines. In what follows, I show that many knowledge systems and legal-political orders offer understandings of "people" (collectives) and/or "personhood" that are not restricted to humanity as it is defined within normative international-legal and political contexts.

However, beyond the anthropocentrism in how its objects (and subjects) are framed, several other features of the UNGC definition and broader genocide discourses make it difficult to apply to nonhuman and more-than-human communities. For instance, critics of "liberal" accounts of genocide argue that the UNGC definition treats collectives as aggregates of individuals grouped by shared features such as genetics, history, and culture (see Powell 2007). This replicates the logic of species thinking, in which difference inheres in the distinction between the *internal similarity* of a group and its *external definition* from other (internally homogeneous) groups. Such accounts do not adequately reflect the *internal plurality* of communities, including unique constellations of ethnicity, religion, disability, and other elements that shape the human members of a polity. In particular, they do not reflect the *(bio)plurality* of worlds, including the co-constitution of multiple life-forms and other beings, the distributed nature of cognition and experience, or practices of cohabitation carried out by radically different beings (see chapters 2 and 3). These elements make a crucial difference when discussing what constitutes humans, or a particular community. Further, as in the biodiversity paradigm, mainstream accounts of genocide tend to treat the difference embodied by a genos not in terms of singular, irreducible difference but rather as *variations* on—or deviations from—an assumed universal norm of humanity. This line of thinking ignores the possibility of multiple distinct, irreducible ways of being human, *and* legal-political orders in which being human is not as ethically salient as, say, being part of an ecosystem or a particular relational structure.[8] Moreover, the UNGC definition places significant emphasis on the destruction of "peoples" as *nouns* or *objects* rather than lively processes, relational formations, or trajectories of (bio)pluralization. In contrast, Muskogee thinker Daniel Wildcat (2015, 394) argues that genocides target the relational processes and structures that enable the flourishing of Indigenous nations, "even if [they do] not always want to destroy the individuals within the collective or the collective in its totality." Following Wildcat's logic, I argue that attacks on processes of (bio)pluralization (see chapter 2) contribute to genocide even if there is no explicit attempt to destroy the bodies or material structures associated with the genos.

The latter sections of this chapter will argue that this mainstream account of genocide focuses too narrowly on liberal-international norms of "humanity" that are currently dominant (see Mitchell 2014a), failing to reflect other worlds and cosmovisions, the conditions of (bio)plurality, or systemic violence against it. I also describe how several knowledge systems and legal-political orders offer different accounts of what constitutes a people, personhood, or ethical status that are relevant to the crime of genocide as it is currently defined. First, though, I want to critically examine

Genocide, Eliminative Violence, and Extinction   165

another concept rooted in Western rights-based thinking that has, since the 1970s, been touted as a means for bringing the gravity and legal force of genocide to bear on harms to nonhumans: ecocide. Proponents of this approach claim that its institution as a "fifth crime against humanity" will make it possible to prevent, punish, and account for some of the most egregious ecological harms. With this in mind, I ask whether this proposed law could adequately and appropriately address eliminative violence against life-forms and the systematic destruction of (bio)plurality.

ECOCIDE

Since the 1970s, a small but determined group of scholars, activists, legal experts, and policymakers has been working to formalize ecocide as the "fifth crime against peace" (Higgins 2010, 61). Originally used by American bioethicist Arthur Galston at the 1970 Conference on War and National Responsibility, and again by Swedish prime minister Olaf Palme in 1972, the concept arose in the aftermath of the U.S. military's use of ecologically destructive strategies in Vietnam. This included the broadcasting of defoliants such as Agent Orange; large-scale bulldozing of jungle, farmlands, and wetlands used to cultivate rice; intensive aerial bombardments of forests; and even attempts to modify patterns of rainfall to disrupt agriculture (see Falk 1973).

Jewish American international law scholar Richard Falk (1973, 80) coined the term "ecocide" to describe these (and similar) military strategies in which "the environment [is] selected as a military target appropriate for comprehensive and systematic destruction," which he regarded as "an Auschwitz for environmental values." His aim was to establish an international moral and legal framework for outlawing and prosecuting acts of ecological violence that would carry similar weight to the law of genocide but apply to nonhumans and environments. Included in Falk's definition of acts of genocide were the use of nuclear, bacteriological, chemical, or other weapons of mass destruction; chemical herbicides; bombs and artillery to a sufficient degree of quantity, density, or size to decrease soil quality or promote diseases affecting humans, animals, or crops; bulldozing with the intention to destroy forest or cropland; attempts to affect rainfall; and the forcible removal of humans or animals from their places of habitation. It is important to note that in this context, the "-cide" in "ecocide" does not necessarily refer to the total destruction of a particular life-form or community but rather refers to the attempt to defeat or dominate a

166   Genocide, Eliminative Violence, and Extinction

community by compromising its ecological base. In this sense, the concept is more inclusive of nonhumans than that of genocide, but it reduces emphasis on specifically *eliminative* (versus more generalized) forms of violence. In addition, all of these examples pertain to *military* actions, except for the last, which Falk identified as being used for "military or industrial objectives" (Falk 1971, 81). This definition recognizes the destruction of nonhumans and (certain) ecosystems as an egregious act. However, nonhumans are not recognized as the direct objects of violence or as capable of being violated in themselves. Rather, harm is defined in terms of its impact on humans (for instance, the loss of food, safe drinking water, or agricultural land).

The predominantly military focus of Falk's concept of "ecocide" shifted in the 1990s, refocusing on the role of corporations in creating ecological harms on large scales during times of peace. In this context, unmarked Canadian/Australian scholar Mark Allan Gray (1996) argued that acts such as the global logging of ancient rainforests, trade in endangered species, the Chernobyl nuclear disaster, and the Exxon Valdez oil spill all possessed the requisite gravity to be considered acts of ecocide (based on the number of people and species negatively affected). Gray (1996) sought to distance his idea of ecocide from the criterion of intentionality, arguing that ecocidal harms may be deliberately inflicted but may also arise from recklessness, negligence, inappropriate planning, and other causes, with their full consequences only becoming clear over time. However, some legal scholars worried that too much imprecision might dilute the effectiveness of a potential law of ecocide. An influential report by the International Law Commission (ILC) (Tomuschat 1996) argued that although an anti-ecocide law could account for distributed responsibility (e.g., within a supply chain), it must still specify a distinct corporate actor as responsible (rather than pointing to the accumulation of separate actions by multiple actors such as polluters). This report also cautioned that only the "worst occurrences" of ecological harm should be prosecuted as ecocides, and only if the requirements of addressing them exceeded the capacity of any individual state. Crucially, it also specified that the crime of ecocide should not be used to protect individual species from extinction or to "preserve existing ecosystems as such" but only to prevent and punish major acts of acute and grievous harm against ecosystems. In other words, the ILC approach frames genocide in terms of egregious *acts* that cause sudden disruptions rather than ongoing processes that engender long-term harms.

Genocide, Eliminative Violence, and Extinction   167

The ILC report also clearly states that the primary goal of any potential law of ecocide would be to guarantee "peace and security" among *states*. As such, like the CBD and many other pieces of international law, it presumes the sovereignty and prioritizes the survival of the Westphalian state system (including the invasive states described in chapter 4).

Meanwhile, in the 1990s another norm—human security—began to rapidly gain international traction, adding new dimensions to discussions of ecocide. Discourses of human security depart from traditional ideas of physical security and war between states to focus on providing multiple kinds of security: food, health, economic, environmental, personal, community, and political (see UNDP 1994). Drawing on this discourse, Gray (1996, 203) argues that a crime of "ecocide" could be grounded in two established human *rights* (to life and health, respectively) but that it *ought* to be defined more broadly, in terms of human security. Specifically, he argues that a law of ecocide should protect "family and property"; provide the right to food, safe drinking water, and a "clean" environment; ensure the cultural and religious rights of Indigenous peoples; and prevent the destruction of societies, institutions, livelihoods, and identities linked to particular environments.[9] He also insists that "the natural world's beauty, complexity and fragility suggest that it and its components in their own right have interests worthy of protection" (Gray 1996, 225). The ILC report echoes these ideas to some extent, urging attention to "long-term repercussions that undermine the substantive bases of life in conditions of good health and individual and collective dignity" (Tomuschat 1996, 22). Importantly, all the definitions of ecocide discussed so far foreground instrumental notions of "habitat" as a resource or base for life-forms rather than the conditions of cohabitation discussed in chapter 3. Further, the report introduces imaginaries of total destruction (see chapter 6): naming "genetic injury," the possibility of entire regions becoming uninhabitable, and even a scenario in which "humankind may become threatened with extinction" (Tomuschat 1996, 22).[10] In so doing, these discourses began to converge with the apocalyptic discourses I return to in chapter 6.

The movement to create an international crime of ecocide gained prominence again in the 2010s, largely through the late unmarked Scottish barrister Polly Higgins's campaign to add it to the Rome Statute as a "fifth crime against humanity." Higgins and her colleagues decried the fact that, due to gaps in international law, it is "not a crime to cause mass destruction or loss of ecosystems" (Higgins, Short, and South 2013, 17) but rather

168 Genocide, Eliminative Violence, and Extinction

an increasingly normalized element of global capitalism. With this in mind, Higgins (2010, 1) proposed a new definition of "ecocide," as

> extensive damage to, destruction of or loss of ecosystem(s) of a given territory, whether by human agency or by other causes, to such an extent that peaceful enjoyment by the inhabitants of that territory has been or will be severely diminished.

This definition gained significant international traction: it was submitted to the UN in 2010; it was the subject of a European Union plebiscite that gathered more than one million signatures; and in 2019, Pope Francis called on the international community to recognize it in his address to the International Association of Penal Law. To date, ten states (in the former USSR and Ecuador) have implemented national ecocide policies based on this definition, and at the December 2019 session of the Assembly of States Parties to the Rome Statute of the International Criminal Court, the states of Vanuatu and Maldives called for its addition in their official statements, while France and Belgium also indicated interest in promoting its formal adoption.

In Higgins's 2010 definition, "ecocide" is a crime of strict liability, meaning that the *individual* with supreme authority over an organization (whether a CEO or a sovereign) can be held responsible for acts undertaken by that organization, whether or not they have knowledge of those acts. Further, there is no requirement to prove *mens rea* (criminal intent); the harms in question must simply be a *foreseeable outcome* of an action. What's more, the definition does not prohibit specific categories of activity (for instance, coal mining as a whole); rather, it is designed to allow for the prosecution of *any* activity that produces outcomes that meet the criteria, whatever the intentions of the actors engaging in it. This shift in emphasis is intended to *prevent* ecocidal crimes by making them prohibitively costly for CEOs and other corporate interest holders. However, drawing on interventionist norms of the 1990s and early 2000s (for instance, the Responsibility to Protect), Higgins's definition would also make it incumbent upon states to *intervene* in acts of "ecocide"—including "natural disasters"—as they are expected to do in conditions of genocide.

Higgins's main aim was to extend the "higher morality" applied to the mass destruction of "human life" to all species (2010, 61). At first glance,

Genocide, Eliminative Violence, and Extinction 169

this approach may seem to recognize the ethical status of nonhumans. However, under Higgins's definition, that status would remain linked to utilitarian, Euro-descendent accounts of relationships with nature that stress the "non-use" or "existence value" of nature (Higgins 2010, 66). These are, in fact, colonial notions of value that erase the myriad engagements and relations with and between life-forms and ecosystems that exceed capitalist production. The idea of "non-use value" may also entrench fantasies of inert, unused terra nullius or wasteland to be revalued within global financial systems (see the discussion of conservation as investment in chapter 4). Indeed, perhaps more ambitiously than its forebears, Higgins's account of ecocide entrenches Eurocentric, liberal, and universalist norms of international law and ethics, including in the ways that nonhumans appear in its frameworks. For instance, in a mock trial carried out by the UK Supreme Court intended to test the norm, one of the plaintiffs named was a group of ducks (species unspecified) harmed by the dumping of tailings in the Alberta Tar Sands. Since neither the concept of "ecocide" nor the UK court system recognize the subjectivity of ducks or their potential role as parties to the law, they were represented by humans claiming to "speak on behalf" of ducks, based on their understanding of the ducks' interests. Indeed, within Higgins's account, nonhumans do not have legal standing in their own right but rather must be interpreted and translated within the existing (anthropocentric) international legal system. This approach precludes principles, instruments, and processes from legal systems in which nonhumans have legal standing or different kinds of entitlements and duties. For instance, in the Anishinaabe story/theory of the Hoof Clan discussed in the book's Introduction, both parties' entitlements were linked to collective coexistence (within and between their respective life-forms) rather than an individualized right to life. Further, instead of seeking retribution or justice only for their own kind, the form of justice sought by the Hoof Clan acknowledged the breaking of co-constitutive relationships between life-forms and demanded their restoration. In contrast, by naming "ducks" as the plaintiff in isolation from their relational webs, the ecocide mock trial parceled out harms to discrete life-forms, ignoring the destruction of (bio)plural *relations* and *conditions of cohabitation*.

In addition, while it critiques existing systems of global capitalism, Higgins's notion of ecocide affirms and bolsters other global structures of domination—in particular the system of Westphalian nation-states. For instance, Higgins's interventionist approach constitutes a significant extension of claims to ecological sovereignty (M. Smith 2011) by states. Under the broad flag of conservation, it creates opportunities for states to engage in the forceful and neocolonial (see chapter 6) expansion of their control over the biodiversity within other states through intervention, including in non-self-governing territories (see also Eckersley 2007). What's more, Higgins's (2010, 74–75) "'ecocide' framework" hinges on the notion that states play a "sacred" role of holding the planet in "trust." This model is drawn directly from John Locke's (1980) arguments regarding how British colonizers ought to manage lands on behalf of the Indigenous inhabitants from whom they were expropriated. In other words, this approach opens up additional leeway for states to use conservation, backed by an international law of ecocide, to justify ongoing colonial and/or imperial control over global ecosystems. Finally, Higgins's account of "peaceful enjoyment" (whether or not intentionally) affirms settler claims to land annexed through colonization. Namely, in an attempt to cut off loopholes that might allow perpetrators to escape prosecution, she asserts that since the "inhabitants of a particular place *change over time,*" the law should apply to "those who live there at any given time" (Higgins 2010, 67, emphasis mine). In so doing, the proposed law masks the ongoing structures of violence through which a given group of inhabitants may have come to occupy a particular place or displace others from it. Meanwhile, the language of "peaceful enjoyment"—usually applied to private property—affirms colonial claims to the ownership of invaded lands on the basis of occupation and glosses over the contestation of land rights.

Efforts to elaborate the concept of ecocide have continued since Higgins's death in 2019. In 2021, the Stop Ecocide Foundation, on the request of Swedish parliamentarians, convened an expert panel of twelve international lawyers (along with "outside experts" and a public consultation including international "legal, economic, political, youth, faith and indigenous perspectives"[11]) to develop the following amended definition:

> unlawful or wanton acts committed with knowledge that there is a substantial likelihood of severe and either widespread or long-term damage to the environment being caused by those acts.[12]

The language of this definition differs substantially from Higgins's original formulation. Narrower and more precise (legally speaking), it adopts

Genocide, Eliminative Violence, and Extinction   171

several features of the Rome Statute, including the criteria that damage be "widespread," "wanton," and "severe." It also includes a proportionality test (all developed to apply to military contexts and adapted to ecocide discourses). The meanings of several of these terms, and the ways they are framed by the panel, call for careful attention.

The specification that actions must be "unlawful" is intended to distinguish between activities that break existing *national* and other *state-based* laws from "activities that are legal, socially beneficial and responsibly operated to minimize impacts that nonetheless cause (or are likely to cause) severe and either widespread or long-term damage to the environment" (SEF 2021, 7). In other words, the law is intended to prevent harms to the environment that stem from actions that are deemed unjust or undesirable, without jeopardizing activities that are deemed relevant to sustainable development. This definition affirms the laws upheld by and entrenched in Westphalian nation-states (to which existing norms and institutions of international law are tied) as determinant of ecocide. As such, it precludes legal ideas, processes, instruments, or other ways of determining harm emerging from other legal orders and systems, including those actively oppressed by nation-states (e.g., Indigenous, landless, and stateless groups). In addition, this state-based approach leaves untouched the colonial, imperial, and other forms of power in which these states are rooted and effectively offers an additional tool for exercising it. Also recall that, as discussed in the previous chapters, many of the phenomena associated with extinction are defined as the unintended consequences of activities that are considered benign or desirable, at least by a particular, and often dominant, group or society. As such, this law would have very limited applicability to the systematic, distributed forms of harm and violence, described in the previous chapters, that are carried out legally within and *by states* or even directly aided by them.

Furthermore, "wanton," according to the panel, refers to "reckless disregard for damage," which would be "clearly *excessive* in relation to the *social and economic benefits anticipated*" (SEF 2021, 5, emphasis mine). This framing immediately raises two questions: what constitutes "excess," and who determines this? As Liboiron (2020) shows, colonial and Eurocentric environmentalist attempts to limit harms such as pollution or contamination almost always involve *allowing*, and in essence *normalizing*, a certain amount of harm that is determined acceptable by lawmakers.[13] In the same vein, the 2021 definition of ecocide measures the acceptability of harms against *intended benefits* of an act, declaring ecocide only in cases where the former is thought to outweigh the latter. Who, then, decides what constitutes an "excessive" (and an acceptable) amount of harm or benefit, and on what bases? The panel specifies that in the case of "socially beneficial" projects such as housing developments and transport links, or other initiatives that promote "sustainable development," such harms might be allowable—indeed, they aver that much of existing international and environmental law seeks to strike this balance. While there are many strong arguments for the importance of projects such as these, the panel bases its argument on an uncritical enshrinement of *one specific* idea of "the good life" and "human flourishing" (see Mitchell 2014a)—"sustainable development." Although it is assumed to be universal, this norm may conflict with other ideas of how humans should cohabit with other beings, and what is considered acceptable and/or harmful within multiple legal-political and relational orders. For instance, the idea that human needs could be measured *against* those of a separate "environment" is anathema to many cosmovisions and legal-political orders, including those I discuss in the following sections of this chapter.

The framing of the term "widespread," which specifies transboundary harms as a possible criterion, further entrenches the existing system of state sovereignty by treating *state* boundaries as criteria of consideration without including other relevant ecopolitical boundaries (for instance, the shifting boundaries of ecosystems, migration routes). It may also complicate claims of ecocide between nested political entities (e.g., plurinational states) and/or in cases where the sovereignty of one party is ignored or not recognized—for instance, in the case of the Canadian state's actions on Wet'suwet'en territory (described in chapter 4). In addition, the term "widespread" is framed in a way that specifies harms to "an entire ecosystem or species," which could potentially describe some of the harms associated with the systematic destruction of (bio)plurality. However, the wording remains firmly entrenched within Western scientific paradigms of ecosystems and species that do not reflect—or protect—the singularity or internal plurality of these entities (see chapter 2). The same issue is reflected in the framing of the term "nature" provided in the commentary on the new definition. "Environment," it specifies, "means the earth, its biosphere, cryosphere, lithosphere, hydrosphere and atmosphere, as well as outer space" (SEF 2021, 4). This mode of segmenting the earth into separate, interacting systems (and earth from outer space; see Bawaka Country et al. 2020) is a hallmark of modern European philosophical thought that cannot be generalized to all cosmovisions and knowledge systems. Indeed, in citing this definition of the environment, the panel refers to a *single* academic paper (Steffen et al. 2020) written by authors noted for their work on popularizing the specific framework of earth systems science (and without reference to the substantial debates surrounding this idea), allowing it to stand in for "scientific consensus." In so doing, the panel treats as universal and takes for granted what is in fact a historically and culturally specific way of thinking about and relating earth and other beings.

So, like its 2010 precursor, this revised definition of ecocide does not diverge greatly from a reliance on Eurocentric scientific, cultural, and legal touchstones—for instance, the framing of legal concepts in ancient Greek terminology; and the attribution of responsibility for harms to individuals (or "corporate individuals") instead of broader structures, cultures, or systems. Further, it continues to use terminology that frames the relations between humans and the environment in instrumental terms. For instance, in defining "severe" harms (to which the law is intended to be applied exclusively), the panel describes "very serious adverse changes, disruption or harm to any *element of the environment,* including grave impacts on *human life, or natural, cultural or economic resources*" (SEF 2021, 8, emphasis mine). This wording is drawn directly from the idea of severity used in the 1976 *Convention on the Prohibition of Military or Any Other Hostile Use of Environmental Modification Techniques (ENMOD).* The direct *substitution* of the term "cultural resources" for "assets" (*ENMOD*'s term for objects of harm) is intended to be more respectful to "indigenous 'ways of thinking,'" yet it reflects an instrumental and often exploitative and/or extractive relationship with nonhuman beings that is at odds with many Indigenous knowledge systems.

For these reasons, the proposed law of ecocide may be useful in prosecuting harms in which there is evidence of clear individual or corporate culpability and discrete victims. It may also be effective in offering remedies that reflect *Eurocentric* conceptions and experiences of harm, relational models, and notions of violence. However, it is not helpful addressing the *systematic destruction of (bio)plurality,* which is systemic, diffuse, and distributed across relational orders. In addition, by defining harms, violence, their subjects and objects, and possibilities of response solely in Eurocentric terms, discourses on ecocide either ignore other legal-political orders or force them to work within currently dominant systems. With these

174   Genocide, Eliminative Violence, and Extinction

problems in mind, let's now revisit the concept of genocide from the perspective of several other knowledge systems and legal-political orders.

GENOCIDE, ELIMINATIVE VIOLENCE, AND NONHUMANS

Eliminative violence is experienced differently within each life-form and world, so it is well beyond the scope of this book to discuss it comprehensively. Instead, I examine three contexts in which eliminative violence against nonhuman life-forms converges with (and diverges from) genocide, as it is framed in existing international law. The first example involves genocidal acts against a human community that were carried out through systematic attacks on a nonhuman life-form integral to their ways of life. Although the primary goal of this type of violence is to eliminate particular human ways of life, it is realized through targeted attacks on the *relations* between humans and their nonhuman kin. The second example discusses attempts to eliminate a life-form whose human/nonhuman status is ambiguous and fluid, giving rise to forms of collective power that threaten dominant actors. This mode of eliminative violence aims to neutralize challenges by eliminating particular modes of more-than-human life and kinship. In the third example, certain nonhumans are recognized as persons/people(s) or nations and hold formal status within relevant laws, treaties, constitutions, or other arrangements. I argue that acts of eliminative violence against these groups constitute genocide under existing international law without significant modification—if the relevant legal-political orders and their definitions of "peoples" are respected. Each of these examples is unique to the worlds it describes. Yet each one also provides insight into the broader uses of eliminative violence against nonhumans and conditions of (bio)plurality, including deliberate efforts to bring about the extinction of certain life-forms.

THE QIMMIIJAQTAUNIQ

All genocides are attacks against more-than-human peoples, in the sense that all human groups are co-constituted by and with other life-forms and beings. However, in this section I focus on forms of eliminative violence that specifically target the *co-constitutive relationships* between a human group and another life-form. Often, this type of violence is analyzed in instrumental terms: it is understood as an attempt to harm a human group by eliminating its most fundamental *resources*. However, to take this argument at face value would be to reproduce the logic of substitution discussed in

Genocide, Eliminative Violence, and Extinction 175

chapter 2. Namely, it would suggest that the effects of the violence could be reversed or erased if an equivalent amount of a similar resource (or financial restitution) were provided. However, as this section will show, the use of eliminative violence against nonhuman kin-species does not simply destroy resources. On the contrary, it erases *unique, irreplaceable* histories; shared knowledge; interspecies intimacies; cohabitats; lifeways; temporalities; and desired futures shared by and distributed across the human and nonhuman members of a world. In short, it targets specific ways of *being more-than-human.*

Importantly, these relations are targeted by aggressors because they threaten, challenge, and/or resist the power of dominant actors and political systems. For instance, in colonial contexts, logics of eliminative violence have often conflated human and nonhuman groups as existential threats to the settler state and society. Indeed, in the Massachusetts Bay colony in the seventeenth century, Indigenous people and wolves were placed in the same category and subjected to identical tactics of violence. Colonists were banned from using guns to shoot anything "except an Indian [*sic*] or a wolf" (Stannard 1994, 41); they were encouraged to set out poisoned meat for wolves and to trade contaminated goods to Indigenous people, and they raided dens to kill wolf pups while they abducted Indigenous children.[14] It is unlikely that many of the colonizers who carried out these acts had a nuanced understanding of the depth and complexity of connections between wolves and specific Indigenous communities. It is much more probable that they simply lumped the two groups together as threats to their dominance.

However, in other cases, aggressors appear to understand—and to directly target—the co-constitutive relations between human groups and other lifeforms. An argument of this kind is set out in the report of the Qikiktani Truth Commission (QTC 2013c). QTC is an Inuit-led organization in Eastern Nunavat that was created to investigate the qimmiijaqtauniq, or "sled dog slaughter," in which it is estimated that thousands of ᕿᒻᒥᖅ (Qimmit or sled dogs) were killed by agents of the Canadian state. Like dingoes and wolves, Qimmit are a unique canid life-form, distinguished from so-called domestic dogs by their distinct genealogy and by adaptations stemming from generations spent as members of Inuit kinship and social structures. Targeted killings of Qimmit took place between 1950 and 1975, a period that coincides with the Canadian government's efforts to force seminomadic Inuit communities into permanent settlements and wage-based

176   Genocide, Eliminative Violence, and Extinction

employment, ostensibly to increase their access to health and welfare services. The rationale provided for these killings was often "dysfunctional behaviour" that was caused by removing the dogs from their traditional lifeways and forcing them into sedentary, urban settings.[15] In its *Analysis of the RCMP Sled Dog Report, 1950–1975*, the QTC (2013a) critiques the Royal Canadian Mounted Police's (RCMP) own internal inquiry on the incident, pointing out that it does not deny the killings nor mount any moral or ethical defense. On the contrary, the RCMP argues that the killings of Qimmit were, at the time, *legal*—an argument that has been used in many cases of egregious mass and/or eliminative violence (see Arendt 1973).[16]

The QTC (and the RCMP's own report) also shows that RCMP officers had a decades-long history of interaction with Inuit communities and, as such, must have had a working knowledge of the nature of the relationships between Inuit and Qimmit. It is likely that federal employees involved in designing and implementing relevant policies also possessed some such knowledge. Indeed, the QTC quotes a 1954 communication in which a white teacher in Coral Bay asks permission of the Arctic Division in Ottawa to kill Qimmit, to which the government employee replies:

> It has been noted by people who have studied primitive cultures and the impact of civilization that when one thread in the fabric of the culture is disturbed the whole weave is affected . . . [so] we cannot lightly issue orders in such a matter as the restraining of dogs. We must remember that these animals are important to the Eskimo [*sic*] in many ways, that they have always run [freely]. (QTC 2013a, 59)

This correspondence shows that however rudimentary, chauvinistic, and simplistic their knowledge might have been, agents of the state had some understanding of how integral Inuit and Qimmit lifeways were to each other. It also shows that these actors could have reasonably foreseen the deeply negative impacts of their actions, as indeed the Ottawa-based correspondent did.

Qimmit, descendants of an ancient genetic line derived from Siberian gray wolves (Skoglund et al. 2015), are distinct from the more common Huskies and Malamutes employed by the RCMP in the Eastern Arctic and are often misleadingly labeled as "sled dogs." Long before the arrival of those breeds—for at least twelve thousand years—Qimmit adapted socially and behaviorally to their Arctic cohabitats in close collaboration with Inuit.

Genocide, Eliminative Violence, and Extinction 177

Across this shared history, they became indispensable to the land-based, seminomadic lifeways embodied by most Inuit until the imposition of the settlement policies in the mid-twentieth century. Until that point, the majority of Inuit lived in more than one hundred ilagiit nunagivaktangit (camps), to which particular kinship groups moved seasonally to take "advantage of weather conditions, animal migrations and cultural linkages" (QTC 2013b, 9). Teams of Qimmit made it possible to travel efficiently over the immense snow- and ice-covered distances between these sites. They were not considered pets or even "working dogs" in the sense assumed by many southern Canadians. Instead, they were understood by their Inuit kin as partners engaged in a system of mutual nourishment aligned with seasonal changes and needs. Specifically, Qimmit supported Inuit travel and hunting practices in the winter in exchange for a share of the food, water, care, and companionship. They were virtually self-reliant in the summer months, when they could hunt and scavenge on their own (McHugh 2013).

Although they took different forms throughout the year, the relationships between Inuit families and their Qimmit are far from casual. Individuals and groups of Qimmit are intimately bonded to specific Inuit families, throughout their life cycles and across generations—and vice versa. Papikattuq Sakiagaq, from Salluit, describes the intimacy of the lifelong relationships formed between Inuit and Qimmit:

> In raising a dog team, while they're still puppies we had to stretch the legs, and rub their underarms, tickle them in order for them to get used to the harness. . . . While they're becoming adolescent dogs, we would have to take them for walks with their harnesses on. . . . When they are harnessed they are irritated if they were not tamed in this way while they're still puppies, and they are not comfortable to run if they are not used to being stretched on their forepaws, and feeding them with soup, making sure that they don't get into the habit of being hungry. (quoted in McHugh 2013, 160–61)

The relationship described by Sakiagaq is a deeply personal, embodied one, in which Inuit are integral to the care of Qimmit—feeding, massaging, socializing, helping them learn to use their limbs and get accustomed to harnesses—and to the development not only of individual dogs but also of teams. According to unmarked American scholar Susan McHugh (2013), Inuit hunters acted as elders to young Qimmit, helping guide them through various life stages. In turn, for Inuit, the process of working with Qimmit

178　　　　Genocide, Eliminative Violence, and Extinction

was central to their social development, providing some of their most formative relationships, skills, and lessons in childhood and adolescence.

Importantly, these relational practices generate a unique mode of co-cognition that is distributed across Inuk and Qimmit bodies (see chapter 3), in which micro-decisions are sourced across the group instead of being made by one actor and transmitted to the others (McHugh 2013). In this context, the collective intelligence, instinct, sensory data, and knowledge of the team are pooled in order to make split-second, precise, and life-changing decisions—for instance, in responding to threats such as cracking ice or predators, or succeeding in a hunt. So integral is this form of intersubjectivity to Inuit worlds that, according to some QTC respondents, government-run schools—including the residential schools used across the country to sever Indigenous children from their cultures—forbade children from even talking about or drawing pictures of Qimmit (QTC 2013c). What's more, during periods of starvation in isolated ilagiit nunagivaktangit, Inuit would sometimes eat their dogs as a second-to-last resort (before eating their clothes); and Qimmit would, in rare cases, eat humans (see McHugh 2013). These relations of reciprocal digestion (see Haraway 2008) reflect the profound, embodied forms of co-constitution and kinship of these beings, and the inseparability of their bodies. In contrast, qallunaat (southerners, usually white), ignoring the deeper context of this relationship, drew on reports of rare attacks by Qimmit on humans to justify the restraint and killing of the animals (QTC 2014a).[17]

The policies supporting these killings reflected a gradual intensification of the Canadian settler state's efforts to assert sovereignty in the eastern Arctic through the agency of the RCMP (see chapter 4). This organization (initially called the North West Mounted Police) was formed in 1873 and deployed by the fledgling settler state as a paramilitary unit whose explicit aim was to suppress Indigenous communities in its newly annexed Western territories (see Ladner 2014). In creating this force, Canada's first prime minster, John A. MacDonald, drew direct inspiration from the Royal Irish Constabulary—an organization made infamous by its brutal oppression of Irish resisters to British colonial rule.[18] During the twentieth century, the RCMP's arctic units were given enhanced governmental authority, so that by 1920 they performed almost all governmental roles in the Baffin region. As representatives of state and sovereign, the RCMP detachments in the eastern Arctic enforced the federal laws, regulating and controlling relations between Inuit and international traders (ostensibly to protect the former);

Genocide, Eliminative Violence, and Extinction   179

patrolling the region to provide (and regulate use of) basic services; and monitoring people and wildlife (QTC 2013a). In reality, this form of governance involved imposing Canadian law over Inuit law and substituting new social development policies for Inuit legal, political, and social orders. As the QTC (2013a, 32–33) notes, many Inuit understood the RCMP presence and remit as "a formal challenge to Inuit law, custom, and practice. They were designed in part to avenge or protect Qallunaat who were punished by Inuit for transgressions against Inuit law."

Until the 1950s, federal policy encouraged Inuit to stay on the land and maintain their traditional lifeways, an arrangement that minimized the cost of government services and infrastructure in the region (see QTC 2013c). This strategy changed abruptly in the 1950s, possibly due in part to international embarrassment when U.S. military forces stationed in the region reported on the apparent destitution faced by Inuit communities (McHugh 2014). However, the federal government had already been moving toward a policy of centralization, which culminated in the forced sedentarization of Inuit communities, including the compression of more than one hundred ilagiit nunagivaktangit into just thirteen permanent settlements (QTC 2013c). As a result of this policy, Inuit extended families, including Qimmit, were compelled to abandon their land-based lifeways, to move into European-style housing, and to enter the capitalist labor market, often through employment at military bases. Officially, the policy was intended to improve access to government services such as healthcare and education by concentrating Inuit communities in places that were deemed relatively accessible and comfortable for providers relocating from southern Canada. As the centralization policy unfolded, southerners continued to rely on the RCMP to implement policy, including the restriction of hunting (to encourage sedentary living) and the removal of children and ill people to southern residential schools and medical centers (QTC 2013a).

For Qimmit, this policy involved a rapid change from a seminomadic, seasonally calibrated life to a static everyday existence and material conditions that were fundamentally "inhospitable" for dogs (QTC 2013a, 41). In these conditions, Qimmit were unable to roam and forage, and, as a lifeform deeply bonded to their more-than-human kin but wary of outsiders, many became neurotic and anxious around relatively large groups of unknown people (QTC 2013a). Forced to live in close quarters with dog teams from other families, Qimmit fought more frequently than usual in order resolve conflict and maintain their social orders. This fed into qallunaat

180   Genocide, Eliminative Violence, and Extinction

stereotypes of "out-of-control" strays, derived from specious comparisons to the Euro-descendent categories of pets and working animals. At the same time, traditional ways of caring for Qimmit, including allowing them to forage freely during the summer, were labeled as negligence (QTC 2013a). Indeed, just prior to the commencement of its formal centralization policy, Ottawa instituted the (Northwest) Territory's Ordinance Respecting Dogs, which

> effectively outlawed traditional ways of handling dogs, wherever this seemed to conflict with the needs or practices of a growing Qallunaat population. . . . The standard government policy was to assume Inuit must, at their own expense, accommodate newcomers' needs and wants. While the Ordinance Respecting Dogs was clear to those who enforced it, hunters understood it as illogical, unnecessary, and also harmful; Inuit and dogs had existed together for uncounted generations without such restrictions being necessary. (QTC 2013a, 15)

The ordinance laid the groundwork for a set of policies that would implode distinctly Qimmit ways of life. For instance, it required that dogs be muzzled and chained while their human kin performed wage labor; those that remained unchained were deemed to be stray and impounded, if not killed on the spot. As the QTC (2013a, 45) points out, "tying, chaining, or confining them in pounds was not good for the dogs themselves. Chained dogs could not exercise, socialize, or forage, and employed Inuit could not hunt for [food for] them"—conditions that caused many dogs to starve. Restrained by muzzles and chains, Qimmit were also unable to eat snow to stay hydrated and became vulnerable to larger predators such as polar bears (McHugh 2013). In addition, Qimmit were increasingly exposed to other canines that carried pathogens to which they were not immune. As a result, many Qimmit were rounded up for inoculation campaigns whose primary aim was to protect the other species of dogs brought to the region by qallunaat (QTC 2013a). Whereas the Inuit practice was to give sick dogs time to recover, Qimmit diagnosed with canine diseases were shot immediately as a matter of "public health and safety" (QTC 2013a, 23). Qallunaat also railed against the Qimmit practice of scavenging of garbage and carrion, which the former considered unhygienic—even as it reduced the exposure of humans to predators attracted to these food sources such as polar bears and wolverines (QTC 2013a). Still other Qimmit found themselves

Genocide, Eliminative Violence, and Extinction 181

abandoned and killed when their human kin were removed to the south for medical care, residential school, or prison and were unable to return (often due to the cost of travel). Even when a team's Inuit kin remained in the settlement, the demands of wage labor made them unable to provide the deep forms of care and attention necessary to the mental, physical, and emotional health and training of Qimmit (QTC 2013c). In short, beyond simply killing Qimmit, these comprehensive policies eroded their social structure, cut off their sources of subsistence and reproduction (social and biological), and immersed them in structural conditions of relentless suffering, terror, scapegoating, and persecution.

The killing of Qimmit was also central to this campaign of elimination. The Ordinance provided a framework of rules whose transgression gave qallunaat the right to shoot dogs on the spot. Based on interviews with 350 Inuit present at the time, the QTC (2013a) estimates that hundreds or even thousands of Qimmit were killed under its directives. Even when Inuit adhered strictly to the rules, some found that their teams were killed as part of efforts at population control. Meanwhile, some temporary visitors to settlements, such as the family of elder Naki Ekho in 1957, were forced to remain permanently after their dog teams were destroyed (QTC 2013a). Indeed, the QTC report shows that many Inuit understood the mass killing of Qimmit as part of a broader effort to remove their mobility and independence, forcing them to rely on the cash economy and government services. For example, Thomas Kublu, who came home from work to find his chained dogs shot, asked:

> "Was it because my hunting was getting in the way of my time as a labourer?"
>
> This was very painful to me as I needed to hunt, and because I was alone with no relatives to help me out with my responsibilities as a hunter and wage earner. . . . A major part of my livelihood was taken away from me, my identity and means of providing for my family. (quoted in QTC 2013c, 42)

According to McHugh (2013), the severe constriction of mobility caused by the killing and constraining of Qimmit forced Inuit to live in conditions that they considered similar to concentration or labor camps. This account is reflected in the QTC (2013a, 40) report, which frames the Qimmiijaqtauniq as the first salvo in a campaign of "interconnected policies and actions, closely linked in time, by which government undermined traditional Inuit ways of living." Indeed, the report notes that acts of formalized violence

182 Genocide, Eliminative Violence, and Extinction

against Qimmit began before the government provided even the "rough beginnings of the housing and other infrastructure a centralized population needs" (QTC 2013a, 40). This suggests not only that Inuit forced into sedentary lifestyles faced dismal living conditions but also that that the destruction of Qimmit-Inuit relations was a precursor for more invasive political, social, and economic interventions. The gradual increase of the intensity and comprehensiveness of violence is a defining feature of many genocides (see Stanton 2016).

Indeed, the Qimmiijaqtauniq exemplifies several features identified by critical accounts of genocide (see the first section of this chapter). For instance, it exemplifies the construction of encompassing relations of genocide, genocidal outcomes (the destruction of traditional Inuit society and of Inuit-Qimmit relations), and the convergence of multiple forms of violence linked by shared eliminative logics. Some individuals, such as the schoolteacher mentioned earlier, expressed explicit and racially motivated enthusiasm for killing dogs. Others, including several RCMP, were saddened or disgusted by having to perform the killings, and still others believed that their actions would improve the lives of Inuit (QTC 2013a). Yet all participated in processes of eliminative violence linked by a common logic: the destruction of a particular more-than-human way of life. In addition, because the acts of violence were targeted (at least explicitly) on dogs rather than directly on humans, many of those involved may not have *understood* their actions as part of a genocide. However, the QTC report articulates its own distinct account of eliminative violence that is not limited to humans. It refuses to accept the labeling of Qimmit as mere instruments or resources, or to discuss reparations in merely financial terms—that is, to reduce the killing of Qimmit to the destruction of property (McHugh 2013). Instead, it states unequivocally that the attack on Qimmit was experienced by Inuit as an attack on their people, their ways of life, and their more-than-human political orders, laws, and sovereignty. This experience is reflected in the words of an Inuk former hunter who spoke to anthropologist Toshio Yatsushiro in the 1950s after his dogs were killed:

> First I thought of killing the policemen. But I don't mind now. Maybe afterwards there won't be so many dogs, since the police are shooting them. In five years there may be none at all. Maybe the police will kill Eskimos [sic] then, just like the dogs. (quoted in QTC 2013a, 45)

Genocide, Eliminative Violence, and Extinction   183

This man experienced the Qimmiijaqtauniq as one stage of a process that might lead to the direct killing of Inuit. His words reflect the dissociative effects of trauma and explicit awareness of the role of the Qimmiijaqtauniq in broader structures of genocide. Moreover, they speak to a phenomenon known in Inuktitut as illira. According to Pond Inlet elder Anaviapik (quoted in QTC 2013a, 62), illira refers to "people or things that have power over you and can be neither controlled nor predicted. People or things that make you feel vulnerable, and to which you *are* vulnerable." In short, it produces, for many Inuit and other co-constituents of their worlds, the same conditions of terror into which Qimmit were plunged, in which their entire history, possible futures, and ways of life may be erased at any moment by forces beyond their control. The institution of an encompassing governmental system rooted in illira is a form of systemic and eliminative violence that undermines existing ways of life. As the QTC articulates, it is a devastating weapon that advances genocidal aims by destroying the relationships between humans and their nonhuman kin.

Shark Culls in Hawai'i

In December 1958, just before Hawai'i was absorbed into the United States—against the will of the vast majority of its Indigenous peoples— Billy Weaver, a haole (white settler) teen died after being bitten by an exceptionally large shark near Lanikai, O'ahu. His death prompted an outcry from the haole community, which quickly mobilized to seek revenge. A citizens' posse was organized to catch the individual shark, while government planes, aided by the U.S. Air Force, surveilled and attempted to shoot several schools of sharks (Goldberg-Hiller and Silva 2011). Members of the U.S. Fish and Wildlife Service set lines to trap sand and tiger sharks, and bounties of twenty dollars per shark and one hundred dollars for any shark larger than fifteen feet were offered to the public by a private citizen and a radio station, respectively (Tester 1960). The Billy Weaver Shark Control Program, a privately funded initiative that later won $300,000 from the new state legislature, was initiated to enhance public safety. It employed fishing vessels equipped with specialized lines to kill 595 sharks around the island of O'ahu in 1959—only 17 of which were tiger sharks, of which species the shark who killed Weaver was most likely to have been a member (Tester 1960). By 1976, state-funded shark control programs stemming from this mobilization had killed 4,668 sharks, although they do not appear to

184   Genocide, Eliminative Violence, and Extinction

have made a significant impact in reducing attacks on humans (Wetherbee, Lowe, and Crow 1994).

Recounting this program of killing in the context of U.S. efforts to destroy Hawaiian sovereignty, American settler scholar Jonathan Goldberg-Hiller and Kānaka Maoli scholar Noenoe Silva (2011) point out the spectacular nature of the violence. During these efforts, sharks were not only killed but also transformed into effigies, their corpses "hoisted on scaffolds near the piers and driven through the streets of Honolulu, where they were photographed as records of vengeance" (Goldberg-Hiller and Silva 2011, 430). Attacks against nonhuman life-forms held responsible for killing individual settlers are common in colonial states. Other examples include the use of the death of Maggie Clay to justify policies for killing Qimmit (see note 17) and the retributive killing of stingrays in Australia after the accidental death of TV personality Steve Irwin in 2006 (P. Lewis 2006). And, as the first sections of this chapter suggest, continuous acts of systemic violence designed to prevent the survival and flourishing of life-forms whose presence threatens (or simply irritates) settler communities are everyday features of such polities. However, Goldberg-Hiller and Silva (2011) show that the ritualized killing of sharks in Oʻahu involved something distinct: an attempt to destroy a being that does not fit easily into Eurocentric models of human/nonhuman distinctions, and the unique form of sovereignty it embodies.

Manō and humans are deeply entwined within Kānaka cosmovisions. Kānaka marine scientist Noelani Puniwai (2020) explains how manō are integral to kinship systems, moʻolelo (histories), and social structure (for instance, only aliʻi or high chiefs could kill niuhi—fierce sharks that may be tiger and/or great whites). Manō also play a role in co-constituting Kānaka temporalities and geographies: one traditional saying suggests that sharks bite when the wiliwili plant is in bloom, connecting sea and land through the mating seasons and reproductive cycles of trees and sharks (Puniwai 2020). Although there are five names for different kinds of sharks in Kānaka tradition, most manō are known for individual traits, their specific life histories, the places where they are born and return, and their individual relationships with human families (Puniwai 2020). In many moʻolelo (stories/theories), certain beings have kino lau (or "many bodies") which means that they are able to take the shape of multiple life-forms. For this reason, many Hawaiian oʻhana (families) include ʻaumākua (ancestors) who are manō (Goldberg-Hiller and Silva 2011). Upon their human deaths, these ʻaumākua are, through ritual efforts on the part of the family and

Genocide, Eliminative Violence, and Extinction   185

the caretaker of a shark deity, transformed into the body of a specific shark with uniquely identifiable markings. This manō is then responsible for protecting members of the oʻhana from drowning, attacks by other sharks, or other marine-based threats. Puniwai (2020, 11) also shares records of human families caring for sharks as family members, as in the case of Kaʻehuikimanōopuʻuloa ("the little red shark who descends from Pearl Island"). His (human) parents, Hōlei and Kapukapu, fed him ʻawa (soup from the kava plant) and breast milk and blessed him with prayers before his journey to Kahiki (Tahiti). In return, the shark offered his parents an abundance of fish. In other moʻolelo, manō are gestated and birthed by human women and may have the capacity to turn into humans (Goldberg-Hiller and Silva 2011). In other words, manō and Kānaka embody a fluid form of co-constitution that does not sit easily within Eurocentric, colonially imposed ideas of the genealogy or proper relations shared between humans and nonhumans.

As Goldberg-Hiller and Silva (2011) show, this form of plurally embodied kinship—common in Kānaka modes of governance—is intensively policed by the settler state. These authors argue that mass killing of manō in the wake of Weaver's death can be understood as an attack on distinctly Kānaka forms of sovereignty—or, more accurately, as retaliation for a perceived attack on U.S. sovereignty by manō, who refused to conform to the rules of the invasive state. Within the Eurocentric framing deployed by the state, the shark slaughter was

> akin to the restoration of sovereignty after the attack on the body of the king. . . . The visceral fear [on the part of haole] of being dismembered by a shark is as much a human terror as it is the horrifying anathema of the sovereign state. (Goldberg-Hiller and Silva 2011, 433)

The attack on manō cannot be understood as purely instrumental: that is, the State of Hawaiʻi and haole citizens did not seek to eliminate sharks from the shores of Oʻahu primarily because they constituted a *resource* for Kānaka (although haole also seized control of traditional food, plants, land, and ocean access) or even because they posed a substantial threat to the lives of settlers. Instead, the direct target of this program of violence was a particular mode of more-than-human being, and its power to disrupt the forms of political order imposed by the settler colonial state. In short, manō embody an Indigenous, more-than-human form of sovereignty that undermines and challenges that of the invasive state. Understood in this way, systemic attacks on the bodies of manō were assaults on the particular forms of autonomy, sovereignty, and ungovernability (by external forces) of Kānaka and their nonhuman kin. In addition, the killing of sharks disrupted not only their biological reproduction with other sharks but also their unique forms of reproduction with/as part of Kānaka ʻohanas. In this sense, the attacks also sought to halt and prevent the future reproduction of a specific more-than-human life-form.

Importantly, systematic attacks on these more-than-human relations were and are not limited to killing; they also continue to be asserted through conservation practices that interfere with the relations through which Kānaka and manō reproduce each other. Indeed, the targeted killing of manō was bookended by bans on shark fishing (see Tester 1960; Goldberg-Hiller and Silva 2011) that interfered with the reciprocal relations of digestion through which some Kānaka maintained their relations with particular manō. Conservation policies implemented by the state since its accession to the United States have been instrumental in severing Kānaka relations with marine life-forms. Traditionally, Kānaka political orders ensured that all family groups had access to strips of land from the ocean up to the mountains, ensuring the availability of all food, water, fibers, and other materials needed for subsistence (Oliveira 2014; D. P. McGregor 2007). However, compounding the privatization and development of most ocean-front properties, recent conservation practices—implemented largely by relatively wealthy retired haole from the mainland United States— include the cordoning of beaches where endangered species such as monk seals and green sea turtles come to shore (Mooallem 2013). Similarly, the creation in 2006 of the Papahanaumokukuakea Marine National Monument around the leeward islands, in which hunting and fishing are restricted, was perceived by some Kānaka as a "massive aquatic landgrab" (Mooallem 2013) that interrupts their relations (including hunting and eating) with life-forms that have been designated for protection by the state. In response, there have been several reported killings of monk seals on the basis that they are valued by, and as symbols of, colonial conservation (Moallem 2013) and the forms of sovereignty that underpin it. From the perspectives discussed in this chapter, these killings could be understood as direct mirroring of the kinds of symbolic and ritual violence against particular life-forms as embodiments of sovereignty carried out by the invasive state against Kānaka-manō kinship.

Genocide, Eliminative Violence, and Extinction 187

Viewing historical and ongoing acts of eliminative violence against manō through this lens, it can be understood as genocide—not only against Kānaka as *human* groups but also against a particular way of being more-than-human or, specifically, of being Kānaka-and-manō. If the UNGC definition accounted for Kānaka knowledge, histories, and political-ethical principles and, accordingly, recognized manō as an integral part of Kānaka communities, then the deliberate attacks on them could be understood as genocide under *existing law*. In addition, accounting for Kānaka-manō relations makes it possible to understand the collective destruction—and in some cases the conservation—of manō as symbolic and ritual violence that targets conditions of (bio)plurality to make way for settler colonial sovereignty.

Buffalo Genocide

Within certain knowledge systems and legal-political orders, genocides may also be committed against *nonhuman peoples* or *nations*—that is, life-forms that hold formal status as persons, humans, or similar within the laws governing the worlds of which they are co-constituents. As "rights of nature" discourses gain ground in international politics, multiple categories of nonhuman beings—including rivers, plants, cetaceans, forests, or "nature" in itself—have recently been recognized as persons under national (that is, Westphalian state) law.[19] In some political-legal orders, nonhuman peoples have been continually recognized as such for centuries or even millennia. This argument is articulated powerfully in Nêhiyaw scholar Tasha Hubbard's (2014) discussion of the attempted elimination of buffalo from the Great Plains region by the nascent Canadian and U.S. governments in the nineteenth century (and in less explicit ways since; for instance, as a result of the construction of roads or mining operations). Ranging from the northern part of what is currently called Saskatchewan to Mexico and numbering between thirty and sixty million in the late nineteenth century, this unique life-form was reduced to a handful of herds comprising just a few hundred animals through militarized campaigns of killing. According to Hubbard, those mass killings were integral, but *not reducible,* to concurrent genocides of Indigenous peoples of the plains. From her perspective, "the slaughter of the buffalo constitutes an act of genocide" (Hubbard 2014, 293) *in itself.* More specifically, she avers, "Euro-Western governments and their representatives undertook *buffalo genocide* in order to consolidate political power in the Great Plains" (295, emphasis mine).

188   Genocide, Eliminative Violence, and Extinction

In making this argument, Hubbard adheres closely to the existing UNGC definition, but with a crucial distinction: one of the peoples in question is not human but rather the buffalo nation. Within a Nêhiyaw epistemological framework, Hubbard (2014, 294) explains, "being a 'people' is not a domain exclusive to humans." As such, she reasons, the concept of "genos" extends beyond human groups "to include other-than-human animals" (294). Indeed, for many Indigenous peoples of the plains, the buffalo are considered to be First People, ancestors, older siblings, and protectors. In fact, Hubbard (2014, 291) interprets the deaths of tens of millions of buffalo at the hands of invaders as a protective act of self-sacrifice made by the buffalo "on the front line in the genocidal war against Indigenous peoples." What's more, Hubbard shows that the strategies and techniques of destruction used against the buffalo nation mirror those described in the UNGC. First, these mass killings were undertaken with the clear and deliberate intention to destroy an entire life-form. She further argues that the U.S. government created a public discourse that framed buffalo as obstacles to its progress and incentivized their wholesale destruction. Ostensibly, buffalo were hunted for their hides, which were used to produce belts and other elements of military uniforms, but the scale of the killing and the inefficient use of hides reveal an eliminative impulse.

Drawing on work by David Smits, Hubbard contends that the extermination of the buffalo nation was an unofficial policy of the U.S. Army starting from the middle of the nineteenth century and part of its notoriously brutal so-called Indian Wars—a series of military campaigns designed to eliminate and/or displace the Indigenous peoples of the continent.[20] For example, General Phillip Sheridan encouraged troops to "kill every buffalo you can!" on the basis that "every buffalo dead is an Indian [sic] gone" (quoted in Hubbard 2014, 296). Similarly, arguing against a proposed bill to protect buffalo in the Texas legislature in 1875, Sheridan argued that the hunting of buffalo had

> done in the last two years and will do more in the next year to settle the vexed Indian question than the regular army has done in the last thirty years. . . . For the sake of a lasting peace, let them kill, skin and sell until the buffaloes are exterminated. (quoted in Hubbard 2014, 297)

These statements reflect several of the dynamics of eliminative violence already discussed in this chapter, including the destruction of life-forms

Genocide, Eliminative Violence, and Extinction   189

to starve and/or impoverish Indigenous communities, and the elision of human communities with (despised) nonhuman life-forms. Indeed, General George Armstrong Custer, infamous for his brutal killing of Indigenous peoples during the "Indian Wars," was known to have used buffalo as target practice to train new recruits who were frustrated that they had not (yet) been authorized to shoot Indigenous people (Hubbard 2014). These statements also mirror the symbolic, ritualistic violence used to destroy forms of governance, sovereignty, and resistance made possible by (bio)plural relations, as in the case of the mass killing of manō. I do not mean to suggest that state or private actors involved in these mass killings had a deep or nuanced understanding of co-constitutive relations between buffalo and Plains peoples. However, they were clearly aware that in killing one group, they were undermining not only the material but also the spiritual, social, and political foundations of the other.

In this case, there was also evidence of attempts to destroy the buffalo as a distinct collective with its own social structures. This included attempts to frustrate the interaction between herds, and the manipulation of their social, kinship, and communicative dynamics, ostensibly to expedite killings. For example, hunters would surround the waterways on which the buffalo relied or force multiple herds together so that they would trample each other, creating conditions in which "instead of living cooperatively in their herd society, the buffalo were tortured prior to their death" (Hubbard 2014, 300). In other cases, hunters would use the emotional connections between members of a buffalo family to kill entire herds. According to Hubbard's traditional teachers, buffalo grieve for their dead and stay with deceased family members, attempting to revive them by issuing sounds of grief. White hunters exploited buffalo mourning traditions by shooting down one animal so that the body would draw the others, taking the opportunity to more efficiently massacre the entire herd (Hubbard 2014). In some cases, the goal of killing buffalo was to clear them from land on which their presence gave Indigenous people the right to hunt. In addition, it helped create space for the importation of the millions of cattle used to construct the settler polity (see chapter 4), whose continuing presence impedes the traditional range of the buffalo nation. Further, the U.S. military and private actors disrupted the reproduction—in biological and social terms of the buffalo nation—by removing calves from their herds. Hubbard (2014) cites a report detailing how cavalry troops rounded up one hundred buffalo calves, feeding them inadequately and often with

190 Genocide, Eliminative Violence, and Extinction

inappropriate foods so that few of them survived for a week. Other calves were kept as pets, curiosities, or, in the case of very young infants, simply left to starve to death beside the bodies of their deceased mothers. At the same time, the army engaged in efforts to fragment and physically separate herds, reducing their viability and the diversity of their gene pool by preventing meetings between families and reducing their populations. According to Hubbard (2014, 299), these acts "broke down the family relationships of the buffalo" and contributed to the destruction of its unique social and political order.

Despite the systematic, violent nature of this genocide and the clear attempts of a particular group of people to orchestrate and carry it out, Hubbard (2014) points out that the decimation of the buffalo nation—and of many of its Indigenous kin—are often described, and naturalized, as "extinction." As discussed throughout this book, this term often carries the connotation of the unintended consequences of desirable activities. Hubbard highlights the danger of this lexical move: it hides the role of genocidal violence in driving the systematic destruction of (bio)plurality and of the unique life-forms and worlds it nourishes. In addition, as discussed in chapter 1, mainstream accounts of extinction stress its irreversibility, an assumption that plays into genocidal narratives of elimination (see chapter 7). Indeed, the survivance and regeneration of peoples is sometimes perversely used as evidence to deny that genocide and/or genocidal acts took place (Fontaine 2014, ix). Thankfully, most modern genocides, including that of the buffalo, did not fully achieve their aims, and therefore return is possible—and an important strategy of political, social, and spiritual resurgence. Hubbard (2014, 302–3) holds open that possibility, arguing that, even in their reduced numbers,

> the buffalo remains with us. . . . Their bodies were destroyed; their spirits were not. Our stories, still told and still understood, tell us that the buffalo will return one day.

Hubbard's statement honors the survivors of buffalo genocide and their human kin resurging against similar acts of violence but also their ability to generate open-ended futures—a possibility denied by discourses of extinction. As I argue in chapter 7, this power and labor of revenance is among the most profound forces for dismantling the structures that systematically destroy (bio)plurality.

SO, IS EXTINCTION GENOCIDE?

The examples discussed in the preceding sections offer important insights into the relationships between extinction and genocide. First, they confirm that there are important conceptual and practical convergences between genocides against humans and those targeted on nonhumans and/or more-than-human communities. In each of these cases, the existing international legal definition of genocide could be applied without modification to some nonhuman groups—*if* the legal, political, and ethical systems of the relevant worlds were taken into account. In the first two examples, this would involve recognizing the unique forms of co-constitution with particular nonhumans that define Inuit and Kānaka communities, respectively. In the third, it would require recognizing the status of buffalo as a people under Nêhiyaw law. This analysis suggests that, instead of relying exclusively on Eurocentric international legal principles and state-based law, it is crucial to consider the legal-political frameworks that are relevant to the place, peoples, kinship structures, and/or worlds in which the harms take place. Doing so can offer a much more accurate account of the nature and scope of the harms caused by eliminative violence as they are experienced in and by singular worlds (see Woolford 2009). This strategy also enables responses to eliminative violence that include but are *not limited to* applying the legal framework of genocide, without forcing affected communities to translate their experiences and grievances into Eurocentric, colonial, imperial, and/or state-based frameworks.

At the same time, framing these forms of violence in terms of the relevant legal-political orders provides insight into how they might be more effectively recognized, prevented, and redressed in ways that are meaningful within the relevant world and can best support its restoration. For instance, possible responses to the harms discussed in this chapter could include direct efforts to promote the flourishing of Qimmit, manō, and buffalo, *and* of their relations with Inuit, Kānaka, and Nêhiyaw (among other) communities. Such responses might also involve relevant ceremonies, protocols, and traditions (ancient and/or emerging) to recognize, witness, and mourn the violence in question. Potentially, these practices could form part of any justice processes undertaken by states or other actors, if they were desired by the community in question. The legal-political orders of the worlds most directly affected by eliminative violence may also offer models for consequences to be applied to aggressors, strategies

192   Genocide, Eliminative Violence, and Extinction

for restitution, or justice processes that satisfy not only international or state laws but also laws between life-forms (where applicable). This approach would make it possible for agents of eliminative violence to be held accountable by, within, and in terms of the worlds they have harmed, and it might also contribute to the restoration of ecopolitical (not only human) relationships (see this book's Introduction).

From this perspective, it is vital to create frameworks of response to eliminative violence that are as (bio)plural as the worlds they affect. However, the lesson here is *not* that any particular legal-political system or concept should be alienated from its world, repackaged as universal, and projected onto other worlds. Instead, I am arguing that if and when crimes of genocide against non- and more-than-human groups are prosecuted by international bodies, they should be framed in terms of definitions and/or knowledge related to "people," "genos," and other key terms relevant to directly affected worlds. Nor should the political-legal systems of directly affected worlds simply be instrumentalized to supplement or augment Eurocentric legal frameworks.[21] At the same time, it should not be assumed that any and every legal-political instrument or remedy can be applied across all Indigenous groups, regardless of its source; this is another facet of colonial logics that erases the distinctness of peoples and worlds. However, there may be value in efforts to strengthen and proliferate direct connections between communities affected by similar forms of eliminative violence against non- and more-than-human communities. This could enable the sharing of knowledge, experience, and resources, and perhaps the co-development of strategies for holding aggressors accountable, dismantling global structures of eliminative violence, and preventing future occurrences. Such an approach may be particularly helpful in situations where the same actors—such as multinational mining companies (see chapter 3)—engage in similar forms of violence across multiple worlds on a global scale.

Certain forms of eliminative violence against non- and more-than-human groups may qualify as genocide (and could potentially be prosecuted as such), and the frameworks surrounding genocide offer important insights into the nature of this kind of violence. However, genocide and extinction should not be elided, conceptually or descriptively, for another reason: the concept of genocide does not comprehensively address the systematic destruction of (bio)plurality. It may be mobilized to redress particular concentrations of violence in which the destruction of (bio)plural relations are intense and targeted. It is also important to recognize that many of the

Genocide, Eliminative Violence, and Extinction

dynamics and forces that erode (bio)plurality—including the breaking of social relations, the instrumentalization of bodies, sexual violence, eugenics, and racism—are key weapons of genocide. However, not all instances of the destruction of (bio)plurality are eliminative in nature. For instance, as discussed in chapters 2, 3, and 4, some forms of violence that target (bio)plurality work to sustain life-forms and/or particular relational models in order to exploit and derive value from them. In addition, many forms of violence that destroy (bio)plurality target the *conditions* and underlying *relations of cohabitation* that sustain worlds, rather than particular life-forms and/or non- or more-than-human peoples. Further, in each of the cases discussed here, destructive acts were targeted against a particular group by an identifiable actor. This is not the case for many of the forces, structures, and processes that break down (bio)plurality on a global scale (as proponents of the law of ecocide point out). As discussed in the first section of this chapter, such harms could potentially be considered genocide if they produced genocidal outcomes. However, ecological harms can be immense and grave without producing genocidal outcomes, and so defining extinction as a subcategory of genocide would be inaccurate.

It is for these reasons that theorists should be careful in using the terms "genocide" and "extinction" in metaphorical ways to describe each other. Doing so without precision can undermine the legal, ethical, and political meaning and impact of either or both frameworks. Nor is it necessary or useful to create new frameworks, such as ecocide, that continue to inscribe Euro- and state-centric assumptions over already existing legal-political orders. Instead, I have argued for a careful, nuanced, and world-specific engagement between the two concepts, and across multiple different legal-political systems, that can reflect the complexities of eliminative violence. At the same time, other efforts are required to address the destruction of (bio)plurality more generally. This undertaking demands large-scale social, political, cultural, economic, and other transformations, including collective (re)worlding and collective movements toward purposefully (bio)plural relations. One of the major obstacles to this latter goal is the framing of extinction—and conservation—in nihilistic and apocalyptic terms, to which I turn in the next chapter.

POSTSCRIPT

Across the city, flying foxes are pushed from site to site, hooked and tangled, speared, bitten, and crushed.[22] But they also reclaim these

FIGURE 1. Lin Onus, *Fruit Bats*, 1991.

structures as perches and nests, and as hunting-, breeding-, and playgrounds. They find unexpected pools of shade and shelter under overpasses, chattering and throwing shreds of stone fruit across close-clipped lawns. And here, in an immaculate tract of polished concrete and white walls, the work of Yorta Yorta artist Lin Onus witnesses this resistance. Onus's fiberglass flying foxes, each one unique, are shaped and painted with the cross-hatching he was authorized to use by his Murrungun-Djinang mentors.

The bats hang neatly from the geometric filaments of a Hills Hoist Clothes line (a symbol of white settler Australian life). Below them, circular, intricately painted droppings cement the bats' presence, spreading their futures across the smooth field of suburban cleanliness. This is the shit that has so often incited settlers' disgust, hatred, and fear of rampant disease. But it also carries the seeds that shift and regenerate entire Eucalypt future forests on which myriad life-forms

Genocide, Eliminative Violence, and Extinction

and worlds depend. These bats, like their furry kin outside, are shitting all over the structures designed to destroy them, gorgeously, with purpose, with intent, with meaning and right. In a stroke of ironic genius, Onus's bats have found themselves centered in the permanent collection of one of the most exclusive art galleries in the country. Certainly, this is an example of the dominant culture letting itself be seen to support Aboriginal and Torres Strait Islander art, and benefiting from it. But at the end of the day, the bats, and their deeply reviled droppings, are there on the polished concrete floor and stark lighting, at the center of things, holding on tight. They're not going anywhere.

6 Apocalyptic Conservation

From "Human Extinction" to "Half-Earth"

> What happens here on Earth, in this century, could conceivably make the difference between a near eternity filled with ever more complex and subtle forms of life and one filled with nothing but base matter.
>
> —MARTIN REES, *Our Final Hour*

> We can be the founders of a global movement that changed our relationship with the planet, that saw us secure a future for all life on Earth, including our own. Or we can be the generation that . . . let Earth slip away.
>
> —MARCO LAMBERTINI, "A New Global Deal for Nature and People Urgently Needed"

According to the two stories / theories quoted here, humanity is at an unprecedented crossroads. Making the right choices could secure a vibrant future in which (at least some) life-forms could survive and flourish. Meanwhile, the wrong choices could lead to the end of all life on earth. The first epigraph is drawn from Martin Rees, one of the key thinkers in the field of "existential risks" or "global catastrophic risks." Rees's work focuses on threats that are relatively low-probability but massive in their potential impact—in particular, the extinction of humans.[1] Meanwhile, the second epigraph is from one of the flagship publications of mainstream global conservation: the 2018 WWF *Living Planet Report* (*LPR*) (Grooten and Almond 2018). In this chapter, I show how these two very different discourses are converging into a new narrative of *apocalyptic conservation*. Within this narrative, conservation is refigured as a key weapon in the fight to save humanity from existential risk. While the choice offered by these apocalyptic conservation discourses may seem obvious, I argue that the pathways they offer toward "secur[ing] a future for all life" are rooted in oppressive and violent logics—including those that drive the systematic destruction of (bio)plurality. Among these logics is a strain of hyperhumanism that seeks, at all costs, to protect and produce (see chapter 2) currently dominant norms of humanity. It is sharpened by fears among *dominant* groups that they may soon face the same kinds of existential threats that they have historically offloaded onto marginalized communities. In this context, some of the most powerful, privileged, and protected people on the planet are expressing abject horror and outrage at the possibility of futures that do not include, let alone center, them.

So who and what, exactly, are dominant actors anxious to secure and conserve? Although discourses on human extinction and global conservation claim to be concerned with the future of humans in general, a closer look shows that they work to protect and enhance *certain* forms of human life at all costs, while consigning others to destruction. As this chapter argues, discourses of apocalyptic conservation are deeply invested in whiteness, Eurocentrism, (hyper)ableism, Western gender binaries and hierarchies, capitalism, colonization, and genocide. They align with, sustain, and deepen several of the forms of systemic violence discussed in the previous chapters and, as such, help accelerate the systematic destruction of (bio)plurality. Apocalyptic conservation also calls for the redoubling of investments in existing power structures, including the accumulation of private property and the policing of BIPOC, disabled, gendered, queer, and/or nonhuman bodies. Furthermore, many of the practices promoted in this discourse—including surveillance, racialized forms of population control, and even the purging of half of the earth's surface of human activity—work to suppress, oppress, and preclude modes of (bio)pluralization that might fuel global ecopolitical transformation. Addressing these issues, this chapter offers a brief overview of mainstream discourses on existential risk and human extinction. Then, it shows how these discourses are shaping mainstream conservation priorities, logics, practices, narratives, and imperatives—and the potentially devastating consequences for (bio)plurality.

HUMAN EXTINCTION

When best-selling science journalist Alan Weisman (2008) imagines a climate-altered, extinction-wracked, eerily empty *World without Us*, who is the "us" he has in mind? Weisman describes the disappearance of rainforest ecosystems and the halting of bird migrations, viral pandemics, and many other catastrophes, but the centerpiece of his analysis is the collapse of modern Western(ized) cities and infrastructure. Like many mainstream discourses on human extinction, Weisman's declared subject is humanity, people, or the planet, but in fact his anxiety centers on the potential collapse of Western/northern ways of life, centers of power, and the structural conditions that sustain them. Given his positionality and the epistemic systems in which Weisman is enmeshed, this is perhaps unsurprising. As Aadita Chaudhury and I have argued (Mitchell and Chaudhury 2020), most influential contributors to discourses of human extinction are rooted in Euro-American and/or settler colonial and/or imperial societies, and the vast majority of their interlocutors are white and male. Even much of the research that critically engages with apocalyptic discourses, including my own earlier work (see, for instance, Mitchell 2017b), draws primarily on white authors and sources. Beyond concerns with representation, the composition of these epistemic ecosystems means that its most influential thinkers are invested in (see Harris 1993) and benefit from existing global structures based on whiteness, colonization, genocide, abled privilege, wealth, and other forms of privilege rooted in oppression. This feature not only reduces the rigor of discourses on human extinction by excluding myriad other sources and forms of knowledge, lived experience, and practices of imagination; it also supports the *preservation* of dominant systems (whether or not this is the *explicit* intention of authors).[2]

These tendencies are reflected in the parameters, central questions, and assumptions of mainstream discourses on human extinction. For instance, in these narratives, the boundaries of Western and Eurocentric thought—in particular, the natural sciences and knowledge related to politics and/or policy—are frequently elided with the limits of *human* thought. For example, unmarked Canadian scholar Thomas Homer-Dixon (2007) contends that "we" (meaning humans) are inept at addressing "slow-creep" problems, helpless without access to (contemporary Western) technology, and limited to utilitarian forms of reasoning. Meanwhile, unmarked American journalist David Wallace-Wells (2019) argues that "we" (again, referring to "humans" in general) assume that the planet is "okay" because we collectively lack longitudinal data about the earth beyond the scope of "mythology and theology." Both arguments ignore the multigenerational processes of systematic observation and theorization of ecological change carried out in many BIPOC knowledge systems and transmitted in various forms—from oral histories to land-based practices—over hundreds or even thousands of years (see Introduction and chapters 1, 2, and 3). And indeed, many of these communities face ongoing violent oppression from states and corporate actors for asserting and providing ample evidence that the planet is *not* okay. At the same time, authors interested in human extinction tend to enshrine white, cishet male, (hyper)abled figures of colonial-capitalist dominance as heroes—that is, as saviors, survivors, rebuilders of worlds.[3] For example, Homer-Dixon (2007) idealizes oil workers on the Canadian prairies (drawing on his own brief employment in that industry). In other cases, writers on human extinction laud oppressive systems and structures as blueprints for the future survival of humans. For instance, science writer Annalee Newitz (2013) chooses the notoriously racist settler colonial society of Saskatchewan as a model for future postapocalyptic communities based on her perception that its people embody "frontier" attitudes and aptitudes. This statement implies that the values, physical attributes and skills, relational norms, and ways of thinking that enabled the genocidal colonization of the Great Plains (see chapter 5) ought to shape survival strategies and future political and social-political orders. Similarly, Wallace-Wells points to unmarked American agronomist Norman Borlaug as a model of future-oriented thinking. Borlaug's so-called Green Revolution in the 1950s and 1960s, which Wallace-Wells (2019, 58) calls "almost too-perfect," caused massive ecological collapse, structural suffering, impoverishment, and political oppression across the Global South—the effects of which continue to cascade at the time of writing.[4]

In addition, the existential privilege (see chapter 1) evinced by many thinkers in this field is reflected in their surprise, discomfort, or shock at the idea that they, too, may have to face threats to their worlds. For instance, unmarked American scientists Anthony Barnosky and Liz Hadley (2016, emphasis mine) state, "If you are *anything like we are,* you probably think of pollution as somebody else's problem. After all, you probably don't live near a tannery, mine, dump or any other source of pollution."[5] As chapter 3 shows, BIPOC, disabled, and poor people (not to mention other life-forms) *are,* in fact, disproportionately exposed to these forms of pollution as a result of environmental racism and ableism, colonialism, and economic marginalization (see chapter 3). Based on this quote, these communities are clearly not the intended readers of Barnosky and Hadley's book—that is, they are not the subjects to whom these authors call as agents of change and future leadership.

At the same time, Barnosky and Hadley overemphasize threats to white people, effectively adopting the logics of "all lives matter" or "color-blindness" by erasing vastly unequal distributions of harm and threat.[6] For instance, in narrating the ecological and social devastation observed during their international travels for scientific research and leisure, Barnosky and Hadley (2016, emphasis mine) seem shocked and sobered to realize that "no one was escaping the impacts . . . *including us.*" This statement reflects the degree to which loss of existential privilege and safety is unexpected and jarring for the authors and their imagined audience. However, it also shifts the narrative to *center* people like the couple, or those with whom they share similar life circumstances. For instance, they draw equivalencies between the temporary flooding of the New York subway system in 2012 and a flood in Pakistan that displaced twenty million people and killed two thousand. Similarly, Wallace-Wells (2019) compares the effects of mudslides in suburban California to the genocidal "camps" into which Rohingya refugees have been forced, and the potential submersion of entire countries in the Global South to that of the White House or Facebook HQ. In the same vein, although they recognize that the youngest girls affected by endocrine disruption in the United States are Black and Latinx/e, Barnosky and Hadley (2016, emphasis mine) are at pains to point out that "the most dramatic *increase* is in Caucasian girls." In this analysis, ableist fears of disability, used as vague metaphors for unwanted futures (see Kafer 2013), merge with racialized assumptions about who is *expected* to absorb such changes and for whom this would be a jolting deviation from the norm. They also converge with cultural panics about perceived increases in disability among communities previously assumed to be immune to and/or relatively protected from it (e.g., unfounded fears about "autism epidemics" affecting white children). In such contexts, the use of relative statistics such as ratios and comparisons across subject groups make the perceived threat *appear* to be advancing more rapidly "toward" populations who are least affected and/or most structurally privileged, while increasing fear of groups most affected and marginalized (see A. McGuire 2016; Mitchell 2022).

The *explicit* intention of these authors is to spur their readers to take action to stop ecological crises. Yet the unexamined assumptions and implicit biases permeating their work have the effect of significantly overemphasizing threats to white, nondisabled, middle- or upper-class, Global North–dwelling people versus racialized, colonized, disabled, poor, and Global

South–dwelling people. They also assume and privilege the survival of the former group, while framing harms to the latter group as expected and unremarkable. At the same time, by appealing to "a universal human frailty" (Gergan, Smith, and Vasudevan 2020, 91), many authors writing about human extinction avoid questions of differential culpability and responsibility between these groups. For instance, when Newitz (2013, 13) argues that "assigning blame [for ecological harm] is less important than figuring out how to . . . survive," she sidelines questions of responsibility that are crucial to transforming and transcending existing structures of violence. Perhaps most dangerously, by placing disproportionate focus on harms to the most privileged and protected groups, these discourses invert the actual distribution of threat. This, in turn, can frame policy problems and decisions in ways that favor the most privileged while continuing to marginalize—and/or demonize—those most affected.

Indeed, emerging discourses of human extinction fixate on the desire to strengthen, protect, and ensure the survival of *dominant norms* of humanity at all costs. As unmarked Australian theorist Claire Colebrook (2014, 142, 203) puts it:

> humanity has been fabricated as the proper ground of all life—so much so that threats to all life on Earth are being dealt with today by focusing on how man may adapt, mitigate and survive. . . . Nothing is more valuable or definitive of value than human life's capacity to maintain and define itself.

As a result, she claims, responses to world-disrupting events and forces are dedicated to the conservative process of shoring up existing structures and ways of life instead of transforming them or transcending their oppressive elements and structures (see also Braidotti 2013). Wallace-Wells (2019, emphasis mine) sums up this attitude neatly in stating that "the world could lose much of what we think of as nature, so far as I cared, so long as *we could go on living as we have* in the world left behind." In other words, he appears to be willing to accept the wholesale destruction of most worlds other than his own (glossed here as "nature") as long as he has continued access to the conditions in which he is invested, and from which he disproportionately benefits.

Within this hyperhumanist logic, subjects who align with dominant norms of humanity are invested with the power to determine the future of earth, including the right to make decisions about who gets to survive and in which ways. For instance, these discourses assign current generations of adults—that is, younger Boomers, Gen X, and the oldest millennials—immense power and authority to determine the course of the future for all humans and other life-forms. Indeed, Wallace-Wells (2019) argues that climate change has effectively "compressed the entire story of human civilization" into just three generations: his parents' (the destroyers of the planet), his own (the last generation who might save it), and his daughter's (who will witness the "greatest story ever told" as their parents battle for her generation's future). Note that Wallace-Wells casts his generation in the role of "humanity" from the story/theory discussed in the book's introduction: the beleaguered, imperfect hero fighting for collective survival against an indifferent or hostile universe. This act of temporal compression erases the agency and entitlement of older (including ancestral), younger, and far-future generations—not to mention beings other than humans—to play a role in shaping earth's possible futures. In so doing, it marks the acts of currently powerful people as historical events and breaks in time (see chapter 1). This, in turn, erases the continuity between their actions and existing structures and processes of power, uncritically granting them sovereignty over all possible futures.

Another facet of this form of hyperhumanism is anxiety over the loss of the perceived potential for human "improvement." This is often framed in terms of "enhancements" to human bodies and cognition through technologies such as artificial intelligence, genetic engineering, and nanotechnology. A set of distinct but deeply linked and partially overlapping theories, which unmarked American philosopher Émile Torres calls TESCREAL, have emerged largely among philosophers and students at the Universities of Oxford and Cambridge.[7] They have grown to influence major actors in Silicon Valley, statespeople and policymakers, international organizations (such as the UN), and popular discourses. Although distinct, the theories in the "TESCREAL bundle" significantly overlap (Torres 2023), presenting a comprehensive set of priorities for the future of humans. These include efforts to "enhance" the biological, genetic, cognitive, and other aspects of human bodies (often rooted in ableist norms of capability, intelligence, health, and so on); fuse human bodies with specific technologies; increase the longevity of humans and/or "cure death"; maximize the impact of philanthropic interventions (by comparing elements such as cost of living and Disability Adjusted Life Years, or DALYs); and more.[8] TESCREAL thinkers, activists, and donors seek to extend their ideal of human life (rooted in rationalist and often utilitarian forms of ethics) across the entire human species and into deep time. Aside from the many other ethical issues they raise, these approaches discount all other currently existing and possible future modes of human (co)existence in favor of realizing the worlds they desire. Indeed, some members of TESCREAL-type movements and related discourses have explicitly stated that they would accept enormous levels of harm and destruction to see their visions realized. For instance, one of the most influential thinkers in the transhumanist and existential risk communities, unmarked Swedish-British philosopher Nick Bostrom (2013, 18), has famously stated that the value of potential future forms of artificial intelligence is so high that it would be ethically defensible to allow a billion human deaths in the present in order to ensure its future realization. Meanwhile, many effective altruists (EAs) argue that charitable donations are better focused on poorer countries, where they have greater economic value (although the conditions of global economic inequality or the often imperialistic dynamics of global altruism are rarely analyzed or critiqued in EA discourses). However, prominent longtermist Nick Beckstead (2013) contends that saving lives in "poor countries" is less likely to bring about a transhumanist future than investing the same resources and effort in rich countries. Some of Beckstead's colleagues even suggest that the further concentration of wealth among the rich, or the transfer of wealth from the poor to the rich, would be more effective in reaching desired human futures (Torres 2021).[9]

Crucially, longtermism, transhumanism, and many other currents of TESCREAL thought embrace eugenicist values, including the artificial selection of "desirable" genetic traits such as "intelligence" and/or "cognitive ability" (based on neurotypical norms). In so doing, they echo and massively amplify existing global discourses of ableism—for instance, the UN's characterization of developmental, neurological, and intellectual disabilities as a threat to "sustainable development" and, possibly, future human flourishing (see Mitchell 2022). Such narratives discount all modes of intelligence, sentience, and ways of knowing that do not fit with existing norms of "humanity," and they contribute to deep-seated efforts to eliminate, suppress, sequester, and demonize diverging bodyminds (A. McGuire 2016; Clare 2017; Mitchell 2022). Many liberal and/or humanist commentators on human extinction also promote eugenicist and/or geographically determinist narratives of this kind. For instance, Wallace-Wells (2019) cites statistics claiming that the gestation of babies in high temperatures and rainy weather in India and Taiwan have produced children of "shorter stature" who perform less well at school and achieve "lower earnings" as adults. He also warns that rises in global temperature will reduce the "cognitive capacity" of people in the North by pushing them beyond the "optimal" mean of 13°C (55.4°F)— a temperature above which most of earth's human population lives.[10] His argument uncritically presents differences in neurocognitive profile, body, and genetic traits as dystopic. It also reduces (racialized) bodies in which these kinds of difference are expressed to mere warning signs intended to spur the world's most privileged and/or abled people to protect themselves against possible future disability (Kafer 2013; Fritsch 2017).

In other cases, discourses on human extinction frame periods of intense threat as opportunities for humanity to rid itself of what are framed as flaws or weaknesses. For example, many TESCREAL-related discourses draw on thought experiments and speculation regarding the "re-evolution" of humans after a near-extinction event. In this scenario, catastrophic events and subsequent efforts to regenerate the species spark a process of genetic "honing" (see Leslie 1996). Presumably, this would occur because those who were too "flawed," "weak," or structurally disadvantaged to weather the catastrophic event(s) perished or could not reproduce in its aftermath. In a variation on this narrative, unmarked American economist Robin Hanson (2008) calculates that if one hundred humans survived a global catastrophic disaster, they could strategically move through the stages of human development, returning to the so-called hunter-gatherer stage within just twenty thousand years and then progressing well beyond current conditions at an expedited pace. Within these imaginaries, the large-scale destruction of existing worlds is framed as an opportunity for the reengineering of a "better" human species.

Other scholars of human extinction focus less on biological reproduction and more on the possibilities for preserving and/or extending dominant social, political, and economic orders. For instance, unmarked Canadian scholar Elizabeth Finneron-Burns (2017, 37, emphasis mine) notes that some scholars argue that human extinction ought to be prevented lest what they regard (and enshrines) as "rational life," "knowledge," and "civilization" is *prevented from progressing.*" Taking this logic further, Homer-Dixon (2007) frames global collapse as an opportunity for a form of large-scale social, political, and economic renewal that he calls "catagenesis." He insists that

> Western civilization is not a lost cause. . . . Using *reason and science* to guide decisions, paired with extraordinary leadership and exceptional goodwill, *human society* can progress to higher and higher levels of well-being and development. . . . But that requires resisting the very natural urge . . . to become less cooperative, less generous and less open to reason. (quoted in Nuwer 2017, emphasis mine)

According to Homer-Dixon's narrative, *Western* civilization—tellingly elided with "human society"—can salvage and reclaim the future using several of its trademark features, including "reason," "leadership," "goodwill," and "development," to overcome its more base "urge[s]." Actively developing minds, bodies, and social orders that embody and promote these values, Homer-Dixon (2007, 109–10, emphasis mine) claims, will make it possible to "turn breakdown to *our* advantage." From this perspective, *near*-extinction scenarios offer opportunities for "improving" human society through a kind of trial by fire—in which countless people and other life-forms would necessarily suffer, perish, or be eliminated.

Indeed, although it may not be the intention of all their proponents, many TESCREAL-related discourses involve or rely on eliminative imaginaries (see chapter 5). That is, while they may not directly call for genocides or other explicit attempts to destroy communities, life-forms, or worlds, the futures they desire are nonetheless *contingent upon* and / or *accept* the destruction of other worlds, ways of being, and the conditions of (bio)plurality. For instance, many discourses on human extinction evoke troubling narratives of purification in which future humanity emerges from its existential trial cleansed of imperfections and ready to fully realize its potential. For instance, in his seminal book on "human extinction," unmarked Canadian philosopher John Leslie (1996, 137) states that

> misery and death for billions [caused by an ecological crisis] would be immensely tragic, but might be followed by slow recovering and then a glittering future for a human race which had learned its lesson.

Considering global demographics and structural inequalities, it is clear that the "billions" expected to suffer or die in these scenarios are disproportionately likely to be BIPOC, poor, disabled, and otherwise marginalized people (not even speaking of other life-forms). And indeed, authors working in the human extinction genre offer predictions about which countries, regions, and demographic groups are mostly likely to be destroyed. For instance, Homer-Dixon (2007, 110–11) claims that Western capitalist societies proved "most adaptive" to the tumult of the twentieth century, and societies in sub-Saharan Africa, Asia, and Latin America less so, while Haiti and Somalia "completely succumbed." For these reasons, he implies that it is obvious that the former countries are better placed to survive future ecopolitical shocks. Similarly, unmarked American historians Naomi Oreskes and Erik Conway (2014, 33, emphasis mine) imagine communities in the "northern inland regions of Europe, Asia and North America, and high-altitude parts of Latin America" as being able to "regroup and rebuild" while "the human populations of Australia and Africa, *of course,* were [will be] wiped out." Again, these comments are most likely *intended* to highlight the disproportionate threat to specific communities. Nonetheless, they reflect the ease with which the total elimination of marginalized peoples and worlds can be imagined as a matter "of course"—while the destruction of the currently dominant norm of "humanity" continues to be framed as intolerable or even unthinkable (Colebrook 2014; Mitchell 2017b).

Discourses on human extinction also express concern with *reversals* of what they perceive as human "progress." In particular, currently privileged groups worry about being forced to inhabit the ecological, social, political, and economic conditions that they have long imposed on others (see Fishel and Wilcox 2017) and considered to be part of *their* past histories. In many cases, this anxiety is expressed in calls to defend, bolster, or protect the ways of life associated with privileged and/or dominant groups. For example, Oreskes and Conway (2014, 78, emphasis mine) frame their best-selling book *The Collapse of Western Civilization* as "a call to protect the *American way of life* before it's too late." Similarly, Weisman (2013, 34) worries about the loss of a "European lifestyle" (available, of course, only to a minority, even in the wealthiest countries). Meanwhile, Wallace-Wells (2019, emphasis mine) announces that the rapidly closing window for "everything *we* know as history, value and progress, and study as politics" is contained by the Holocene epoch (which several continuously existing Indigenous societies predate).[11] Reflecting the preoccupation of Eurocentric civilizing discourses with public order, he cites a study (Burke, Hsiang, and Miguel 2015) that claims that rises in mean temperature will result in increased conflict and violent crime in northern countries, including police shootings. This latter argument sidesteps the role of structural racism, ableism, and gendered violence in Northern police cultures (see Alexiou 2020), attributing police violence to *victims'* physiological responses to heat (another example of the logic of DARVO; see chapters 3 and 4). Similarly, upon witnessing a knife fight in the mountains of Nepal, Hadley (Barnosky and Hadley 2016) asks whether she is seeing the past or the future. Her association of contemporary Global South communities with violent, unruly pasts *and* potential reversionary futures reveals the civilizational impulse integral to many human extinction narratives.

Such arguments are rooted in a teleological, stadial view of history that places modern, Western societies at the pinnacle of social-political development. In some cases, this assumption is extended (in a gross misrepresentation of Darwinian thought) to the evolution of humans. Hanson (2008), for instance, sets out four stages in the development of humanity, starting with the animals with enlarged brains, to hunter-gatherers, then to agricultural societies and finally technology-driven industrial models. This account echoes a twentieth-century scientific paradigm claiming that human nature and liberal values emerged from the transcendence of hunter-gatherer brains and social structures (Milam 2018). Similarly, Homer-Dixon (2007, 80, 55, 65, 255, emphasis mine) notes that without the emergence of modern petro-capitalism, *"we* would still be hunter-gatherers, surviving on grubs, roots and local game," and that "returning" to this state would grind "engineering marvels, political institutions and *our* culture and great art . . . into dust." He and others working in the field (Oreskes and Conway 2014; Barnosky and Hadley 2016) worry that this perceived reversion would mark the destruction of liberal democracy and the rise of authoritarian regimes. These statements dismiss marginalized forms of legal and political order—including consensus-based and multi-life-form democratic orders (see the book's Introduction)—as pre- or antidemocratic, potentially authoritarian, and pre- or not fully human. Simultaneously, they cast contemporary hunter-gatherer societies, including many Indigenous and land-based groups, as part of an inferior human *past* rather than recognizing them as coexisting ways of life and/or alternative models for future ecopolitical relations. Similar stereotypes are reflected in the uncritical use of the fates of ancient Indigenous societies as cautionary tales or indicators of the future of contemporary BIPOC communities.[12] For instance, Barnosky and Hadley (2016) argue that the collapse of hydroscapes in some Puebloan communities are predictors of current and future conditions in Sudan, Somalia, and Gaza. Such narratives tap into racial, colonial, and imperial stereotypes that misleadingly frame BIPOC communities as poor stewards of the environment (see Cone 2000). In addition, in these frameworks, Indigenous and/or hunter-gatherer societies are framed *in contrast* to future human survival and flourishing rather than being recognized as skilled, knowledgeable, and resourceful survivors of multiple waves of catastrophe (see chapters 1 and 3).

Based on these perceived threats to the future of normative humanity, scholars of human extinction often propose strategies and responses rooted in invasive measures designed to control the (bio)pluralizations of marginalized communities, including population growth and mobilities. For instance, although it is widely projected that global populations of *Homo sapiens* will flatten by 2050 (see UN 2019), many discourses of human extinction frame overpopulation as a major existential threat. Yet a closer look at the arguments put forward by scholars of human extinction shows that they do not necessarily fear increases in the global population of *Homo sapiens* in general but rather with *"relative* population sizes" (Homer-Dixon 2007, emphasis mine). Namely, many of these authors are specifically concerned with the decline of *white* populations and increases in BIPOC births and survival rates. For instance, Homer-Dixon (2007) warns of a future 3:1 demographic ratio between North Africa / West Asia and Europe, along with 70 percent growth in Bangladesh, 140 percent growth in Kenya, and a doubling of the populations of Iraq, Saudi Arabia, Pakistan, and Nigeria. His argument is presented as purely descriptive; however, he immediately goes on to list (without further explanation or context) a series of international news reports on clashes between Indigenous communities in Kenya, riots in Shanghai, and rising murder rates in Mexico. This reflects the uncritical association between BIPOC communities and physical violence linked to the civilizing discourses discussed in the previous paragraphs. In such discourses, it is also common to see BIPOC reproduction described in dehumanizing and/or violent terms, such as "unremitting population growth" following "the doctrine of the cancer cell" (physician John Guillebaud, quoted in Weisman 2013, 65, 114) and the "explosion" of populations (demographer Paul Demeny, quoted in Homer-Dixon 2007, 65).

In such discourses, Black and Brown bodies coded as "female" within colonial-racial gender binaries (see A. Simpson 2014) and the perceived hyperfertility of those bodies (in comparison to white females) are framed as key targets for control. For example, Weisman (2013), who begins his treatise on "over" population by contrasting the birthrates of Palestinians with those of Israelis, posits high infant survival rates as a "dilemma." Namely, he argues that although it would be "unconscionable" to withhold vaccines for malaria, HIV, and other pathogens, making them freely accessible would cause population increase; instead, he suggests the use of family planning to control population sizes.[13] According to Weisman (2013, 47), controlling the reproductive choices and practices of BIPOC people is justifiable because "there's no vaccine against extinction." With this seemingly breezy phrase, he equates the growth—and survival—of racialized and Global South communities with extinction and frames them as pathologies requiring a vaccine. Weisman also seems to assume that his argument would only be racist and/or eugenicist if it caused direct harm to existing humans; he does not seem to realize that acts to prevent the future existence of racialized groups serves the same logic. In a context in which such statements are considered to be common sense, it is not surprising that many communities of color expressed hesitancy over accepting state-provided vaccines for Covid-19, only to be widely criticized for this choice (see Quinn and Andrasik 2021). Similarly, disabled people (and especially disabled people of color) whose differences are genetic and/or heritable are actively discouraged from reproducing in wealthy countries, and their desire to have children is often framed as selfish or antisocial (see Kafer 2013). Others are (and have long been) subjected to legal processes of non-consensual sterilization (Clare 2017; NWLC/AWAN 2021). These practices are undergirded by prevalent beliefs—promoted by influential thinkers such as Australian settler ethicist Peter Singer (1979)—that disabled lives are not "worth living" or even merit prevention for the "social good" (see S. Taylor 2017) but also that they are a drain on social services, healthcare infrastructure, and political-economic systems. In a context in which these systems are understood to be deeply beleaguered, the survival and reproduction of disabled people are increasingly framed as antithetical to future human flourishing (see Mitchell 2022).

Many theorists of human extinction issue calls to limit the movement of marginalized groups into spaces currently designated as white, rich, and/or nondisabled for fear that it will reduce the standards of living or ways of life discussed in previous paragraphs.[14] For example, Oreskes and Conway (2014) imagine a near-future Northern Hemisphere wracked by the scorching of crops, leading to global food riots; the mass northward migration of people and insects, producing outbreaks of typhus, cholera, dengue fever, yellow fever, and retroviruses; and the eventual global breakdown of the international system of states—all starting in what they refer to simply as "Africa."

Similarly, Wallace-Wells (2019) suggests that the more than one million refugees "unleashed on Europe" from Syria are essentially carriers of a political nihilism and "explosive" terrorism he glosses under the label of "the Middle East." Similarly, Wallace-Wells and unmarked Canadian scholar Eric Kaufmann (2019) blame the movement of BIPOC into white-dominated spaces for the rise of destabilizing, extremist, "populist," and especially racist movements—a textbook use of the DARVO technique, this time on a global scale.[15] In this vein, Wallace-Wells (2019, 8, emphasis mine) surmises, "*when* Bangladesh floods," "the world" (meaning receiving countries) are likely to be less welcoming "the browner" those refugees are. Again, while ostensibly expressing empathy for migrants and *anti*-racist beliefs, such arguments not only normalize racist and xenophobic attitudes but also fail to explicitly critique the structures that support them and may contribute to policies that intensify them. For instance, following this kind of logic, Kaufmann (2019) argues that the best way to prevent such racist reactions is to block permanent pathways for settlement in white-majority countries rather than addressing the global structural issues forcing people from their homes *or* tackling white supremacist cultures in receiving countries.

In an effort to protect white-dominated spaces from these feared changes, many authors advocate for preemptive disciplinary measures. For instance, Weisman (2013, 43) reviews strategies for reverse-engineering "liveable" populations that allow for a "global standard of living roughly equivalent to a European level, pre-[2008 financial]crisis." Drawing on influential work by Gretchen C. Daily, Anne H. Erlich, and Paul Ehrlich (1994), he suggests limiting the global population to ensure that all humans have access to Western-style food, shelter, education, healthcare, and political orders— but without "ending inequality" (this is dismissed as "unrealistic") or adopting a "pastoral, preindustrial existence" akin to the "hunter-gatherer" lifestyles discussed earlier in this section (2013, 92).

Many authors working in this field call for forms of "anticipatory" discipline and governance (Evans and Reid 2014) based on surveillance and multiscale interventions into marginalized bodies and/or the planet. For instance, Bostrom (2002, 2013) fantasizes about the creation of a unitary form of government in the form of an artificial intelligence that controls every aspect of collective existence. Meanwhile, Newitz (2013, 271, emphasis mine) avers that "if we want our species to be around for another million years, . . . *we* must take control of the *earth*" through various forms of geo-engineering, bioengineering, or the colonization of other planets. In the social-political realm, Homer-Dixon (2007, 282) outlines an "aggressively proactive" approach that includes family planning "in countries that *still* have high fertility rates," conservation of "resources," transitions to cleaner energy globally, postconflict reconstruction, building resilience of governments in "poor" countries to reduce the movement of immigrants and disease, and targeted efforts to destroy "extremist groups."[16]

Still other contributors to human extinction discourses suggest the deliberate instrumentalization of BIPOC bodies, knowledges, and labor to the project of securing existing global structures of oppression. In a stunning display of white possessive logic (Moreton-Robinson 2015), Hanson (2008, 374) suggests that, in the case of global crisis, it

> might make sense to stock a refuge with real hunter-gatherers and subsistence farmers, together with the tools they find useful. Of course, such people would need to be disciplined enough to wait peacefully in the refuge until the time to emerge was right.[17]

Here, Hanson quite literally advocates for the imprisonment and enslavement (including forced reproduction; see chapter 5) of BIPOC in order to bring about the re-evolution of a humanity whose starting point is modern Western whiteness. His ideas are eerily similar to the plot of Métis author Cherie Dimaline's (2017) dystopic novel *The Marrow Thieves,* in which Indigenous people are hunted and interned for their bone marrow in order to ensure the future survival of white people (see chapter 7). According to Whyte (2016, 219), the instrumentalization of BIPOC knowledge to futures of resurgent whiteness is already well underway, as commentators on "the Anthropocene" demand that Indigenous communities perform the role of the "last remaining Holocene survivors" whose purpose is to teach them "how the rest of humanity can save itself."

Indeed, this is what mainstream human extinction discourses aim toward: protecting, bolstering, and ensuring the ongoing dominance of a specific, currently dominant form of humanity at *all* costs—including the wholesale elimination, instrumentalization, and/or exploitation of other beings, life-forms, and worlds. In the next section, I show how this logic is increasingly expressed in the norms, language, strategy, and practice of an increasingly apocalyptic model of global conservation. To this end, I offer close readings of two influential texts considered to fit well within the mainstream: the *Living Planet Report* (2018 and 2020) published biennially by the Worldwide Fund for Nature (WWF) (Grooten and Almond 2018; Almond, Grooten, and Petersen 2020); and the recent work of the late Edward O. Wilson, in particular his book *Half-Earth* (2016).

THE LIVING PLANET REPORT, 2018–2020

The WWF's *Living Planet Report* (*LPR*), released biennially since 1998, analyzes data from the Living Planet Index (LPI), a database through which it tracks and monitors 27,127 populations of 4,773 species. Since 2014, the *LPR* has shaped international headlines by reporting on global crashes in wildlife populations, including, in 2020, a 68 percent decrease since 1970 (Almond, Grooten, and Petersen 2020). These figures are central to WWF's ongoing call for dramatic and rapid escalations of conservation efforts on a global scale. As WWF executive director Marco Lambertini (2018, 126) puts it, "we all need to embrace this ambition. . . . Not much time is left." I show how these sentiments are converging with the narratives on human extinction discussed in the first part of this chapter—in particular, in their shared fear of the destruction of Eurocentrism and whiteness, global capitalism, colonial sovereignty, and imperial power.

It is important to note that WWF's history and organizational structure emerge from, and remain deeply embedded in, those same systems of power (see the Introduction and Adams 2004). WWF is by far the world's largest global conservation organization, operating in one hundred countries with an annual budget of US$308.3 million in 2019. This budget is more than double that of the next largest conservation NGO, Conservation International (US$150.2 million), and more than triple that of the Nature Conservancy (US$90 million). Prominent colonial political figures and corporate executives have held leadership roles in the WWF throughout its history, shaping its values and priorities. For instance, one of WWF's early presidents was John H. Loudon, a CEO of Royal Dutch Shell—a company infamous for, among other ecological atrocities, the ongoing devastation of the Niger Delta ecosystem through long-running oil spills and participation in the intimidation and extrajudicial killings of protestors. What's more, WWF's leadership reflects entrenched patterns of white, male, colonial, and imperial power. For instance, it has included royal patrons such as Prince Bernhard of the Netherlands (president from 1972 to 1976) and the notoriously racist late Prince Phillip of the UK (president of WWF-UK from its founding in 1961 to 1982, of WWF International from 1981 to 1996, and later serving as president emeritus for WWF until his death in 2021).[18] As British scholar Bill Adams (2004) contends, WWF's founding in 1961 was, in many ways, a means for pooling wealth and political power to finance these men's colonially based passions for (hunting) "wildlife."

More recently, the organization has been a leading proponent of the shift toward financialized conservation, as reflected in its leadership and governing principles. For instance, WWF International's president (at the time of writing) Pavan Sukhdev is an international banker and environmental economist best known for developing the "Economics of Ecosystems and Biodiversity" agenda (see chapter 2). Similarly, the current president and CEO of WWF in the United States, Carter Roberts, is a Harvard Business School graduate and former executive for pharmaceutical giant Procter and Gamble. Rooted in corporate and global-financial cultures and models, today's WWF uses the LPI much in the same way that a stock market index tracks the value of a set of shares or a retail price index tracks the cost of a basket of consumer goods (Almond, Grooten, and Petersen 2020). Indeed, the most recent *LPR* embraces British-Indian economist (and key member of Cambridge's Center for Existential Risk[19]) Partha Dasgupta's suggestion that "humanity," and especially governments, ought to

> view nature as an asset, just as produced and human capital are assets . . . acknowledge that we are failing to manage our assets efficiently . . . [and] understand that the loss of nature is an asset management problem. (Almond, Grooten, and Petersen 2020, 100)

We can see this kind of thinking reflected prominently in the 2020 *LPR*, which emphasizes the finding that "our global stock of natural capital has declined by nearly 40% since the early 1990s." This phrasing simultaneously casts "biodiversity" quite literally as a shrinking form of capital while claiming entitlement to manage and profit from it (Almond, Grooten, and Petersen 2020, 7).

However, it is not simply the organization's links to neoliberal finance that expose its investment in existing power structures but also its centering of Eurocentric, colonial, and imperial social-political and relational models. Consider how the 2018 *LPR* frames biodiversity as "a prerequisite for our *modern, prosperous human society* to exist, and to continue to thrive" (Grooten and Almond 2018, 6, emphasis mine). It goes on to state that everything that has built *modern human society, with its benefits and luxuries,* is provided by nature.... Its resources have *enabled people to dominate the planet*.... To sustain modern human society we will continue to need the resources of nature. (Grooten and Almond 2018, 12–13, emphasis mine)

These statements are explicit about the kind of society they associate with humanity and seek to protect: modern societies, including "benefits" and "luxuries" (whose radically unequal distribution goes unnoted) rooted in a relationship of domination over "nature" and the exploitation of the "resources" it provides. These norms are reflected in Figure 2, which purports to represent "the importance of nature to people" in a universal way.

The graphic depicts detached, European-style houses, set apart from an entirely unpopulated (or depopulated) forest and organized around geometric, intensive, apparently monocultural and industrial farming systems (reflected in the uniform color, shape, and texture of the fields). Interestingly, it also taps into consumer aesthetics and corporate marketing strategies by adopting the graphic design principles popularized by search-engine giant Google: land marked by flat, pale green and blue sections divided by smooth lines (see P. Hall 2014). Agricultural land is clearly separated on one side from a modern city, designated by skyscrapers and a large factory, and from the forest, including one solitary, out-of-proportion

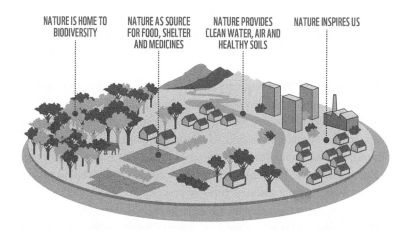

FIGURE 2. "The Importance of Nature to People," from the *Living Planet Report 2018* (Grooten and Almond 2018).

elephant.[20] Captions are used to draw the reader's attention to key elements of a functionally segmented relationship between nature and people. For instance, the phrase "nature is home to biodiversity" (not, the image implies, to human communities), hovering over the forest, ignores and precludes the idea of (bio)plural urban and agricultural spaces and models, and of human cohabitation of ecosystems. This framing maps directly onto the "land-sparing" (vs. "land-sharing") models of large-scale conservation that I discuss in the paragraphs to follow. Meanwhile, the statement "nature provides clean water, air and healthy soils," connected to the bright-blue river, places "nature" in a secondary role as a support service for the urban and agricultural spaces. The image and its labels also impose clear norms regarding proper or correct separation of functions. For instance, farms are presented as a different kind of nature that has been instrumentalized as a "source for food, shelter and medicines," in contrast to a "home to biodiversity." At the same time, urban dwellers are expected to relate to nature (presumably the pristine area marked "home to biodiversity") as a source of abstract inspiration rather than a direct source of food, fuel, fiber, medicines, and other basic needs, let alone as kin.

These images are intended to function as universal symbols of a healthy, balanced, and sustainable ecosystem. But what they actually visualize and promote is the rationalized, segmented, Eurocentric model of relations that underpins modern Western/Northern capitalist, state-based societies. The fact that the high-canopied trees and lone, disproportionate elephant evoke tropical settings suggests a desire to see this relational model entrenched across earth. Images like this are powerful tools for enclosing possible futures within particular aims, goals, and formations of power. Indeed, as the 2020 *LPR* states, "our imagination creates the new worlds we could live in," and there is no longer any question of "'what kind of future world . . . *we* want'—this seems evident: one in which humanity not only survives but thrives, which means a planet on which nature *also* survives and thrives" (Almond, Grooten, and Petersen 2020, 112, 115). What is not evident, and what demands critical thought, is why these futures are assumed to conform to existing norms and structures of power.

In addition, the geographic distribution of the data on which the *LPR* is based, by its own admission, reproduces a Euro-American bias. Figure 3—in which dots indicate data collection sites, recently added populations, and recently added species—shows the concentration of data in Europe and

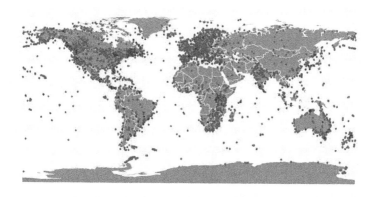

FIGURE 3. Sites where data on species populations was collected and used in the 2018 *Living Planet Report*.

areas where ongoing settler colonialism and imperialism continue to be significant structuring forces.

The editors of the *LPR* explain that this bias is due to a paucity of data from other regions that meet their requirements. Consider, however, the types of sources from which data are drawn for inclusion in the LPI: primarily published reports, data sets, and written records legible within Western scientific and scholarly discourses. As mentioned throughout this book, many BIPOC knowledge systems collect and store information in oral, embodied, practical, political, legal, artistic, and other forms, often crossing the boundaries of life-forms. So despite the systematic, longitudinal nature of Indigenous ecological knowledges (Geniusz 2015)—most vastly predating Western scientific data-collection processes—there is no mention of their deliberate inclusion in the LPI. Any data from Indigenous and land-based knowledge systems that have been *translated* into WWF's data are not identified as such nor is their provenance mentioned. Meanwhile, even as it sidelines Indigenous knowledge systems for not meeting its requirements, the LPI relies heavily on "citizen science"—data of inconsistent scientific quality collected using Western scientific methods by volunteers with varying levels of training and expertise (see, for instance, Gardiner et al. 2012; Aceves-Bueno et al. 2017). It also draws from historical sources whose adherence to contemporary Western scientific standards cannot be verified (see Almond, Grooten, and Petersen 2020). This differential attitude toward sources of data reflects a hierarchy of knowledge systems within the reports. Specifically, BIPOC knowledge systems are glossed as "storytelling" or "informal education" (Grooten and Almond 2018, 76)—that is, as supplementary to Western science and the goals of conservationists (Whyte 2016). Meanwhile, WWF heartily advocates for efforts to educate BIPOC communities about biodiversity and conservation projects taking place on their own lands.

The language of the *LPR* also reflects the existential privilege of its main intended audience. For instance, Lambertini (2018, 16, emphasis mine) states:

> The spiritual, intrinsic, aesthetic and scientific cases for the protection and restoration of nature can *seem remote* or to have *little immediate relevance*. But as it becomes more widely recognized that natural systems underpin *our health, wealth and security*, the impetus to protect and restore nature is much more powerful.

These words call out to subjects who are accustomed to and comfortable within the kinds of relations visualized in Figure 2 and who treat them as universal goods. These are subjects who regard themselves as separate from, and served by, nature and who feel the relevance of ecological harms only when their *own* "health, wealth and security" are threatened. And, as in the human extinction discourses outlined in this chapter, it is *these* subjects who are exhorted to direct the future of the planet in order to secure these conditions. As Lambertini (2018, 4–5) puts it,

> Few people have had the chance to find themselves on the cusp of a truly historic transformation. . . . We can be the founders of a global movement that changed our relationship with the planet, that saw us secure a future for all life on Earth, including our own. . . . We are the first generation that has a clear picture of the value of nature and our impact on it.

Here, as in discourses of human extinction, tens of thousands of years of BIPOC and land-based knowledge, world building, and leadership are ignored in order to frame as heroes and saviors the current adult generation of globally privileged people—all with the aim of motivating us/them to act (largely to protect the conditions that benefit us/them).[21] This "we"— assumed to be so disconnected from other life-forms that they have "little immediate relevance to it"—is anointed and empowered with the authority to decide the fate of earth and its multitude of worlds.

Indeed, mirroring discourses of human extinction and TESCREAL frameworks, the *LPR* seeks to inspire and mobilize its target audience by highlighting threats to the future of humanity. Unless earth's resources are conserved and managed in rational ways, its authors declare, it is not clear "whether continuing human development is possible" (Grooten and Almond 2018, 11). Crucially, this form of development is presumed to hinge on the "incalculable potential future value of benefits we might derive from future discoveries" (Grooten and Almond 2018, 16)—that is, the ongoing extraction of new and additional value from ecosystems as existing resources are exhausted. Similarly, the LPI also expresses palpable fear that failure to implement large-scale conservation strategies could result in the *reversal* of the conditions on which humanity has come to depend. Quoting (white, male, British, septuagenarian) IPBES chairman Sir Robert Watson, the 2018 *LPR* states that "we must act to halt and reverse the unsustainable use of nature, or risk not only the future *we* want, but even the lives *we* currently lead" (Grooten and Almond 2018, 20, emphasis mine).

Although presented more subtly than in mainstream discourses on human extinction, the *LPRs* also associate the possibility of reversal with the growth, change, and movement of BIPOC worlds. Like the discourses discussed in this chapter, they use the violent imagery of "explosion" to discuss the rise not only in trade and consumption but also of "human population growth" over the past five decades (Almond, Grooten, and Petersen 2020). Echoing Weisman (2013) and Wallace-Wells (2019), the 2018 *LPR* argues that increases in global health, access to food, and other elements that affect life chances are

> to be celebrated. . . . However, these exponential health, knowledge and standard-of-living improvements of the Great Acceleration have come at a huge cost to the stability of the natural systems that sustain *us*. (Grooten and Almond 2018, 24, emphasis mine)

Although referring to the Industrial Revolution as a starting point and to the "Great Acceleration," the time period specified (the past fifty years) clearly identifies the Global South as the primary source of these changes, since the majority of rapid industrialization during that period occurred in that part of the planet. By referring obliquely to these trends, these statements gloss over the roles of colonialism, neo-imperialism, neoliberalism, and Cold War geopolitics in driving them. The 2020 *LPR* (Almond, Grooten, and Petersen 2020, 52) also states that patterns of migration since 1970 have "changed the face of our planet," linking this trend with the loss of biodiversity yet offering no further context or justification, beyond the emergence of "economic gaps" within countries. The latter inference maps onto misleading stereotypes that poor and/or BIPOC people do not prioritize biodiversity and that their movement into white-dominated spaces is a force for ecological disorder (see the previous section).

In particular, the imperative to feed a rising population in BIPOC-majority polities and the forms of "land-use change" associated with this task are framed as leading causes of the destruction of biodiversity.[22] For example, the 2018 *LPR* (Grooten and Almond 2018) points to major increases in food crops such as wheat, maize, soy, and rice (the latter three in particular are staple goods in many traditional global majority diets). In the 2018 report, statistics intended to illustrate this "runaway *human* consumption" are superimposed over a large image of monocultural palm oil plantations in Malaysia (Grooten and Almond 2018, 26–27, emphasis mine). Meanwhile, the 2020 edition presents an image of a starkly divided landscape with a caption reading "pristine *Asian* rainforest alongside an oil palm plantation" (Almond, Grooten, and Petersen 2020, 78–89, emphasis mine). Although its authors are likely aware of the powerful global economic forces and structures driving agricultural land-use change, only the generic "Asianness" of these images is emphasized.[23] At the same time, even when national, regional, or global influences and markets are acknowledged, land degradation and habitat destruction are described as resulting from "inappropriate management" and as "typically *local*" (Grooten and Almond 2018, 42, emphasis mine). "Local" is commonly used by international organizations as an umbrella term (and/or a euphemism) for Indigenous, BIPOC, or other communities who are labeled as such by actors who distinguish themselves as "international" (see Richmond and Mitchell 2011). Meanwhile, within the *LPR* publications, the transmission of infectious diseases—including HIV, the Ebola virus, and, it is suggested, possibly Covid-19—are directly linked to areas of

> high human population density and high wildlife diversity, and is driven by . . . deforestation and the expansion of agricultural land, the intensification of livestock production, and the increased harvesting of wildlife. (Almond, Grooten, and Petersen 2020, 78)

The first part of this statement describes conditions most commonly associated in conservation discourses with the Global South, in particular the proximity of densely populated urban spaces to areas of "high biodiversity." Meanwhile, the latter section telegraphs practices of agro-forestry, hunting, and consumption of wild terrestrial meats typically linked in these discourses with BIPOC and/or land-based communities. This analysis ignores entrenched and continuing histories of sport hunting by white settlers in colonial contexts (see Adams 2010). It also brackets off the role of northern investments, tourism, and other interventions in driving urbanization and conditions of poverty that increase the hunting of wild animals. Here, as in discourses on human extinction, the intimacies of BIPOC relations with nature—including conditions of digestion (see chapter 5)—are implicitly framed as inappropriately intimate in contrast to Eurocentric forms of detachment and instrumentality. What's more, they are construed as irresponsible acts that threaten the overall health of humanity. Further, in the security-driven language of global conservation (see chapter 4), areas of habitat destruction are described in military language, such as "deforestation fronts" (Grooten and Almond 2018, 52–53). While this terminology is used to describe the destruction of ecosystems, it frames the actions of those who are seen to disrupt conservation processes as violent enemies of biodiversity—and, in this rubric, possibly of "humanity."

At the same time, like the apocalyptic discourses discussed in this chapter, the *LPRs* frequently refer to BIPOC and land-based peoples, and to their other-than-human kin, as instruments or resources for ensuring the survival of humanity. For instance, Australian settler and former agribusiness owner turned climate activist David Shelmerdine (quoted in Grooten, Dillingh, and Petersen 2020, 36), whom the *LPR* names as a "voice for a living planet," identifies "Aboriginal People" as "stewards of *our* diverse ecology" whose role is to "teach" settlers how to care for the planet.[24] The latter statement naturalizes the presence of settlers and assumes our/their entitlement to the educational, cognitive, social, and physical labor of Aboriginal and Torres Strait Islander people—with the ultimate aim of sustaining the *invasive* polity. Writing to one's own direct biological descendants (a common trope in mainstream futurisms; see also Barnosky and Hadley 2016; Wallace-Wells 2019), Shelmerdine describes the "sad" depopulation of the Australian outback since 1778 as the loss of a resource that is essential to securing "our" (his and his descendants') future, without mentioning the causes of this "decline." Similarly, the *LPR* highlights varieties of Andean potatoes considered to be "fundamental to the health of Indigenous communities" and nurtured through their agricultural knowledge as promising tools in fighting the "next global hunger crisis"—that is, if they can be bred by Western scientists (Almond, Grooten, and Petersen 2020, 96). In other words, the value of the tubers is understood to be released only by the intervention of Western scientists and the application of *their* knowledge systems. The Indigenous people who have co-created these potatoes are not only expected to freely relinquish the plants and knowledge regarding them; they are also framed as mere temporary stewards of something rightly belonging to humanity as a whole and only selfishly withheld. Both quotes demonstrate how threats to "humanity" are used in conservation discourses to justify the continuation of colonial relations of extraction, exploitation, and theft on a global scale.

Just like mainstream discourses on human extinction, the *LPRs* advocate for forms of governance rooted in the surveillance, mapping, control, and policing of the planet, in particular in areas identified as targets for conservation. For example, emerging technologies are heavily featured as tools for achieving the surveillance and control of areas of "high biodiversity." For instance, major emphasis is placed on the use of big data, sophisticated computing systems, and satellite and/or drone technologies to track and model actual and potential changes in areas of concern, including the 25 percent of earth's surface designated by the *LPR* as "pristine" or "intact" "wilderness" (Almond, Grooten, and Petersen 2020, 66). This (sexualized) language refers to measurements of the integrity of an ecosystem in relation to its "pre-impact" state, including the Biodiversity Intactness Index derived from the Planetary Boundaries framework. To qualify as "wilderness," an area must have no "human footprint" score—that is, to *appear* (to Western scientists at least) to be unaltered by human activities (Almond, Grooten, and Petersen 2020, 66). With the overarching desire to conserve these areas, the *LPR* tracks regions where the most change is occurring: "the world's tropical and subtropical grasslands, savanna and shrubland ecosystems, and the rainforests of Southeast Asia" (Almond, Grooten, and Petersen 2020, 66). The *LPR* also describes wilderness areas as being concentrated in Russia, Canada, Australia, and Brazil (Almond, Grooten, and Petersen 2020, 66), its maps uncritically affirming only the boundaries of settler colonial states and ignoring Indigenous place-names, land tenure, and/or conflicts over sovereignty.

At the same time, the *LPR* boasts that

Apocalyptic Conservation

using a network of satellites combined with bottom-up census and crowd-sourced data, allows us to quantify and locate even sparse human settlements, low-intensity agricultural farming and road construction, and other forms of human pressure. (Almond, Grooten, and Petersen 2020, 66)

Essentially, this means that conservation actors (often supported and/or funded by states and private organizations) are able to perform intensive and detailed surveillance of communities living in areas they wish to conserve. Such data can easily be instrumentalized by states and corporate actors to pursue other aims, such as resource acquisition and the suppression of BIPOC resistance—including the global trend of increasing arrests, abductions, rapes, and targeted killings of BIPOC land and water defenders.[25] At the same time, the overarching goal is to incorporate data about these areas into a comprehensive account of human pressure on global biodiversity, equating what the authors admit are low-impact activities of remote communities with the broader structures of colonial capitalism.

Similar strategies are used to track and manage areas deemed to be rich in biodiversity as assets in the context of financial conservation strategies. One such program uses the European Commission's (EC) Copernicus satellite program to calculate the biodiversity value of particular regions through remote sensing and vegetation mapping. It is intended to influence supply-chain management but is also tied to the financial paradigm of biodiversity, in particular the practice of taking "inventory" of biodiversity. Similarly, initiatives such as the Global Surface Water Explorer developed by the EC's Joint Research Team and Google's Earth Engine Team track the changing use and characteristics of bodies of fresh water across the planet (Grooten and Almond 2018, 56–57). Mirroring the tactics, imaginaries, and language of European colonizers—including the naming and categorization of lands, waters, life-forms, and worlds in their own terms—these conservation actors lay claim to perceived resources for "humanity." At the same time, enabled by hypercapitalist actors such as Google, they enable the further extension of forms of sovereignty, power, and governance into areas not yet thoroughly penetrated by colonial and extractive structures.

Similar tactics are carried out through practices of modeling: mathematical projections of future trends based on past and current data (see chapter 1), often used to predict and prepare for threats. For example, the 2020 *LPR* highlights two projects: the Europe-based Food, Agriculture,

Biodiversity, Land-Use and Energy Consortium (FABLE) and the IMAGE-GLOBIO Framework. Both projects assess E. O. Wilson's proposal to dedicate half the earth's surface to conservation, euphemistically calling this approach "land-sparing." FABLE's findings suggest that it is possible to achieve this reallocation of land by 2050 while ensuring food security, reducing carbon emissions, promoting reforestation, and planning the governmental interventions required to achieve this end (Almond, Grooten, and Petersen 2020, 134–35). Its authors highlight Ethiopia as a possible candidate for this approach, showing that 60 percent of its land "could support biodiversity in 2050" if increases in "crop productivity" were achieved, allowing for "afforestation and natural vegetation regeneration" (Almond, Grooten, and Petersen 2020, 135). In so doing, they casually advocate for the effective annexation (by conservation) and top-down zoning of a country in which efforts to consolidate centralized governance continue to result in eliminative violence.[26]

Meanwhile, the IMAGE-GLOBIO project assesses both the "half earth" proposal and an alternative plan based on "land-sharing," which would allow for human activities in areas slated for conservation. They find that both approaches could, in combination with efforts to mitigate climate change and safeguard food security, significantly "bend the curve" of "biodiversity loss" by 2070, although their data show the half-earth model achieving a quicker point of "peak extinction" (Grooten and Almond 2018, 129). As I show in the next section, the half-earth model exemplifies the convergence of contemporary conservation discourses with human extinction, TESCREAL, and other apocalyptic narratives that bolster the forms of structural violence that systematically target (bio)plurality.

E. O. WILSON'S HALF-EARTH

Edward O. Wilson was one of the most influential figures in the global conservation movement and beyond—indeed, he was named by *Time* magazine as one of its "25 Most Influential Americans" and by *Foreign Policy* as "one of the world's 100 leading intellectuals." Wilson received more than 150 international awards, including the National Medal of Science in the United States; two Pulitzer Prizes for nonfiction; and the Crafoord Prize (given by the Royal Swedish Academy for contributions not eligible for the Nobel Prize). He also sat on the boards of many major international conservation organizations, including the Nature Conservancy, Conservation International, and the WWF. A white American man born and raised in

Alabama during the Jim Crow era, Wilson spent the majority of his career at Harvard University, where he established an international reputation as an authority on ants. Seminal publications such as *Biophilia,* which sought to explain an innate tendency among humans to seek connections with nature, and editorship of the seminal book *BioDiversity* established him as an eminent thinker in the wider area of conservation biology. Yet, like many of the authors contributing to public discourses on human extinction, his most famous contributions address subjects that lie well beyond his main areas of expertise, training, and research. This includes his theory of "socio-biology," which frames altruism and social organization as evolutionary outcomes. Upon its publication in the 1970s, this book was denounced by many of Wilson's colleagues and critics as having authoritarian or even fascist implications. However, in recent decades, its arguments have migrated into the mainstream and play a central role in one of his last books, *Half-Earth* (2016). The book revolves around a seemingly simple thesis: in the face of the wholesale destruction of biodiversity by humans, the best chance for saving life on earth is to annex one-half of the planet's surfaces in a network of "nature reserves" stripped of human presence. As we have seen, this proposal is being given serious consideration by major conservationist organizations (Almond, Grooten, and Petersen 2020) and proponents of conservation (Barnosky and Hadley 2016). For this reason, its underlying logics, possible implications, and imaginaries of the future call for careful examination.

Mirroring the discourses discussed in this chapter, *Half-Earth* is written in an overtly apocalyptic tone. According to Wilson (2016, 1), as Western scientific evidence of a "sixth mass extinction" grows, "for the first time in history a conviction has developed amongst those who can think more than a decade ahead that we are playing global endgame." And, like discourses on human extinction, Wilson's concern is primarily with the survival of a particular ideal of humanity that he assumes to be universal. Indeed, *Half-Earth* opens with Wilson's (2016, 1) musings on the self-posed question "what is Man [*sic*]?," to which he responds:

> Storyteller, mythmaker and destroyer of the living world . . . mind of the biosphere . . . born with the capacity to survive and evolve forever, able to render the biosphere eternal also. Yet arrogant, reckless, lethally predisposed to favour self, tribe and short-term futures. Obsequious to imagined higher beings, contemptuous towards lower forms of life.

This model of humanity bears many of the hallmarks of Eurocentric subjectivity: a divide between humans and nature; the predominance of individualism, self-interest, and exclusive group identity (negatively referred to as "tribes"); an emphasis on "mind(s)" distinct from other elements; and a form of spirituality that places humanity at the peak of a cosmological hierarchy. According to Wilson, this subject also shares a set of goals (also apparently held in common with "the family dog"):

> an indefinitely long and healthy life for all, abundant sustainable resources, personal freedom, adventure both virtual and real on demand, status, dignity, membership in one or more respectable groups, obedience to wise rulers and laws, and lots of sex with or without reproduction. (Wilson 2016, 48)

This language expresses clearly what kinds of humans and human lives are considered desirable in the future imagined by Wilson. Specifically, the "half-earth" proposal is intended to secure healthy (nondisabled, nonsick) bodies and lives whose quality is expressed in their longevity (a key aim of many proponents of TESCREAL); ample, consistently available resources; access to "lots of sex" and on-demand adrenaline-producing activity; a hierarchical, centralized society run by intellectual and/or technocratic elites and sustained by collective obedience (another cherished goal of some TESCREAL thinkers); and access to "respectability" (a term often applied oppressively in racist, homophobic, ableist, and other ways).[27] Further, Wilson's critique of humanity, and particularly the ecomodernists whom he inaccurately describes as "Anthropocene" thinkers, is that "we" see "ourselves" as "rulers of the biosphere and its supreme achievement . . . entitled to do anything to the rest of life we wish" (Wilson 2016, 12).[28] Just like the discourses described earlier in this chapter, Wilson's audience, and the subjects in whom he invests agency, are clearly people and societies who conform to Eurocentric understandings of separation from, and domination of, nature.

Like many of the narratives on human extinction and TESCREAL frameworks discussed in this chapter, Wilson's work is also deeply concerned with the loss of humanity's future potential. His goal is to protect what he considers to be the peak achievement and ultimate end of evolutionary processes—current forms of humanity—while securing evolution as a process and the *future* developments it promises. In articulating these views, Wilson echoes the neo-eugenicist language and imagery found throughout human extinction narratives. He remarks that all extant life-forms "including *us*" are "champions in a club of champions . . . the best of the best" (Wilson 2016, 156, 21, emphasis mine). In so doing, he describes evolution in oversimplified terms, as a process in which the virtuosity of "the best" life-forms is revealed through their survival and through elimination of inferior ones. In reality, extinction and survival are shaped by multiple factors—including random genetic mutations and physical locations during geological events—that are not reducible to fitness, adaptability, or the ability to withstand crises. Also mirroring several of the TESCREAL-related theories discussed in this chapter, Wilson imagines the re-evolution of humans after an extinction event. Specifically, he contends that, were *Homo sapiens* to be eliminated, remaining extremophiles might eventually evolve back into a "human-grade metazoan" (Wilson 2016, 130). In so doing, he grafts a teleological end—the production of normative humanity, or something resembling it—onto the open-ended, complex phenomenon of evolution. By this logic, echoing the longtermist approaches discussed in this chapter, Wilson presents the preservation of evolution and its potential as "an investment in immortality" for "Man" (Wilson 2002, 133).

In order to achieve this goal of human "immortality," Wilson (2016, 49) insists that it is necessary to reduce patterns of violence, greed, and "tribalism."[29] He argues that modern "Man" (as he prefers to call his subject) emerged through social-evolutionary processes in which group interests gradually displaced those of individuals, creating "eu-social" superorganisms—and eliminating "older," more animalistic traits. This theory maps onto the colonial and racialized narratives discussed in this chapter, in which relational orders and practices regarded as "primitive" are treated as barriers to be overcome in the achievement of fuller or more perfect humanity. Indeed, Wilson (2004) famously argued that if these processes were nurtured, humanity might eventually transform into a cosmopolitan superorganism (not unlike the singularity imagined by Bostrom and others). Like Homer-Dixon and others discussed in this chapter, Wilson's image of this future humanity is shaped by European Enlightenment ideals, heavily laced with ideas of civility, classic liberal ethics, and capitalist economic structures. Indeed, Wilson (2016, 191) argues that, if allowed to continue with minimal interruptions, the "evolution of the free market system, particularly in the technology sectors," will produce more efficient and less costly ways of life "just as natural selection drives organic evolution." In so doing—and mobilizing his substantial authority in the biological sciences as discursive leverage—he naturalizes accelerating processes of capitalism as akin to evolutionary processes. An important requirement for protecting this developmental trajectory, Wilson (2016) argues, is the maintenance of a diverse human "gene pool," which he likens to the importance of maintaining biodiversity across species. Here, diversity is valued in purely instrumental, eugenicist terms: as a means for ensuring the continued development of normative forms of humanity.

Meanwhile, BIPOC cosmovisions and knowledges receive no mention in *Half-Earth*, except indirectly, in references to "myths." Instead, the book is dominated by Wilson's impassioned advocacy for traditional Western scientific knowledge production, including Linnaean taxonomy and, in particular, the binomial system based on Greek and Latin. He regards this system as the "key to finding everything that has been learned by science" about life on earth, "the basis of a hierarchy suited to the way *the human mind* actually works . . . and the way *we all* most readily communicate" (Wilson 2016, 159, emphasis mine).[30] Dismissing the vast bodies of knowledge and strategies for organizing and transmitting it embodied in the world's many other knowledge systems, he states:

> If this hierarchical system did not exist, and was not subjected as it has been to the strict, internationally sanctioned rules of zoological and botanical literature, knowledge of Earth's biodiversity would quickly descend into *chaos*.
> (Wilson 2016, 159, emphasis mine)

So dedicated is Wilson to this way of organizing knowledge that, when running out of Greek and Latin words to classify the new species that he describes himself as "discovering," he substitutes the names of famous personal friends such as actor Harrison Ford and long-term Conservation International president Peter Seligmann.[31] This form of naming and claiming not only reflects the centrality of white male privilege within global conservation practice but also reflects the degree to which this group feels entitled to assert ownership over biodiversity. In a similar regard, Wilson (2016, 166) wants to privilege classic forms of naturalism, including the militaristic (and ableist) notion of "boots on the ground" research as the only legitimate form of biological knowledge (as opposed to modeling).[32] Signaling the colonial practices of collection and appropriation through which these techniques developed and continue to be practiced, Wilson (2016, 166) calls Western naturalists the "masters of the logos" and the rightful bearers of the "stories" of earth's life-forms. Wilson (2016, 99) sees these individuals as members of a particularly laudable community, describing them as humble; immune to competition, negative ambition, and gossip; harder working than other scientists; willing to take risks for less reward than their peers; courageous; persistent; and entrepreneurial.

Members of this privileged group, singled out as the saviors of the planet, are portrayed as being much like Wilson himself: white, mostly male, over the age of fifty (and often of Wilson's own generation), Euro-American, English speaking, possessing significant social status and/or wealth (regardless of their upbringings), and often from rural and/or southern U.S. backgrounds. Wilson identifies many of them as personal friends, a detail that reflects the high concentration of power within limited networks of socioeconomic, racial, gender, and other forms of privilege within global conservation structures (like the TESCREAL epistemic circles discussed in this chapter). For example, Wilson (2016, 137) asks "eighteen of the world's senior naturalists" to identify the "best places in the world" to conserve, and, although he does not provide an exhaustive list, the individuals he names (Mark Moffett, Adrian Forsyth, Stuart Pimm, and Diana Wall) possess many of the identity factors listed here. In Wilson's view, these individuals are among those best placed to assign relative values to particular areas of earth and to decide what should be protected—and targeted—for conservation. Wilson's ideal conservationists must also develop and maintain appropriately objective relationships with the elements of nature to which they are devoted. According to Wilson (2016, 164),

> an authentic scientific naturalist is devoted to his group of species. He feels responsible for them. He *loves them,* not the literal earthworms or liver flukes or cavernicolous mosses he might be studying, but the research that reveals their secrets and the place of those chosen organisms in the world.

In Wilson's view, the love conservationists ought to feel for "their" species is of a particular kind: it is based on the ability to discover, dominate, and reveal their secrets, to extract data and to make it available as a resource for humanity (indeed, one of Wilson's main anxieties is that humanity will not be able to catalog all of biodiversity). It is not the intimate love of co-embodiment or sensuality discussed in chapter 3 (which he dismisses as "literal") but rather the Western scientist's love of the knowledge they are producing—in other words, a kind of love of self.

230 Apocalyptic Conservation

Like the ideal future survivors imagined in human extinction discourses, Wilson's champions of conservation embody hyperhumanism, reprising the heroic role of "humanity" discussed in this book's Introduction. Poised at a cosmological turning point, these subjects are willing to choose goals that are "potentially game-changing and universal in benefit. To strive against odds on behalf of all life," reflecting "humanity at its most noble" (Wilson 2016, 4). Wilson's ideal conservationists are risk takers, embodying rugged appetites for "exploration" and "adventure" linked with Eurocentric ideals of masculinity, colonial prowess, and (hyper)abled capabilities (see D. Taylor 2016; Jaquette Ray and Sibara 2017; and note 3 in this chapter). For instance, he applauds the Explorers Club of New York for turning its attention toward biodiversity when faced with a "shrinking supply of unclimbed mountain peaks, unwalked polar ice sheets and unvisited Amazonian tribes. . . . The exploration of biodiversity offers scientists and adventurers alike the greatest physical adventures that remain on planet earth" (Wilson 2016, 121). This passage displays the degree to which colonial appropriation and ecological research are linked for Wilson: when colonial imperatives run through the existing supply of land and peoples to conquer, biodiversity research is considered a promising new frontier on which to exercise these desires. Indeed, Wilson avers that all conservation projects rely on an individualistic, rugged ethos of heroism. Specifically, he states that they

> start with a heroic age [in which a] few individuals push forward, risking failure and harm to their own security and reputations. They have a dream that does not fit the norm. They accept long hours, personal expense, nagging uncertainty and rejection. When they succeed, their idiosyncratic views become the new normal. Their individual stories are then rightfully seen as epics. They become part of environmental history. (Wilson 2016, 176)

Wilson has specific individuals in mind when describing his ideal heroes of conservation. One is M. C. Davis, a white settler based in Miramar Beach, Florida, who attained his substantial wealth through gambling, mining, and the sale of property and mineral rights (see Block 2015). Davis apparently possessed many of the features valued by Wilson and the apocalyptic thinkers mentioned in this chapter: entrepreneurial skills and resulting wealth; a rugged form of abled white maleness, complete with a "good old boy southern drawl"; a commitment to Western science, including an outdoorsman's approach to conservation; and, crucially, the financial and political power to acquire land on which to impose his visions (Wilson 2016, 177). Davis's conservation strategy involved buying up large sections of land along the Florida coastline that were ecologically denuded and could be purchased cheaply. On this land, he planted more than a million long-leaf seedlings and worked to create a "wildlife corridor" of lands held privately, by the state or by the military, in a perpetual trust. This strategy relies on established tools of domination: annexation and sometimes multiple remortgaging (see Kay 2018) of private property by white males, made possible through wealth accrued through resource exploitation, on lands from which BIPOC have been expelled, dispossessed, and/or subjected to genocide. In many cases, these strategies build on—or reinvigorate—entrenched patterns of racialized and genocidal land control such as segregation and apartheid (Koot, Büscher, and Thakholi 2022). Indeed, Davis's vision of creating a "precontact" broadleaf forest free of human activity is an eliminative one that rehearses American frontier settler colonialism while erasing evidence of its harms (by re-creating a simulacrum of "precontact wilderness"; see chapter 4). Meanwhile, the legal framing of the land trust permanently excludes any possibilities of future land return (see chapter 7 and the Conclusion), contributing to ongoing patterns of dispossession (see chapter 4). Land trusts can, of course, be designed to promote land return, especially when they are initiated by BIPOC communities seeking to reclaim their ancestral lands. For instance, the Sogorea Te' Land Trust in what is currently called Northern California works to increase access to land and relations with nonhuman relatives for Ohlone people who have no current land base, including through a voluntary tax paid by some settlers.[33] In contrast, Davis's vision, and Wilson's proposed global expansion of it, would further entrench and temporally extend the dispossession of Indigenous lands and their control by non-Indigenous actors.

Another hero of conservation enshrined by Wilson is his close friend and supporter Gregory C. Carr, technology entrepreneur and the scion of what Wilson describes as a "pioneer family" from Idaho. Carr is best known for his efforts to redevelop the Gorongosa National Park in Mozambique after the 1978–92 civil war, which claimed more than one million human lives. Wilson devotes just one sentence to this devastating war and its colonial roots, stressing instead the "heavy poaching" that occurred in its wake, and which he claims destroyed "almost all the megafauna." He also laments the "once sacred slopes of Mount Gorongosa, [where] *local* people had begun to cut away the rain forest" (Wilson 2016, 179, emphasis mine). Notably, Wilson does not offer any context regarding why or to whom those slopes are or were sacred. Instead, Wilson congratulates Carr's mission to restore Gorongosa to what he calls its "original condition"—that is, the state of the park when it was formally designated as a 1,000 km² hunting reserve by the Portuguese-state-supported Mozambique Company in 1920.[34] Once again, the idea of "restoration" is linked not to its Indigenous cultural heritage but rather to previous postcolonization conditions, or even prehuman conditions. Indeed, Indigenous and "local" people are depicted by Wilson as despoilers of the area (see chapter 4).

Carr's interventions in Gorongosa involved a substantial transformation of the landscape and built environment. Starting in 2004, Carr invested millions of dollars to rebuild the central camp, add laboratories and museums for scientific research, and create infrastructure that "vastly increased tourist numbers" (Wilson 2016, 179–80). Wilson also applauds Carr's contributions to the "welfare of people living in and around Gorongosa," which involved providing opportunities for wage work, largely in low-wage roles such as laborer, construction worker, restaurant staff, and park ranger. He holds up as a visionary example of Carr's largesse and altruism that "a Mozambican was named park warden" by Carr and that "another Mozambican was made director of conservation" (Wilson 2016, 179–80). His emphasis on the nationality of these staff (unnamed by Wilson but including forestry specialist Pedro Muagura, who is Black) suggests that it is a remarkable and benevolent act to name locals to senior roles. Meanwhile, employees' ability to engage with what is, for at least some, their own ancestral land is controlled and constrained by their white male American benefactor, with support from the state. This model, which blatantly centers neo- (and paleo-) colonial imperatives, capitalist investment in conservation, and racialized sociopolitical hierarchies, is held up by Wilson (2016, 180) as "an initiative that *pioneers* an example for parks around the world."

Indeed, Wilson's plan for protecting and regenerating the planet does not involve any fundamental changes to the existing global order. Throughout the book, he makes it clear that his half-earth proposal

> does not mean dividing the planet into hemispheric halves or any other large pieces the size of continents and nation-states. Nor does it require changing ownership of any of the pieces, but instead only the stipulation that they be allowed to exist unharmed. (Wilson 2016, 189)

In fact, Wilson is at pains to reassure statespeople, policymakers, corporations, and wealthy benefactors of conservation that their property and/or claims to sovereignty will not be disturbed. Instead, following the logic of real estate speculation, his proposed strategy involves existing political, legal, and economic power structures to buy up, allocate, annex, or otherwise acquire "premier terrestrial wildlands [linked] into a single global circuit" (Wilson 2016, 153)—that is, to vertically integrate global conservation. Notably, Wilson does not comment on what is to become of the remaining land, which he and his colleagues have not identified as being of high conservation value.

Although Wilson's plan involves clearing half of earth's surface of *human* presence and activity, his language, imagery, and examples imply that it is BIPOC and/or land-based communities who most threaten his vision. For instance, Wilson (2016, 187, emphasis mine) argues that although "every sovereign state" has some form of land-based conservation program, the relatively small proportion of earth's land comprised by these programs "should be considered unacceptable by *civilized peoples.*" In so doing, he associates land-intensive conservation with civilization, casting other kinds of relations with nature, or resistance to this form of conservation, as its opposite. Perhaps the most visceral expression of this attitude is the inclusion of the engraving *The Green Sea Turtle* by nineteenth-century German zoologist Alfred Edmund Brehm. Although plates by Brehm and European contemporaries are placed at the start of each chapter, most of these images show illustrations of plants, animals, and their habitats, conforming to the orderly aesthetic of Eurocentric science and mapping (see King 2018). In contrast, the focal point of *The Green Sea Turtle* is two semiclothed Black men aggressively spearing a large sea turtle on a tropical beach, while a white figure dressed in safari gear moves rapidly toward them holding a stick. No context is offered regarding the specific place or peoples depicted, their relationships with turtles, or the presence of the white man (is he joining the hunt? Trying to prevent it?). Instead, presented as a stand-alone statement, the image offers a stark reflection of Wilson's assumptions about the primary direction of violence against biodiversity.

Indeed, throughout *Half-Earth*, BIPOC communities are presented as aggressive, violent, backward, and hostile or indifferent to the survival of other life-forms. For example, in his discussion of the already effective or impending extinction of several subspecies of rhinoceros, Wilson (2016, 30, emphasis mine) says the following:

FIGURE 4. Alfred Edmund Brehm, *The Green Sea Turtle*, 1892, engraving featured in E. O. Wilson's *Half-Earth* (2016).

Apocalyptic Conservation

The whittling away of their numbers began with *sporting* hunters of the colonial era. Then came poachers harvesting rhino horn to make the shafts of ceremonial daggers, principally in Yemen but also in other parts of the Middle East and in North Africa. Finally came the *crushing blow*, the *huge appetite* in China and Vietnam for powdered rhino horn as a pharmaceutical of Chinese medicine. The increased consumption was fueled through the favouring by Mao Zedong of traditional Chinese medicine over Western medicine. . . . *China's population has risen by 2015 to 1.4 billion.* So even though only a tiny percent sought rhino horn, the effect on rhinos turned *catastrophic.*

In this narrative, the massive effects of European colonial elites in decimating megafauna and creating the property laws in which poaching is framed (see the Introduction) is dismissed in a single sentence and in positive terms such as "sporting," or conforming to elite manners. The bulk of the blame for declining rhino populations is placed on BIPOC communities, signified through negative and violent terms such as "crushing," "huge appetite," and "catastrophic," along with references to population growth. Similarly to the apocalyptic discourses discussed in this chapter, Wilson also uses historical examples of environmental harm involving BIPOC communities as apparent evidence of their lack of ability to manage biodiversity. For example, Wilson (2016, 39) refers to the Pacific archipelagos as a "killing field" whose biodiversity was devastated by the "rapid reproduction of colonists"—by whom he means Pacific Islanders rather than more recent European and Asian immigrants. He rehearses the popular narrative in which movements of Pacific Islanders to the Western Polynesian archipelagos (including Fiji, Vanuatu, and New Caledonia) approximately 3,500 years ago are claimed to have wiped out approximately 10 percent of existing bird species on earth at the time "during a *single episode of colonization*" (Wilson 2016, 38–39, emphasis mine). Like the state of Aotearoa / New Zealand's justification of its biosecurity policies (see chapter 4), Wilson equates the movement and worlding practices of Polynesian Indigenous peoples with the multi-episodic, cross-century, massive-scale, systemic changes wrought by European colonialism. Indeed, Wilson argues that the former event caused more extinctions (45) than the latter (25), without offering further contextual details.[35] He uses these numbers to argue that the ecosystems in question "had the most to lose when the Polynesian voyagers first came ashore" and were only dangerously altered with the "later help of *Europeans and Asian colonists*" (Wilson 2016, 39, emphasis mine). Here, it is notable that he refers to white colonizers simply as "Europeans" but to Asians—and, indeed, Indigenous Pacific Islanders—as "colonists." Indeed, Wilson valorizes the efforts of "squads" of largely haole conservationists (Mooallem 2013) to remove invasive plants brought to Polynesia by European settlers from "uncultivated areas" in Hawai'i (Wilson 2016, 38). This example of desirable conservation is juxtaposed against his description of Indigenous hunters in Vanuatu killing a Pacific imperial pigeon to sell to a tourist restaurant. Wilson condemns their action but fails to consider its context, traditional practices, the conditions of poverty imposed by colonialism, or the effects of global tourism on the hunters, while asserting the stereotype that BIPOC do not care about nature.

What's more, mirroring narratives of human extinction, Wilson is preoccupied by changes in human population, and especially by the growth and mobilities of BIPOC communities. Opining that "our population is too large for comfort" (Wilson 2016, 1)—although *whose* comfort is not specified—he worries that growing numbers of humans will lead to water shortages, extreme pollution, and other negative changes. Through this lens, Wilson points to the relatively small population sizes of Indigenous peoples as their primary virtue—without considering the role of colonial genocides in continually affecting those numbers. At the same time, he praises the low population growth associated with Global North countries as a model of good ecological citizenship, stating that

> in every country where women have gained some degree of social and financial independence, their average fertility has dropped by a corresponding amount through personal choice. In Europe and among native-born Americans, it has already reached and continued to hold below the zero-growth threshold of 2.1 children per woman surviving to maturity. (Wilson 2016, 190)

He goes on to state that "given even a modest amount of personal freedom and expectation of future security," women choose to give birth to smaller numbers of "healthy, well-prepared offspring" rather than larger numbers of less-well-prepared progeny (Wilson 2016, 190).[36] In this quote, Wilson applies r/K selection theory to humans, importing an idea from the Western biological sciences (and formulated to describe other species) that compares the production of fewer offspring with a greater chance of survival (K) to higher numbers with lower survival rates (r). In so doing, he suggests that it is the reproductive strategies of "women"—and not structural factors such as poverty; access to healthcare, food, and water; barriers to reproductive rights; sexual violence; or gender norms, many implemented through colonization—that affect birth rates. Instead, education, financial and social development, personal freedom, security, and individual choice—all ideals associated with Western political systems—are championed as means of (ironically) controlling the reproductivity of women. However, Wilson (2016, 190, emphasis mine) contends,

> there also *remain high-fertility countries,* with an average of more than three *surviving children* born to each woman. . . . They include Patagonia, the Middle East, Pakistan, and Afghanistan, plus all of sub-Saharan Africa exclusive of South Africa.

So, just like the apocalyptic discourses discussed in this chapter, Wilson's narrative pits the goals of conservation against what he presents as BIPOC hyperfertility and implies that the mere *survival* of their children to adulthood is a threat to humanity. Indeed, Wilson (2016, 134) is so concerned with (relative) population growth that he appears to be offended by the inclusion of people in the marketing materials of conservation organizations, which he believes should show only "nature." It is perhaps unsurprising that the materials on which he comments feature BIPOC people. For instance, commenting on a recent report by Conservation International literature, Wilson (2016, 134) complains that

> almost every photograph and block of photographs in the text features people, their habitations and their domestic animals [including a small Mongolian boy riding a horse] . . . [and] salmon fillets hanging in an Alaskan smokehouse. . . . In contrast, the view of experienced naturalists and conservation biologists is focused on the two million other known species on Earth, and the more than six million others still thought undiscovered.

This statement pits BIPOC and land-based communities and their ways of life against not only the apparently virtuous work of conservation biologists but also the *survival of other species* and the richness of biodiversity. Notably, Wilson does not express any similar concern about the inclusion of images such as skyscrapers or modern cities in the images used in key conservation documents such as the *LPR,* presumably since he does not see these places as sources of valued biodiversity. Instead, he is preoccupied with the ongoing presence of BIPOC people in areas that he believes ought to be (potential) pure wilderness. So, when Wilson calls for the removal of human activity from half of earth's surface, it is clear which groups of humans he believes ought to be removed.

Ironically, Wilson's eliminative imaginary—which would remove Indigenous and other POC communities from their ancestral lands and lifeways—is intended to re-create what he regards as the "species composition immediately prior to the first major shift that can be ascribed to human activity" (2016, 182). For instance,

> for Gorongosa National Park, it is the late Pleistocene prior to *invasions by Neolithic people from Western Africa*. On the US Gulf of Mexico coast, it would be just before either the start of the European incursion or the later clear-cutting of the longleaf pine. (Wilson 2016, 182)

In other words, Wilson's desire to erase the ecological effects of "human" activity on the ecosystems he counts as valuable not only erases and obscures the sources of the ecological destruction. It also presents a powerful and detailed eliminative imaginary in which entire peoples, life-forms, histories, and (bio)plural relations are replaced with a system of global ecopolitical segregation. This kind of thinking is at the troubled core of the emerging, powerful, and highly funded current of apocalyptic conservation.

～

The apocalyptic tone of contemporary conservation reflects a deep fear that the survival of humanity is at risk—but also that the best way to address this threat is to retrench and intensify existing structures of power, oppression, and violence. In particular, discourses on human extinction, TESCREAL, and conservation alike are concerned with the potential *irreversibility* of ecological changes. In response, their proponents are working urgently to ensure that the futures *they* want, and that reflect *their* perspectives, experiences, needs, identities, and preferences, are realized in irreversible ways—that is, immutably, universally, and into the deep future. One of the key tools employed by these discourses to increase urgency and mobilize support is the assumption that these are the *only* possible responses, ways forward, or kinds of futures available. In the two remaining chapters of this book, I will argue not only that many other alternatives are available but also that their construction is already well underway. This chapter has discussed how discourses of human extinction and apocalyptic conservation embrace many of the forms of systemic violence discussed in the previous chapters, corroding conditions of (bio)plurality and preventing (bio)pluralizations. Among the latter are practices and processes of *revenance*—the return of violenced, silenced, and eliminated life-forms—which many currently marginalized communities are working as, alongside, and/or in support of. In the next chapter, I argue that the logics and practices of revenance, and the distinct ecologies it creates, are an indispensable counterbalance to global structural violence, including problematic narratives of human extinction, apocalyptic conservation, and what Western science calls "extinction."

7 Revenant Ecologies

Practices of Reversal and Return

I am not at the end of things, but the beginning.

—LOUISE ERDRICH, *Future Home of the Living God*

Cedar Hawk Songmaker, the pregnant, twenty-six-year-old Indigenous protagonist of Louise Erdrich's (2017) novel *Future Home of the Living God*, speaks these words from a near-future Minneapolis where the first winter has passed without snow, the maple trees no longer produce sap, and "sabre-toothy tiger things" stalk suburban streets. One of the nightmares of scholars of human extinction (see chapter 6) has come true: evolution is reversing itself, and not in an orderly manner but in unpredictable spurts and jolts. As Cedar moves through the stages of pregnancy, the state around her contracts into a vice grip. Property is seized, streets are renamed for biblical passages, the postal service is militarized, and a disembodied character called Mother broadcasts demands for total compliance with new policies. Among these rules is "female gravid detention," which involves the arrest of pregnant women of color and, eventually, the drafting of all people categorized as female into reproductive servitude to the state. Detention and birthing centers work rapidly to identify and separate potentially "devolved" babies from those regarded as "normal" or of value to potential human (re-)evolution efforts. Yet, despite her increasing entanglement in this system, Cedar is not afraid—in fact, she marvels in the sublime experience of being alive to watch things "return to their beginning." Instead of seeking to protect existing structures and conditions at all costs, she generates gratitude and receptiveness for what is to come, while refusing to succumb to oppression or passively accept her fate. She prepares to welcome and, crucially, to *love* her offspring—whatever kind of being they may turn out to be—so much that she kills and, eventually, dies in order to protect them.

242 Revenant Ecologies

This narrative critiques apocalyptic fears of, and oppressive responses to, mainstream narratives of (human) extinction. Drawing on Anishinaabe knowledge pluralized with Catholic theology and Western science, it centers the possibilities of *return*, not as a linear *reversion* but as a homecoming and reclamation of other possible futures.[1] I call this practice and mode of comportment *revenance*, the beings who embody it *revenants*, and the ecosystems and modes of cohabitation they create *revenant ecologies*.[2] Revenants do not romanticize or celebrate disaster, nor do they allow for the erasure of the harms involved in its production or its consequences. But, at the same time, they refuse to succumb to imposed nihilism or to the closure of worlds and futures in the effort to protect the status quo. Instead, in revenant ecologies and practices, possibilities of return, emancipatory reversals, restorations of worlds, rhythmic collective motions, and embodied resurgence make way for *(bio)pluralizations*. These multiple reworldings confound narratives of singular, linear, mutually exclusive progress or devolution, playing with temporalities and relational arrangements to make space for their worlds to continue.

Revenants and revenant ecologies offer a very different mode of comportment toward extinction than the apocalyptic narratives of conservation discussed in the previous chapters. Although practices and processes of revenance are not always gentle or entirely nonviolent, they directly confront the forms of global structural violence described in previous chapters. That is, they are anti-oppressive, resisting closures around single futures and the forcing of currents of coexistence into single directions, and actively inviting the (re)generation of (bio)plurality.

In this chapter, I discuss several stories/theories that center revenants and revenant ecologies, examining how they confront what Western science calls "extinction" and how they (re)turn toward multiple, alternative futures. In particular, I pay attention to how these beings and collectivities theorize global structural violence; the forms of agency they embody; and the practices through which they create and nurture revenant ecologies, including distinct relational orders. Rather than offering precise prescriptions or pathways forward (since forward is not the only direction in which possible futures lie), my aim is to fall into rhythm with revenants in their efforts to refuse extinction—and the narrow, "there is no alternative" ultimatums pushed by apocalyptic narratives of (human) extinction and conservation.

NOTES ON SOURCES

In what follows, I engage with just a handful of contributions to a rich and immense body of thought and practice through which multiple marginalized communities have long been actively worlding and (re)turning against ecological destruction—*and* against oppressive responses to it. This does *not* suggest that *all* BIPOC, land-based, queer, disabled, poor, or otherwise marginalized communities or thinkers (including those cited here) oppose conservation or other strategies discussed in this book. Rather, it highlights how these communities practice and generate alternative modes of comportment and response to global patterns of ecological violence—in particular, eliminative violence and the systematic destruction of (bio)plurality. It is also important to note that the works by Indigenous and Bla(c)k thinkers discussed here are contemporary expressions, interpretations, and retellings of collective stories/theories refracted through the worlds and experiences of their authors.[3] While they most certainly are embodiments of Indigenous knowledge, non-Indigenous readers need to be careful not to homogenize or reify them as a kind of generic "traditional ecological knowledge" (see Introduction). Instead, it is important to honor the singularity of each (telling of a) story/theory *and* the infinite potential for transformation and difference encompassed by living, growing collective knowledge systems. In the same vein, stories/theories that center revenance should not be understood solely as *reactions to,* and even less as *products of,* global structures of violence. Even as their interactions with such structures are world altering, these stories/theories are independent, irreducible forms of worlding that have existed and will exist long before, throughout, and after the violent ascendance of existing global systems of domination.

The stories/theories discussed in this chapter speak to the themes of a burgeoning and vital field that is becoming known in terms such as Indigenous, Afro-, Asian, BIPOC, queer, crip, and other forms of futurisms and/or science fiction (see Mitchell and Chaudhury 2020).[4] Specifically, they imagine—each from their distinct cultural, ancestral, and lived-experiential grounds—alternative futures beyond current and near-future dystopias created by global power structures. However, few of the authors whose work is discussed in this chapter are known primarily for their work in these fields; most of them are best known for their works of literary fiction. Perhaps for this reason, their aesthetic is often realist, and their dystopias reflect *established and continuing* conditions imposed on BIPOC communities and their *intensification and innovation* in conditions of global ecological crisis. In this sense, these stories/theories are speculative realisms that reflect lived experiences not only of oppression but also of the modes of responsiveness nurtured by plural cosmovisions. For instance, these narratives are shaped by ancestral forms of agency, guidance, and disruption; the braiding of multiple temporalities (see Dillon 2012); subjects enlivened by the fluidity and hybridity of heritage, gender, body type and disability, sexuality, and species (see brown 2017); and forms of knowledge that include attunement, intimacy, sensuality, labor, love, and multiple embodiment. What's more, these stories/theories are works of *global political theory*, examining multiscale forms of power, governance, and political action, and I read them as such (rather than through the lens of literary criticism, in which I am not professionally trained).

The Swan Book (2015), by Waanyi writer Alexis Wright, is a magnificently nuanced work that blends Aboriginal and Torres Strait Islander knowledge systems, Bla(c)k political praxis, global dystopian theory, eco-criticism, decolonial thought, and much more into a saga of destruction and return. The complexity of its themes, events, and relational structures shifts upon each reading, so instead of looking for a linear plot, I follow several of its strands: the role of revenant and ancestral agents in leading a response to ecological devastation; the reversal of destruction; the reclamation of home(lands); the rhythms of revenance; and the embodied labor of loving future beings, life-forms, and worlds. From *Future Home of the Living God* (2017), by Anishinaabekwe novelist Louise Erdrich, whose plot is briefly described at the beginning of this chapter, I draw on themes of cyclical return, unconditional love for revenants, and possibilities of reclamation (including land return) in the face of ecological rupture. I also engage with Métis author Cherie Dimaline's (2017) *The Marrow Thieves*, a multinational postapocalyptic love story/theory and fable of reclamation; and Haisla/Heiltsuk writer Eden Robinson's *Trickster Drift* (2018), which highlights the vengeance of life-forms harmed by global ecological violence. Importantly, these two sources are marketed as young adult fiction, which may seem out of place in a Western academic text about global political ecology. In fact, I argue that these sources are highly relevant precisely *because* they address future adults and future generations. They actively transmit knowledge, warnings, deep historical experience, the value of lifelong learning, and guidance for survival, reaching out to plural futures with love, empathy, and concern for those who inhabit them. I also discuss

Revenant Ecologies 245

sources such as Laguna Pueblo writer Leslie Marmon Silko's *Almanac of the Dead* (1992), which addresses global-ecological politics of resurgence and return on a deep time and multicontinental scale; and Inuit artist and writer Tanya Tagaq's *Split Tooth* (2018), which brings ancestral time into contemporary creation stories in the face of destruction. These works provide rich sources for critiquing mainstream structures of violence and apocalyptic escalations—and for building more intimate relations with earth and its plural worlds.

ECOLOGICAL HARMS AND AUTHORITARIAN RESPONSES

Stories/theories of revenance offer trenchant critiques of global structural violence and the systematic destruction of (bio)plurality, including the narratives of human extinction and apocalyptic conservation discussed in chapter 6. In each of the works mentioned in the previous section, earth is deeply damaged, depleted, poisoned, and in various states of collapse. Meanwhile, the states and governments described in these stories/theories are imploding, leaving millions homeless and subject to increasingly brutal, targeted forms of policing and eugenicist control (see chapter 6). Rather than imagining distant futures, these stories/theories drop subtle hints that they are set mere decades from the time of their publication (the late 2010s and early 2020s). For instance, *The Swan Book* references a camel who is "unhappy to be sat down in the mud in the 21st century" (A. Wright 2015, 313). Similarly, in *The Marrow Thieves* (Dimaline 2017, 176), the protagonist, a teenager called Frenchie, finds a government-issued health card stating his mother's birth date in 2027 and its issuance in 2049. Yet, even in these temporally proximate worlds, earth is radically changed. In *The Swan Book,* the Northern Hemisphere and the cooler southern reaches of Australia have been thrown into chaos as a result of climate change, pushing millions of migrants into seemingly endless global motion, renaming Mother Nature as

> the Mother Catastrophe of flood, fire, drought and blizzard. These were the four seasons she threw around the world whenever she liked. . . . In every neck of the woods, people walked in the imagination of doomsayers and talked the language of extinction. They talked about surviving a continuous dust storm under the old rain shadow, or they talked about living out the best part of their lives with floods lapping around their bellies; or they talked about tsunamis and dealing with nuclear fallout on their shores and fields

forever. Elsewhere on the planet, people didn't talk much at all while crawling through blizzards to save themselves from being buried alive in snow. . . . They hardly talked while all around the world governments fell as quickly as they rose in one extinction event after another. (A. Wright 2015, 6–7)

The impact of these ecological conditions thoroughly pervades the characters' experiences. Belladonna, a white European woman (who may be a ghost), "invades" the northern Australian swamp homeland of the novel's protagonist, Oblivia Ethyl(ene), after wandering for years through the emptied, snow-smothered villages of Europe.[5] Meanwhile, throughout the novel, Oblivia is dragged up and down the length of a ravaged continent of rapidly expanding desert, marshlands where forests used to stand, and a flood-sodden coastal city (possibly what is currently called Sydney) in which people must press their ears to the concrete to listen for the approach of deadly king waves. According to Rigoletto, a world-traveling monkey and political theorist who travels with Oblivia, the frequency of the waves "was really just as natural as seeing water flooding in the lanes of Venice, Bangladesh or Pakistan" (A. Wright 2015, 284). In her journey, Oblivia also encounters many relics of extinction, such as an abandoned shop in the flooded city owned by the president's advisors and full of "rare and valuable parrots" from "other wild places in the world," whose residents "preserved the entire history of their species inside their heads" (260–61). They embody the last fragments of their life-forms, histories, languages, and worlds—and the futility of efforts to conserve them through biopolitics or as private property.

Similarly, the characters in *The Marrow Thieves* navigate a world destabilized by climatic, biological, and geological disruption so profound that entire coastal areas of Turtle Island have sheared into the ocean, and (what is most likely) Lake Ontario has become so toxic that it is fenced off on all sides.[6] Miig, an Anishinaabe man who acts as mentor to the novel's teenage protagonists, tells them that

the earth was broken. . . . She went out like a wild horse, bucking off as much as she could before lying down. A melting North meant the water levels rose and the weather changed. It changed to violence in some cases, building tsunamis, spinning tornados, crumbling earthquakes, and the shapes of countries were changed forever, whole coasts breaking off like crust. And all those pipelines in the ground? They snapped like icicles and spewed bile over forests, into lakes, drowning whole reserves and towns. . . . People died in the millions when that happened. The ones that were left had to migrate inward. (Dimaline 2017, 87)

In each of these worlds, invasive states (see chapter 4) have responded to ecological collapse with increasingly authoritarian policies organized along intensified racial boundaries. For instance, Erdrich (2017) critiques the uncritical, fear-driven responses of apparently moderate white liberals as a factor in the rise of authoritarian and far-right-wing politics in response to global-ecological chaos.[7] For example, Cedar's adoptive parents, Sera and Glen, are both lawyers (in the reproductive health and environmental fields, respectively) and self-described liberals. Sera, an "anti-vaxxer" worried for her daughter's immune system, represents the liberal branch of white middle-class discourses of the bodily "purity" of children (see Shotwell 2016), a position the racialized Cedar critiques as such:[8]

For you, not vaccinating me was a class thing. Upper class delusionals can afford to indulge their paranoias only because the masses bear the so-called "dangers" of vaccinations. (Erdrich 2017, 67)

These anxieties and inequalities come to a head as the family watches a news broadcast reporting on what is understood as the nonlinear reversal of evolution, including speculations on which species of hominid humanity might devolve (back) into. Hearing that it is unlikely to be *Homo neanderthalus* due to a relative lack of shared genes, Sera exclaims: "Dear God. There goes poetry. There goes literary fiction. There goes science. There goes art" (Erdrich 2017, 62).[9] Her fears are symbolized by a series of infographics on the screen, in which "humanoids hunch as they walk backwards into the mists of time, while in the background, Beethoven's 5th symphony dissolves into a series of hoots and squawks" (59). When Glen points to the value of cave paintings and the possibility that future humans may have their own kinds of intelligence, Sera bursts out: "You're PC even about the *foraging* apes our species may become in only a few generations" (62, emphasis mine). Sera, like the mainstream apocalyptic theorists discussed in chapter 6, understands the prospect of multiple types of intelligence (whether Indigenous, neurodivergent, or more-than-human) and the practice of foraging as signs of degeneration. When threatened with losing the elements of elite Western culture that she so dearly values, her egalitarian politics vanish to reveal a profound fear of what she regards as inferior forms of humanity, or as not-quite-humans. In an effort to self-calm, Sera reaches for the ideas of hyperhumanity discussed in chapter 6, musing that "maybe this is just humanity's biggest challenge" to overcome and master (61).[10] Later in the book, when Cedar asks Sera what she thinks hell will be like, Sera replies that living through devolution *is* hell. When Cedar insists that "turning around to the beginning. Maybe that's not the same thing as going backward," Sera replies, "Well, it is for me" (251). This exchange exposes the rift between white, Western liberal fears of revenance as *reversion* and the openness of other knowledge systems to its multivalent possibilities.

Throughout the novel, the set of attitudes expressed by Sera are embodied in multiple levels of government and society, intensifying as processes of devolution appear to pick up speed. One of the first indicators that Cedar notices is a comprehensive form of racialized erasure: suddenly, there are "no brown people anywhere. Not in movies, not on sitcoms, not on shopping channels or on the dozens of evangelical [Christian] channels" (Erdrich 2017, 50). Soon, she becomes aware of a new government policy called "female gravid detention" (85), which involves apprehending pregnant women—in particular, women of color, two whose sudden arrests Cedar witnesses. It appears that pregnant people of color are being targeted because they are more likely to be gestating "normal" fetuses, over which the white-dominated state wishes to gain total control in order to protect its desired norm of humanity.

More specifically, these bodies and their potential are construed as threats to the *future* of humanity and possible drivers of its extinction. The shadowy figure Mother releases regular broadcasts exhorting pregnant women to volunteer to "save the country we love" (Erdrich 2017, 90), while bounty hunters are incentivized to apprehend them at gunpoint. When Cedar discovers that she herself is pregnant and attends an ultrasound appointment, she hears the doctor examining her fetus's developing brain say tearfully, "We've got one." The doctor asks Cedar if she has "any special ethnicity" and warns her that, if so, she should tape him to the chair, flee, and refuse to tell anyone that she is pregnant (58). Soon after, Cedar learns from her fetus's father, Phil, that it is now illegal to harbor or assist a pregnant woman, and rewards are offered for turning them in (indeed, Phil eventually turns in Cedar to prevent his own arrest). Later, Phil justifies his own action and

Revenant Ecologies 249

the government's policies on the basis that "it's a global crisis. It's the *future of humanity*" (296). Later, when Cedar is imprisoned in a "birthing center," she stares at a wall of memorial photos of women captioned "they served the future" as one of Mother's broadcasts tells the inmates that they can "completely win back God's love" by helping secure the future of humanity (310). These scenes echo the belief espoused by many mainstream apocalyptic futurists that immense suffering and oppression—borne by BIPOC, women and other genders, and other marginalized people—are justifiable in the context of efforts to secure the future of humanity. And, like those discourses, *Future Home of the Living God* shows how some people seek to profit from the inequalities and vulnerabilities accentuated by ecological collapse. For instance, Glen, on first hearing about the possibility of devolution, adopts something very like the "prospective mind" championed by Homer-Dixon (2007), looking to benefit from the overturning of existing order. He muses that he "should invest in one of those genetics companies. They'll try to turn this thing around with gene manipulation. It will be big" (Erdrich 2017, 61). The same attitude is expressed by Phil, a conservationist who "took a vow to . . . save nature" and believes that Cedar might be carrying "one of the originals" (a nondevolved fetus) (96). He pleads with her that "if our baby is normal, we could be in charge of things. Rich. Super rich. We'd be safe. If we somehow worked out genetically. . . . I mean, to have a normal child, the sky would be the limit for us" (295). Both men's arguments reflect a culture in which control over the means to embody and reproduce normative models of humanity—and over the bodies deemed capable of doing so—is a primary source of wealth, power, security, and privilege.

Similar themes of racialized, ableist, and eugenicist oppression run through *The Swan Book*. The swamp homeland of Oblivia's people has been seized by the military (after many previous acts of expropriation) and transformed into a detention center for Aboriginal and Torres Strait Islander people forced from their lands. Within the detention center, internees are graded into an "upper scale," whom the army believes can "be educated," and a "lower scale," who "just needed some dying pillow place to die" (A. Wright 2015, 50). As truckloads of people arrive, the swamp becomes home to a lively and generative mix of peoples, their ancestors, and their nonhuman kin, from which "ungovernable thoughts unfur[l] into the atmosphere" (51). We learn that the military was sent by the federal government to

250 Revenant Ecologies

save babies from their parents.[11] . . . Ever since the wave of conservative thinking began spreading like wildfire across the twenty-first century, when among the mix of political theories and arguments about *how to preserve and care for the world's people and environment,* the Army was being used in this country to intervene and control the will, mind and soul of the Aboriginal people. . . . The internment camp excluded the swamp people from the United Nations' Universal Declaration of Human Rights. (A. Wright 2015, 49–50, emphasis mine)

In this world, the militarized detention, control, and exclusion from legal protection and human rights of Aboriginal and Torres Strait Islander peoples is unquestioned by the mainstream society. This is precisely because it is framed as a means of satisfying global norms of conservation by controlling BIPOC reproduction, mobility, and land tenure. Indeed, many stories / theories of revenance refer to governmental attitudes that frame the flourishing or even survival of autonomous BIPOC communities as threats to humanity and global ecosystems (see chapter 6). For instance, in *Almanac of the Dead,* Clinton, a Black army veteran who is working to mobilize a transnational movement of the homeless, feels

suspicious whenever he hear[s] the word *pollution.* . . . Human beings had been exterminated strictly for "health" purposes by Europeans too often. . . . [Environmentalist] ads blamed earth's pollution not on industrial wastes— hydrocarbons and radiation—but on overpopulation. . . . "Too many people" meant "too many *brown-skinned* people." (Silko 1992, 415)

Similarly, in *The Swan Book,* the swamp community—composed of people who refuse to adopt either white lifestyles or stereotypes of traditional life fetishized by white politicians—is framed by the state and dominant culture as a sink of pollution simply awaiting elimination. Warren Finch, the mixed-race president of Australia, lauded by white politicians and the international community, destroys the swamp that he knows "contained [Oblivia's] whole world" (A. Wright 2015, 130). When Finch explains this to Oblivia, whom he claims as his "promise wife" and removes from the swamp,[12] he insists that the inhabitants were

returned to homelands where their real laws and governments exist. . . . They were doing nothing to change things for themselves for the future

Revenant Ecologies 251

so they had given up the right of sovereignty over their lives. (A. Wright 2015, 230)

In this world, BIPOC lives must conform to global norms of humanity—including essentialized images of "good" Indigenous peoples—in order to earn their existence and rights to any land. In this world, BIPOC, and especially people "from the north" (of Australia)—a region that, throughout the novel, is associated by white characters with dangerous Indigeneity *and* with their own salvation—are heavily criminalized. Indeed, Belladonna warns her less-than-consensually adopted charge, Oblivia, that if she leaves the swamp she will be immediately targeted as

one of those Aboriginals from up North, a terrorist . . . one of those faces kept in the Federal Government's *Book of Suspects* . . . brown- and black-coloured criminals, un-assimilables, illegal immigrants, terrorists—all the undesirables. (A. Wright 2015, 55)

Themes of BIPOC detention and instrumentalization are echoed in *The Marrow Thieves* (Dimaline 2017). In this story/theory, the Canadian government abducts Indigenous people en masse, placing them into institutions modeled on the residential schools of the nineteenth and twentieth centuries, in which their bone marrow is systematically extracted from the rest of their bodies, relational webs, and cohabitats (see chapter 4). In the novel, Indigenous peoples' bone marrow is believed to hold the capacity for dreaming, a skill that white people lost during the ecological collapse and that is connected throughout the novel to ancestral knowledges, blood memory, survival skills, and collective futuring. As Miig explains to his young mentees, this new form of extreme extraction emerged in stages: first the Church and scientists worked to find a cure; then, white people (in the manner of New Age cultural appropriation) asked to be included in ceremony before "they changed on us . . . looking for ways that they could take what we have and administer it themselves" (Dimaline 2017, 89–90). Soon after, government scientists began conducting research to make Indigenous ceremonies and medicinal practices "more efficient," calling on eco-politically traumatized communities to offer up "volunteers" with "Indigenous bloodlines and good general health" to participate in local trials in exchange for food, board, and a small honorarium. Failing to achieve the desired numbers of participants, the government turned to the prisons, which were "always full of our [Indigenous] people" (89–90) and where they could experiment with impunity, since "there weren't enough people worried about the well-being of prisoners" (89). For inspiration and technical knowledge, governments "turned to history to show them how to best keep us warehoused, how to best position the culling. That's when the new residential schools started growing up from the dirt" (89–90).

Dimaline follows to its horrifying but logical conclusion the violent forms of reasoning emerging among dominant white cultures when their futures appear threatened—logics in which "harvesting a race" (2017, 50) is made to seem justifiable. In these stories, BIPOC, gendered, violenced, poor, and disabled bodies are disciplined, controlled, instrumentalized, and collectively destroyed in order to safeguard entrenched power structures. However, they also enact and offer conditions for creative modes of pluralization through which oppression is rejected and in which worlds and cohabitats are remade.

FUTURE ANCESTORS

Within mainstream Western scientific thought, evolution—and extinction—moves in one, irreversible direction. Meanwhile, in revenant ecologies, some life-forms and worlds that have withdrawn as a result of violence resurge, return, and even (r)evolve in unpredictable ways. Many revenants are ancestral and/or extinct beings who emerge to help (re-)create indeterminate futures. Extrusions of ancestral time that puncture Eurocentric existential rhythms, the returns of ancestral beings and worlds are not neat reversals. Instead, they embody the mingling and sometimes jarring conflict between dominant and oppressed temporalities.

For instance, in *Future Home of the Living God* (Erdrich 2017), Cedar watches as chickens come to resemble large "pale iguanas" (305) and as large, long-toothed cats devour domestic dogs. In this context, "devolved" domestic and farm animals live alongside familiar ones. In *The Swan Book* (A. Wright 2015), as Oblivia is driven through the desert center of Australia by her new husband and his advisers, they pass a region densely populated by grass owls. At the time of writing (summer of 2023), the eastern grass owl is classified by the IUCN (2020) as being of "least concern" for extinction, but in the near-future time of *The Swan Book*, it has long "been regarded as one of Australia's scarcest owls, rarely seen" (A. Wright 2015, 165). The advisers or "genies," Aboriginal men who are equal experts in Western

Revenant Ecologies 253

and their own ancestral knowledge systems, explain that populations of owls and snakes have blossomed in response to the millions of rats and insects migrating inland to escape coastal flooding. Similarly, the "seemingly never-ending trail of bats" (242) that Oblivia watches when she reaches the flooded city are, despite their precarious status at the time of writing (see chapter 6), ragged and ill but adamantly extant. Far from signs of the decay of urban places (see Weisman 2008), these beings are actively regenerating their ancestral Country. Indeed, observing the owls, one of the genies, Edgar Mail, sings to Country, asking for insight into the owls' "special stories of origins and creation, *return and renewal*, which are as old as they are new" (A. Wright 2015, 184, emphasis mine). These words suggest that this is not the first time his people have witnessed the contraction and expansion of such life-forms, even in places that appear to be empty or denuded.

Indeed, in the glittering, arid pan of a dried-up salt lake, Mail and his companions sense immense and plural presences:

> the quietness of a resting serpent spirit fellow . . . listening deeply to hear even an insect perching on its skin, coming there to recite a song. The landing of butterflies. The feet of a lizard pounding on crystals of salt. . . . Battalions of stink beetles crawling over each other and the salt. . . . Plague grasshoppers jum[ping] away at the coming of strangers. Moth storms swe[eping] across the lake. Crimson and orange chats whistl[ing] away from the heath of spinifex, pittosporums, mulga and eremophila scrubs. . . . Green twisting clouds of budgerigars . . . [and] up high, harriers and kites [crying] out as they glid[e] in the thermals. (A. Wright 2015, 190)

In this place, viewed by Western science as lifeless and climate ravaged, a riot of beings—some dormant and some active, some visible only to those with the requisite (ancestral) knowledge—are resurging and pluralizing their creation stories. When the group wakes one morning to find the desert filled with lilies, Finch tells Oblivia that some people regard these flowers as

> a fragment of life from another era, when there might have been a different language that once described the wetlands and rainforest in the heart of the country, before it disappeared. The living fossil was all that was left of those times. . . . It was a ghost place. (A. Wright 2015, 200)

The return of these plants—whose physical existence is ambiguous—shows the continued presence and episodic reemergence of rainforests long declared "extinct." In this context, "ghost place" does not carry the same connotations of abandonment as the North American "ghost town"; instead, it speaks to the rich inhabitation of the place by spiritual beings undetected by the Western sciences.

Similarly, in *The Marrow Thieves* (Dimaline 2017), Miig insists that his teenage co-travelers hone their hunting skills, despite their protests that there are no animals left to hunt. He responds simply, *"They'll be back,* and you need to be ready" (33–34, emphasis mine). This exchange calls to mind the story/theory of the Hoof Clan discussed in this book's Introduction: by renewing their traditional relationships and agreements with the hoofed animals in the form of respectful hunting practices, the teenagers may collaborate in their (possible) return. Frenchie practices this ethos when he encounters a lone moose and must decide whether to kill it to feed his hungry adoptive family. He eventually decides to leave the moose, reasoning that

> it was like he was a hundred years old, like he had watched all of this happen. Imagine being here through it all—the wars, the sickness, the earthquakes, the schools—only to come to this. . . . I couldn't let it come to this, not for him and not for me. (Dimaline 2017, 50–51)

Even in a moment of near-starvation, Frenchie honors law and respectful relations between life-forms, placing them above his and his family's immediate needs for survival. This respect is reciprocated by the moose, who visits him in a dream to block the path between Frenchie and the brick wall of a school, an intervention that protects the teenager from being captured and "harvested."

In some of these stories/theories, the human protagonists are themselves revenants. Indeed, many of the characters in *The Swan Book,* including Oblivia herself, are at least semi-ancestral, moving between states of life, death, mortality, and eternal presence. In fact, it is not clear whether Oblivia is alive in the Western scientific sense. She interacts seamlessly with ghosts and spirits, one of whom, learning of her fear of being abandoned in the desert, reassures her that she is "already dead" (A. Wright 2015, 79). At the same time, Oblivia is part of an ancestral origin story, in which she is a young Aboriginal woman named Emily Wake, a "closing-the-gap

Revenant Ecologies 255

baby" and survivor of gang rape who has withdrawn into a tree to heal—
and, at the same time, she *is* the tree.[13] This particular giant Eucalyptus is
the last of a group of "dikili ghost gums old as the hills [that] once grew
next to a deepwater lake fed by an old spring-spirit relative, until they had
all slowly died . . . during the massive storms that cursed the place after the
arrival of strangers from the sea" (8). As the tree, the traumatized Oblivia
embodies the return of a whole and integral world that predates the invasions of colonizers and climate refugees from the Global North. She becomes an ancestral being in which

> all the stories of the swamp were stored like doctrines of Law left by the
> spiritual ancestors . . . a place so sacred, it was unthinkable that it should
> be violated . . . like all of the holiest places into the world rolled into one.
> (A. Wright 2015, 79)

When trapped in the flooded southern city, groups of (non-Indigenous)
street children immediately recognize Oblivia as a "spiritual ancestor" and
"the first Aboriginal spirit they had ever seen" (272). What's more, having
returned to the swamp at the end of the novel, Oblivia is described as a
will-o'-the-whisp, a glowing light who occasionally appears around the
swamp screaming "*kayi, kayi kala-wurru nganyi, your country is calling out
for you*" (334). Embodying all these beings and times at once, ancient and
young all at once, Oblivia is a bearer, leader, and co-creator of futures in
a form that overturns the norms of pure, rugged, hyperabled, idealized
male leaders enshrined by apocalyptic narratives (see chapter 6). Regardless of how damaged Oblivia's bodymind may seem to the colonial state
and those who accept its logics, she is nonetheless a formidable ancestor
whose presence helps welcome and ease the return of alternative futures.

However, Oblivia's reemergence from the tree—from which she is eventually yanked by Belladonna, and which is then bulldozed by the army—
releases destructive acts and painful memories. In the wake of her removal
and the tree's destruction,

> elders and their families whose ancestors had once cared for the old dried
> and withered, bush-fire burnt-out-trunk of a giant eucalyptus tree through
> the eons of their existence . . . were too speechless to talk about a loss that
> was so great, it made them feel unhinged from their own bodies, unmoored,
> vulnerable, separated from eternity. . . . The reciprocal bond of responsibility

256 Revenant Ecologies

that had existed between themselves and their ancestors . . . was what held all times together. (A. Wright 2015, 79)

So, when Oblivia is released suddenly, it is as though she has skipped through time, "by-passed history" (85), and the fragile temporal and social ecosystem is disrupted. Upon her return, many of her swamp kin ask, "Why can't she stay lost? All this searching . . . and the only thing they discovered was shame. . . . They found no lost child . . . [only] new tracks of possibilities for things that had once happened and should stay buried with the past" (85). So, as a revenant, Oblivia's presence and the many layers of violence that bring it about is deeply ambivalent and retraumatizing as well as hopeful and generative.

In *The Marrow Thieves* (Dimaline 2017), human revenants often take the healing form of elders, whose presence is not so much a reemergence as it is the product of their unrelenting return in and through younger generations. For instance, Rose, a Black Indigenous teenager who is part of Miig's group, was raised by "old people" in traditional ways after her parents were abducted. When she speaks in their tones and language, her friends feel "surrounded on both ends—like we had a future and a past all bundled up in her round dark cheeks and loose curls" (32). Meanwhile, Minerva, the disabled female elder traveling with the group, works assiduously to preserve elements of her people's song, ceremony, medicines, and language using what is available—including tin cans to make jingles.[14] When she sacrifices herself to the "recruiters" to protect her family and is forcefully attached to neural probes, Minerva summons her blood memory and sings

> with volume and pitch and a heartbreaking wail that echoe[s] through her relatives' bones, rattling them in the ground under the school itself. Wave after wave, changing her heartbeat to drum, morphing her singular voice to many, pulling every dream from her own marrow and into her song. And there [are] . . . words in the language that the conductor couldn't process, words the Cardinals couldn't bear, words the wires couldn't transfer. As it turns out, every dream Minerva had ever dreamed was in the [ancestral] language. (Dimaline 2017, 174)

Flooded by the overwhelming power of Minerva's song and dreams, the system designed to extract them short-circuits and the school burns down. The Indigenous people from multiple communities, camped around the perimeter, use the smoke of the burning building as a ceremonial smudge, "pull[ing] the air over their heads and faces, making prayers out of ashes and smoke" (174). Minerva, who depends on her younger charges for physical assistance and wields her power through song and dreams, is very far from the young-to-middle-aged, hyperabled, self-sufficient, super-rational heroes framed by mainstream apocalyptic discourses (see chapter 6). Yet her ability to embody and channel collective ancestral power makes her able to lead multiple generations toward the renewal of their worlds.

A spectacular narrative of large-scale ancestral revenance is reflected in *Almanac of the Dead* (Silko 1992), whose deep-temporal frame follows the northward migration across Turtle Island of millions of living, dead, and spectral beings of many life-forms killed and oppressed by five centuries of colonization. This process is described by the charismatic public speaker Wilson Weasel Tail at an international conference of Indigenous peoples concerned with ecological destruction. He interprets the revenance of the migrating dead—and other phenomena such as anxiety, depression, addiction, and violence eroding the settler society—as the continuation of Wovoka's Ghost Dances, in which the dead were expected to return to help repel the forces of invasion.[15] Europeans, argues Weasel Tail, assumed that the Ghost Dances did not work because the dancers were shot dead while wearing their protective Ghost Shirts and the colonizers continued unimpeded. What the invaders failed to grasp were the scales in which the effect of the dances would unfold—over the following centuries and across multiple continents—and the powerful agency of the dead, perhaps especially as revenants. Another important revenant who appears in this story/theory is a thirty-foot stone snake who appears overnight among the mining tailings near a Laguna Pueblo village, his head "looking south, in the direction from which . . . the people would come" (Silko 1992, 763). The snake reminds those who see him that

> Spirit beings might appear anywhere, even near open-pit mines. The snake didn't care about the uranium tailings; humans had desecrated only themselves with the mine, not the earth. Burned and radioactive, with all humans dead, the earth would still be sacred. (Silko 1992, 762)

This revenant is not coming back to save humanity—in fact, he does not appear to be much concerned with its fate at all. His purpose is to help usher in conditions that can halt the destruction of his ancestral lands.

Indeed, not all revenants are warm and fuzzy: they often take frightening, ambiguous, hostile, or even vengeful forms. For instance, in *The Marrow Thieves* (Dimaline 2017), Frenchie notes that the "animals making their way back [to the city] were different. Too much pollution and too much change. Miig said if we gave them another half century, they'd take everything back over and we would be the hunted" (91). A similar theme is found in *Trickster Drift* (Robinson 2018), in which the young Haisla/Heiltsuk protagonist, Jared, is stalked by a group of river otters hell-bent on eating him. Eventually, we learn that they are relatives of the millions of beavers killed to meet European demands for fur (see chapter 4). While the beavers have rebounded, "other fur-bearers, like the otters, generally loathe humans for the genocide they perpetrated, and will take human form to lure the unsuspecting to their death" (Robinson 2018, 288). Having been forced to live in human bodies since the European hunters stole their furs, the otters hope to force Jared into helping them with their task of retrieving their skins. These beings are not "extinct"—or "endangered"—with the passive connotations that these words imply. Instead, these otters are vengeful revenants fighting to the death to continue their collective worlds, restore their bodily integrity, and reclaim the lands they and their furry relatives co-created.

In some cases, however, even terrifying or vengeful revenants can become allies to people seeking to rebuild their worlds in the wake of ecological collapse. In Métis filmmaker Danis Goulet's short film *Wakening* (2013), the young warrior Weesegeejak makes their way through a North American cityscape wracked by military occupation, while a male, Canadian-accented voice drones through a loudspeaker that no one can own lands unless authorized by the state.[16] They enter an abandoned theater that echoes with voracious growls and the sound of crunching gristle, where a handful of people tied to chairs warn Weesegeejak that the monster Weetigo is devouring them. Running through the dark theater, Weesegeejak hunts down Weetigo, a monster with a deer's head, whom they know from previous ancestral conflicts. The warrior tells the monster that his hunger, previously feared throughout the land, has been supplanted by the violence of the occupiers. Weetigo responds that he was compelled to come to the city to eat people because "the forests are all dead." But Weesegeejak persuades him that the colonizers tricked him and are simply using him for their own oppressive ends. Angered by these words, the monster growls and begins to chase Weesegeejak, who flees to the sound of pulsing drumbeats until

Revenant Ecologies 259

they stop short of two armed guards thrusting the muzzle of a gun into the back of a hooded figure. Just as the guards shine their flashlights at Weesegeejak, the monster looms up and we see only the warrior's horrified face as they watch Weetigo kill the gunmen. After a brief flash of the monster's blood-spattered but soft-eyed deer's face, the film ends with Weesegeejak watching the flapping plastic curtains through which Weetigo has exited. Weetigo is not an obvious hero; windigos appear throughout the knowledge systems of the Anishinaabe, Nêhiyaw, and many peoples of the plains as cannibals, signs of social corrosion, and often embodiments of colonial violence. Yet in Goulet's narrative, the reappearance of Weetigo in response to the destruction of the forests makes it possible for Weesegeejak (who is also a revenant, weaving seamlessly across time periods) to convince the monster to turn its power against the forces of their common oppression.

In some cases, it is not clear whether a revenant presents a threat or is a potential ally (or to whom, exactly). This is the case in Melissa K. Nelson's (2013) discussion of the reappearance of Mishipizhu, a water being with a lynx's face and a scaly, often copper-colored body. He, or beings like him, are also found in Arikara, Cree/Nêhiyaw, Delaware, Dakota, Fox, Mandan-Hidatsa, Omaha, Potawatomi, and Ponca worlds and are related to the Feathered Serpent of the Southwest, Mexico, and Middle America (Nelson 2013, 20–21). According to Nelson, this ancestor is currently (re)appearing with greater frequency and force in the form of floods, droughts, and other water-related calamities as climate change brings him into conflict with his traditional enemies, the Thunderbirds. Drawing on the work of esteemed Anishinaabe elder Basil Johnston, Nelson (2013, 213) describes Mishipizhu as "a protector of natural resources and a mediator between the water, land and sky beings . . . reappearing to punish anyone who attempts to upset the balance of eco-social relations." She contends that, with the disruption of practices that feed the waters—including ceremony and the offering of tobacco—Mishipizhu is

> creating climate disruption to renew the ecologies of Ojibwe homelands. He is taunting and agitating the Thunder Beings, so storms and rain come too soon, too much, or not at all. He is travelling through the underground waterways to evaporate fertile wetlands, stunting vital medicines and freezing wild-rice lakes. With his long copper tail, he is whipping up and disturbing the layers between earth and sky to disturb climatic patterns. (Nelson 2013, 228)

In other words, it seems that Mishipizhu's mobilization of this destructive form of revenant agency is a direct response to the fact that "humans have forgotten how to revere and pay tribute to him" (Nelson 2013, 227). From some perspectives, Nelson (2013, 226) argues, his actions can be seen as those of a victim—"another creature on the list of endangered native species . . . [who] will not survive climate change in the next twenty years." However, Nelson (2013, 222) points out, when he is treated and recognized appropriately, Mishipizhu can bestow blessings such as healing, protection, and good health. From this perspective, the chaos he creates is ultimately a set of

> healthy shifts to clean and renew ecosystems. . . . Climate change is, perhaps, simply part of a larger cycle of planetary change and eco-mythic regeneration. Mishipizhu is not a victim, but a creative destroyer and regenerator. He reminds us that we must acknowledge and revere *real* power. (Nelson 2013, 227)

For these reasons, instead of understanding Mishipizhu's revenant presence as a sign of *inevitable* and *irreversible* apocalypse, she suggests that we listen to this powerful water being and ask ourselves, "How shall we relate to water and protect and nurture it for future generations?" (Nelson 2013, 229). This story/theory suggests that mainstream apocalyptic writers may be correct to fear revenants, in the sense of respecting their power, but that efforts to control and suppress them are only likely to produce more destruction. Instead, Nelson's work stresses the importance of forming respectful relations to these beings and the worlds they are (re-)creating, which begins with recognizing that their presence is both possible and real. To do this, it is necessary to question the unidirectional movement of Western secular time and, in particular, the rule of irreversibility on which it rests.

REFUSING (AND REFUTING) IRREVERSIBILITY

Revenants are not bound by unidirectional, path-dependent Western secular time. On the contrary, the revenants discussed in this chapter scramble and graft together different kinds of time, sometimes reversing its direction so that "pasts, presents and futures . . . flow together like currents in a navigable stream" (Dillon 2012, 3). I certainly do not mean to suggest that *all* BIPOC physics and metaphysics involve the *same* kinds of temporalities or time-space relations or that *none* of them includes unidirectional modes of time. The point is rather that what is considered impossible in Western

Revenant Ecologies 261

secular temporal frameworks is commonplace in *many* other worlds and their temporal orders. For instance, in *Almanac of the Dead* (Silko 1992, 629), places are "living organism[s] with time running inside [them] like blood, unique to that place alone." Revenants move across temporal assemblages just as they navigate physical space—with skill, improvisation, responsiveness, and specificity—not in abstract obedience to one kind of temporal rhythm. In so doing, they regularly revisit "moments of divergence" between possible trajectories, reopening alternative presents and futures (Dillon 2012, 4). Where mainstream apocalyptic thinkers perceive *only* the possibility of destructive reversals of progress, revenant perspectives often intuit opportunities for rebalancing or correcting destructive trajectories, and the renewal of ecological relations. For example, in *Future Home of the Living God* (Erdrich 2017), Cedar questions whether the forms of "intelligence" valued by Western scientists are good survival strategies, reasoning that the relatively unintelligent dinosaurs "lasted so much longer than we have or probably will." Eurocentric norms of intelligence could, in fact, be "a maladaptation, a wrong turn, an aberration" (Erdrich 2017, 64), she reflects, pointing to other evolutionary possibilities in the past, present, and future.[17] Indeed, the cover art for a 2018 reprint of the novel appears to show two entirely different paths of evolution proceeding from an explosive cosmic event—one following a Western scientific narrative in which a humanoid emerges from mammals, fish, and snakes; and the other beginning with microorganisms, crickets, and songbirds but ending with a doglike figure and bipedal hominid, neither of which are recognizable within Western scientific taxonomies. The symmetry and circularity of the field they traverse, and their meeting at its center, speak to the contingency of evolution and time and of cyclical, iterative, temporal trajectories.

The contingency of evolution is raised in a broadcast by a paleontologist watched by Cedar and her adoptive parents toward the beginning of the "devolution" event. He argues:

> "We do not have a true fossil record of human evolution . . . or any other species' evolution, for that matter. What we have are bits and pieces that have survived and surfaced over millions of years. . . . That's like playing 52 pickup with one deck of cards flung over the entire planet and expecting to come up with a full and orderly deck. So if evolution has actually stopped . . . and evolution is going backward . . . then we would not see the orderly backward progression of human types that evolutionary charts are so fond of

presenting. Life might skip forward, sideways, in unforeseen directions. We wouldn't see the narrative we think we know. Why? Because there was never a story moving forward, and there wouldn't be one moving backward. . . . We might roll back adaptation through adaptation, the way canines will revert to type left on their own until they reach a wild dog-slash-wolflike status. Or we might skip straight to a previous hominim." (Erdrich 2017, 62)

In this near-future world, "devolution" would not involve a simple reversal but rather the indeterminate recombination of possibilities existing virtually and ancestrally within extant (and extinct) life-forms. At the same time, the development of life-forms may move in multiple directions simultaneously and at different scales. For instance, the pregnant Cedar tells her fetus that it has passed through an "age of miracle" (conception), "gone from tadpole to vaguely humanoid," lost its embryonic tail, and grown a permanent brain (Erdrich 2017, 54). That is, the fetus has performed on a micro-scale the linear stages of development observed by Western science, even though they may be developing into a form that is both a "reversion" and the beginning of an unprecedented future. Sensing this, Cedar experiences her pregnancy as "a directionless flow of time, moving backward through corridors and hallways, as if this one room . . . has opened out into the farthest stretches of the universe" (Erdrich 2017, 50).

The multidirectional flow of time, flesh, genes, and forms of political order attuned to broader cosmic patterns is a common idea within stories / theories of revenance. Indeed, Cedar, while reconnecting with her Anishinaabe heritage in response to the devolution event, also becomes fixated on the Catholic idea of incarnation (the fusing of spirit and flesh). In contrast, in her novel *Split Tooth* (2018), Inuit artist Tanya Tagaq's young female protagonist actively embodies the "welcoming of spirit into the flesh" as an act of rebellion *against* the violent strictures of colonial Christianity. For Tagaq, this involves not only sex and sensuality but also the broader erotic metabolism of earth and the cosmos. As her narrator states,

the earth calls us back into her, just as the earth is being pulled back into her origin [accompanied by the sound of deep, rasping exhalation].[18] In one giant breath the universe exhaled us all out [deep breath sound] . . . therefore the universe will inhale all back in again. Upon our deaths, the earth welcomes us back into her bosom, turns us into plants and oil and wind, churns us into more life. (Tagaq 2018, 78)

Revenant Ecologies   263

For Tagaq, the linearity imposed by colonial cultures—including the irreversibility of death and the desire to avoid it at all costs—is a violent refusal of the cosmic material (re)cycling of energies and matters. Similar imagery is used in *Almanac of the Dead,* in which Mosca, a drug runner who spends a great deal of time in the desert lands, tells his colleagues that he would prefer that his remains be left in the desert, like the "old people" who raised him:

> that way they started "living" again within a matter of hours, surging through the blood veins of a big coyote as she raced across the desert to suckle her pups. . . . [Mosca] didn't mind being coyote shit because the rain carried the shit to the desert roots and seeds, and all kinds of beings and life. Fed back to the earth, Mosca believed he would bound and leap in the legs of mule deer and soar in the wings of the hawk. (Silko 1992, 609)

Within this cosmovision, death is part of a constant energetic exchange (see chapter 1) between different kinds of cohabitating bodies (animal, plant, soil) made contingent by circumstances such as weather conditions and particular relations of metabolism (see chapter 5). The Yaqui characters in *Almanac* also describe this multidirectional interabsorption of bodies and life on a deep temporal scale. According to the elder Yoeme's history of the coming future,

> once the earth had been blasted open and brutally destroyed, it was only logical the earth's offspring, all the earth's beings, would similarly be destroyed. . . . The humans would not be a great loss to the earth. The energy or "electricity" of a being's spirit was not extinguished by death; it was set free from the flesh. Dust to dust or as a meal for pack rats, the energy of the spirit was never lost. Out of the dust grew the plants; the plants were consumed and became muscle and bone; and all the time, the energy had only been changing form, nothing had been lost or destroyed. (Silko 1992, 718–19)

From this perspective, what the apocalyptic discourses described in chapter 6 understand as the dysfunction of planetary systems is actually earth's attempt to *regulate* in response to the harms caused by systemic violence by redistributing energy and life. As Cedar speculates in *Future Home of the Living God*:

> perhaps we are experiencing a reverse incarnation, a process where the spirit
> of the divine becomes lost in human physical nature. Perhaps the spark of
> divinity, which we experience as consciousness, is being reabsorbed into the
> boundless creativity of seething, opportunistic life. (Erdrich 2017, 76)

It is not "earth" that is at risk in these disruptions but rather particular
configurations of matter, energy, and power that certain polities are unwilling to relinquish. This process might very well involve many of the outcomes that mainstream apocalyptic thinkers fear, including the collapse of
currently dominant systems for *managing* and *exploiting* earth, its beings,
and its worlds. The difference is that, from within these cosmovisions, the
continuity of *currently existing* norms and structures—and perhaps even
physical embodiments—of humanity is not presumed to be the only priority. As Whyte (2017a, 159) puts it, many Indigenous peoples "do not tell our
futures beginning from the position of concern with the Anthropocene"
and its preoccupation with the destruction of particular ecosystems. Their
concern is not to protect or secure current conditions but rather to reworld
and to restore good ecological relations after the catastrophes of colonization, and within broader sweeps of time.

However, the fact that what Western science calls "extinction" may
be understood as multidirectional does *not* mean that cohabitants of this
world find it, or the forms of violence driving it, normal or acceptable. On
the contrary, these accounts show that current ecological tumult is a *logical*, foreseeable (and widely *foreseen*) consequence of the violation of earthly
laws and agreements that require restitution. Here, reversal takes on an
important political purpose. Global structures of violence such as colonization, globalized capitalism, and (neo-)eugenics are intended, by those who
benefit from them, to follow irreversible trajectories. As such, for many of
the worlds they oppress, disruptions or even reversals of these processes are
experienced as possibilities for restoration and renewal. Recall Hubbard's
(2014) argument, discussed in chapter 5, that the destruction of the buffalo
nation constitutes genocide. In this context, the return of the buffalo does
not erase the violence done against them or reduce its gravity. Instead, their
refusal to be eliminated recalls and underscores the severity of the violence
while—and *by*—refuting its irreversibility. Within revenant ecologies, restitution does not involve the *erasure* of harms, let alone their justification,
but rather the *healing* of the traumas they have caused, the reestablishment
of continuities, and the activation of different relationships.

In this vein, stories/theories of revenance foreground the labor of scrambling linear modes of violence and of picking up severed paths of continuity to move forward in new directions. For instance, Miig in *The Marrow Thieves* (Dimaline 2017) shares with his young mentees a future origin story/theory that speaks to continual renewal, rebuilding, and reworlding. He starts with the story of the movement of Indigenous peoples across the earth, followed by the arrival of European invaders and the genocides of Indigenous cultures on Turtle Island. "But we got through it," he says. "We returned to our home places and rebuilt, relearned, regrouped. We picked up and carried on" (23–24). Then, he speaks of a period of renewal in which—despite racist exclusion, incarceration, and struggles with addiction—his people "sang our songs and brought them into the streets and into the classrooms. . . . We moved ahead. We were back" (25). This period marked the beginning of a time of ecological and political chaos, including international water conflicts and the construction of giant "metal straws" to transport water, along with melting ice caps and tectonic shifts that left his people "scattered, lonely and scared. On our knees again, only this time there was no home to regroup at" (25). This is the point at which the novel begins: with Indigenous people from across Turtle Island and other places (e.g., two characters from the Caribbean) heading north to regroup, rebuild, and reworld. In the face of this challenge, Miig tells the teenagers, "We've survived this before. We will survive it again" (32–33). Instead of succumbing to apocalyptic narratives of the kind long imposed on Indigenous peoples by their oppressors, he stresses that, and how, BIPOC peoples have survived multiple end times against huge odds and welcomed the return of their worlds.

A similar theme emerges in *The Swan Book*'s ingeniously adaptive swamp community. They find little sense in Belladonna's talk about the wars, sea level rise, and political collapse in the Northern Hemisphere; it "mean[s] nothing to overwhelmed swamp people who had always been told to forget the past by anyone thinking that they were born conquerors. They already knew what it was like to lose country" (A. Wright 2015, 40). Having already survived multiple destructions of their worlds, the multinational swamp community is not interested in predictions of doom. Instead, they are concerned with recovering their connections to Country, however polluted, dried-out, and toxified it may have been rendered by the most recent waves of destruction. Similarly, Cedar in *Future Home of the Living God* (Erdrich 2017, 60) responds to her adoptive parents' terrified reactions to news reports on devolution by thinking to herself, "I feel so sorry for them. They are devastated on such a fundamental level." Meanwhile, Cedar herself is grateful to be alive in her time and present for a new beginning. Cedar's Anishinaabe stepfather, Eddie, with whom Cedar corresponds throughout the novel, concurs that the world is "always going to pieces" and that his people "have been adapting since before 1492, so I guess we'll keep adapting" (32). When Cedar protests that "this is different!" Eddie replies that "it's always different. We'll adapt" (32). These exchanges undermine an important assumption of mainstream apocalyptic thinkers: that there is only one world, and only one possible future for that world, tied to an inevitable forward trajectory. Eddie's arguments do not ignore the severity of ecological harms or the suffering and death caused by them. But at the same time, they refuse to accept the limits to agency and response imposed by mainstream apocalyptic thought. Instead, they focus on remembering and innovating the multiple survival strategies that they and their kin (including ancestors in deep time) have used to adapt to unique yet resonant world-destroying events. Eddie is even able to see the beauty of devolution. Sharing pages of his "suicide journal"—a compilation of reasons to stay alive in the face of disaster—he lists

> the opportunity to witness the working of the design unravelling, the sheer thrill of the plan coming to light in each detail. Who says any complexity is irreducible? IT IS BEING REDUCED ALL AROUND US RIGHT NOW. I have the chance each day to marvel at the vast dismantling. (Erdrich 2017, 168)

For Eddie, the historical moment in which the characters find themselves is sublime, not because he revels in destruction but because he feels privileged to be alive in a time when it is possible to gain a deep intimacy with earth and its workings. Adopting an ethos of reverence toward earth (whatever it becomes) and actively choosing to participate in the return of its multiple possible futures by simply staying alive is a powerful expression of agency. Against a backdrop of apocalyptic hyperhumanism in which the survival of currently marginalized communities is frequently framed as a threat to humanity (see chapter 6), it is also a powerful act of resistance.

REVENANT FORMS OF AGENCY

Mainstream apocalyptic discourses often inaccurately frame resistance or proposed alternatives to their narratives of inevitability as passivity—as simply sitting back and waiting for the worst to happen. In addition, they mobilize ableist, racist, and gendered stereotypes of "laziness," "short-sightedness," "slowness," or "stupidity" as antithetical to the rapid, aggressive, forceful forms of agency that they demand. Revenance (and revenants) could not be less passive. However, the kinds of agency they embody often diverge from those recognized by colonial, white supremacist, ableist, heteronormative, and anthropocentric norms—that is, instrumental, linear, object-related, intentional, individualized (and/or self-interested) action. Indeed, they often embody what adrienne maree brown (2017) calls "emergent" theory and practice. This involves movement without a clearly centralized force, coordinated through flock-like attunement across a variety of bodies (normative and divergent) and animated by instinct, distributed intelligence, adaptability, and the capacity to ride waves of complexity. Instead of employing force to control unfolding trajectories of change, these kinds of emergent agency work to align, embody, and move *with* currents of (bio)pluralization.

In many cases, this involves responding to calls for action, participation, or collaboration issued by other life-forms, land, or ancestors. For example, for a considerable part of *The Swan Book*, Oblivia leads a large group of (living and dead, human and other) migrants from the flooded south to the north of Australia. Leading the group but disappearing within it, she, in turn, surreptitiously follows a flock of black swans. The swans, meanwhile, are moving "as if the ancestors had pulled [them] across the skies . . . towards a sacred rendez-vouz, a tabula rasa place, where all the world's winds come eventually and curl in ceremony" (A. Wright 2015, 324). The swans and Oblivia are connected viscerally *and* spiritually; they follow her to her swamp home at the beginning of the novel and lead her back at its end. When these different beings connect, they find

> each other's heartbeat, the pulse humming through the land from one to the other, like the sound of distant clap sticks beating through ceremony, connecting together the spirits, people and place of all times into one. They were her swans from the swamp. There was no going back. She would follow them. They were heading north, on the way home. (A. Wright 2015, 303)

Journeys like these (in particular, northward migrations), which run through many stories/theories of revenance, refuse regimens of containment and spatial-racial purity imposed by existing power structures (see chapter 6).

268   Revenant Ecologies

While responding to acute ecological disruptions, many of these journeys—like those of the swans—are foretold, anticipated, welcomed, prophetic, or (re)iterative. Their direction, rhythm, and destinations often reflect traditional pathways such as migration, hunting, trading, or transport routes, retraced as an assertion of survivance (see L. Simpson 2020). Indeed, Oblivia's migration with the black swans is "a journey foretold, clear in the oldest swan to the youngest cygnet" (A. Wright 2015, 323).

In this way, stories/theories of revenance subvert racist and xenophobic panics about mass migration from the south to the north, framing these collective movements as forces of renewal and recognizing migrants of all kinds as powerful agents of futuring. Indeed, Oblivia's future-ancestral migration is carried out with a group of people who lack citizenship, "having failed the rigid nationality test for maintaining a high level of security in the country" (A. Wright 2015, 305). Instead, having scraped together money to pay for their passage, they are "travelling incognito on unofficial and illegal crossings through the swamps," prey to unscrupulous "human removalists": former "intergenerational environmentalists" whose prior aim was to "save a multitude of furry or feathered threatened species" (305). This detail reflects the increasing fusion of environmentalism and policing in apocalyptic conservation discourses (see chapter 6). Similarly, the characters in *The Marrow Thieves,* like many of their ancestors, are forced to migrate almost constantly as they lose their homes and are compelled to dodge agents of the state, while those who are caught are forced into sedentary imprisonment (Dimaline 2017, 46–47). In *Almanac of the Dead,* northward collective movement is the profound, multicentury force through which global strategies of racialized containment, dispossession, and genocide are turned on their head. The procession of the living and dead migrants follows a pair of twin brothers from the mountainous Chiapas region of Mexico who are, simultaneously, sacred macaws. As they move north, gaining revenant followers, their collective motion reclaims Indigenous homelands and those of peoples with whom they are in solidarity, creating a multinational (and multi-life-form) procession of resurgence. The Barefoot Hopi, another prophetic speaker who appears in the novel, describes it as such:

> In Africa and in the Americas, too, the giant snakes, Damballah and Quetzalcoatl, have returned to the people. . . . The snakes say this: From out of the south the people are coming, like a great river flowing restless with the spirits

Revenant Ecologies

of the dead who have been reborn again and again all over Africa and the Americas, reborn each generation more fierce and more numerous. Millions will move instinctively; unarmed and unguarded, they begin walking steadily north, following the twin brothers. (Silko 1992, 735)

This movement, too, is understood to be a reprise of previous collective journeys. Indeed, the procession of the revenant dead follows the path of a group of children in the distant past who were sent north to carry their people's almanac in order to ensure that the "days and years" that passed before their people's demise would "return again" (Silko 1992, 257). The almanac carries instructions of the ancestor being Quetzalcoatl, who predicts the destruction of worlds by European invaders but also instructs the people to wait for the arrival of a story from the south that will signal the return and rebirth of their peoples. By attuning themselves to the revenant ancestor beings Quetzalcoatl, Damballah, and the twin macaw brothers, and to each other's instinctive movements, the procession works to reverse five centuries of the destruction of their worlds.

The movement carried out by these beings is not only a flight but also a homecoming, a reunification with land and ancestors—including homes that no longer or do not yet exist. It produces its own distinct ecologies by knotting together links between the extant and returned, the living and the yet-to-become. Indeed, the movement of revenants into spaces ravaged by violence and ecological harms restor(i)es them *as* homes and as cohabitats (see chapter 3). In this vein, Grace Dillon (2012, 10) draws on the Anishinaabe concept of biskaabiiyang ("returning to ourselves") to describe the skill and practice of Indigenous peoples creating and restoring their homes on apocalypsed lands. Often, this includes generating a collective ethos of welcome for the recently returned—a sharp contrast to the frightening imagery of zombies and vampires that often attend mainstream white apocalyptic images of BIPOC resurgence (see Fishel and Wilcox 2017; Gergan, Smith, and Vasudevan 2018). For example, when the large birds suddenly descend on their community, the swamp people of *The Swan Book* must learn how to welcome and live with the "first swan[s] ever seen on this country" (A. Wright 2015, 13). Displaced from their own Country in the far south of Australia—just like many of the people living in the swamp—they "ha[ve] no storyline for taking them back" (15)—that is, no direct kin relation to this part of Country. Nonetheless, "the swamp people [think] that the swans had returned to a home of ancient times, by following stories for

Country that had always been known to them" (67). The people speculate that the swans may have retrieved stories of "their ancestors of long ago, when great flocks might have travelled their law stories over the land through many parts of the continent" (15–16). For this reason, the people respect the swans and refuse to eat them (despite rampant food insecurity in their community), allowing the birds to "place [themselves] within the stories of this country" (16). In this story/theory, the appearance of exogenous beings and their movement across territories are treated not as "invasion" but as a homecoming. As discussed, the swans later reciprocate this welcome by bringing the swan's daughter/ancestor, Oblivia, back to her ancestral Country. Through these practices and ethics, the swamp community, the swans, Country, and the ancestors connecting them co-create a distinctly revenant ecosystem: a cohabitat that is at once ancient and unprecedented.

The Marrow Thieves, too, is concerned with homecoming. When the group of protagonists finally reunites with a handful of exiled elders in the north, one of the elders, Clarence, says that in order to heal from all the harms they have endured, Indigenous peoples simply need "the safety to return to our homelands" (Dimaline 2017, 194). Hearing this, Frenchie is confused. "How can you return home when it's gone?" he asks, referring to the ecological and political ruptures that have altered his family's traditional lands beyond recognition (194). Clarence responds by telling him that simply being on that land and working to heal it will reconstitute it as their home. From this perspective, "home" is a specific place of origin and kinship but also the *living relationships* that co-constitute it—not so much a static place or thing as a set of conditions that one (re)makes every day. Miig puts this belief into practice when he risks his life to break into a school where he believes his husband may be detained, stealing vials of bone marrow from deceased detainees and pouring them into a lake. "I tried to take them home," he says. "I drove to the lake, one of the last ones I knew still held fish. . . . I sang each one of them home when I poured them out. It rained, a real good one, too. So I know they made it back" (145). Homecoming, for Miig, is about the reunification not just of the living but also of the dead, with their land and loved ones, and their ability to combine their bodies with the land in death, continuing their cohabitation. This message is powerfully affirmed by the elder Minerva, who, after burning down the school in which she is detained, escapes and is shot by government agents. As she dies, she leaves Miig and the teenagers with the resounding message "kiiwen"—"you must always go home" (211).

In these stories/theories, homecoming is an act of reclamation. In moments of rupture that crack existing power structures, revenants work in creative, improvisational, yet deeply remembered ways to retake stolen and occupied worlds and to nurture ecologies back into existence. This work forms an important subplot of *Future Home of the Living God,* particularly through Eddie's communications with Cedar and his repeated invitations for her to return home (to her Anishinaabe community and the reserve, where she has never physically lived). At one point, he writes that "quite a number of us [members of his tribe] see the governmental collapse as a way to make our move and take back the land. Right now" (Erdrich 2017, 111). When Cedar visits the reserve, she finds that Eddie has won an election and is presiding over a meeting discussing plans to redistribute land from wealthy cottage owners to the members of the tribe. He displays a hand-drawn real-estate map marking out land parcels colored in green, yellow, and purple, which mark off the land "lost through incremental treaties" (255), sold through the Dawes Act (which extinguished communal property), and/or allocated to settlers for farms and, in many cases, vacation homes.[19] Eddie tells the assembled members of the community that "over the next months, you will see this map change" (256) as they secure state land at first, then begin to reclaim and distribute privately owned land. These properties are to be distributed by lottery to unhoused community members, including relatives returning from cities and underhoused people. Through this work of reclamation, the community hopes to attract more members back, and Eddie has developed plans for creating a big farm to meet food security needs, while creating a local "compassionate" police force and diverting criminal activity to farm work. In Eddie's eyes, the community is "being reasonable. We are not taking back the whole top half of the state, or Pembina, Ontario, Manitoba, or Michigan—all of our original stomping grounds. We're just taking back the lands within the boundaries of our original treaty" (256). He goes on to tell Cedar that they were planning to conduct a "compassionate" process to take back land from non-Indigenous people, but this had not been necessary, as the latter had all "removed themselves" (256). At a subsequent community meeting, he asks the community to bow their heads and offer prayers for the plight of the white people now returned to the cities, countering the common belief among white settlers that Indigenous peoples wish them/us harm (see Shotwell 2016). Ironically, Eddie is convinced that within a single generation, all this work will be undone, and the wealthiest and most powerful will once again seize land, capital, and control. Still, in this moment, reclamation matters: it asserts the survivance of his people and enables them to welcome home their relatives, human or "devolved."

The Swan Book, too, is a story of revenant ecopolitical reclamation; indeed, Oblivia understands her story and her journey as "the quest to regain sovereignty over [her] own brain," not least by traversing her ancestral Country (A. Wright 2015, 4). The swamp and its people are skilled revenants, having rebuilt their community and retained their cultural autonomy despite multiple governmental incursions. Swamp elders share stories about previous unsuccessful struggles "to get back what was theirs in the first place," including the extinguishment of their Native title when they were forced to leave for the cities (10). Despite the fact that their land and waters have long been marked by the toxic pollution of military refuse, including the hulks of huge navy vessels sunk in the lagoon, the people of the swamp "flatly refus[e] to have junk buried among the ancestral spirits" (11). So, they simply decline to see, taste, smell, or otherwise acknowledge the presence of this pollution. Their dedication to sensing and caring for Country *as* Country—regardless of how it has been violently altered—is a way of reclaiming it or, more to the point, refusing to accept colonial malfeasance and wastelanding (see chapter 3). The swamp reciprocates this work of reclamation, as the people watch "life triumph. Hadn't they witnessed the growth of an enormous flock of swans on their country? The swans had thought it was ok to live there" (116). Even a place declared dead and destroyed by colonial powers is, from their point of view, a place for nurturing life, afterlife, and whatever kinds of thriving might become possible (again).

Beings other than humans also play important roles in the revenant reclamation of land, law, and relations. For example, in *The Swan Book,* Oblivia observes that "much of the city had cracked. . . . This had happened a long time ago and now the natural landscape was quietly returning and reclaiming its original habitat" (A. Wright 2015, 209). She sees mature native trees sprouting orange fungi, ferns, and moss-covered walls and hears frogs croaking in the drains. Many settler residents of the city regard these multi-life-form movements as evidence of collapse—and indeed, the regrowth witnessed by Oblivia mirrors much of Weisman's (2008) imagery

Revenant Ecologies 273

of a humanless future. Oblivia, however, understands it as the return of Country to its ancestral forms after being buried and arrested beneath the colonial city for centuries.

Reclamation of stolen land by nonhuman kin and ancestors is also a central theme in *Almanac of the Dead*, epitomized in a speech by Weasel Tail:

> You think there is no hope for indigenous tribal people here to prevail against the violence and greed of the destroyers? But you forget the inestimable power of the earth and all the forces of the *universe*. You forget the earth's outrage and the trembling that will not stop. Overnight, the wealth of nations will be reclaimed by the earth. . . . The rain clouds no longer gather; the sun burns the earth until the plants and animals disappear and die. . . . Next to thirty thousand years, five hundred years look like nothing. The buffalo are returning. . . . Fences can't hold them. Irrigation water in the Great Plains is disappearing, and so are the farmers and their plows. . . . Year by year the range of the buffalo grows a mile or two larger. (Silko 1992, 224, 728)

From this perspective, the ecological changes that currently occur may appear, within Western secular time (e.g., time measured in centuries) to be the end of all life on the planet. But placed in a deeper time frame and different cosmovision, they involve the earth's reclamation of itself in preparation to be remade. At the end of the novel, looking out over his reserve and the massive uranium mine, the Laguna man Sterling reflects that these forces have been moving in their rhythms of reclamation for many years. He reflects that

> as long as [he] did not face the mine, he could look out across the grassy valley at the sandstone mesas and imagine the land a thousand years ago, when the rain clouds had been plentiful and the grass and wildflowers had been belly high on the buffalo that had occasionally wandered off the South Plains. . . . The buffalo were returning to the Great Plains. . . . The buffalo herds had gradually outgrown and shifted their range from national parks and wildlife preserves. . . . [They] had begun to roam farther as the economic decline of the Great Plains had devastated farmers and ranchers and the small towns that once served them. Sterling . . . did not care if he did not live to see the buffalo return; probably the herds would need another five hundred years to complete their comeback. What mattered was that after all the groundwater had been sucked out of the Ogalala Aquifer, then the white

people and their cities of Tulsa, Denver, Wichita, and Des Moines would gradually disappear and the Great Plains would again host great herds of buffalo and those human beings who knew how to survive on the annual rainfall. (Silko 1992, 758–59)

From Sterling's viewpoint, the buffalo—and the land as it was one thousand years earlier—were never fully destroyed. They are *still there* and beginning to resurface, at least for those who know how to detect them. The buffalo, grasses, and other beings were not rendered extinct by colonial processes but were only *dormant* and are now reawakening and on the move, reshaping the continent's ecosystems by traversing their ancient pathways. Importantly, Sterling does not demand that he survive in order to see the buffalo return; it is enough for him to know that this return is possible and underway. This idea is mirrored in *The Marrow Thieves* when one of the teenagers tries to explain why Minerva has sacrificed herself to the government agents in order to protect them: "sometimes you risk everything for a life worth living. Even if you're not the one that'll be alive to live it" (Dimaline 2017, 152).

For these characters, reclamation is not about possession or improving their own conditions but rather about righting damaged relations so that (other) life-forms and worlds can continue. These stories/theories embrace profound transformation as a condition of cohabitation with earth and acknowledge the consequences of systems that interfere with the planet. Instead of seeking to protect existing conditions at all costs and to engineer the direction of time, they aim to move with earth and its changes. At the same time, while these stories/theories imagine and even welcome the fall of currently dominant systems, they do not wish for the elimination of specific peoples or attempt to limit the conditions of their survival. On the contrary, many of the revenants described in these stories/theories—including Oblivia, Miig, and Cedar—love, care for, and offer guidance or protection to people of all heritages, nationalities, and genealogies (and indeed, several of the revenants described in these stories/theories are of mixed, ambiguous, or multiple heritage, gender, disability, sexuality, and/or species). The revenant ecologies they work to create include people, life-forms, and beings from multiple worlds and shaped by diverse forms of violence.

All these forms of revenant agency are deeply embodied and involve difficult, risky, often painful labor. Indeed, the work of migration involves the reciprocal bearing, carrying, and caring for other life-forms across time, space, and the boundaries of life-forms. For example, while Oblivia undertakes the long collective walk home, she carries in her arms a "heavy fledgling swan who had refused its destiny" (A. Wright 2015, 308). In so doing, she becomes a carrier of swan pasts and futures, reciprocating the guidance of the swans and their contributions to her survival (and that of the group she leads). Similar labor is performed in *Future Home of the Living God* by Cedar, who comes to terms with the fact that, by carrying a potentially devolved (or potentially "normal") fetus, she may be carrying "two species in one body . . . straddling not just millennia but epochs" (Erdrich 2017, 76). By nurturing and protecting this indeterminate being within her own body, she forms a profoundly co-embodied relationship with the uncertain futures unfolding around her *and* with her ancestral past.

So, even as they directly face what Western science calls "extinction," these revenants respond by carrying, co-embodying, and offering cohabitats to each other, and to the future beings who will carry on beyond them. In some cases, this takes place through interpersonal relations; in other cases, through the sharing and mingling of genes, energy, and matter; and still in other situations, through the transmission of stories/theories, knowledge, and memory. Tagaq's (2018, 121) protagonist understands this relation as follows: "we are not individuals but a great accumulation of all that lived before. They are with us. They lift us. We will lift them later"—whether as humans, insects, or fossil fuels. Similarly, Robinson (2017, 159) states that

> our bodies are transitory vessels built from recycled carbon like every other living being on this planet. Bits and parts of you have probably been a cricket or a dinosaur or a single blade of grass on the prairies. . . . Let me speak to the creatures that swim in your ancient oceans, the old ones that sing to you in your dreams. Encoded memories so frayed you think they're extinct, but they wait, coiled and unblinking, in your blood and your bones.

These perspectives offer a dramatically different response to extinction than those found in mainstream apocalyptic narratives. Instead of a competition to the death to secure one's own survival or even that of one's life-form, they reconceptualize earthly life as a cross-epochal, multi-life-form relay whose participants constantly lift, remake, and reanimate one another. In so doing, they continually pull life (back) out of extinction not in the form of particular individuals or species but rather in (bio)plural bodies composed of multiple beings, life-forms, and worlds. This is an entirely different way to understand revenance: not as the return of the particular life-forms (or phases thereof) reified by Western ecology but rather the partial and endless reembodiment of beings in different forms, relationships, and modes of cohabitation.

A final, and defining, form of revenant agency is love—more specifically, unconditional love for revenants and returning futures, whatever they may become, without expectation of reciprocation or certainty. In many ways the stories/theories of revenance discussed here are, in Oblivia's words, "really deadly love stor[ies]" (A. Wright 2015, 344) about commitment to kin and land, however changed or harmed.[20] Plural forms of love surge through these narratives: familial, spiritual, ancestral, friendship, sibling, co-conspiratorial, ideological, erotic, parental, romantic, (pluri-)sexual, asexual, platonic, and more. They surge across the barriers erected by oppressive social-political structures between life-forms; between the living, dead, and nonliving; and between the extant and extinct. Various forms of love are nourished throughout the plot of The Marrow Thieves, including adoptive kinship; intergenerational love; love and respect for the land, air, water, and other life-forms; collective love for and through one's people, ancestors, languages, stories, and song; and romantic love (including queer love) that opens up futures worth living for. The plot is framed by the poignant love story of Miig and his husband, Isaac, who was taken into the schools and assumed to be dead until he is reunited with the group near the novel's conclusion. Isaac's homecoming reflects the power of love to overcome comprehensive systems of violence, erasure, and elimination. Tellingly, the marriage tattoos on Miig's and Isaac's hands are buffalo, cherished kin whose return is yearned for, and symbols of revenance as an act of love. When the pair is reunited, Frenchie watches as Isaac

[holds] his hands out, palms turning upwards in a slow ballet of bone, marrow intact after all this time, under the crowded sky, against the broken ground. . . . And I understood just what we would do for each other, just what we would do for the ebb and pull of the dream, the bigger dream that held us all. Anything. Everything. (Dimaline 2017, 231)

What Frenchie describes is a profound form of unconditional love, for which one would do "anything" and "everything," a kind of love that holds

Revenant Ecologies 277

peoples together and "intact," despite the ways in which systemic violence and its ecological effects have pulled them apart.

An important element of revenance as unconditional love is the willingness to welcome and care for returning beings, however unfamiliar or even frightening they might be. For instance, as Oblivia and the swans move northward in *The Swan Book,* they reach a place filled with the noise of flies, moths, and birds. Oblivia recognizes this motion as "land screaming with all of its life to the swans, Welcome to our world" (A. Wright 2015, 327). In other words, this is Country opening itself in welcome—in accordance with its own law—to beings whose presence marks its radical transformation. In *Future Home of the Living God,* Cedar is overwhelmed not by fear but by love for her ending world, absorbed by its beauty although fully aware that she may be living out its final seasons. Enjoying an evening on the porch with her adoptive parents, she reflects that

> all of this is terminal. There will never be another August on earth. Not like this one. . . . The deep orange gold of the sun is pure nostalgia. An antique radiance already sheds itself upon this beautiful life we share. (Erdrich 2017, 69)

At the same time, she prepares to welcome a deeply uncertain being into the world and to love it no matter what. Despite the fears and warnings permeating social discourse, when Eddie learns that Cedar is expecting a child, the news brings him joy, despite the fact that "we do not know what this child will be like" (Erdrich 2017, 51). Cedar, too, begins to feel this sense of wonder, telling Sera that she is "happy at the very pit of [her]self. She feel[s] this stupid joy, a sense of existence, a pleasure in the senseless truth. We happen to be alive" (251). Instead of resentment at the truncation and constraint of her life, or the potential difference of her offspring, she is filled with love for her indeterminate progeny. Steeling herself against the increasingly millenarian public discourse, she insists that "the children born during this time will be possessed of souls, whether or not they are capable of speech, and should be considered fully human" (248).[21] Here, she points to the fusion of ableism and colonialism, linking fears over the neurocognitive difference of potential newborns to the debate between sixteenth-century Catholic bishop Bartolome Las Casas and humanist scholar Juan Ginés de Sepulvéda (and other church leaders) regarding the souls (and human status) of Indigenous peoples.[22] At the close of the novel, when she is trapped at the birthing center, postpartum and awaiting forced insemination, she imagines herself and her baby playing in the now-absent snow, and thinks, "I am here, and I was there. . . . Where will you be, my darling, the last time it snows on earth?" (Erdrich 2017, 332). She does not fantasize that the world as she knows it will be saved; she accepts that snow *will* fall for the last time, in the near future. But she and all the people she cared for will have existed, and her child may still exist, in worlds nonetheless worth inhabiting and loving.

A similar kind of intense but unromanticizing love is found among the black swans of *The Swan Book*, who will have the final word here. Each day, the migrating swans risk death by dehydration and heat exposure, driven by their "infatuation—[their] love affair with the northern skies" (A. Wright 2015, 92). Like the Canada geese in Leanne Betasamosake Simpson's *Noopiming* (2020), they undertake this perilous journey as an act of love and commitment to their nation, its elders and future generations, and to their ancestral law. When they arrive at the tiny and toxic oasis of the swamp for the first time, the flock produce only one egg: "their ode to the swamp," an expression of their love and gratitude for its existence (A. Wright 2015, 92). The swans work for weeks to create an intricate nest, cradling and adjusting the egg to ensure that it is perfectly placed and evenly warmed. Eventually, it is clear that the egg will not hatch, yet the flock continue to build ramshackle nests filled with plastic rubbish. They embrace their new home for what it is, engaging in new forms of reproduction, worlding, and cohabitation that integrate elements of their new home into their traditions. Even as dogs begin to attack and kill the swans, they remain on their nests, where they are lovingly buried by Oblivia, completing their union with the land. And eventually, through these acts of multi-life-form and multibeing love and procreation, the swans are rewarded: "when the rains finally came, all of the winngil, big rain . . . the old lake reappeared again . . . [and] the breeding nests were full of half-grown cygnets" (92). In that moment, the immense effort of this damaged, toxic, potentially deadly (in both senses of the term) love nonetheless makes a future possible for these beings and their kin. They will continue making this journey, recommitting to the land and to earth despite its increasing hostility, giving it their bodies and their young, come what may. As the climate continues to warm, the swans continue their pilgrimage:

> in the hotter sky, their wings beat faster in desperation until finally, they become completely disoriented. They lose faith in their journey. They lose

Revenant Ecologies

each other. The remaining swans fly in every direction in search of the last drying water holes. They stand on baked earth and hiss at the sky they cannot reach, then the time arrives when no more sound comes from their open beaks. The weak, feather-torn necks drop to the ground, and eventually, with wings spread they wait for the spirit flight. (A. Wright 2015, 328)

At first reading, this passage sounds like a hopeless description of impending death and, possibly, extinction. Yet the swans' love for the north, for Country, and for their ancestral migration routes never ceases. Their leader, who is the last of his kind, "found being alone unbearable. . . . [He] never stopped looking for the other swans. . . . [The] continuous clicking of his beak exaggerated an even greater number of swans he anticipated would return in his ghostly rendition of what life once was" (332). Even though he is aware that he is an endling (see chapter 1), this swan never stops repeating his migration, his search, or his physical expression of hope that the swans, their kin, and their worlds will return. "Well," sums up Oblivia, "talk about acts of love" (333).

∿

Revenants, and the distinct ecosystems they co-create, surge back against nihilistic narratives of extinction and apocalyptic discourses, which frame intensifying oppression as the only means for securing the survival of humanity. Revenance—as an ethics, a form of labor, a mode of love, and an ecological strategy—is not a matter of accepting destruction or doing nothing, as apocalyptic narratives suggest of most alternative approaches. On the contrary, it involves actively participating in reversals *as* part of the work of continuities, cultivating and mobilizing radical love for what is to come (back), and living in the humility of fighting for (bio)plural futures even if one cannot benefit from them. Revenants of all kinds—those returning, those supporting the return of others, ancestors, future kin, living and dead—reject the notion of a single future and take advantage of moments of contingency to furiously (bio)pluralize, to (re-)create worlds and ecosystems. These are not salvation stories: revenance does not necessarily involve the reversal of harms, let alone their erasure or automatic forgiveness for those responsible. Yet these *are*, unmistakably, love stories. Specifically, they are narratives of unconditional love and the profound desire to get relationships right regardless of whether doing so will save currently existing worlds.[23] In the wake of the possible end of *a* world—

one constructed and sustained by colonization, capitalism, enslavement, racism, ableism, eugenics, gendered oppression, and, indeed, the systematic destruction of (bio)plurality—they generate new ecologies of return. These are not calls to conserve jealously guarded resources or to control complexity in order to ensure that one's own desired future comes to pass. Instead, they are expressions of love for earth, kin, and worlds, without expectation or demand. They are fierce and powerful refusals of extinction, as a discourse and as a destiny.

Conclusion

Returning Futures

In the years when I first started writing this book, I noticed discussion among seedkeepers, Indigenous gardeners, academics, and regional media about a certain plant and her unexpected return from extinction.[1] One story/theory about this squash explains that her seeds were found in a small clay ball unearthed by archaeologists conducting a dig on Menominee land in what is currently called Wisconsin (Lentz 2015).[2] The archaeologists gave the seeds to renowned Anishinaabe economist and food sovereignty leader Winona LaDuke. She named them "Gete Okosomin" ("really big" or "really cool" old squash in Anishinaabemowin) and identified them as members of a species that had been extinct for at least eight hundred years. According to this story/theory, the seeds were deposited in the White Earth Seed Library and some were shared with the Central Mennonite University (CMU) in Winnipeg, Canada, where a group of students successfully grew them (Hageman 2014; Garrick 2020). Settler academic Kenton Lobe of CMU confirms that he was given the seeds by the White Earth Seed Library for the students to grow and distribute to schools, communities, farms, and gardens, including several Indigenous communities (CMU 2015). However, Lobe, along with retired settler professor David Wrone, question the story of the clay ball and the idea that the squash grown by the students sprouted from centuries-old seeds. They maintain that the seeds were given to Wrone in 1995 by female seedkeepers from the Miami Nation of Indiana and that he shared them with the White Earth Seed Library, from where they made their way to CMU and beyond (Fessenden 2016). Teasing out the

281

tangled vines of these stories, Diné journalist Alysa Landry (2017) contends that, far from being discovered by settler archaeologists, Gete Okosomin were painstakingly held in existence through the intense intergenerational labor of Miami seedkeepers and their kin. Across centuries of colonial violence, she contends, the plants were sustained and their distinct lineage preserved through meticulous practices of hand pollination and companion planting. According to this story/theory, contemporary Gete Okosomin plants are the carefully guarded descendants of a never-extinct life-form.

Some of these seeds came into my hands in autumn 2017 as a gift from a treasured teacher and mentor, Anishinaabekwe Lynx Clan grandmother Dr. Judy Da Silva of Asubpeeschoseewagong / Grassy Narrows First Nation.[3] Her community survives ongoing colonial genocide, forced relocation, and the continuous (for more than six decades) mercury poisoning of their river system and waters. For several decades, Judy has played an integral role in caring for the water and land, supporting the community, holding governments to account, and restoring relations with other life-forms. In autumn 2017, I joined one of the gatherings that Judy organizes annually for Indigenous women and Two-Spirit folks, along with their kin and supporters,

FIGURE 5. Gete Okosomin seeds.

Conclusion

to connect, heal, laugh, eat, make medicine, and connect with the land and water. I attended at the request of a friend, who was moving through two parallel processes of return: the reclamation of her Haudenosaunee roots, to which she had been denied access as a survivor of the "Sixties Scoop"; and the final stages of her life.[4] She had asked me to work with Judy and the other attendees to make medicine to help ease her passage. That weekend, Judy taught us how to find and prepare a powerful pain medicine from the inner bark of a particular tree. This knowledge was itself a revenant memory that had recently returned to one of her family members in a dream.[5] We worked through the night to produce a huge bag of this medicine for our mutual friend in order to ease her suffering and prepare her for her transition. As I left, Judy also gave me and a friend who was traveling with me a small bag of seeds. They had been pulled from the slippery flesh of a Gete Okosomin that the whole group had cooked and eaten on the last night of the gathering. Judy had received some of the seeds from an Indigenous gardener and had been growing them for a few years. She wanted to help them return to Indigenous communities and asked us to pass them through our networks and grow more to share. That winter, we (and many others) sent little parcels of the seeds out through the mail or passed them from hand to hand to people who were making trips to visit family and friends or to participate in frontline struggles. A small palmful of seeds was reserved for our mutual friend, but she completed her journey through the Western door in February 2018, before they could be planted. I grew those seeds in her honor.

Over that winter, I dried them, tentatively turning each seed, trying not to disturb the papery outer coating that I had been warned never to remove before planting. Anxious to keep the seeds in circulation, I covered the first springy seedlings with netting to protect them from squirrels, racoons, crows, and baby skunks. Within a few weeks, the animals had pulled down the mesh so that when I tried to remove it, I damaged the plants. I will never forget seeing a dark-eyed junco killed by a cat because its foot became caught in my ill-advised netting. I had not listened, not understood that the squash should share herself and use her own body as she pleased, on her own terms. Soon after, a new friend began an Indigenous food garden nearby, and I brought three seedlings to grow among their siblings—glassy purple and red corn, flapping tobacco, and purple-blossomed beanstalks, all under the gaze of enormous, ancient Haudenosaunee grandfather sunflowers.[6] This is typical of how Gete Okosomin moves and grows: spreading out tendrils in all directions, grabbing and coiling, pulling kin and strangers close, reuniting and binding them with vines that are fragile but strong enough to move heavy stones. She twines together the people who grow her, the other plants and soils with whom she flourishes, the animals who eat her and whose bodies she will help digest, the times we all differently occupy. With them, she knits together different kinds of knowledge and language, old and new relationships, recipes, plant histories, the paths of ancient trade routes, co-planting methods, soil acidity data, climate change prognostications, and moon knowledge. Like many of her cucurbit kin, she produces both male and female blooms, so that a single plant can pollinate itself, with the help of insects and, often, human hands (the male blooms can be rubbed against the female ones to share pollen). After carrying out this intimate work, I spent the whole summer worrying over the tiny fruits swelling from the base of her brilliant yellow blooms. I started to pay close attention to the insects that stalked along her vines, wondering which ones would carry her future generations in the dirtied fur of their legs and which ones would drill out and wither her hollow body. I learned to identify the insects to whom she offers her bodies as nourishment and shelter, including the solitary bees and returning fireflies. I also learned which ones she needed me to kill to ensure her survival, including the striped southern squash beetles now flourishing in the warming northern summers.

I wished I could witness the motion of her growth, the movements of this being who lives so much slower *and* so much faster than me, who is a hundred seasons younger and thousands of years older than I will ever be. Gradually, each of her fruits fell away, gnawed by thirsty or curious squirrels, dried out by squash beetles, or broken off by my clumsy attempts to care for her. I did not manage to grow any fruit that year (although others with whom I had shared the seeds did). I felt that I had failed at the task given to me and the commitments I had made to the living and the dead. But that squash did not need me, specifically, and she was not broken by my problematic love. I was just one of a multitude of vehicles she passed through on a much bigger and more complex return journey. Gete Okosomin has everything she

Conclusion 285

needs, every gender and gene uncurling in the length of her tendrils, unbroken histories stretching out behind and beyond her yearning vines, and millennia of love stored in her seeds. She refuses to be made extinct, one way or another. She is and has been and will be here, always vibrantly reaching, grasping, creeping, binding, blossoming, offering herself into futures that I cannot feel but nonetheless believe. She is taking (back) her time, her space, her land, her lives, preparing the ground for change. My only role in her return is to love her, and when I can, to help hold open the futures she is busy growing (Michell 2017).

I open this final chapter with reflections on Gete Okosomin because she embodies, and has helped to teach me, so many of the ideas discussed in the previous chapters. In the face of mainstream narratives of extinction and conservation, apocalypse and control, Gete Okosomin offers countertheories and practices of violence and survivance, revenance and unconditional love. Not least, the multiple stories/theories surrounding her extinction, her return, and her renewed movement across the continent offer insights into the creative work through which life-forms and worlds struggle to maintain continuity. When her seeds first came into my life, I asked some collaborators and other growers about their thoughts on the stories of the squash's return from extinction. At first, I was surprised to hear that the story/theory of the clay ball resonated so strongly with LaDuke and many other Indigenous seedkeepers (see Parker 2015; Lentz 2015). With its focus on settler scientists and their apparent "(re)discovery" of Indigenous worlds, I had wrongly assumed that they might find it insulting or harmful. But from another angle, I learned, this story/theory speaks to the immense power of the squash and her kin to *confound* those discourses, sprouting up green and fertile after eight hundred years in protective exile, reversing the condition of extinction imposed violently upon her. Gete Okosomin's (re)emergence asserts that neither the most comprehensive forms of violence nor the imposition of boundaries—such as "living," "dead," "extant," and "extinct"—can break the bonds of cohabitation and multi-life-form love that hold worlds flexibly together. In the context of the clay ball story/theory, this squash is a revenant: not (just) a *descendant* of an ancestor plant but (also) the ancestor *herself*. She embodies the continuous presence of an uncolonized world; she withdrew in refusal of colonial violence and is now, perhaps, returning to hasten its unraveling.

286   Conclusion

Maybe she is taunting her so-called discoverers with her own seemingly impossible existence and miraculous growth, teasing the edges of Eurocentric knowledge systems and their presumption of power over plants and planet. Or perhaps she is working to renegotiate relations with the beings among whom she finds herself—including by strategically leveraging settlers' bodies, labor, and networks to hasten her return. However, the story/theory centering the Miami seedkeepers also attests to the refusal of worlds to submit to destruction and extinction. By turning attention toward the careful, iterative, multigenerational labor of caring for, consuming, and keeping the squash against immense odds, this story/theory, too, centers the power of kinship, more-than-human relations, laws, treaties, and love to survive and flourish beyond the intended ends of worlds. Beyond all this powerful work, Gete Okosomin also supports returns that are both personal and collective, helping to twine communities together, to compost grief into new relationships, and to bring knowledge back its roots in the soil.

Gete Okosomin's return also directly contests mainstream discourses of irreversible extinction and apocalyptic conservation. Her recent public appearances draw attention to the difference between the distinctly revenant ecologies she co-creates and nourishes and those centered by discourses and practices of biodiversity. She is, of course, an object of biodiversity: her participation in knowledge production in Western institutions, concerns about the genetic purity of her lineage, and the debate around her extinction mark her as such. In addition, she is drawn into discourses on conservation, as reflected in the work of the academics attempting to grow, distribute, and teach others how to nurture her. This is also reflected in my own ignorant anxieties over whether she would produce enough seeds so that I could complete my task of sharing them and "keeping her alive" (a markedly conservationist concern).

However, the history of her co-creation, kinship, and co-flourishing with Miami and other Algonquian peoples, other peoples, and life-forms; her specific, iterative bodily formations (including the soils, climates, waters, and other plants, animals, and ancestors she grows with); her movement across ancient and contemporary networks; and her vibrant resurgence all speak to conditions of (bio)plurality. Her existence is not only a matter of biological survival, reproduction, functionality in an ecosystem, or value as a resource or commodity. Gete Okosomin—as a life-form, or the particular plants in which it embodies itself—is not substitutable. Each one

Conclusion

holds its own relationships, shapes unique worlds, and makes distinct contributions to the continuity of others. Gete Okosomin is also an embodiment and endless elaboration of relations, knowledge, ethics, labor, skills, love, and law. She brings bodies together in labor, laughter, eating, gathering, mourning, and the trading and sending of seeds, reconnecting flesh to ancestral forms of nourishment while directly embodying future ecosystems. What's more, she generates intense relations of intimacy and even eroticism as she winds (bio)plural beings into her many-gendered, plurisexual, biological, social, cultural, and political processes of reproduction—including the pleasures of eating or plunging one's fingers into her vibrant, slippery flesh. She comports herself to each of us differently—as vessels and vectors, carers and cared for, mode of return and means of futuring; witness to violence and defiance of it. Indeed, Gete Okosomin (re)emerged into a period of increasing apocalypticism and authoritarian attempts to seize control of earth and its futures, reflected in a wave of right-wing extremism across the Global North. I wrote the first draft of this last chapter on the day of the 2020 U.S. election, in which, for nearly a week, the United States teetered at the edge of *re*electing a publicly avowed white supremacist and misogynist who has justified systemic terrorism against BIPOC and reversed more than one hundred hard-fought environmental protections (among many other things). As I revise this text in the summer of 2023, the Supreme Court of the same country has removed life-saving rights from people who can get pregnant, and struck down affirmative action (a key tool in fighting white supremacy in educational systems in the United States). Meanwhile, many states are banning texts that address racial injustice and/or removing protections for (or actively promoting violence against) trans and nonbinary folks. All these acts constitute not *reversals*—the creative inversions and practices of reemergence and tactical resistance practiced by revenants. Rather, they are *reversions*: forceful *arrests* of movements toward deeper forms of justice, violent interventions designed to drive them out of the public sphere, efforts to halt and prevent the return of alternative futures and the conditions from which they can grow. Yet this is also a moment of powerful, multiple, exponentially generative uprisings for social, racial, political, and ecological justice and of global mobilizations of solidarity, to which Gete Okosomin is now offering her body as nourishment.

In this closing chapter, I want to let the main arguments of this book be drawn into, and together by, Gete Okosomin's twisting vines, roots, and leaves. Picking up on these lessons from the squash, her kin, and her many carers and cohabitants, I offer this final chapter as a "manifesting" (see Creatures Collective 2021) aimed at nurturing (bio)plurality, transforming global structures of violence, and keeping good relations with earth's rapidly changing worlds.[7] In particular, I discuss some practical, concrete actions that can be taken to apply and activate these ideas without attempting to prescribe or determine outcomes.

CONTESTING MAINSTREAM STORIES / THEORIES OF EXTINCTION AND CONSERVATION

The main goal of this book is to contest a pervasive understanding of extinction embedded in the vast apparatus of global conservation and wider ecopolitical discourse. It holds that extinction is the unintended consequence of human activities and progress that can be controlled through scientific-managerial and financial methods. The framing of extinction as "death writ large" (chapter 1) is used to justify and promote aggressive forms of biopolitical, racial, and eugenicist control over human and nonhuman bodies (see chapter 7). Further, this discourse frames extinction as an irreversible threat to the *continuation of dominant global orders*. Since the late 1980s, the issue has been framed in the (oddly apolitical) language of the decline of biodiversity—a version of difference that aligns with existing forms of global social, economic, and political power. It defines difference as an external distinction between internally homogeneous groups, erasing the internal plurality and singularity of worlds. This, in turn, undergirds logics such as substitutability, redundancy, and "no net loss," which reflect and facilitate capitalist forms of control over life-forms and worlds (see chapter 2). In so doing, the biodiversity paradigm drives the homogenization of unique worlds and the transformation of their distinct relational orders to fit with logics of commodification, quantification, financial value, and private ownership. Once absorbed into these political and economic systems, life-forms and worlds are treated as the "financial assets" (Almond, Grooten, and Petersen 2020) of individuals, communities, states, or even "humanity" as a whole.

Such logics affirm the currently dominant system of state sovereignty that rests in large part on colonial, (neo-)imperial, and racial geopolitical power dynamics. Conservation has, from its inception, been functionally entwined with capitalism, colonialism, and statism and promoted by their

Conclusion 289

primary beneficiaries. For instance, Jamaican American environmental historian Dorceta Taylor (2016) has shown how conservation in the nineteenth-century United States (which remains the epicenter of global conservation, culturally and financially) was promoted largely by settler business interests and the white elites they served. Conservation has also, Taylor (2016) contends, shaped American modes of governance, including the naturalization of land theft, (dis)possession, and displacement perpetrated upon BIPOC communities and within gendered hierarchies. Today, conservation has grown into a multibillion-dollar industry and vehicle of neocolonial governance that, as West (2016) has argued, remains rooted in processes of global dispossession, accumulation, and neocolonial dominance. Now, as narratives of biodiversity loss converge with increasingly apocalyptic visions of human extinction (see chapter 6), existing efforts to seize control of processes of life, death, and existence are becoming more ambitious, invasive, encompassing, and authoritarian. They range from the use of big data to track and surveil wildlife—and the marginalized communities who care for it—to ambitious schemes for annexing half of earth's surface for the purposes of private and state-based conservation. This narrative is presented in stark, zero-sum terms: humanity can either double down on forms of conservation that extend and entrench existing global power structures or face a mass extinction event that might mark its own end (see chapter 6; Wilson 2016; and Almond, Grooten, and Petersen 2020).

I acknowledge here that many different people and communities—including those marginalized by dominant power structures—engage in mainstream conservation and biodiversity protection and that their choices to do so are varied and complex. My claim is not that working within these frameworks is inherently wrong or bad, especially in cases where they provide one, or the only, feasible or politically expedient means for protecting one's kin or lands. Instead, my concern is that these concepts and practices, being so firmly rooted in global forms of power and oppression, are often counterproductive, forcing people to uphold systems that oppress them and others, while undermining systems of resistance and alternative forms of co-flourishing. Since the nineteenth century, the idea of conservation has achieved such a strong degree of hegemony and material power as to all but monopolize responses to the destruction of life-forms, erasing and crowding out other approaches. In so doing, it has helped concentrate

290   Conclusion

wealth, power, and sovereignty in the hands of those who have for centuries
dominated earth by force and set in motion enormous ecological harms.

However, despite their claims to universality, discourses of conservation and biodiversity are not the only story/theory available for understanding what is happening to earth's worlds. Nor do they exhaust the
spectrum of possible responses, forms of agency, and ethical, political, and
legal orientations toward this complex of harms. Throughout this book,
I have tried to foreground a range of experiences and articulations of the
destruction of life-forms and worlds, along with plural modes of response
and forms of leadership. Upsetting dominant narratives and power structures, these stories/theories expose the *violence* underlying many mainstream claims about extinction and conservation but also their *contingency*
and the ripe possibilities for their transcendence. I now briefly revisit the
key points of contestation raised by these stories/theories and their implications for action.

REFRAMING "EXTINCTION" AS VIOLENCE

When discussing or presenting the ideas outlined in this book, I have often
been met with two questions: "So, you're against biodiversity?" and "Do
you think that extinction is a bad thing?" As I hope this book has shown,
I most certainly do believe that extinction is an egregious harm. In fact,
one of my major concerns is that its gravity and enormity are not adequately reflected or addressed by dominant frameworks—including the
term "extinction." But whether protecting biodiversity should be the primary, let alone the *only,* mode of response to extinction is a different question. As this book has shown, efforts to protect difference *as* "biodiversity"
often promote and amplify logics that destroy other kinds of difference,
one of which—(bio)plurality—I have discussed in depth. Through the lens
of (bio)plurality, difference is not an abstract quality, let alone a commodity or substance that can be substituted, re-created, or separated from its
concrete embodiments. It is *also* the singular expression of irreplaceable,
constantly transforming constellations of relationships—and much more
that exceeds the limits of my knowledge system and capacities. The main
point of this book is that protecting ecosystems means nurturing singular
expressions of difference *in their own terms* rather than only producing a
kind of difference to (bene)fit existing power structures.

Paying attention to different kinds of difference also requires thinking
critically about their destruction, including how it is described. Throughout

Conclusion 291

this book, I have critiqued terms such as "extinction" and "biodiversity loss" as well as abstractions such as "species," "ecosystems services," or processes of mathematical modeling. These frames, I have argued, depoliticize extinction, deflecting attention from the role of violence in driving it. Similarly, the idea of species *loss* frames life-forms and worlds as property that can be owned, accumulated, or depleted; moreover, it is often used to support the territorial claims of states (see chapter 4). This terminology converts the harms engendered by extinction into matters of damage— that is, the destruction or devaluation of *property* rather than of beings and relations. Narratives of biodiversity "loss" also downplay the agency and collaboration of nonhuman beings and more-than-human worlds in resisting destruction. At the same time, such terms cement the divisions imposed on multiple worlds by colonial and imperial knowledge systems— for instance, between living/dead, biotic/abiotic, sentient/nonsentient, and extant/extinct beings (see chapter 1). In turn, these distinctions narrowly define ideas about who and what can be harmed, is integral to an ecosystem, deserves protection, has value, or can be killed, wasted, or discarded (chapter 4).

So what am I suggesting instead? I have tried to shift attention from the framework of extinction, biodiversity (loss), and conservation toward the *systemic destruction of (bio)plurality,* along with the logics and global structures of violence driving it. Where conservation seeks to conserve the status quo, an approach rooted in (bio)plurality is committed to defending, nurturing, and ensuring the conditions for open-ended difference and change, including revenance and the unique ecosystems that emerge from it (see chapter 7). This approach is *structural*: that is, instead of treating extinction as an accumulation of discrete events (e.g., deaths, extirpations), it attends to broader metanarratives and material formations of power and violence. It is also *systemic,* in that it focuses on how dominant actors construct pervasive systems of violence *and* infiltrate existing relational orders to expand and assert power. In addition, this approach rejects purely subtractive definitions of extinction, focusing instead on the material *formations* (e.g., structures, processes, social orders, subjectivities) that attack (bio)plurality—along with the bodies and cohabitats that nurture and protect it.

What motivates systematic efforts to destroy (bio)plurality? As this book has argued, the conditions of (bio)plurality obstruct and resist projects of domination in which one world attempts to subsume (all) others.

292 Conclusion

This includes the European colonial project as well as the global imposition of dominant norms of "humanity," shaped by powerful global currents of racism, ableism, heteropatriarchy, capitalism, and anthropocentrism (chapters 4, 5, and 6). Under this rubric, bodies and cohabitats that refuse to conform to the demands of aggressors are construed as "threats to humanity" and targeted with extreme intensity, often to the point of (attempted) elimination (chapters 3, 4, and 5). What's more, the breaking of relations is one of the primary ways of releasing—or, more accurately, dismembering— valued entities from the broader bodies of which they form a part. This process is integral not only to the massification used by authoritarian states but also to extractive capitalism (see chapters 1, 2, and 4).

Starting from the analysis of multiscale structural and systemic violence, this book calls for a conscious divestment and diversion of attention, energy, solidarity, and resources from the global conservation industry. More than this, it calls for the purposeful *redirection* and *redistribution* of these energies and resources to support multi-life-form communities who are resisting the systematic destruction of (bio)plurality. In some cases, this may mean fighting *against* mainstream conservation projects. Importantly, I do not mean to suggest that *marginalized* communities should be criticized for participating in mainstream conservation. My call to divest from conservation is aimed primarily at the highly privileged groups who created this system and hold power within it. Nor do I mean to suggest that marginalized communities should be supported only if their actions align with the ideas I have described in this book. On the contrary, terms such as "(bio)plurality" and "revenance" (and indeed, "beings," "life-forms," and "worlds") are simply tools for loosening compacted ways of thinking about how we can respond to extinction. They are not intended to be reified, universalized, or superimposed over the ways that particular worlds understand their relations. I also invite others to hack, rework, critique, and transform them to whatever extent this assists in their own struggles to protect their worlds.

What, then, do I hope will be done with the arguments presented in this book? Perhaps most of all, I hope that readers might reconsider the kinds of activities and struggles they associate with efforts to stop extinction. Simply put, since colonialism, capitalism, racism, ableism, heteropatriarchy, and anthropocentrism drive the systematic destruction of (bio)plurality, *struggles against these forms of oppression are efforts to halt extinction.* Mainstream (and emerging apocalyptic) conservation strategies appear to be doing the opposite, doubling down on responses that further entrench and protect existing power structures while driving the homogenization of relational models, ecosystems, and worlds. In contrast, this book argues that one of the most important ways to fight extinction is to actively participate in struggles against systemic violence but also *for* justice, (bio)plurality, and (bio)pluralizations. If, as this book has argued, extinction is driven by the breaking, perversion, and weaponization (see Todd 2022) of relations, then anti-extinction efforts should focus on remaking, repairing, standing accountable to, and building good relations within and across worlds.

To be very clear, this argument in no way suggests human needs must be met before nonhumans are considered. On the contrary: worlds are internally plural, including multiple life-forms and kinds of beings. At the same time, racism, ableism, anthropocentrism, colonialism, capitalism, and heteropatriarchy cut across multiple life-forms, beings, and worlds, often instrumentalizing them against one another (see chapter 3). As such, to effectively fight the systematic destruction of (bio)plurality, struggles against oppression and for justice must reach across life-forms and worlds.

A multitude of communities marginalized by global power structures are already, and have long been, doing this work. With this in mind, the call to *change* directions is directed predominantly toward those of us who most benefit from and are invested in existing global structures such as conservation, colonialism, extractivism, and, indeed, mainstream norms of humanity. It is also crucial for people who occupy positions of privilege to become skilled in following the leadership of racialized, Indigenous, disabled, queer, nonhuman (including, where appropriate ancestral), and other currently marginalized beings and communities. This involves recognizing forms of power, wisdom, knowledge, and authority that diverge from Eurocentric norms of individual rationality and are embodied in plural ways. For instance, it might mean learning from the ways that groups of nonhumans communicate and coordinate with each other (see chapters 2 and 5). It could involve attuning to distributed forms of emergent, collective, decentralized social mobilizations (brown 2017) led by those who diverge from dominant norms of humanity (see chapter 7). Or it could entail valuing and learning from forms of cognition that are distributed, embodied, or nonlinguistic (see L. Simpson 2017; see also chapters 2 and 7). At the same time, such efforts must acknowledge, generate accountability for, and work to redress the violations of laws, agreements, and relationships between peoples, other life-forms, and other beings (see the Introduction and chapters 3 and 7). This includes contesting universalist claims to occupy enormous areas of earth's ecosystems in the name of mainstream conservation or, indeed, of "humanity."

Crucially, addressing the systematic destruction of (bio)plurality requires ethico-political responses to violence that are not always totally nonviolent, at least from the perspective of states, police, or military actors (see chapter 4). For instance, as discussed in chapter 4, actions such as blockades and protests—often undertaken in response to the breaking of laws and treaties by the state—are regularly framed by states as acts of violence. Precisely because they disrupt the forms of order imposed by structures of domination—including the smooth functioning of colonial sovereignty and extractive capitalism—acts of resistance to the destruction of (bio)plurality are often defined as threats (see chapter 7). For this reason, these mobilizations should not be judged in terms of the definitions of "order," "peace," and/or "lawfulness" defined by the actors responsible for the destruction. Rather, they ought to be understood in terms of the laws, ethics, and political orders of the worlds in which they are embedded (see chapter 5). It also bears repeating that the logic of DARVO (see chapters 3 and 6)—the attempt to reverse the perceived direction of a threat by making aggressors appear to be victims—is a powerful tool used to vilify and criminalize resistance (see chapter 7). Actions that challenge dominant forms of power—such as the use of conservation areas for traditional practices or refusal to respect rules put in place by conservation organizations—should not be automatically criminalized. Instead, they too need to be understood in the legal-political and historical contexts in which they take place. Bearing all this in mind, I will now briefly sketch out *some* possibilities of response to the forms of violence discussed in this book.

EARTH/BODY VIOLENCE: RECOGNIZING VIOLENCE, HEALING (BIO)PLURAL TRAUMA, QUEER(ING) RELATIONS

The attempt to sever co-constitutive bonds between bodies and/or cohabitats (chapter 3) is one of the most pervasive and fundamental weapons used to destroy (bio)plurality. Far beyond the degradation of habitat—defined as a substrate, a background, or a set of resources for life—this form of violence toxifies conditions of cohabitation. It converts the homes that radically different beings make for one another into places of harm and

Conclusion

trauma. Earth/body violence also works to impede, prevent, and punish many forms of (bio)pluralization that enable continuities across life-forms and worlds. These include love, care, corporeal integration (including co-digestion or burial in the earth), reproductive and nonreproductive forms of eroticism, play and rivalry (including ancestral conflicts; see chapter 7), and a multitude of intimacies between beings. As this book has shown, bodies and cohabitats that engage in and derive power from (bio)pluralizations are targeted with particular force by invasive states and economic orders (see A. Simpson 2014; Goldberg-Hiller and Silva 2015). Mainstream conservation, with its focus on managing life and death processes—not least through programs of (en)forced biological reproduction (chapters 1, 3, and 4)—does little to address these forms of violence and, as this book has shown, often works along with them. An approach informed by earth/body violence would call for very different strategies.

First, it would require efforts to identify and hold aggressors to account for intersectional forms of harm based on race, gender, sexuality, disability, economic status, and/or life-form, and to link these directly to ecological harm. Second, such approaches ought to be *trauma informed*: that is, shaped by awareness of how trauma is inflicted, how it manifests in diverse bodies (and cohabitats), and how it impacts the ways that they cohere and relate to one another. As this book has argued, harm and trauma are not located in individuals. Instead, they are distributed—radically and unevenly—across bodies, relational structures, cohabitats, and worlds. For instance, harm and trauma can spread through entire ecosystems (see Mitchell 2014a), impeding interactions, severing or blocking connections, and causing breakdown or collapse (see chapter 3). In invoking the language of trauma, I am not suggesting that Western psychological methods should be applied to situations of ecopolitical violence (although they may be useful in some cases). Rather, my point is that efforts to address extinction should recognize the role of trauma caused by earth/body violence and support modes of caring for and healing trauma that are relevant to the impacted worlds. For instance, in its report on the effects of environmental violence, NYSHN (2016) provides a set of healing practices that include land-based activities, conversation prompts, and the use of traditional medicines to heal trauma that is distributed across bodies, lands, and life-forms. Efforts to support healing from earth/body violence may also include acknowledgment by aggressors and beneficiaries of the harms, along with the (re)allocation of resources to support the restoration of relationships. Although it is desirable in itself and should not be treated in purely instrumental terms (especially by outsiders), the healing of traumatized relationships makes it possible for conditions of (bio)plurality to be restored and for cohabitats to return to a state of thriving.

Third, responses to extinction informed by earth/body violence would embrace queer(ed) understandings of the relations between bodies, life-forms, and worlds. In this context, "queer(ed)" does not *only* refer to relations that fall within 2SLGBTQIA+ identities, relationships, and practices. It also includes any and all relations that challenge, resist, subvert, and confront—that is, actively *queer* (as a verb)—dominant relational norms.[8] Eurocentric, colonial-capitalist systems of governance (including most mainstream conservation projects) define "proper" relations between beings and life-forms in narrow ways, including heterosexual and/or nuclear family structures among humans, and the instrumental use, commodification, consumption, domination, and waste of nonhumans. As this book has shown, these relational norms are imposed and maintained through (often lethal) force. Responses to extinction informed by earth/body violence would explicitly embrace the multitude of relations, including intimacy, eroticism, care, respect, and love (see chapter 7), that contribute to the integrity, richness, continuity, and beauty of worlds. They would also recognize the importance of love, care, and erotic connection in generating and sustaining the conditions of (bio)plurality along with the continuity and well-being of ecosystems. Emotional, sensory, somatic, and other forms of relational labor (including grieving, ceremony, and reckoning with aggressors) would be recognized as integral elements of protecting and nurturing ecosystems. Importantly, such approaches would recognize the importance of restoring relations of *pleasure* and *enjoyment* (see brown 2017) between lifeforms and within cohabitats, such as the sensory joy derived from direct connection with land and water or from caring for multiple generations of another life-form. Approaches informed by earth/body violence would confront heteropatriarchal norms that frame sexuality (and survival) only in terms of biological reproduction, including conservation practices based on coercive reproduction, gendered and sexual violence, and/or eugenics (see chapters 1, 4, and 7). They would acknowledge the role of gendered and sexual norms—and the destruction of entire relational orders—as drivers of extinction and support efforts at rebuilding these relationships within affected worlds.

CONFRONTING INVASIVE POLITIES: GLOBAL LAND RETURN, REPARATIONS, AND DIVESTING FROM CONSERVATION

The alloyed logics of invasion and extraction are powerful solvents of (bio)plurality. They align tightly in their shared goal of breaking down relationships and relational orders, for different but compatible reasons. Colonialism, and settler colonialism in particular, seeks to remove any and all barriers to the acquisition of land and the assertion of sovereignty by extinguishing resistance and alternative forms of power. Extraction, a logic at the heart of global capitalism, involves the violent dissolution of cohabitats and the dismemberment of multi-life-form bodies into commodifiable parts and waste. Within invasive states, these logics work in mutually supportive ways. Namely, states create and sustain legal and political environments that support and rely on extraction, using military and police force to ensure its smooth functioning. Meanwhile, extractive industries provide the material and financial basis for the expansion and accumulation of (global) power by states, while benefiting from the financial, political, and physical support of states for their projects. As this book has shown, these dynamics contribute to the systematic destruction of (bio)plurality by fragmenting and destroying cohabitats, transforming relational orders to fit their own purposes (including by recasting them as biodiversity), and halting or commandeering (bio)pluralizations. For this reason, one of the most important goals of those concerned with stopping extinction should be to fight capitalism, colonialism, and state sovereignty over "nature." From this perspective, *intersectional* and *(bio)pluralistic* movements against capitalism, extractivism, racism, ableism, and police / military violence and *for* racial, social, disability, ecological, multispecies, and other forms of justice, equity, and inclusion are among the most important defenses against extinction. This is not to suggest that all these movements, in their current forms, embrace the kinds of antiviolence and (bio)plurality described in this book; indeed, many social and / or environmental movements embed powerful currents of racist, ableist, gendered, heteronormative, and anthropocentric violence (see, for instance, brown 2017; Jaquette Ray and Sibara 2017; L. Simpson 2017, 2020). For this reason, many social movements are working to address lateral and horizontal violence (aggressions within their movement and among members of other movements). Many are also working to seed solidarities across different groups affected by similar forms of violence (e.g., BIPOC and / or disabled communities affected by pollution)

298   Conclusion

and/or similar groups facing different kinds of violence (e.g., Indigenous communities linked by kinship facing different forms of extractive violence and/or negative impacts of conservation). Because it helps to strengthen defenses for (bio)plural worlds and the relationships on which they rely, this kind of work is indispensable in the fight against extinction.

Crucially, confronting the systematic destruction of (bio)plurality also requires transforming the land-intensive focus of conservation. Specifically, it means moving from a global logic of land grabbing to one of *land return* and *reparations*. As this book has shown, mainstream conservation projects are increasingly implicated in the claiming and appropriation of enormous tracts of land, often as a form of investment and/or development (chapter 6). In so doing, they contribute to the displacement of Indigenous, land-based, and other marginalized peoples, while concentrating control over land in the hands of already dominant actors and institutions. The most ambitious of these projects, including Wilson's (2016) "half-earth" proposal and more modest yet similar "land-sparing" scenarios (Almond, Grooten, and Petersen 2020), would necessitate the mass displacement of primarily BIPOC, land-based, and poor people. Even critics of such approaches tend to promote forms of ecopolitical transformation that are ultimately homogenizing. For instance, unmarked scholars Bram Büscher and Robert Fletcher (2019) propose a model of "convivial conservation" as an alternative to existing capitalist and financial approaches. Their model includes "historic reparations" for those harmed by colonialism, and "conservation basic income schemes" that would encourage "interaction with biodiversity" and *"biodiversity-friendly* livelihood pursuits" (Büscher and Fletcher 2019, 292, emphasis mine).[9] In so doing, it recognizes the issue of land grabbing, avoids calls to remove humans from conserved areas (see Wilson 2016 and chapter 6), and contests extractive and/or developmental models of conservation. Nonetheless, it aims to remake global ecosocial relations in alignment with the ideas of unmarked Austrian theorist Ivan Ilich, the (nearly hegemonic in some fields) work of unmarked American scholar Donna Haraway, and the fraught practices of TEK (see the Introduction and chapter 1). In so doing, it calls for the extension of a specific model of ecopolitical relations across the planet. The call for the return of land to Indigenous peoples is also qualified; the authors champion *either* this radical form of change *"or* at the very least . . . co-ownership of or co-management responsibilities" (Büscher and Fletcher 2019, 291, emphasis mine). The latter would amount to the mere *modification* of existing conservation approaches (many of which already, and often problematically, involve "co-management" programs).

This book calls for a more radical paradigm shift in which the ownership, control, development, and consolidation of land for and by conservationists is actively contested and in which changes in ownership of and access to land are considered indispensable to fighting extinction. More precisely, it proposes that much of the resources and energy now devoted to conservation be redirected toward the *global-scale return of land to Indigenous and land-based communities* and to supporting the restoration and/or revenance of their ecopolitical orders.[10]

Opponents of land return often start from the assumption that it would be overly complex or contentious (i.e., that many communities might conflict over how land should be returned or used in the future). It is indeed important to note that Indigenous and land-based communities are far from monolithic; they engage with land in many different ways—including, in some cases, support for extraction and other ecologically harmful projects. However, as discussed in chapter 4, Indigenous and land-based communities across the planet have for millennia employed arrangements such as shared access, diplomacy, what European legal theory calls "usufruct," seasonal rotation, kinship responsibilities, nomadic movement, the hosting of guests (including many invasive communities), and many other techniques to enable multiple communities to live on and care for the same lands. The point is not that the process of negotiation required for global-scale land return would be simple, easy, or uncontentious. Rather, the point is that such a task is possible, vital, and has a deep history and set of precedents within many communities.

In fact, a project of similar scale but with very different motivations is already underway in mainstream conservation. Specifically, major conservation organizations have begun planning in fine-grained detail (including the creation of maps, milestones, and benchmarks; see Dinerstein et al. 2019) strategies for annexing enormous areas of land for "conservation (investment)" on a global scale. This includes negotiating access by multiple groups for different forms of use (e.g., scientific, recreation, and leisure) and developing terms of ownership. Mainstream conservationists, governments, and billionaires are lining up behind the idea of "setting aside" 30 percent of earth's surface for "nonuse." So, the issue does not appear to be concern over scarcity of land or the complexity of negotiating access, rights, and use when the actors involved are governments, corporations, NGOs, investors, philanthropists, or universities. More than this, the idea of engaging in large-scale transfers and/or changes in ownership and control of land seems to be regarded as feasible by mainstream conservationists—as long as the transfer moves in the direction of existing forms of power.

So, if large-scale changes in land ownership and access are already on the table, then why are processes of *land return* not given the same consideration? And why do proposed solutions focus on transferring *more* land into the hands of the actors and institutions driving extinction rather than to communities recognized to have the knowledge, skill, and capabilities to ensure the long-term thriving of ecosystems? The latter question is especially relevant considering the degree to which conservation organizations rely on the knowledge, resources, and labor (including unacknowledged relational labor) of BIPOC, poor, and land-based communities in order to carry out their projects.

The analysis of apocalyptic conservation discourses in chapter 6 offers some insight into these questions. Namely, that chapter discusses the racist, anti-Indigenous, and other assumptions that underpin these discourses, including the false beliefs that marginalized communities do not prioritize environmental issues and/or that their flourishing threatens privileged ways of life. Further, proposals for land return on national or subnational scales are often met with irrational fears on the part of groups currently in power, which are linked to the narratives of reversion and/or the reversal of threat discussed in chapter 6. Among these is the assumption that white people would be subjected to violence and/or rendered homeless if land in North America were returned to Indigenous peoples (see Shotwell 2016). Simply because invaders used and continue to use these techniques to seize and dominate lands does not mean that others would do the same. On the contrary, the stories/theories discussed in chapter 7 explicitly imagine forms of solidarity, care, and protection across multiple communities; however, they are not led by, nor do they center the priorities of, groups currently in power. Indeed, every chapter in this book includes examples of alternatives to conservation rooted in the leadership and ways of worlding of land-based peoples and their more-than-human kin. While some of these proposals involve changes in relationships and access to land, in contrast to historical and contemporary modes of conservation (and other forms of governance), none of these alternatives involves killing, eliminating, or preventing the flourishing of another group.

In addition to shifting the focus toward land return, supporting the work of revenance and protecting (bio)plurality also requires *reparations* in the sense described by Queen Quet, leader of the Gullah Geechee nation.[11] From her perspective, reparations are not mere payments of money that extinguish ongoing responsibility. They also involve investment of labor, moral support, and energy into the rebuilding of worlds in which harmed beings can once again flourish—not necessarily exactly as they were but as their communities want them to be.[12] Understood in this way, reparations do not simply involve a kind of quid pro quo but also include the desire and continued commitment to the flourishing of others.

Some techniques that may support reparations of this kind include the creation of urban farming systems and the enhancement of access for racialized, Indigenous, disabled, poor, and 2SLGBTQIA+ people to land; the reinstitution of practices such as silviculture, swidden farming, and controlled burning; practices of living with other animals that include hunting but also legal and/or ethical agreements to ensure their continuity; the restitution and protection of migration routes and traditions, including practices for supporting migrants, whether human or nonhuman; and much more.[13] Reparations and the labor and effort invested in them would involve a very different kind of "land-use change" from that envisioned by the framers of the LPI (see chapter 6). Namely, instead of coercing and/or paying people to stop using land, it would encourage the proliferation of collaborative, multi-life-form practices of cohabitation *on* and *with* the land, not least in response to rapidly changing climatic conditions. Crucially, this form of reparation(s) would also involve materially supporting—rather than criminalizing and punishing—the creation of solidarities among people who have sustained similar kinds of harm and who wish to work together to address injustices and negotiate future conditions (see Adisa-Farrar 2020). It is very possible that these future arrangements might employ (some) techniques of conservation or use this language, but they would not be compelled to do so by external or internalized power structures or as a requirement for receiving support.

As mentioned previously, the first step in achieving these goals would be to divest and redirect the immense amounts of effort, energy, knowledge, labor, public support, and, indeed, money currently invested into conservation and biodiversity protection. As this book has discussed, conservation is a multibillion-dollar global industry, whose major actors are focusing their operations on large-scale investment and expropriation that concentrate more wealth and power—and control over possible futures—in the hands of the mega-rich. In addition, a recent report shows that billionaires—including Amazon founder Jeff Bezos and Anders and Anne Holch Povlsen (the largest landowners in Scotland)—are donating and/or endowing record-breaking amounts of funds to (private) conservation projects that reflect their personal values and goals (Greenfield 2021).[14] Similarly, a record US$5 billion was donated to support the goal of protecting 30 percent of earth's land and water by 2030 as part of a "global deal for nature" championed by major conservation actors such as the UN's Environment Program and the WWF (Dinerstein et al. 2019).[15] Importantly, several of the donors highlighted as part of this "green era of giving" (Greenfield 2021) engage in private rewilding. For instance, the Holch Povlsens have bought up large areas of the Scottish highlands (lands that have been subject to significant anti-colonial struggles over several centuries) for this purpose. Similarly, the late Douglas Tompkins, founder of leisure brand the North Face, bought up huge tracts of land in Chile and bequeathed them (under the name of Pumalín Park) to the Chilean state. Most recently, in 2022, Patagonia CEO Yvon Chouinard and his family donated their stake in the company (worth US$3 billion) to "fighting climate change."[16] This donation involves creating an NGO and trust dedicated to promoting that particular (white, Euro-descendent, settler) family's environmental values and model for ecological futures. If it is possible to "give away" one's company, why, then, is it not possible to give back these resources to the communities from whose lands its profits were derived?

The sheer size of the conservation investments mentioned here, and the central involvement of billionaires—who increasingly influence global governance and future planning—are moving conservation markedly toward the apocalyptic models described in chapter 6. In this context, it is crucial for those who care about earth's life-forms and worlds to divest from these efforts and direct support toward a wider range of ecopolitical movements. Of course, such efforts must also involve large-scale transformation to systems of production, global finance, consumption patterns, and the role of states in promoting them. The huge and rich literature and public discourse on divestment to address climate change discusses many of these concerns. However, divestment also involves efforts to relinquish cultural, social, and popular beliefs and ideas that shape our actions and relationships. For example, this book highlights the need for privileged people concerned

Conclusion 303

with conservation to release attachment to ideas such as biodiversity and the financial value of life-forms (see chapter 2). Another example of cultural investment in conservation is the tendency of white, northern people to mourn and lay claim to life-forms with which they have no direct relationships but only colonial or consumerist connections (see Mitchell 2017a). For many of us who care about other life-forms and worlds, divesting from such ideas will involve processes of learning, relearning, and critically confronting our own assumptions, goals, and (often implicit) frames of reference. It also demands careful, critical scrutiny of the aims, practices, leadership, cultures, and messaging of organizations one supports. Put another way, fighting against the systematic destruction of (bio)plurality requires many of us to turn against discourses in which we may have invested a great deal of hope and effort. But we can do so out of love for the peoples, beings, and worlds with whom we cohabitate and out of the active desire for future coexistence.

ANTI-ELIMINATION AND (BIO)PLURAL FUTURES

Among the most salient concepts discussed throughout this book are genocide and eliminative violence. As chapter 5 argues, the concepts of genocide and extinction are deeply entwined, in theory and practice. Both terms speak to the total and irreversible destruction of unique collectives. At the same time, both involve eliminative forms of violence that exceed physical and biological forms of killing, attacking the collective flourishing and possible futures of a unique life-form or world. As chapter 5 shows, tactics of genocide are often used to target not only human groups but also more-than-human communities and nonhuman peoples. In some cases, existing legal frameworks and concepts may be useful in preventing and holding actors accountable for egregious harms, where this is deemed appropriate by the affected community. Chapter 5 argues that, if international law were to account for multiple legal, political, and ethical orders beyond, it should allow for the prosecution of genocide cases in which the plaintiff is nonhuman or more-than-human. It should also recognize multi-life-form genos, and/or nonhuman peoples when they exist in relevant legal-political systems. Indeed, this book argues that responses to eliminative violence must be rooted in the legal, political, and ethical contexts of the *worlds in which harm has taken place*—not (only or necessarily) in the abstract, universalizing, and Eurocentric frameworks of international law. In many cases, honoring the relevant legal and political orders involves recognizing harms to nonhumans, attending to collectives co-constituted by radically different beings, and respecting laws, agreements, and other arrangements with nonhumans (see chapter 1). At the same time, there are important discussions and negotiations to be had about the kinds of sentences, punishments, or other (nonjudicial/nonpenal) responses that might emerge from such cases, again within the context of relevant legal, political, and ethical systems.[17]

Another argument made in this book is that processes of extinction include forms of elimination that are embodied by a complex mix of structural and systemic forms of violence. Even in cases where there is no evidence of *intentional* or *centralized* targeting or in which harms appear to be indirect (e.g., a result of extraction), the forces driving extinction are guided by eliminative *logics*. These logics may be deeply internalized, especially for those of us embedded within invasive and/or dominant cultures. For instance, they might involve the uncritical acceptance of biosecurity policies that insist that some life-forms must be exterminated for others to thrive. They also lurk in the (often subconscious) beliefs of many white and non-disabled communities that population growth among BIPOC and/or disabled communities threaten the future survival of humanity (see chapter 6).

In order to address the systematic destruction of (bio)plurality, *eliminative imaginaries in all their forms need to be actively resisted, discredited, and disempowered*. All of us who care about stopping extinction—and especially those who are not members of groups directly targeted for elimination— need to become skilled, sensitized, and knowledgeable about identifying eliminative logics and intervening to challenge them. It is crucial to believe, ally with, and actively support communities who are resisting eliminative violence in any form.

At the same time, a key priority for anyone concerned with protecting (bio)plurality and/or fighting extinction should be to generate a politics of *desire for co-existence* (Kafer 2013) with radically different others. In particular, there is an urgent need to actively imagine futures that include life-forms and worlds who are currently simply expected to "go extinct"— and to figure out how to realize those futures.[18] For people with significant privilege, this means redistributing access to the conditions that support survival and thriving, whether material, social, economic, or relational (see L. Simpson 2020). For those interested in the futures of "humanity," it means releasing rigid norms and cultivating openness to different ways of *being* human and more-than-human. As chapter 7 discusses, it also involves learning with and from revenants who embody an ethos of welcome toward new worlds and ecosystems, even if these movements unsettle, challenge, or shift one's desires, hopes, and expectations. Another term for this (in English) is *unconditional love*—for difference, for earth, and for the multiplicity of worlds. Crucially, it is possible—and essential—to cultivate love for these worlds whether or not we (as individuals or as collectives) will be the ones who inhabit them. Dreaming these inclusive, (bio)plural futures and cultivating this unconditional love is integral to fighting eliminative violence and extinction. And whatever the results, the fight itself matters.

In pondering these possibilities, I am grateful to Gete Okosomin and her fellow revenants for curling her tendrils into my consciousness and that of so many others. I often wonder what she is up to, and why she is making her return now, of all times. Maybe her roots are tingling with a sense of political contingency infusing the soil, water, and air, and she is offering herself to aid in the transformations carried out by her kin. Maybe she is sick of being called extinct and wants to make her presence irrefutably known. Or maybe she is fed up with the pollution and enclosure of the earth that nurtures her and is joining her fellow revenants in overturning the systems that suppress them. Perhaps she has no goal beyond the essential work of her continued existence, even if it does not "save the planet." What I sense most intensely in the unfurling of her tendrils and the breath of her blossoms is the thrum of revenance—the fierce, world-creating power of desiring difference and welcoming (bio)plural futures, whatever they might turn out to be.

Notes

INTRODUCTION

1. I am indebted here to Christina Sharpe's (2016) work on the *ongoing* wake of white supremacist violence embodied in slavery, settler colonialism, and other structures of oppression. This book argues that global patterns of extinction are another wave in this wake.

2. The term "story/theory" affirms that stories may crystallize generations of iterative knowledge, experimentation, and observation and offer elegant frames for understanding complex worlds (Benton-Benai 2010; Umeek 2012; Doerfler, Sinclair, and Stark 2013; Million 2014). Likewise, theories—whether scientific, philosophical, or otherwise—are stories that help make sense of the world. Neither should be considered more valuable than the other in sharing and elaborating knowledge.

3. BIPOC is an acronym for Black, Indigenous, and People of Color that is frequently used in the context of North America by members of the relevant communities at the time of writing. However, like many identifying terms, this acronym is contested and does not capture the complexity of identities and kinship shared by the communities to whom it refers. I would therefore encourage readers to heed the diversity of groups referred to as BIPOC and to pay attention to changing currents of language and, of course, to each person's practices of self-identification. "Majority world" was coined by writer and photographer Shahidul Alam in the early 1990s to refer to the Black, Brown, and other communities that comprise the majority of earth's human population (Shafaieh 2022).

4. Métis scholar Max Liboiron (2020) writes beautifully about the connection of *all* knowledge to specific places and multispecies communities, and the politics of its travels.

5. See C. Taylor 2007, Bennett 2010, and Mitchell 2014a for discussions of how Western secularity remains infused with Judeo-Christian concepts and frameworks.

6. Extirpation refers to the localized—rather than total or global—extinction of a species.

Notes to Introduction

7. For example, Geraldo Ceballos (2016, 286) reflects on Pope Francis's influential 2015 encyclical *Laudato Si*, citing "unchecked human population growth, *social inequities*, and irresponsible consumption" as causes of extinction (emphasis mine).

8. The United Nation's insistence on protecting state sovereignty caused significant delays to the ratification of the UN Declaration on the Rights of Indigenous Peoples (UNDRIP).

9. The Latin phrase *ex situ* refers to removal from its natural context—e.g., the placement of plants in arboretums. See Chrulew 2011 for an account of the use of this practice by colonial powers.

10. "Subsistence" is not intended to homogenize the immensely diverse range of practices used by Indigenous and small-scale farming communities; instead, it refers to economic models that do not rely on the creation of excess.

11. West (2016) shows that the majority of "international" conservation funding originates from American and European sources and has the explicit aim of benefiting those countries.

12. "Fortress conservation," emerging from conservation projects in sub-Saharan Africa, refers to forms of conservation that rely on keeping all humans out of protected places.

13. For instance, Donna Haraway's (2015) article, which has become seminal within environmental humanities discourses on extinction, mentions the word "extinction" twice but does not offer any further definition or critical analysis, taking for granted mainstream meanings of the term.

14. See West's 2004 and 2016 discussions of how conservation projects function as and often replace governments and/or modes of governance within the communities in which they become embedded.

15. Please note that throughout this book I decline the Western academic convention of italicizing words in languages other than English, which embodies the assumption that these terms are "foreign" (a particular irony in contexts where English is an externally imposed tongue!). The story/theory in this section is paraphrased from John Borrows (2010) and Leanne Betasamosake Simpson (2013). As an outsider to Anishinaabe culture, I have no automatic entitlement to these stories, and I wish to express respect and gratitude for their being shared beyond the community. Following the guidance of Anishinaabe elders and educators Basil Johnston (2010) and Edward Benton-Benai (2010) on appropriate engagement with Anishinaabe stories, I have retold the story in my own words but included as many details as possible from the tellings from which I draw. All errors in the telling and interpretation of these and other communities' stories/theories quoted in this book are mine alone, and readers should always defer to the cited sources if discrepancies occur.

16. The story/theory of Sedna varies considerably across communities and regions. For instance, in some communities, the young woman marries a dog-man or a raven-man. As given here, this story/theory is paraphrased from Ipellie 1993, Leduc 2010, and Martin 2011. Thank you to Tim Leduc for suggesting engagement with this story/theory. All errors are mine.

Notes to Chapter 1   309

17. In some versions of the story, Sedna does not voluntarily control the ways in which she withholds the animals. Instead, this duty is thrust upon her, as a result of the violent act of the severance of her limbs.

18. These protocols can vary across different communities.

19. The Akule is a fish called the goggle-eyed scad in English.

20. The translation of kūpuna most often used in English is "elder." A kuūʻula is a Hawaiian Fishing God stone.

21. It is common in Kānaka Maoli knowledge systems for multiple theories to coexist without necessarily contradicting or negating each other. Many Kānaka Maoli words and stories have multiple meanings, and knowledge of a phenomenon is often derived from multiple versions or interpretations.

22. Following the work of Jarrett Martineau, Leanne Simpson (2017) uses the concept of opacity to describe knowledge that is legible to those immersed within a particular knowledge system but inscrutable to those outside of it.

23. Here, "co-constitutive" refers to logics of violence that ground, support, amplify, and/or may be necessary to each other—for instance, the relationship of colonialism and anthropocentrism (see Belcourt 2015) or that between ableism, racism, and speciesism (Clare 2017; S. Taylor 2017).

24. Ontological expansion is the privilege conferred by whiteness to move with ease in and out of BIPOC spaces, always ensured by the option of exiting into the safety of white privilege (Shannon Sullivan 2019).

25. As articulated by the cited thinkers, resurgence and decolonization involve *Indigenous people* (not others) taking back their land, culture, and lifeways; and Indigenous research is carried out by Indigenous people, in ways that reflect their distinct knowledge systems.

26. I would like to thank Zoe Todd for consistently raising this point in multiple mediums.

27. "Turtle Island" is a term used by *some* (but not all) Indigenous peoples in Canada to describe the continent that is known in colonial terms as North America. The term is frequently used within Haudenosaunee and Anishinaabe communities on the lands where much of this book was written, so I use it here. However, it should not be assumed that all Indigenous peoples of this continent use the term, and its links to the origin stories of specific peoples should be acknowledged.

28. White and/or Euro-American scholars who take offense at being identified as such often adopt philosophies of "color-blindness" or "all lives matter," which undermine distinct BIPOC experiences, including significant inequalities in the distribution of violence, harm, and benefits.

29. This is another effect of settler mobility—see the Preface of this book and Creatures Collective 2021.

1. "MEGADEATH"?

1. To give just a few examples of theorists discussed in this book, Donna Haraway (2008, 2015), Thom van Dooren (2014), Deborah Bird Rose (2011a, 2011b), and Ursula Heise (2016) all offer rich accounts of what extinction does, how it manifests

Notes to Chapter 1

within particular worlds, and elaborations on its meanings. However, they all use the terms "extinction" and "mass extinction" without significantly questioning these definitions or basic logics.

2. Discourses of TEK often impose—and fetishize—criteria such as the perceived age of stories, their use of "traditional" language, or their perceived alignment with Western scientific communicational norms, discounting the contributions of contemporary Indigenous thinkers, the use of colloquial language, humor, satire, and other knowledge practices.

3. The Yarralin community in what is currently called the Northern Territories includes members of the Gurindji, Ngarinyman, Bilinara, and Mudburra peoples. Rose's work does contain some inconsistencies in regard to not conflating extinction with death: for example, she refers to life-forms "dying out" and claims that, with extinction, "we are seeing deaths expand and expand, shifting into another state altogether" (2011b, loc. 2632).

4. It is important to note that for many Aboriginal and other Indigenous peoples in Australia and around the world, textile-related references are not abstract metaphors. Weaving, braiding, and other textile practices are deeply entwined in everyday activity and practice and are part of the entwining of life, death, intergenerational knowledge, and continuity.

5. Although many people who practice Western science follow other religious or belief systems (see, for instance, Ceballos 2016), the biological concepts of life and death expressed within mainstream scientific discourses are strongly Western secular. These positions are not necessarily contradictory: Western secularity is not the absence of religious belief but the conversion of Judeo-Christian beliefs into mundane or earthly forms (see also C. Taylor 2007; Mitchell 2014a).

6. The Copenhagen Zoo maintains a policy of giving individual names to only a select few animals that are likely to live more than fifty years, affirming the others are generic, anonymous units of life or genetic materials.

7. Offers to relocate Marius to zoos in Krakow and Yorkshire were reportedly rejected on similar bases, for failure to meet EAZA's standards for genetic conservation.

8. The so-called Doomsday vault contains copies of seeds held in many other seedbanks around the world.

9. On woolly mammoths, see, in particular, projects led by George Church (Sarchet and Press Association 2017), Henrik Poinar (Kaplan 2015), and Sergey Zimov (Revive & Restore n.d.). On pigeons, see, in particular, the work of the Revive & Restore project of the Long Now Foundation (https://reviverestore.org).

10. Norms of compulsory sociality are profoundly ableist—something I know firsthand as an Autistic person whose disability means that I am often alienated and excluded from social networks and kinship structures but nonetheless live a rich and worthwhile life (see Clare 2017). These norms are also often racist, in that they may undermine the identities, rights, and connections of people who have been removed from their social worlds, such as survivors of the Sixties Scoop in Canada and the Stolen Generations in Australia.

Notes to Chapter 1 · 311

11. This definition, however, reduces the existence of a life-form to its functional role.

12. Including the Alderville, Six Nations, and Walpole Island First Nations, and parts of Wikwemikong/Manitoulin Island.

13. There is some controversy over the threshold of a mass extinction event—for instance, some commentators suggest that it should be placed at 80 percent, and others lower than 75 percent. Nonetheless, consensus has formed around the idea that it should consist of a significant majority of extant species. The short period of geological time could be millions of years but not the tens or hundreds of millions associated with previous mass extinction events.

14. In quantum physics, the term "superposition" means being in more than one state simultaneously.

15. The chapters that follow discuss how different cultures and cosmologies inhabit time/space. In addition, minds/bodies experience time and space in different ways, not only across species but also across *Homo sapiens*. For instance, Autistic people like me often experience time as "longer" or "shorter" than allistics, or in nested scales.

16. The international Genocide Convention stipulates that acts of genocide must be intentional. However, several theorists working in contemporary critical genocide theory understand genocide as a logic, process, or outcome rather than a singular crime committed with intent. I discuss this in greater detail in chapter 5.

17. This principle states that the lack of *certainty* is not an excuse for failing to act in the face of impending and grave harms if there is significant consensus that they are taking place. It is also increasingly used in the context of climate change and related policies.

18. The "golden spike" is a term often used by stratigraphers and others interested in defining geological periods to mark the beginning of a new one.

19. For instance, the Cambrian, Ordovician, and Silurian periods refer to the Latin names for Wales and Welsh Tribes; the Jurassic period was named by a French scientist after a region of the French Alps; the Permian period is named for Perm in Russia; and the Mississippian and Pennsylvanian subperiods are named after these American states. These names were bestowed by European and American scientists working primarily in the nineteenth century based on the places where they observed relevant geological phenomena. As such, they reflect the geopolitical (and personal) interests of these scientists, their institutions, and/or state funders, yet they claim universality.

20. Discourses on the Anthropocene are complex and highly contested, and, unlike the geological discourses of the nineteenth century, they involve diverse interlocutors, including renowned thinkers concerned with the Global Majority (e.g., Dipesh Chakrabarty, Amitav Ghosh, Achille Mbembe, and many others). Nonetheless, the framing of the Anthropocene and the ways in which it is being *formally* negotiated (e.g., through the meetings and reports of the International Commission on Stratigraphy) embody Western scientific assumptions, forms of knowledge making, and structures of epistemic and political power continuous with those of their nineteenth-century European forebears (see Davis and Todd 2017).

312   *Notes to Chapter 1*

21. This claim has, of course, been made before, not least by G. W. F. Hegel (2019), whose claim rested on the perfection of human reason, and his twentieth-century interpreter Francis Fukuyama (1992), who saw this pinnacle of perfection in 1980s liberalism, as well as by multiple Christian and other millenarian movements that see the return of Jesus Christ (or other deities) as the definitive end of history. Predicting the "end of history"—and, indeed, defining history as a linear progression—is a common strategy for claiming the power to determine the parameters of time and humanity.

22. Both Eli Clare (2017) and Alison Kafer (2013) are clear that they do not reject cure wholesale, especially for disabled people who seek relief from pain; what they critique is the imposition of cure on disabled people in order to enforce conformity to norms of humanity. As Clare and Sunaura Taylor (2017) argue, ableism is deeply entangled with racism, heteronormativity, and other forms of oppression.

23. In medical contexts, the term "extinction" is frequently used to express the total suppression of a symptom or behavior.

24. Anishinaabe thinker Gerald Vizenor coined the term "survivance" to describe survival as a form of resistance (and vice versa).

25. A particularly clear example of this is recent work on "ontological security in international relations" (see, e.g., Mitzen 2006; Steele 2007). In these discourses, "ontology" is used to refer to something like the self-identity of states and their persistence through time.

26. To be clear, I am not claiming that I am able to think, write, or speak from "outside" ontology. Having been raised and educated within a Western secular, settler Euro-descendent tradition of thought, I am very much influenced by ontology in the sense I have described it here. However, my aim in this book is to hold open space for other cosmological possibilities, while acknowledging the limitations of my thinking.

27. This group of approximately thirty filmmakers is centered around Belyuen in what is currently called the Northern Territories of Australia.

2. (BIO)PLURALITY

1. "Country" is a term used by many Aboriginal and Torres Strait Islander communities across Australia that refers to the entirety of earth, including subsoil, ocean, and sky—including what Western science calls outer space (see Bawaka Country et al. 2020). Usually, a particular family group or clan is responsible for taking care of a particular part of Country, in this case, the coastal homeland of Bawaka.

2. The "nature's contributions to people" report (Díaz et al. 2018) has been lauded by international organizations such as the Intergovernmental Science-Policy Platform on Biodiversity and Ecosystem Services (IPBES) for accounting for the different ways that various cultures understand the value and importance of nature. Nonetheless, it retains the universalizing belief that all humans have and engage with culture in the way that it is understood in the Western (social) sciences (see the discussion of ontology in chapter 1). It also lumps together "Indigenous peoples," framing them in the Western-universal category of "practitioners" or "knowledge keepers."

Ultimately it evinces the idea that different cultures interpret the same world in various ways (see Introduction); it does not recognize the existence of different worlds.

3. Reduction-oxidation is a basic biochemical process in which one substance or molecule is reduced and another oxidized (that is, an oxygen molecule is lost or gained, respectively) in a complementary way.

4. For instance, as of 2016 (the most recent data available at the time of writing), 832 mammal species were listed as "data deficient" by the IUCN, while 2,890 arthropod species were, suggesting (among other factors) different levels of attention to and investment in protecting these life-forms.

5. "Geontopower" is a form of power derived from a Euro-descendent ontology (see chapter 1) that is grounded in a distinction between the geological (nonliving) and the biological.

6. That is, sameness is given more emphasis in determining the existence of difference and its place in the broader structures of being that define Western philosophy. See chapter 1 for a discussion of ontological accounts

7. Aristotle's is an ontological account that understands "Being" and the characteristics of "beings" to exist on different planes or ranks (see the discussion of ontology in chapter 1).

8. It should be noted that the American chestnut is not, in fact, extinct in a biological sense, although perhaps it is in a functional sense: a small group of individual trees exists, for instance, in southern Ontario (see University of Guelph 2017).

9. Of course, many Indigenous knowledge systems *also* emphasize the importance of what the Western sciences gloss as "function" or "services" of kin life-forms, such as their value as sources of food or protection (and many Indigenous communities adopt Euro-descendent forms of conservation, sometimes in combination with their own approaches). However, these relations are not necessarily *reducible* to abstract ideas or aggregate calculations of services or functions, let alone their alienated economic value, but often emphasize concrete historical interactions and social-political arrangements (see Introduction).

10. See Introduction. My aim is not to replace singular understandings of difference emerging from distinct worlds but rather to support resonances across them and facilitate their critiques of dominant approaches. Wherever a specific community or world offers a different term or concept, this should be given precedence rather than collapsed into the idea of (bio)plurality.

11. With very few exceptions (notably, the more recent work of William Connolly [2011], who has examined in depth processes of plural becoming), political pluralists in fact promote diversity. They point to the interaction of multiple, distinct groups or institutions that may assert competing values, forms of sovereignty, legal systems, and so on *within* a shared political body (see, for instance, Tully 1994). In this approach, difference is a product of the external relations between those entities as they strive to retain their internal integrity and distinction from others (e.g., in the context of multiculturalism within states; see Kymlicka 1992). In international relations, the concept of "pluralism" refers to a situation in which sovereign nation-states are thought to maintain difference by developing and asserting distinct models

of political order (see Buzan 2004; Jackson 2011). In each of these contexts, difference exists *between* internally homogeneous groups acting in / on a shared field, from which they are considered to be distinct (not *as* a co-constituted world, as is the case in the example of Country).

12. The awkwardness of expressing the meanings of plurality in English attests to its marginalization in Anglo-European thought.

13. For instance, the Kija people of the East Kimberley use the term Ngarran-karni (sometimes spelled Ngarrarngkarni); the Ngarinyin people speak of the Ungud (or Wungud); in Martu Wangka, a Western desert language, Dreaming is called Manguny; and some North-East Arnhem Landers refer to the same core concept as Wongar. The use of the term here is not intended to generalize across them but rather to focus on resonances across this massive and varied field of experiences and ways of knowing.

14. Indeed, the same logic allows contemporary, continuing settler colonial states and publics to aver that colonization is part of history or the past.

15. Much of the knowledge about the Rainbow Serpent cannot leave specific communities. Several Indigenous writers have shared aspects of it that are safe to share with non-Indigenous peoples. The Rainbow Serpent is, in different stories, male, female, or both; it sometimes changes genders and is sometimes gender fluid. When paraphrasing particular stories, I use the pronoun furnished by the teller; otherwise, I use gender-neutral pronouns to reflect this multiplicity.

16. The term "totem" is in fact an inaccurate English translation of the Anishi-naabe word "nindoodem," which refers to the animal nations to whom human families are kin. From the late eighteenth century onward, it was taken from this context by English-speaking anthropologists and grafted in a generic way onto many kinship structures that they considered to be "animist." It is often associated with racist stadial schemes that suggest that all humans pass through a totemic "stage." However, like the term "Dreaming," it has also been taken up and used by many Indigenous authors working in English to share their knowledge beyond their communities, as is the case with Goobalathaldin.

17. The term "Bunyip" originates in the Wemba-Wemba language group of south-east Australia, but stories about the creature are found throughout Indigenous nations across the continent. Thought by early settlers to be an undiscovered freshwater marsupial, it is often described as a sinister being.

18. It is important to note that modern Western science is based on a cosmology transformed from Western Judeo-Christian thought. Until the late eighteenth century (and in some cases later), divine power, energy, and order played a substantial role in scientific understandings of phenomena as varied as astronomy and zoology. Indeed, the excision of "divine" agency and its replacement with "natural" agency was a pivotal moment in the transformation of Western secular cosmology (see C. Taylor 2007; Bennett 2010; Mitchell 2014b).

19. Conversation at the workshop "Indigenous Visions of the Global Extinction Crisis," Balsillie School of International Affairs, Waterloo, Ontario, Canada, June 2, 2016.

Notes to Chapter 3 315

20. The practice of planting the placenta on family land has been maintained continuously in some parts of Hawai'i, such as Moloka'i, where Indigenous practices remain strong. A 2006 law allowing women who give birth in a hospital to bring their placentas home (following their designation as "biological waste" in 2005) removed one colonial blockage to the continuation of the practice.

21. Kohn restricts the capacity to embody practical knowledge to "life" (although he extends "life" to include anything that comports itself toward a future).

22. Sheridan and Longboat (2006) use the term "Onkwehonwe" to refer to "traditional" Haudenosaunee people, or Haudenosaunee people who are working toward this way of life (see also Barreiro 2010). Of course, it should be recognized that many Haudenosaunee and other Indigenous peoples have been violently assimilated and/or removed from their cultures by settler colonial states.

23. Vizenor uses the term "Native," so I retain this term when quoting his work.

24. However, where Grosz (2011, 54) describes this process as one of life "interven[ing] into (parts or elements of) matter to give them a different vitality," the pluralizations I discuss here do not necessarily involve this kind of subject/object relationship.

25. It is important, especially as a settler scholar learning with and from Indigenous knowledge systems, to resist the archetype of the trickster that has emerged in Western anthropology. For instance, as Cutcha Risling-Baldy's (2015) excellent work points out, "Coyote" has been homogenized in these discourses as a universal trickster figure, when in fact she or he takes multiple forms and plays different roles within a range of tribes and communities across Turtle Island.

3. EARTH/BODY VIOLENCE

1. The growing field of "extinction studies," carried out largely within the environmental humanities, has accomplished much in discussing the ethical *implications* of extinction and the role of violence between or against particular species/life-forms (see, for example, Heise 2010; Rose 2011a; Hatley 2012; van Dooren 2014). However, few of these accounts have discussed the role of *systematic* violence and how it affects what I have called (bio)plurality, in particular in a global context; or brought their anthropological work into conversation with international law, ethics, and governance.

2. The official title for the superfund program is the Comprehensive Environmental Response, Compensation, and Liability Act of 1980 (CERCLA), part of the Environmental Protection Agency.

3. These statistics do not include communities in British Columbia or the Northwest Territories, and as such, lack of access to clean water in Indigenous communities is significantly underrecorded.

4. The more established term "eco-ableism" refers to ableist practices within or as outcomes of environmental movements—for instance, total bans on plastic straws in public restaurants, which make life more difficult for people who rely on them to eat and drink (see Liboiron 2020). In addition, environmental movements often marginalize disabled bodies by enshrining images of (hyper)abled, "rugged," "energetic" (overwhelmingly white and straight) bodies as the only ones that can and should

316   *Notes to Chapter 3*

engage with nature (see Kafer 2017). Without diminishing the importance of such critiques, I focus here on the distinct issue of the targeting of disabled bodies as dumps for ecological harms and the destruction of disabled practices of cohabitation.

5. The literature on disability in environmental justice is relatively small and recent, not only due to the general prevalence of ableism within environmentalist and some social justice discourses (see also Piepzna-Samarasinha 2018) but also possibly because of the historical overrepresentation of whiteness in disability studies, which may have limited its perceived relevance to struggles against ecological racism.

6. The "medical model" of disability refers to the dominant paradigm, in which disability is understood as a medical and/or biological matter rather than a political, social, or ethical one. In contrast, the "social model" of disability tends to focus on the construction of harms and limitations by social processes that *disable* certain bodies more than others. Still others criticize both models for, respectively, depoliticizing disability or ignoring concrete, embodied experience and seek a nuanced approach (see Shakespeare 2010; Kafer 2013) or one grounded in intersectional demands for justice (Piepzna Samarasinha 2018; Sins Invalid 2019).

7. Cal Montgomery (2012) points out that *all* humans—and indeed, all beings— are dependent on others but that only certain kinds of dependence are deemed inappropriate or excessive.

8. The Porgera mine was originally operated by Barrick's predecessor, Placer Dome, from 1989 until the acquisition of that company by Barrick in 2006.

9. According to Mining Watch (2017), initial payouts were worth approximately C$6,700 (subsequently an additional $13,800 was offered) and included counseling, medical expenses, a one-time business training course, and school fees for dependent children for a few years. Eleven women settled privately with Barrick and subsequently denounced their agreements.

10. In the context of the ongoing epidemic of Missing and Murdered Indigenous Women and Girls (MMIWG), Northern British Columbia (and rural regions of Canada more generally) is a notoriously dangerous place for Indigenous women to travel, exemplified by, but not limited to, the "Highway of Tears" (where between seventeen and eighty-five reported murders of Indigenous women have occurred since 1970). Poverty and inadequate public transport systems force women to hitchhike, leaving them highly vulnerable to predation.

11. In the United States National Park Service and major conservation organizations, the actual number of women (although data are not available for other genders or sexualities) in leadership has increased substantially, but this has not changed the pervasive culture of machismo associated with this type of work (see Gilpin 2016; Jones and Solomon 2019).

12. "Compulsory heterosexuality" is a term coined by poet Adrienne Rich to describe the perceived "male right of access" to female bodies. Forced copulation is intended to produce offspring. However, Salazar Parreñas also describes situations in which immature males incapable of breeding were similarly allowed to harm females.

Notes to Chapter 4

13. Many disabled people are considered unable to give or withhold consent if they are deemed to lack the "autonomy" or "intelligence" to participate in the legal and/or medical processes through which consent is granted.

14. As Umeek [E. Richard Atleo] (2012) argues, all more-than-human communities have their own ways of negotiating consent, even if they do not always use this precise wording.

15. In the terms of this document, "free" means that there is no manipulation or coercion of the communities in question; "prior" requires that consent is sought sufficiently in advance and allowing time for consultation; and "informed" means that "relevant" Indigenous (human) *people* receive information on aspects such as the nature, scope, pace, duration, and reversibility of the project. Similarly, the International Labour Organization's Convention 169 of 1989 mandates *consultation* with Indigenous communities within culturally appropriate mechanisms before a project can take place.

16. I do not mean to suggest that BIPOC communities are or ever were completely devoid of sexual and gender-based violence in the absence of external forces, which is not the case. However, the colonial-racist formations described here work to *replace all existing relations* with their own, creating encompassing cultures of violence.

17. Muskrat is a key actor in the Anishinaabe Creation story and those of several other peoples. After the fall of Sky Woman to the water-covered planet and the failure of several other animal ancestors to find dry land, Muskrat dives to the bottom and then surfaces, almost dead, but with a piece of earth clutched in their paw that ultimately becomes earth.

4. INVASIVE STATES

1. In the context of the Canadian settler state, the term "unceded" usually refers to lands that the federal and/or provincial governments claim and govern as part of their territory but the rights to which have never been formally surrendered to any of these bodies through treaties or other means. Much of what is currently called British Columbia consists of unceded lands. In an effort to formalize its control of these lands, in 1975 the federal government began a "modern treaty process" with the primary intention of negotiating the extinguishment of Native title and the creation of treaties for all remaining unceded lands. While often framed by the state in the language of Indigenous rights, development, and inclusion, the explicitly stated, primary purpose of the project was to extinguish native title to prevent future land claims by First Nations. Many Indigenous nations refused to participate in the process; indeed, all Wet'suwet'en clans had opted out of this process by 2008.

2. The RCMP was originally formed by the nascent Canadian state with the goal of "subduing" Indigenous communities in the northwestern part of the frontier in the late nineteenth century (see chapter 5). In this regard, its actions in Wet'suwet'en territories constitute a continuation of its historical mission.

3. The full text of the letter is available in Real People's Media 2020. The Haudenosaunee nations hold direct treaties with the Crown rather than the federal government of Canada (of which the Crown is the head of state); hence, the Crown, and not the Canadian prime minister, is the Mohawks of Tyendinaga's treaty partner.

318   *Notes to Chapter 4*

4. Many systems of governance do not revolve around, or even necessarily include, the Eurocentric conceptions of "property" or "ownership" that involve exclusive individual or several rights to the use or disposal of the objects in question.

5. Tiffany Lethabo King (2018) points out that theories of settler colonialism tend to originate with and center the experiences and subjectivities of white men. This includes the originator of the term "settler colonialism," Patrick Wolfe (1999), along with Lorenzo Veracini (2010) and other Australian elaborators of the concept. (However, in conflating the Australian experience with these white authors, King somewhat glosses over the importance of Blac(k)ness and Bla(c)k political thought in shaping Australian Indigenous critical discourse.) With this critique in mind, while I draw on these seminal texts on settler colonialism, I try to place more focus on the contributions of BIPOC thinkers whose work reflects lived experience of the logics and structures of invasion. At the same time, King rightly contends that the dominant language used within these discourses—including the term "settler"—is euphemistic, suggesting a gentle process of acclimatization. With this in mind, I use the term "invaders" / "invasive" to point to the much more violent nature of settler colonial political presence.

6. Thank you to Ni Nok Cuma Gook for sharing this insight. It is important to acknowledge that people living in settler colonial polities inhabit a variety of positions in relation to power, domination, and violence. For instance, the relative privilege and benefit experienced by a white, male, cishet person in such a polity may differ greatly from that of a genderqueer hyperexploited healthcare worker or a disabled Black millionaire. For this reason, it is important to attend to the variety of positionalities within invasive polities and the different dynamics of power and violence in which we participate.

7. It is important to note that "subsistence" does not involve living "hand to mouth" or "meal to meal" (as it is often stereotyped in Eurocentric histories). It may, for instance, involve strategically saving enough foodstuffs to survive prolonged periods in which growing, hunting, and gathering are restricted (for instance, cold winters or long wet seasons). In addition, it does not suggest that farmers produce only enough food for themselves or their families; on the contrary, intensive farming often involves complex forms of sharing of land usufruct and produce, including forms of gifting and trade. It is contrasted here with the production of food primarily for sale for profit.

8. *The Columbian Exchange* (TCE) and the author's related work (see Crosby 1986) have been canonized within mainstream Western ecological discourses as seminal and have been exposed to relatively little criticism, especially along the lines of their racialized assumptions. For that reason, some of the author's most salient pseudo-scientific assumptions merit more lengthy unpacking here. For instance, in *Ecological Imperialism*, Crosby quotes Charles Darwin's claim that "the varieties of man seem to act on each other in the same way as different species of animals—the stronger always extirpate the weaker" (Crosby 1986, ix). In so doing, it takes for granted pseudo-scientific social Darwinist and eugenicist racial hierarchies (see Ferreira da Silva 2007; TallBear 2013) that present colonization, genocide, and the domination of BIPOC as

Notes to Chapter 4   319

a matter of "nature." To bolster this claim, Crosby (1972, 21) argues that Indigenous communities across the planet were decimated by diseases that the "stronger" peoples of the Old World had long "accommodated themselves to." In making this argument, Crosby suggests that Europeans were simply selected for survival and dominance through evolutionary processes, ignoring the role of (often extreme) violence in providing them with this advantage. At another point, Crosby (1972, 47) reduces the entire (ongoing) existence of the Arawak people of the Antilles to "a reserve of pestilence . . . from which the conquistador drew invisible biological allies for his assault on the mainland." This kind of biological essentialism once again naturalizes genocide. In the same breath, Crosby (1972, 166, emphasis mine) implies that the deaths of Arawak people were offset by colonization and the slave trade, claiming: "for every Indian [*sic*] who died, a European *or an African* has disembarked and proceeded to found a family." Here, Crosby not only treats races as substitutable (by means of biological reproduction) but also conflates the circumstances of Europeans and Africans. In so doing, he erases the conditions of mass enslavement of the latter and the very different circumstances under which they founded families (including as a means of increasing the capital of those who enslaved people and the instrumentalization in settler colonial economies). Further, Crosby (1972, 21) states as fact, with scarce evidence or argumentation, that "we" (his presumedly white reader and him) are part of a "post-Neolithic" culture, in which "few still living" Indigenous peoples exist in a separate, ahistorical lineage. This statement not only entrenches essentialist racial divisions but also treats as fact widespread colonial narratives that naturalize the disappearance of Indigenous peoples while obscuring the forms of violence responsible (see chapter 5). Racial categories are defined by Crosby (1972, 23) with the use of nineteenth-century proto-eugenicist means such as the measurement of "colour, height, weight, bone formation"; the comparison to derogatory and anachronistic (even for the 1970s) categories such as "Mongoloid peoples"; and entirely subjective speculations about the results of interracial reproduction. Crosby's work also presumes the existence of specific hierarchies among the groups he racializes. For instance, he designates Bantu-speaking peoples (whom, he is at pains to argue, outnumber white settlers in South Africa) as superior to "American, Australian and New Zealand indigenes" due to their possession of iron weapons and their ability to become "indispensable servants" to their colonizers (1972, 146–47). In addition, Crosby's rhetoric is shot through with gendered and sexualized contempt for Indigenous women in particular. To give one example, in discussing the spread of venereal disease in a Sioux community in the late nineteenth century, he laments that the women of that community were "*chaste* until the disappearance of the buffalo" (Crosby 1989, 288, emphasis mine). In so doing, he imposes heteronormative moral judgments on Indigenous women both by presenting their precontact phase as virginal and pious and by blaming them for harms to their community caused not least by sexual exploitation and violence on the part of European invaders.

    These examples raise questions about not only the ethical but also the scientific quality of Crosby's work. Simply put, it is based (often to the exclusion or contradiction of empirical evidence) on race theories that have been roundly contradicted by numerous scholars as baseless and unscientific; and its ideological goals often overshadow its commitment to rigorous empirical scholarship. At the same time, Crosby's work fails to address even in a cursory manner the widespread critiques of racist thinking that were *widely available at the time when he was writing* (which, as a work of ecological *history*, it should address). For these reasons, serious readers of ecological history should approach it with considerable caution and critical attention.

9. The swan is the only nonnative bird species protected under Canadian law.

10. Such events occur when the effects of an invasive species create domino effects that travel across an ecosystem, causing it to lose functional integrity.

11. From a personal discussion with a Kānaka kūpuna who asked to be acknowledged by place but not individually named, Kalihi Valley, Oʻahu, March 20, 2017.

12. "Plantain" refers to the small, leafy plants with elongated stamens known as the common plantain (*Plantago major*) and narrow-leafed plantain (*Plantago lanceolate*) in Western taxonomy, not the banana-like genus *Musa*. Plantains are often referred to in Anishinaabe medicine discourses as "white man's footprint" because of their tendency to be transmitted through invaders' transportation processes.

13. For instance, the frequent labeling of the virus as "Chinese" by white politicians contributed to several waves of physical violence against Asian Americans; and there were vastly different trends concerning infection rates, health outcomes, and access to (and concerns with) vaccination among BIPOC-majority communities.

14. Although some state-led biosecurity policies engage with various forms of TEK (see Introduction), they have not to this date involved the large-scale return of Indigenous lands or the removal of invaders' agricultural and economic systems in favor of pre-existing practices.

15. Ableist language such as "cripple" is often used in political discourses to describe the effects of poor, racialized, 2SLGBTQIA+, and other "undesirable" groups on the normative body politic (see the discussion of environmental ableism in chapter 3) and their undesirability among the robust bodies demanded by frontier life.

16. Field notes based on interpretive signs and guided talk on author's visit to the similar Quarantine Station on Darug territories (Manley, Sydney), New South Wales, Australia, February 2014. It is notable that the Australian state has been widely criticized for its ongoing practice of detaining migrants, especially from its former colony of Papua New Guinea, in offshore detention centers.

17. Here, again, we can see the reliance on ableist discourses, in which exogenous life-forms are understood in terms such as "outbreaks" usually used in epidemiological contexts.

18. It is also worth noting that the Ministry for Primary Industries report (MPI 2016) contrasts Māori culture with social (that is, settler) culture, particularizing the former while abstracting, universalizing, and naturalizing the latter, and treats Māori knowledge systems as a branch of the social sciences, contrasted with Western knowledge that is simply described as "science."

19. Compare this trapper's language to the rhetoric of former U.S. president Donald Trump in his frequent assertions in the late 2010s that Mexico should fund a

Notes to Chapter 4 321

wall intended to block migration. The desire to conscript BIPOC in their own oppression is a key trope of white settler desire.

20. Many, if not most, wildlife rehabilitation centers devote at least some of their efforts to returning animals to their wild habitats. However, as Collard (2014) shows, many released wildlife remain physically close to wildlife centers, enhancing local ecotourism industries by concentrating populations of endangered species in places predictable to tour companies.

21. The term "Tar Sands" was first used by R. G. McConnell, Deputy Minister of Mines and member of the Geological Society, in 1894; it later appeared in the *Geological Survey of Canada, 1891–1910* (McConnell 1910) and was referred to in a Privy Council decision in 1910. In other words, it was created by actors deeply invested in the mining industry with the purpose of facilitating industry in northern Alberta. The term was increasingly applied (along with the term "oil sands") by oil and gas industry professionals and policymakers to refer to both the region and the mining projects taking place there. These terms are euphemistic in that they naturalize the reduction of the landscape to one element (tar or oil) and normalize efforts to extract it (suggesting that the land is "for" the extraction of oil and gas). In so doing, these terms overwrite many other preexisting names and other meanings associated with the land—for instance, Indigenous place-names and the term "muskeg" (from the Cree "mashkiig"), which describes the boggy ecosystem.

22. Colonizers often associated female organs with sexual promiscuity and/or sex work.

23. Some mining installations in the Tar Sands have implemented such measures to avoid prosecution after mining company Syncrude was forced to pay C$3 million in damages for the death of 1,600 ducks who landed on one of its "tailings ponds" in 2008. See CBC News 2010.

24. For instance, the "biodiversity banking" and "no net loss" programs discussed in chapter 2 rely on finding parts of the planet where biodiversity and labor are both more plentiful and "cheaper" (e.g., less expensive to buy or lease) than in the Global North. Value is created in these strategies from the differential between the price of biodiversity in each respective region.

25. Rather than a standing fund, NatureVest is an "investment platform" that seeks to broaden sources of conservation finance beyond state and charitable funding by creating opportunities for investors to connect with NGOs carrying out potentially profitable conservation projects worldwide. Its board of advisors includes financiers from major global firms such as JP Morgan Chase and Goldman Sachs (see Dempsey and Bigger 2019). As of May 2023, NatureVest claims to have helped its partners to "originate, structure, fund and close investment vehicles representing more than $3.1 billion of committed capital," a number that continues to grow (https://www.nature.org).

26. Ultimately A$150,000 in damages was awarded, none of which was directed to the Aboriginal owners of the land but rather to the Northwest Territories state, as the presumptive owners of the land. Povinelli (2016) points out that shortly afterward, the government of the Northern Territories abolished the independence of

the body that oversaw the protection of Aboriginal sites, and the government of Western Australia redefined sacred sites to include only places used for religious purposes, not those associated with myths or stories (including Dreamings). At the same time, the penalties—A$100,000 and twelve months' imprisonment for damage to Aboriginal sites, compared to A$1 million and two years in prison for damage to non-Aboriginal religious sites such as places of worship—demonstrates the profound devaluation of Indigenous sacred sites in comparison with those of invaders.

27. I do not intend to criticize the communities that brought the suit, and I recognize the importance of holding mining companies legally responsible for their actions. My point is that, through the perversions of colonial extractivism, efforts to responsibilize corporations are often instrumentalized *in service of* the extractive relations they promote.

28. These are the two moieties that structure kinship within Laklak's community.

5. GENOCIDE, ELIMINATIVE VIOLENCE, AND EXTINCTION

1. This section was adapted from Audra Mitchell, "Flying Foxes, Moving Futures" Worldly. Online. Available: https://worldlyir.wordpress.com/2019/01/31/flying-foxes -moving-futures/ (2019).

2. While zoonotic diseases, by definition, refer to pathologies spread *between* humans and other life-forms, the nonhuman participants in this dynamic tend to be considered the source and apportioned blame for causing outbreaks—even when it is the actions of certain humans (for instance, in disturbing their habitat, or bringing them into forced contact with exogenous life-forms; see chapter 4) that initiates the transmission.

3. This baby gray-headed flying fox was transferred to qualified rehabilitators. Her wounds healed and she was rereleased to the same community roost within three months.

4. There are several words in Indigenous languages used to describe this life-form, including but not limited to moostoos (Nêhiyaw); linii (singular) and iniiksii (plural) (Blackfeet); tatanka (Lakota); ivanbito (Diné); and Kuts (Paiute). The word "buffalo" is derived from the French "boeuf," originally used by French colonists to describe animals they encountered in various parts of Asia and Africa, and later imposed on the ungulates of what is currently called North America.

5. Mazis (2008) considers "speciocide" to be broader than genocide because the latter seeks to eliminate groups *within* a species, while the former would erase the entire species (although Mazis extends this argument only to nonhuman animals).

6. The UNGC definition of "intentionality" is often interpreted to refer to situations in which individuals make conscious, voluntary, autonomous, reason-directed choices to knowingly carry out an act that will result in the destruction of a people. This understanding of intentionality is based on a culturally specific model of human cognition (see Wynter 2003)—eighteenth-century European philosophy—that does not account for the substantial role of unconscious decision-making (see Max-Planck-Gesellschaft 2008).

Notes to Chapter 5

7. In terms of shared goals, some people may participate in actions contributing to genocide because it is of financial benefit, because they are motivated by racism or xenophobia (without an explicit desire for the total elimination of the other group), or because they believe they are contributing to civilization, development, or other projects. This in no way dilutes their culpability; the point is that people may carry out genocidal acts with different degrees of knowledge, investment, and commitment to the overall project.

8. In this context, it is interesting to note that many Indigenous communities use demonyms that mean something like "the people" (e.g., Anishinaabe, Diné, and Kānaka Maoli all have resonant meanings). Yet all these communities were, and remain, in relation with many other peoples, human and otherwise; and none of them claim to be the only or universal people, or the model against which all other versions of peoplehood or "humanity" ought to be compared.

9. "Clean" is a curiously imprecise word used frequently in these discourses. It seems to refer to fantasies of unpolluted spaces (see Liboiron 2020) but also to notions of (moral) purity and social propriety (see Shotwell 2016) that speak to ideas of cleanliness and the ability to impose mastery or order on the environment (see D. Taylor 2016; Singh 2018).

10. The usage of "genetic injury" is another site for potential environmentalist ableism, in which arguments to protect humanity present genetic divergences automatically and homogeneously as harms. In contrast, crip/disability studies, the neurodiversity movement, and related discourses stress the idea that genetic variations should be understood as part of a spectrum of human *difference* and not prima facie labeled as "harmful" or "undesirable" without taking account of their deeper contexts and meanings (see Kafer 2013; Clare 2017; Walker 2021).

11. The Stop Ecocide Foundation is a nonprofit organization founded by the late Higgins and Jojo Mehta, whose main aim is to create an international law of ecocide. For information on the panel, see "Legal Definition and Commentary 2021," Stop Ecocide International, accessed June 19, 2023, https://ecocidelaw.com/legal-definition-and-commentary-2021/. No further information is provided about the nature of the consultation (e.g., Was it one event or many? How were participants recruited? In what ways were they able to share their input? Did they have opportunities to shape the content or simply to review and respond to materials provided by the panel?).

12. Whereas the definition of genocide requires intentionality, this definition of ecocide invokes endangerment liability (that is, knowledge that an act is likely to result in the above-mentioned harms) rather than requiring evidence of the *materialization* of harm.

13. For instance, in the neighborhood of Montreal where I currently live, the legally allowed amount of mercury in drinking water is 0.001 milligrams per liter, *not* 0; that is, a certain amount of contamination is legal.

14. Both strategies of violence continue to be practiced by the contemporary American and Canadian settler states, in the form of the ongoing removal of Indigenous children from their communities and the large-scale culling of native predator species deemed to threaten agriculture (see chapter introduction).

324 *Notes to Chapter 5*

15. Here, again, ecological ableism (and ableist colonialism) is at work in defining certain canine modes of embodiment, movement, and communication as "dysfunctional" and dangerous against a universalized norm (based on a different species).

16. It is important to note that the RCMP report included only 8 Inuit respondents out of 150, the vast majority of whom were its former or current employees. What's more, the QTC analyzes the language of the report to show how it works to discredit the handful of Inuit witnesses who were included.

17. The QTC refers to the frequently cited (by RCMP and other qallunaat) case of Maggie Clay, an officer's wife visiting from the south who was mauled to death in 1924 while playing with a group of dogs (probably Huskies rather than Qimmit) owned by the RCMP, whom she had treated as pets. This is ony one of such cases of dog attacks recorded in the region.

18. For a discussion of the sources of RCMP culture and structure, see Gerster 2019.

19. For instance, in 2013, India declared dolphins "nonhuman persons" with attendant rights (see also Declaration of Rights of Cetaceans 2011); the 2008 Ecuadorian Constitutions recognized Pachamama ("mother nature") as a person; and the city of Toledo, Ohio, declared Lake Erie a person in 2019 (although the decision was struck down by a federal court in 2020). In addition, some Indigenous communities have created new laws to recognize nonhuman personhood, often in ways that are deliberately legible to and compatible with national and international law. These include the Kichwa of Sarayaku's (2018) declaration of the rights of Kawsak Sacha (the "living forest"); and the 1855 Treaty Authority's (2019) granting human rights to manoomin (wild rice) under tribal law (distinct from traditional Anishinaabe law).

20. Benjamin Madley (2016) points out that it is erroneous to use the term "wars"— which suggests a formal conflict governed by rules of engagement—to describe the largely one-sided campaigns of genocide and terror carried out against Indigenous peoples by settler states.

21. In some cases, Indigenous communities have explicitly requested that their frameworks for addressing ecological harm be adopted by the international community and integrated into existing laws. For instance, the Kichwa people of Sarayaku's (2018) *Kawsak Sacha* ("living forest") framework, which presents an encompassing manifesto for ecopolitical relations, was developed and released for this purpose. However, it should not be assumed that *all* Indigenous or other marginalized legal/political orders can or should be used in this way—especially by state and international actors, who have an ongoing history of appropriating knowledge from colonized groups.

22. This section was adapted from Audra Mitchell, "Flying Foxes, Moving Futures" (2019b).

6. APOCALYPTIC CONSERVATION

1. The field of existential or global catastrophic risks is concerned with a wide range of threats, including biological terrorism, hostile artificial intelligence, and

Notes to Chapter 6   325

gamma-ray bursts, whereas conservation discourses focus more narrowly on ecological disruption.

2. Several of the authors working in the areas of human extinction and existential risk identify as liberal and/or humanitarian and thus might bridle at the assertion that their work promotes, for example, racism or ableism. However, unexamined bias and privilege (to which liberal humanitarian discourses are certainly not immune) can also produce substantial harms. As discussed in chapter 5, one can participate in structures of, for instance, racism, ableism, homophobia, and genocide, even while *explicitly* denouncing these ideas in an abstract sense.

3. "Hyperabled" in this context refers to ideas of "strength," "endurance," "ruggedness," or other indicators of physical robustness that are perceived to exceed what is considered "normal" for human bodies (for instance, people who are able to withstand extremely intense exercise, extended pain, or long periods of time without food or sleep).

4. The so-called Green Revolution involved the extension of agricultural technologies, including the use of irrigation, fertilizers, and pesticides from the United States, to what was then widely referred to as the "developing world," along with economic and political policy recommendations. Its aim was to promote the extensive forms of farming used in the United States (see chapter 4) in order to maximize global food production. It resulted in not only the widespread toxification of soils and waters (including global-scale nitrate pollution) and water shortages but also the centralization and disempowerment of many small-scale farmers to the benefit of large agribusiness corporations. The consequences and legacies of the Green Revolution continue to shape land use and political dynamics at the time of writing. For instance, farmers in the Philippines struggle to maintain ancestral rice breeds due to regulations put in place by the Green Revolution. Meanwhile, in the Punjab region in India, policies based on the Green Revolution led to widespread ecological disaster as a result of pesticide and fertilizer use (resulting in the suicides of many farmers in the 1990s) and the privileging of wealthy landowners. In 2021, farmers in India held a year-long mass protest against policies of privatization directly linked to the legacy of the Green Revolution.

5. Barnosky has been a central figure in discourses on the "sixth mass extinction," and the data collected by his team are used in many of the most influential models for future trends.

6. The phrase "all lives matter" refers to pushback, largely by white men, against the Movement for Black Lives and its guiding slogan, "Black lives matter," which speaks to specific, disproportionate, and targeted Black experiences of violence within white-dominated societies. "Color blindness" is a value that emerged in the late 1980s and early 1990s, largely in the United States, in which white people claim that they "don't see color"—that is, that perceptions about race do not affect how they treat people, erasing the distinctness of BIPOC experiences.

7. TESCREAL stands for transhumanism, extropianism (efforts to improve or perfect the human condition), singularitarianism (the belief and/or desire that humans and technological systems will fuse into one entity, "the singularity"), cosmism (the

desire to cure death), rationalism, effective altruism (a branch of philanthropy that uses utilitarian principles in the attempt to ensure that charitable efforts make the greatest possible impact on human well-being), and longtermism (the idea that influencing the long-term future is a key moral priority of the present). The term "TESCREAL" has also been associated with and used by AI ethicist Timnit Gebru.

8. Calculations based on DALY assume that disabled lives are inherently less enjoyable and/or productive and therefore "worth less" than nondisabled lives (see S. Taylor 2017). Such calculations are often used, for instance, in utilitarian arguments that claim that money is better spent in supporting nondisabled people because they are better able to enjoy or derive productive benefit from a resource, treatment, etc.

9. It is worth noting in this context that proponents of various TESCREAL discourses, EA in particular, have actively courted and received the support of billionaires and individuals with very high levels of wealth.

10. Wallace-Wells's (2019) account often elides (neurotypical) "cognitive capacity" with intelligence and with notions such as productivity, success in school, and other markers of neurotypical norms (see Walker 2021).

11. For instance, many Aboriginal and Torres Strait Islander people's histories reach back more than fifty thousand years.

12. I use the term "impoverished" rather than "poor" to denote that these people have been forced into conditions of poverty by dominant power structures; they are not passively or intrinsically poor but rather have *been* impoverished.

13. This argument should not be construed as a critique of contraception, abortion, or other forms of medical intervention relevant to people with uteruses. On the contrary: the concern is that contraception is being promoted as a means of the eugenicist control.

14. Importantly, perceived "quality of life" is one of the most frequent arguments made for preventing, oppressing, segregating, and prematurely ending disabled lives (e.g., through homicide, neglect, or medical abuse); again, these authors fear being reduced to the conditions to which they consign us. It is important to attend to the racist and ableist dimensions of quality-of-life arguments.

15. Thank you to Aadita Chaudhury for pointing me in the direction of Kaufmann's troubling work.

16. The use of the term "still" here not only refers to differential speeds of decline in birth rates across countries but also relates high birth rates to perceived backwardness or delays in "development." A large literature on "critical peace and conflict studies" suggests that strategies of postconflict resolution are often thinly veiled forms of neocolonialism carried out by Euro-American states (see, for instance, Richmond and Mitchell 2011).

17. It is not clear whether the people in question would *be* disciplined (that is, subjected to discipline) or expected to possess this feature as a desired trait.

18. On Prince Phillip's racism, see, for example, Dabashi 2017.

19. This research center is one of the key sites for the production of contemporary discourses on human extinction and TESCREAL-related theories.

Notes to Chapter 6

20. Elephants are among the "charismatic species" most often used by conservation organizations to stand in for all "wildlife" or biodiversity.

21. I am part of the group interpellated by the WWF and wish to acknowledge this (hence "us/we"); however, I do not want to assume that all readers are part of this group, so I also include "them/their."

22. Recently, there has been a movement away from the term "habitat destruction" toward that of "land-use change" within major conservation discourses. This may signal a need for a wider, less normatively charged descriptor for activities such as agriculture. At the same time, it elides systems such as colonization, industrialization, and development (e.g., the Green Revolution) with subsistence, peasant and Indigenous agriculture, silviculture, and other practices, erasing the role of violence.

23. The concentration of arable land in the hand of a small number of wealthy landowners has increased rapidly since the middle of the twentieth century (partially as a result of the Green Revolution; see note 4). Currently, the largest 1 percent of farms *operate* more than 70 percent of the world's farmland, and a single company—the U.S.-owned BlackRock—owns $7.4 billion of farmland worldwide (Anseeuw and Bardinelli 2020).

24. The phrase that is *currently* considered most respectful (second to using the name of the specific people in question) is "Aboriginal and Torres Strait Islander." This may change in future, so please use the term employed by the relevant community.

25. Since the mid-2010s, reports have shown that up to four land defenders are assassinated each week, with the majority being Indigenous people. For a recent report, see *Al Jazeera* 2020.

26. Indeed, the same year of the report's release, long-standing tensions over regional autonomy and resistance to state control formed the background to a campaign of brutal military violence by the state against the Tigray minority, which many analysts consider to be genocidal in nature.

27. While his qualification that sex may or may not involve reproduction reflects difference in sexual practices, the idea that all humans seek "lots of sex" nonetheless homogenizes the scope of human sexuality, ignoring, for instance, the asexuality spectrum.

28. Wilson uses the term "Anthropocene" in two imprecise ways. First, he reduces the discourse to thinkers and actors associated with ecomodernism (see the Introduction) and, in particular, approaches that advocate for the inclusion of people in conservation strategies. Second, stemming from this, he assumes that all Anthropocene thinkers approach the concept normatively and are working consciously to create it, which is not true of many contributors to this discipline.

29. Wilson uses the terms "tribes" and "tribalism" as catch-all descriptors of self-interested societies that he perceives to lack a cosmopolitan human consciousness. In so doing, he reproduces colonial stereotypes of the "tribe"—a descriptor used by some contemporary BIPOC societies and by many colonial powers to *describe* BIPOC societies—as "uncivilized" and inherently prone to violence.

30. The idea that there is only one kind of "human mind" is an expression of ableism and the dogma of neurotypicality (that is, the idea that all human cognition

328   *Notes to Chapter 6*

should conform to medically determined norms; see Walker 2021). Similarly, the notion that humans communicate in one style is grossly reductionist and can be dehumanizing to people who, for instance, do not speak and/or who communicate through gestures, sounds, and other means.

31. It is worth noting that Seligmann presided over the organization for much of the period during which systematic gendered discrimination was reported. See chapter 3.

32. The idea that valid scientific research requires the ability to walk along with the implied physical stamina and capacity to access all environments precludes many disabled people from fitting the description of his ideal "naturalist." Such ableist assumptions are common in environmental movements (Jaquette Ray and Sibara 2017).

33. See Sogorea Te' Land Trust, accessed June 20, 2023, https://sogoreate-land trust.org.

34. See "Timeline," Gorongosa, accessed June 20, 2023, https://gorongosa.org/timeline/.

35. This reasoning is specious, and especially so coming from a biologist. It is likely that the higher number of extinctions was because some of these life-forms were encountering humans for the first time; by the time European invaders arrived, many such life-forms may have adapted to the presence of larger numbers of humans.

36. Wilson specifies "women" and not people who can give birth, including trans, nonbinary, and genderqueer people. In so doing, he simultaneously genders "women" as the source of the problem (and controlling their reproductivity as the solution) and ignores the diversity of human genders, along with the role of sperm in producing pregnancies. He also assumes the presence of "choice," ignoring significant and unequal barriers to contraception, abortion, and reproductive rights in many places, including his home country.

7. REVENANT ECOLOGIES

1. The narrative mirrors the melding of these knowledge systems in real life through centuries of colonialism and more recent forms of reappropriation that blend Indigenous and Western sciences.

2. "Revenance" is a word used in English and French to connote "return." In English, it is less commonly used, usually to refer to persons or other beings who have returned from the *dead* (e.g., deities, prophets, zombies, vampires); for this reason, it often has religious and/or supernatural overtones. The French "revenir" simply means to "come back" and is used in daily speech—e.g., to indicate that one will come back to see a friend the next day or to pick up a package later (and "revenance," used as a noun, can refer to income, as in "revenue"). In this book, I tap into both predominant meanings of the term: its relevance to metaphysical and/or spiritual forces and inversions; *and* the everyday, often unmarked *labor* of making returns, whether journeys, compensations, reconnections, or renewals, the keeping of promises, or the retracing of steps. Please note that, like all English and Euro-descendent terms used in this book, "revenance/revenant/revenir" is an imperfect frame for

Notes to Chapter 7   329

weaving together complex ideas from multiple knowledge systems—in colonial languages that have been used continuously to oppress them—for the purpose of examining their resonances. As such, it involves its own form of epistemic violence and distortions. Therefore, it should be treated not as a permanent signifier but as a site for critique and, where useful, as a meeting point between knowledge systems (see Introduction).

3. Among Aboriginal and Torres Strait Islander communities, the term "Blak" is often used to describe the distinct experience of Blackness and anti-Black racism in Australia and to connect anti-racist movements in that country with broader international movements (including but not limited to civil rights and the Movement for Black Lives).

4. "Crip" is a term reclaimed from its previous derogatory connotations and used by some disabled scholars to refer to our community, movement, theory, and culture (in the same way, e.g., that "queer" and "gay" have been reclaimed by 2SLGBTQIA+ people). While the term can be used to refer to disabled people who self-identify that way (e.g., "they are a scholar of crip theory"), it should not be used by nondisabled people, especially to describe disabled people.

The term "BIPOC futurisms" refers to a rich and plural field of labor, action, and creative practice that cannot fully be captured here. For example, Afro-futurism uses the lens of science fiction, techno-science, music, and art to critically (re)center Afrocentric cosmologies, histories, and epistemes and to confront ongoing oppressions rooted in anti-Blackness. Indigenous futurisms engage with mediums such as fiction, visual and performing arts, film, video games, social movement organization, ceremony, and other mediums to promote decolonization, critique colonial power structures, and support Indigenous forms of governance, including better relations with earth and other planets. Asian futurisms imagine rich, distinct futures rooted in plural Asian histories and forms of life, while contesting the global instrumentalization and policing of Asian bodies in service of white futures. Rather than formal disciplines, these bodies of thought and action are open-ended movements manifested in the arts, social organizing, spiritualities, and other elements of lived experience.

5. Belladonna is the English (technically, Italian) name for a highly poisonous plant native to Turtle Island, a reference that signals her role as a disruptive pharmakon-like (harmful and beneficial in turns but always potent and transformational) presence in the swamp community.

6. The fact that major cities and landmarks are not named in these books is possibly a rhetorical technique intended to increase uncertainty. However, it could also be read to suggest that the colonial names of these places have been washed away along with the crumbling colonial-capitalist political orders that imposed them.

7. Although the book was published in 2017, in the early days of the Trump administration, Erdrich began writing it in the early 2000s, during the George W. Bush administration, in response to her experience of an increasingly reactionary conservative political culture.

8. "Anti-vaxxer" (anti-vaccination) culture emerged in the late 1990s and early 2000s (when a then pregnant Erdrich first began writing the novel). It was rooted

330   *Notes to Chapter 7*

in claims—later roundly disproven—by British doctor Andrew Wakefield (who was stripped of his license) that immunization for common childhood diseases such as measles, mumps, and rubella "caused autism" (see Silberman 2015). Many Autistic and critical disability/crip thinkers, including me, understand anti-vaxxer culture as a profoundly ableist political movement that pathologizes neurological and physical difference. This movement has taken on new and complex dimensions in the context of the Covid-19 pandemic; shifting beyond the spheres of "health and wellness," large-scale anti-vaxxing protests are now often associated with far-right-wing politics. For instance, in the winter of 2021–22, a group of mostly white and far-right conservative truckers and their supporters (inspired by the storming of Congress by right-wing activists in the United States in 2021) occupied the Canadian capital of Ottawa for weeks in protest of government policies related to vaccination. On the other hand, marginalized communities have also resisted some government vaccination efforts as a result of ongoing histories of violence such as medical experimentation, forced sterilization, and other violations by government actors via the medical system (see Quinn and Andrasik 2021)—to which Cedar's comments allude. In the context of Erdrich's book, it appears to refer to the complexities and ironies of liberal people who nonetheless pursue very narrow ideas of what constitutes "'good' human life."

9. Sera's comments are based on a form of neuro-deterministic thinking in which the different brains of hominids are believed to have been the precursors to specific capacities, such as those for creative and abstract thought. This quote once again reflects (if not consciously) the anti-neurodivergent ableism found in many mainstream future discourses.

10. Narratives of "overcoming" and "mastery" are often uncritically imposed on disabled/crip bodies, as if there were no other ways of living a worthwhile or valuable life (see Clare 2017).

11. This comment references the Stolen Generation, a policy in which it is estimated that one in three Aboriginal and Torres Strait Islander children were removed from their families of origin and placed with white families as a strategy of cultural destruction, assimilation, and genocide.

12. In the story, the marriage between Finch and Oblivia is described as the culmination of an ancestral arrangement based on their respective kinship with specific groups of nonhumans.

13. "Closing-the-gap baby" refers to a set of federal government policies claiming to raise health outcomes and life expectancies of Aboriginal and Torres Straight Islanders to equal those of non-Indigenous citizens of Australia but often experienced by those communities as invasive, assimilationist, and/or oppressive.

14. Jingle dancing, in which a dancer wears regalia covered with small cymbal-like attachments, is part of the culture of many Indigenous peoples across Turtle Island.

15. The Ghost Dance was the central practice of a spiritual movement adopted in the late nineteenth century by numerous Indigenous groups across the Western part of Turtle Island, led by the Paiute prophet Wovoka. He had received a vision that the dance could reunite the living with the dead, who would stand with their

Notes to Conclusion 331

living relatives to stop colonization, create peace, and renew earth. Ghost shirts were garments worn by some Lakota practitioners of the Ghost Dance and believed to repel bullets; Silko's reference to their failure to stop bullets relates to the 1890 massacre of three hundred Sioux by the U.S. Army at Wounded Knee, South Dakota.

16. Weesegeejak (there are multiple spellings of this name) is a character central to Nêhiyaw and other Indigenous cosmovisions who is human and a trickster, and although a prominent hero, often makes mistakes and learns important lesson from them. Weesegeejak is variously depicted as male or female, and the gender of the protagonist in *Wakening* is not made obvious, so I use gender-neutral pronouns to describe them here, but they may appear in different genders across various stories/theories.

17. Similarly, the neurodiversity paradigm stresses that a variety of cognitive styles and bodyminds are not pathologies, "hangovers," or reversions but rather have been integral to the evolution of *Homo sapiens*—and, I have argued, to alternative possible futures (Mitchell 2022).

18. Tagaq is a throat singer, and her novel, when listened to in oral form, is punctuated by song and rhythmic stanzas that add an embodied element to the text.

19. In much of what is currently called North America, waterfront land on lakes ("cottage country") is owned by wealthy, predominantly white urban dwellers who buy property as holiday homes and/or investments. These dwellings are often used for only a few weekends or a couple of weeks per year during the summer months. Yet property boundaries—including access to beaches and shorelines—are often heavily policed, cutting off Indigenous peoples' access to traditional waterways and food sources, for instance fishing or wild ricing grounds (see L. Simpson 2017).

20. In many Aboriginal and Torres Strait Islander discourses, "deadly" means "amazing" or "great"—but here it simultaneously speaks to the conditions of danger that the characters face.

21. In dominant ableist societies, like capacity for "true language use" and "intelligence," speaking is often used as a divider between those regarded as "human" and "nonhuman"—denying many nonspeaking disabled people from the status of "human" (see Mitchell 2022).

22. This argument, called the Valladolid Debate after the Spanish city in which it was held in 1550–51, did not result in a clear decision on the part of the judges.

23. Miigwech to Kyle Powys Whyte for articulating this point so clearly.

CONCLUSION

1. This section was adapted from Audra Mitchell, "Sister" (2018).

2. In most cases, seedkeepers refer to this squash as female, some denoting the ovary-like seeds through which it reproduces.

3. Information about Judy's work and Grassy Narrows is available at https://freegrassy.net. For a summary of Judy's accomplishments and impacts, see Mitchell 2019a.

4. Like many other members of the "Sixties Scoop" generation, my friend was removed from her family of birth, adopted into a white family, and raised as a white woman with no knowledge of her heritage. She only learned of her Haudenosaunee

roots in her forties, after hearing from relatives about her birth mother's passing. Before her own passing, she had the opportunity to reconnect with some family members, participate in traditional healing ceremonies, and take courses in the Mohawk and Cayuga languages.

5. Like many members of their generation, Judy's family member had been taken from their family and forced into "residential school" in which much of their ancestral and traditional knowledge was suppressed and punished. Through years of ceremony and healing, they were able to recover some of this knowledge and return it to the community.

6. From 2018 to 2020, Anishinaabe scholar Dr. Andrew Judge Mkmosé built the garden Minjimendan to provide nutritious traditional foods to the many urban Indigenous people in the Cambridge-Kitchener-Waterloo region of Ontario, including heritage sunflower, corn, sweetgrass, and many other foods. Andrew invited hundreds of Indigenous and non-Indigenous people from all over the world (including members of my research group from as far away as Northern Australia) to help construct the garden and share plant knowledge. Squash of many varieties are a key part of the "Three Sisters" system of coplanting that is the centerpiece of Haudenosaunee and other Indigenous growing traditions.

7. In contrast to a manifesto, which often makes broad, universalizing claims and prescriptions on behalf of collectives, a "manifesting" (Creatures Collective 2021) is a clear and impassioned statement of commitments, norms, and responsibilities emerging from a singular set of relations. It is deliberately contingent, dynamic, and open to transformation. While inviting mobilization and solidarity around shared aims, a manifesting does not assert itself as the only possible or valid approach, nor does it claim to speak on behalf of comprehensive groups (e.g., "humanity") but rather aims to diffract and spark generative dissonance.

8. Here, I take inspiration from Nick Walker's (2021) idea of "neuroqueer(ing)," which she uses as a verb to describe the limitless range of ways in which difference (in this case, neurological) is used to challenge and produce alternatives to oppressive norms, not least through (but not limited to) relational, gender, and sexual practices.

9. The reference to "historic" reparations also seems to ignore the ongoing nature of (settler) colonial projects and processes of land grabbing.

10. In using the term "land-based peoples," I am referring to, for instance, small-scale farmers or peasants, silviculturists, contemporary hunter-gatherer communities, and some un- and underhoused communities, depending on the context (the term "Indigenous" does not capture all communities whose land has been annexed through colonization and global capitalism).

11. This definition of "reparations" was offered in an online public talk hosted by the NGO A Growing Culture, June 21, 2021.

12. "Investment" in this context does not refer to the injection of capital with the aim of producing profit but rather the nonspeculative vesting of labor, energy, and other supports into a project with the aim of achieving it.

13. Many of the "land-sparing" projects described in chapter 6 seek to protect migration routes by creating zones from which all humans are excluded instead of

encouraging multiple communities to support migrations (e.g., by providing nesting boxes, planting edible plants, offering water, or limiting fishing during certain periods). At the same time, land-sparing proposals would make migration more difficult for human migrants, further limiting mobilities and increasingly policing and buttressing existing regimens of border control. The approach outlined here would involve creating and strengthening networks of mutual aid to support migrants of all life-forms (including with food, shelter, and medical care along traditional and emerging migration routes).

14. Similar to the private "rewilding" projects described in chapter 6, the Holch Povlsens are engaged in "rewilding" large tracts of privately owned land.

15. The "30% by 2030" goal was launched by a UN initiative, the High Ambition Coalition for People and Nature, with the aim of inspiring large-scale action to increase conservation.

16. A white, French American enthusiast of hiking, climbing, and other outdoor sports, Chouinard reflects the image of the "rugged environmentalist" enshrined in many conservation discourses (see chapter 6). His "love of nature" reflects his access to and enjoyment of lands stolen from Indigenous peoples and rendered inaccessible to many others.

17. While I do not wish to generalize, it is likely that the use of punishments such as imprisonment may clash with many legal, political, and ethical orders in their approach to addressing harms. These practices may also undermine the goals of movements to abolish state, police, and military violence.

18. I am influenced here by the work of Kafer (2013), who actively refuses futures that are defined in and by the absence of disabled and queer people.

Bibliography

ABC News. 2017. "Tasmanian Tiger: Trio Release Footage They Claim Is Sighting of Thylacine." September 5. http://www.abc.net.au.

Absolon, Kathleen E. (Minogiizhigokwe). 2011. *Kaandossiwin: How We Come to Know.* Halifax: Fernwood.

Aceves-Bueno, Eréndira, Adeyemi S. Adeleye, Marina Feraud, Yuxiong Huang, Mengya Tao, Yi Yang, and Sarah E. Anderson. 2017. "The Accuracy of Citizen Science Data: A Quantitative Review." *Bulletin of the Ecological Society of America* 98, no. 4: 278–90.

Adams, William M. 2004. *Against Extinction: The Story of Conservation.* Abingdon, UK: EarthScan.

Adams, William M. 2010. "Conservation PLC." *Oryx* 44, no. 4: 482–84.

Adisa-Farrar, Teju. 2020. "How Can Fibersheds Shape Alternative Futures?" *Fibershed Soil to Soil Podcast,* October 29. https://fibershed.org/podcast/.

Agamben, Giorgio. 1995. *Homo Sacer: Sovereign Power and Bare Life.* Stanford, Calif.: Stanford University Press.

Agathangelou, Anna, and Lily Ling. 2009. *Transforming World Politics: From Empire to Multiple Worlds.* London: Routledge.

Ahmed, Sara. 2013. "Making Feminist Points." Feministkilljoys, September 11. http://feministkilljoys.com.

Alaimo, Stacy. 2017. Foreword to *Disability Studies and the Environmental Humanities: Toward an Eco-Crip Theory,* edited by Sarah Jaquette Ray and Jay Sibara, x–xv. Lincoln: University of Nebraska Press.

Alexiou, Gus. 2020. "No Justice, No Speech: Autism a Deadly Hazard When Dealing with Police." *Forbes,* June 14. https://www.forbes.com.

Al Jazeera. 2020. "'More Dangerous Every Day': Land Rights Defenders Killings Surge." July 29. https://www.aljazeera.com.

Almond, Rosamund, Monique Grooten, and Tanya Petersen, eds. 2020. *Living Planet Report—2020: Bending the Curve of Biodiversity Loss.* Gland, Switzerland: World Wildlife Fund.

Bibliography

Aluli, Noa Emmett, and Davianna Pomaika'i McGregor. n.d. "'Aina: Ke Ola O Na Kanaka 'Oiwi." *A Voyage to Health: Land: The Health of Native Hawaiians.* National Library of Medicine. Accessed July 6, 2023. https://www.nlm.nih.gov.

Amnesty International. 2016. *Out of Sight, Out of Mind: Gender, Indigenous Rights and Energy Development in Northeast British Columbia.* London: Amnesty International.

Angermeier, Paul L. 1994. "Does Biodiversity Include Artificial Diversity?" *Conservation Biology* 8, no. 2: 600–602.

Annahatak, Betsy. 2014. "Silatuniq: Respectful State of Being in the World." *Études/Inuit/Studies* 388, nos. 1–2: 23–31.

Anseeuw, Ward, and Giulia Maria Bardinelli. 2020. *Uneven Ground: Land Equality at the Heart of Unequal Societies.* London: International Land Coalition and Oxfam.

Arendt, Hannah. 1973. *The Origins of Totalitarianism.* New York: Houghton Mifflin.

Arendt, Hannah. 1998. *The Human Condition.* Chicago: University of Chicago Press.

Australian Bureau of Meteorology. 2014. "The Rainbow Serpent." Indigenous Weather Knowledge. http://www.bom.gov.au.

Badiou, Alain. 2009. *Being and Event.* London: Bloomsbury.

Barnett, Michael. 2016. *Eyewitness to a Genocide.* Ithaca, N.Y.: Cornell University Press.

Barnosky, Anthony. 2014. *Dodging Extinction: Power, Food, Money, and the Future of Life on Earth.* Oakland: University of California Press. e-book.

Barnosky, Anthony, and Elizabeth A. Hadley. 2016. *Tipping Point for Planet Earth: How Close Are We to the Edge?* New York: Thomas Dunne Books.

Barnosky, Anthony D., Nicholas Matzke, Susumu Tomiya, Guinevere O. U. Wogan, Brian Swartz, Tiago B. Quental, Charles Marshall, Jenny L. McGuire, Emily L. Lindsey, Kaitlin C. Maguire, Ben Mersey, and Elizabeth A. Ferrer. 2011. "Has the Earth's Sixth Mass Extinction Already Arrived?" *Nature* 471:51–70.

Barreiro, José, ed. 2010. *Thinking in Indian: The Collected Essays of John Mohawk.* Denver: Fulcrum.

Barta, Tony. 2000. "Relations of Genocide: Land and Lives in the Colonization of Australia." In *Genocide and the Modern Age,* edited by Michael N. Wallimann and Isidor Dobkowski, 237–52. 2nd ed. Syracuse: Syracuse University Press.

Bateson, Gregory. 1972. *Steps to an Ecology of Mind.* Chicago: University of Chicago Press.

Bauman, Zygmunt. 1992. *Mortality, Immortality and Other Life Strategies.* Stanford, Calif.: Stanford University Press.

Bawaka Country, Sarah Wright, Sandie Suchet-Pearson, Kate Lloyd, Laklak Burarrwang, Ritjilili Ganambarr, Merrkiyawuy Ganambarr-Stubbs, Banbapuy Ganambarr, and Djawundil Maymuru. 2016. "Co-becoming Bawaka: Towards a Relational Understanding of Place/Space." *Progress in Human Geography* 40, no. 4: 455–75.

Bawaka Country, Audra Mitchell, Sarah Wright, Sandie Suchet-Pearson, Kate Lloyd, Laklak Burarrwanga, Ritjilili Ganambarr, Merrkiyawuy Ganambarr-Stubbs, Banbapuy Ganambarr, Djawundil Maymuru, and Rrawun Maymuru. 2020. "Dukarr Lakarama: Listening to Guwak, Talking Back to Space Colonization." *Political Geography* 81, no. 1: 102218.

Beal, Cara. 2017. "Some Remote Australian Communities Have Drinking Water for Only Nine Hours a Day." *The Conversation,* November 9. https://theconversation.com.

Beckert, Sven. 2015. *Empire of Cotton: A Global History.* New York: Vintage.

Beckstead, Nick. 2013. "On the Overwhelming Importance of Shaping the Far Future." PhD diss., Rutgers University, Rutgers, N.J.

Belcourt, Billy-Ray. 2015. "Animal Bodies, Colonial Subjects: (Re)locating Animality in Decolonial Thought." *Societies* 5, no. 1: 1–11.

Belcourt, Billy-Ray. 2016. "A Poltergeist Manifesto." *Feral Feminisms,* no. 6, 22–31.

Bellard, Céline, Phillip Cassey, and Tim M. Blackburn. 2016. "Alien Species as a Driver of Recent Extinctions." *Biology Letters* 12, no. 2: 20150623.

Belmaker, Genevieve. 2018. "Calls for Change in Handling Abuse Allegations at Top Conservation Group." Mongabay, April 2. https://news.mongabay.com.

Bennett, Jane. 2010. *Vibrant Matter: A Political Ecology of Things.* Durham, N.C.: Duke University Press.

Benton-Banai, Edward. 2010. *The Mishomis Book: The Voice of the Ojibway.* Minneapolis: University of Minnesota Press.

Besser, Linton. 2021. "Dead White Man's Clothes." ABC News, August 11. https://www.abc.net.au.

Blackburn, Tim M., Céline Bellard, and Anthony Ricciardi. 2019. "Alien versus Native Species as Drivers of Recent Extinctions." *Frontiers in Ecology and the Environment* 17, no. 4: 203–7.

Block, Melissa. 2015. "Gambler-Turned-Conservationist Devotes Fortune to Florida Nature Preserve." NPR, June 17. https://www.npr.org.

Bohn, Thomas, and Per-Arne Amundsen. 2008. "Ecological Interactions and Evolution: Forgotten Parts of Biodiversity." *BioScience* 54, no. 9: 804–5.

Borrows, John (Kegedonce). 2010. *Drawing Out Law: A Spirit's Guide.* Toronto: University of Toronto Press.

Bostrom, Nick. 2002. "Existential Risks: Analyzing Human Extinction Scenarios and Related Hazards." *Journal of Evolution and Technology* 9:1–36.

Bostrom, Nick. 2013. "Existential Risk Prevention as Global Priority." *Global Policy* 4, no. 1: 15–31.

Braidotti, Rosi. 2013. *The Posthuman.* Cambridge, UK: Polity.

Braidotti, Rosi. 2022. *Posthuman Feminism.* Cambridge, UK: Polity.

Brand, Stewart. 2013. "The Dawn of De-extinction: Are You Ready?" TED Talk, March 13. https://www.ted.com.

Brand, Stewart. 2015. "Rethinking Extinction." Aeon, April 21. https://aeon.co.

Brockington, Daniel. 2002. *Fortress Conservation: The Preservation of the Mkomazi Game Reserve, Tanzania.* Indianapolis: Indiana University Press.

Brockington, Daniel, and James Igoe. 2006. "x." *Conservation and Society* 4, no. 3: 424–70.

Brook, Barry W., and John Alroy. 2017. "Pattern, Process, Inference and Prediction in Extinction Biology." *Biology Letters* 13, no. 1.

brown, adrienne maree. 2017. *Emergent Strategy: Shaping Change, Changing Worlds.* Edinburgh: AK Press.

brown, adrienne maree. 2019. *Pleasure Activism: The Politics of Feeling Good*. Chico, Calif.: AK Press.

Brown, James H., and Dov F. Sax. 2004. "An Essay on Some Topics Concerning Invasive Species." *Austral Ecology* 29, no. 5: 530–36.

Burarrwanga, Laklak, and family. 2013. *Welcome to My Country*. Crows Nest, Australia: Allen and Unwin.

Burke, Marshall, Solomon Hsiang, and Edward Miguel. 2015. "Global Non-Linear Effect of Temperature on Economic Production." *Nature* 527:235–39.

Büscher, Bram. 2013. "Nature on the Move I: The Value and Circulation of Liquid Nature and the Emergence of Fictitious Conservation." *New Proposals: Journal of Marxism and Interdisciplinary Inquiry* 6, nos. 1–2: 20–36.

Büscher, Bram, and Robert Fletcher. 2019. "Towards Convivial Conservation." *Conservation & Society* 17, no. 3: 283–96.

Buzan, Barry. 2004. *From International to World Society: English School Theory and the Social Structure of Globalization*. Cambridge: Cambridge University Press.

Cain, A. J. n.d. "Taxonomy." *Encyclopedia Britannica*. Accessed July 29, 2020. https://www.britannica.com.

Caplan, Art. 2013. "New Zealand's Solution for Rising Health Costs? Deport Fat People." NBC News, August 11. https://www.nbcnews.com/.

Cardinal, Jesse. 2014. "The Tar Sands Healing Walk." In *Drawing a Line in the Tar Sands: Struggles for Environmental Justice*, edited by Toban Black, Stephen D'Arcy, Tony Weis, and Joshua Kahn Russell, 127–33. Toronto: Between the Lines.

Carey, Peta. 2003. "Making Possums Pay." *New Zealand Geographic*, May–June. https://www.nzgeo.com.

Carson, Rachel. 2022. *Silent Spring*. Boston: Mariner Books Classic.

Cassey, Phillip, Tim M. Blackburn, Richard P. Duncan, and Steven L. Chown. 2005. "Concerning Invasive Species: Reply to Brown and Sax." *Austral Ecology* 30, no. 4: 475–80.

Castree, Noel. 2003. "Commodifying What Nature?" *Progress in Human Geography* 27, no. 3: 273–97.

CBC News. 2010. "Syncrude to Pay $3M Penalty for Duck Deaths." October 22. https://www.cbc.ca/.

CBD (Convention on Biological Diversity). 2010a. *Global Biodiversity Outlook 3*. Montreal: Secretariat of the Convention on Biological Diversity.

CBD (Convention on Biological Diversity). 2010b. *Nagoya Protocol on Access to Genetic Resources and the Fair and Equitable Sharing of Benefits Arising from their Utilization to the Convention on Biological Diversity*. Montreal: Secretariat of the Convention on Biological Diversity.

Ceballos, Geraldo. 2016. "Pope Francis' Encyclical Letter *Laudato Si'*, Global Environmental Risks, and the Future of Humanity." *Quarterly Review of Biology* 31, no. 3: 285–96.

Ceballos, Geraldo, Paul R. Ehrlich, Anthony D. Barnosky, Andrés García, Robert M. Pringle, and Todd M. Palmer. 2015. "Accelerated Modern Human-Induced Species Losses: Entering the Sixth Mass Extinction." *Science Advances* 1, no. 5.

Bibliography

Chen, Mel Y. 2012. *Animacies*. Durham, N.C.: Duke University Press.

Christie-Peters, Quill. 2018. "Kwe Becomes the Moon, Touches Herself so She Can Feel Full Again." *Guts*, March 26. http://gutsmagazine.ca/.

Chrulew, Matthew. 2011. "Managing Love and Death at the Zoo: The Biopolitics of Species Preservation." In "Unloved Others—Death of the Disregarded in the Time of Extinction," special issue, *Australian Humanities Review*, no. 50, 137–56.

Clancy, Kathryn B. H., Robin G. Nelson, Julienne N. Rutherford, and Katie Hind. 2014. "Survey of Academic Field Experiences (SAFE): Trainees Report Harassment and Assault." *PLOS One* 9, no. 7.

Clare, Eli. 2017. *Brilliant Imperfection: Grappling with Cure*. Durham, N.C.: Duke University Press.

Claxton, Nick XEMŦOLTW̱. 2018. "The SXOLE (Reef Net Fishery) as an Everyday Act of Resurgence." In *Everyday Acts of Resurgence*, edited by Jeff Corntassel, 93–98. Olympia, Wash.: Daykeeper Press.

CMU (Canadian Mennonite University). 2015. "Seed-Saving at CMU Leads to Relationships between Mennonites, Indigenous Peoples." CMU Archives, November 10. https://www.cmu.ca.

Colebrook, Claire. 2014. *Death of the Posthuman: Essays on Extinction, Vol. 1*. Ann Arbor, Mich.: Open Humanities Press.

Collard, Rosemary-Claire. 2014. "Putting Animals Back Together, Taking Commodities Apart." *Annals of the Association of American Geographers* 104, no. 1: 151–65.

Collard, Rosemary-Claire, and Jessica Dempsey. 2017. "Capitalist Natures in Five Orientations." *Capitalism Nature Socialism* 28, no. 1: 78–97.

Colman, Zach. 2019. "Nature Conservancy President Resigns in Wake of Sexual Harassment Probe." Politico, May 31. https://www.politico.com.

Cone, James H. 2000. "Whose Earth Is It Anyway?" *CrossCurrents* 50, nos. 1–2: 36–46.

Connolly, William. 2011. *A World of Becoming*. Durham, N.C.: Duke University Press.

Corntassel, Jeff, et al. 2018. *Everyday Acts of Resurgence*. Olympia, Wash.: Daykeeper Press.

Costanza, Robert, Ralph d'Arge, Rudolf de Groot, Stephen Farber, Monica Grasso, Bruce Hannon, Karin Limburg, Shahid Naeem, Robert V. O'Neill, Jose Paruelo, Robert G. Raskin, Paul Sutton, and Marjan van den Belt. 1997. "The Value of the World's Ecosystem Services and Natural Capital." *Nature* 387: 253–60.

Coulthard, Glen Sean. 2014. *Red Skin, White Masks: Rejecting the Colonial Politics of Recognition*. Minneapolis: University of Minnesota Press.

Cox, Lisa. 2019. "More than 2,000 Flying Foxes Die in Victoria's Extreme Heatwave." *The Guardian*, January 29.

Cox, Sarah. 2020. "The Complicated Tale of Why B.C. Paid $2 Million to Shoot Wolves in Endangered Caribou Habitat This Winter." *The Narwhal*, April 25. https://the narwhal.ca/.

Craft, Aimee. 2017. "Giving and Receiving Life from Anishinaabe Nibi Inaakonigewin (Our Water Law) Research." In *Methodological Challenges in Nature-Culture and Environmental History Research*, edited by Jocelyn Thorpe, Stephanie Rutherford, and L. Anders Sandberg, 105–19. London: Routledge.

Creatures Collective (K. J. Hernández, June M. Rubis, Noah Theriault, Zoe Todd, Audra Mitchell, Bawaka Country, Laklak Burarrwanga, Ritjilili Ganambarr, Merrkiyawuy Ganambarr-Stubbs, Banbapuy Ganambarr, Djawundil Maymuru, Sandie Suchet-Pearson, Kate Lloyd, and Sarah Wright). 2021. "The Creatures Collective: Manifestings." *Environment and Planning E: Nature and Space* 4, no. 3: 838–63.

Cronon, William. 1983. *Changes in the Land: Indians, Colonists, and the Ecology of New England.* Rev. ed. New York: Hill and Wang.

Crosby, Alfred W. 1972. *The Columbian Exchange.* Westport, Conn.: Greenwood.

Crosby, Alfred W. 1986. *Ecological Imperialism: The Biological Expansion of Europe, 900–1900.* Cambridge: Cambridge University Press.

Cruikshank, Julie. 2004. "Uses and Abuses of 'Traditional Knowledge': Perspectives from the Yukon Territory." In *Cultivating Arctic Landscapes: Knowing and Managing Animals in the Circumpolar North,* edited by David G. Anderson and Mark Nuttall, 17–32. London: Berghahn Books.

Crutzen, Paul J. 2002. "Geology of Mankind." *Nature* 415:23.

Cummings, William. 2019. "'The World Is Going to End in 12 Years if We Don't Address Climate Change,' Ocasio-Cortez Says." *USA Today,* March 12.

Czachor, Emily Mae. 2022. "Another Giant African Snail Sighting Forces Florida County into Quarantine." CBS News, July 7. https://www.cbsnews.com/.

Dabashi, Hamid. 2017. "The Priceless Racism of the Duke of Edinburgh." *Al Jazeera,* August 13. https://www.aljazeera.com.

Daily, Gretchen C., Anne H. Ehrlich, and Paul R. Ehrlich. 1994. "Optimum Human Population Size." *Population and Environment* 15, no. 6: 469–75.

Darug Country, with Sophie Adams, Tasmin-Lara Dilworth, Sarah Judge, Kate Lloyd, Patrick McEvoy, Audra Mitchell, Harriet Narwal, Emily O'Gorman, Jo Anne Rey, Sandie Suchet-Pearson, Sabiha Yeasmin Rosy, and Thomas Wicket. 2017. "Lifework Part II." *Worldly* (blog), April 9. https://worldlyir.wordpress.com.

Daschuk, James. 2013. *Clearing the Plains: Disease, Politics of Starvation, and the Loss of Indigenous Life.* Regina: University of Regina Press.

Dauvergne, Peter. 2016. *Environmentalism of the Rich.* Cambridge, Mass.: MIT Press.

Davis, Heather, and Zoe Todd. 2017. "On the Importance of a Date, or, Decolonizing the Anthropocene." *ACME: An International Journal for Critical Geographies* 16, no. 4: 761–80.

Declaration of Rights for Cetaceans. 2011. "Introduction to the Declaration of Rights for Cetaceans: Whales and Dolphins." *Journal of International Wildlife Law & Policy* 14, no. 1: 76–77.

de Groot, Rudolf, et al. 2012. "Global Estimates of the Value of Ecosystems and Their Services in Monetary Units." *Ecosystem Services* 1, no. 1: 50–61.

de la Cadena, Marisol, and Mario Blaser, eds. 2018. *A World of Many Worlds.* Durham, N.C.: Duke University Press.

Deleuze, Gilles. 1994. *Difference and Repetition.* Translated by Paul Patton. New York: Columbia University Press.

Delong, Don, Jr. 1996. "Defining Biodiversity." *Wildlife Society Bulletin* 24, no. 4: 738–49.

Deloria, Vine, Jr. 2003. *God Is Red.* 30th anniversary ed. Denver: Fulcrum.

Dempsey, Jessica, and Patrick Bigger. 2019. "Intimate Mediations of For-Profit Conservation Finance: Waste, Improvement and Accumulation." *Antipode* 51, no. 2: 518–38.

Descola, Philippe. 2005. *Beyond Nature and Culture.* Chicago: University of Chicago Press.

Dhillon, Jhaskiron. 2017. *Prairie Rising: Indigenous Youth, Decolonization, and the Politics of Intervention.* Toronto: University of Toronto Press.

Diamond, J. M. 1984. "'Normal' Extinctions of Isolated Populations." In *Extinctions,* edited by M. H. Nitecki, 191–246. Chicago: University of Chicago Press.

Diamond, J. M. 1989. "The Present, Past and Future of Human-Caused Extinctions." *Philosophical Transactions of the Royal Society of London, Series B: Biological Sciences* 325, no. 1228: 469–76.

Díaz, Sandra, et al. 2018. "Assessing Nature's Contributions to People." *Science* 359, no. 6373: 270–72.

Dillon, Grace, ed. 2012. *Walking the Clouds: An Anthology of Indigenous Science Fiction.* Tucson: University of Arizona Press.

Dimaline, Cherie. 2017. *The Marrow Thieves.* Toronto: Dancing Cat Books.

Dinerstein, E., et al. 2019. "A Global Deal for Nature: Guiding Principles, Milestones and Targets." *Science Advances* 5, no. 4.

Doerfler, Jill, Heidi Kiiwetinepinesiik Sinclair, and Niigaanwewidam James Stark, eds. 2013. *Centering Anishinaabeg Studies: Understanding the World through Stories.* Lansing: Michigan State University Press.

Duffy, Rosaleen. 2014. "Waging a War to Save Biodiversity: The Rise of Militarized Conservation." *International Affairs* 90, no. 4: 819–34.

Eckersley, Robin. 2007. "Ecological Intervention: Prospects and Limits." *Ethics & International Affairs* 21, no. 3: 293–316.

1855 Treaty Authority. 2019. "Chippewa Establish *Rights of Manoomin* on White Earth Reservation and throughout 1855 Ceded Territory." Press release, January 11. https://healingmnstories.files.wordpress.com.

Elkin, A. P. 1943. *The Australian Aborigines and How to Understand Them.* Sydney: Angus & Robertson.

Erdrich, Louise. 2017. *Future Home of the Living God.* New York: HarperCollins.

Esposito, Roberto. 2013. *Immunitas: The Protection and Negation of Life.* Cambridge, UK: Polity.

Evans, Brad, and Julian Reid. 2014. *Resilient Life: The Art of Living Dangerously.* Cambridge, UK: Polity.

Falk, Richard A. 1973. "Environmental Warfare and Ecocide: Facts, Appraisal, and Proposals." *Bulletin of Peace Proposals* 4, no. 1: 80–96.

Farmer, Paul E., Bruce Nizeye, Sara Stulac, and Salmaan Keshavjee. 2006. "Structural Violence and Clinical Medicine." *PLOS Medicine* 3, no. 10: 1686–91.

Ferreira da Silva, Denise. 2007. *Toward a Global Idea of Race.* Minneapolis: University of Minnesota Press.

Fessenden, Maris. 2016. "An Ancient Squash Dodges Extinction Thanks to the Efforts of Native Americans." *Smithsonian Magazine,* June 27.

Finneron-Burns, Elizabeth. 2023. "What's Wrong with Human Extinction?" *Canadian Journal of Philosophy* 47, nos. 2–3: 327–43.

Fishel, Stefanie, and Lauren Wilcox. 2017. "Politics of the Living Dead: Race and Exceptionalism in the Apocalypse." *Millennium* 45, no. 3: 335–55.

Fletcher, Maggie. 2003. "Dreaming: Interpretation and Representation." PhD diss., Flinders University, Adelaide.

Fontaine, Theodore. 2014. Foreword to *Colonial Genocide in Indigenous North America,* edited by Andrew Woolford, Jeff Benvenuto, and Alexander Laban Hinton, vii–x. Durham, N.C.: Duke University Press.

Foucault, Michel. 1995. *Discipline and Punishment: The Birth of the Prison.* New York: Vintage.

Foytlin, Cherri, Yudith Nieto, Kerry Lemon, and Will Wooten. 2014. "Gulf Coast Resistance and the Southern Leg of the Keystone XL Pipeline." In *A Line in the Tar Sands: Struggles for Environmental Justice,* edited by Stephen D'Arcy, Toban Black, Tony Weis, and Joshua Kahn Russell, 181–95. Toronto: Between the Lines Books.

Freyd, Jennifer J. 1997. "Violations of Power, Adaptive Blindness, and Betrayal Trauma Theory." *Feminism & Psychology* 7, no. 1: 22–32.

Fritsch, Kelly. 2017. "Toxic Pregnancies: Speculative Futures, Disabling Environments and Neoliberal Biocapital." In *Disability Studies and the Environmental Humanities: Toward an Eco-Crip Theory,* edited by Sarah Jaquette Ray and Jay Sibara, 359–80. Lincoln: University of Nebraska Press.

Fujii, K. 2012. "Towards Disability Inclusive and Responsive Disasters and Emergency Response and Management through Promoting Accessibility." Conference presentation, Building Inclusive Society and Development through Promoting ICT Accessibility: Emerging Issues and Trends, Tokyo, Japan, April 19–21.

Fukuyama, Francis. 1992. *The End of History and the Last Man.* New York: Free Press.

Galtung, Johan. 1996. *Peace by Peaceful Means.* London: SAGE.

Garcia Cano, Regina. 2015. "Cleanup Underway for Nearly 3M-Gallon Pipeline Saltwater Spill in ND." *Petoskey News-Review,* January 22. https://www.petoskeynews.com/.

Gardiner, Mary M., Leslie L. Allee, Peter M. J. Brown, John E. Losey, Helen E. Roy, and Rebecca Rice Smyth. 2012. "Lessons from Lady Beetles: Accuracy of Monitoring Data from US and UK Citizen-Science Programs." *Frontiers in Ecology and the Environment* 10, no. 9: 471–76.

Garrick, Rick. 2020. "Building Indigenous Food Sovereignty in 14 First Nations in Northern Superior Region." *Anishinabek News,* September 25. https://anishinabeknews.ca/.

Geniusz, Mary Siisip. 2015. *Plants Have So Much to Give Us, All We Have to Do Is Ask: Anishinaabe Botanical Teachings.* Minneapolis: University of Minnesota Press.

Geniusz, Wendy Makoons. 2009. *Our Knowledge Is Not Primitive.* Syracuse, New York: Syracuse University Press.

Gergan, Mabel, Sara Smith, and Pavithra Vasudevan. 2020. "Earth beyond Repair: Race and Apocalypse in Collective Imagination." *Environment and Planning D: Society and Space* 38, no. 1: 91–110.

Bibliography

Gerster, Jane. 2019. "The RCMP Was Created to Control Indigenous People. Can That Relationship Be Reset?" *Global News*, June 15. https://globalnews.ca.

Gibson, G., K. Yung, L. Chisholm, and H. Quinn with Lake Babine Nation and Nak'azdli Whut'en. 2017. *Indigenous Communities and Industrial Camps: Promoting Healthy Communities in Settings of Industrial Change*. Victoria, B.C.: The Firelight Group. https://firelight.ca/assets/publications/reports/firelight-work-camps-feb -8-2017.pdf.

Gilpin, Lyndsey. 2016. "The National Park Service Has a Big Sexual Harassment Problem." *The Atlantic*, December 15.

Ginn, Franklin, Uli Beisel, and Maan Barua. 2014. "Flourishing with Awkward Creatures: Togetherness, Vulnerability, Killing." *Environmental Humanities* 4, no. 1: 113–23.

Goldberg-Hiller, Jonathan, and Noenoe K. Silva. 2011. "Sharks and Pigs: Animating Hawaiian Sovereignty against the Anthropological Machine." *South Atlantic Quarterly* 110, no. 2: 429–47.

Goldberg-Hiller, Jonathan, and Noenoe K. Silva. 2015. "The Botany of Emergence: Kanaka Ontology and Biocolonialism in Hawai'i." *Native American and Indigenous Studies* 2, no. 2: 1–26.

Goobalathaldin [Dick Roughsey]. 1988. *The Rainbow Serpent*. Milwaukee: Gareth Stevens.

Gray, Mark Allan. 1996. "The International Crime of Ecocide." *California Western Law Journal* 26: 215–71.

Greenfield, Patrick. 2021. "Record $5bn Donation to Protect Nature Could Herald New Green Era of Giving." *The Guardian*, September 29.

Grooten, Monique, and Rosamunde Almond, eds. 2018. *Living Planet Report 2018: Aiming Higher*. Gland, Switzerland: World Wildlife Fund.

Grooten, Monique, S. Dillingh, and Tanya Petersen, eds. 2020. *Voices for a Living Planet*. Living Planet Report 2020 special edition. Gland, Switzerland: World Wildlife Fund.

Gross, Lawrence William. 2002. "The Comic Vision of Anishinaabe Culture and Religion." *American Indian Quarterly* 26, no. 3: 436–59.

Grosz, Elizabeth. 2004. *The Nick of Time: Politics, Evolution, and the Untimely*. Durham, N.C.: Duke University Press.

Grosz, Elizabeth. 2011. *Becoming Undone: Darwinian Reflections on Life, Politics, and Art*. Durham, N.C.: Duke University Press.

Guthrie, Kate. 2016. "Possums and More Possums: Is a Fur Trade the Answer?" Predator Free New Zealand, July 22. https://predatorfreenz.org/.

Habedank, Daniel. 2012. "The Trails of the Rainbow Serpent." YouTube. https://www.youtube.com.

Hageman, William. 2014. "Rare Squash Is Born Again." *Chicago Tribune*, June 22.

Hall, N., M. C. Barbosa, D. Currie, A. J. Dean, B. Head, P. S. Hill, S. Naylor, S. Reid, L. Selvey, and J. Willis. 2017. "Water, Sanitation and Hygiene in Remote Indigenous Australian Communities: A Scan of Priorities." Global Change Institute discussion paper. Water for Equity and Wellbeing series, University of Queensland, Brisbane.

Bibliography

Hall, Peter Alec. 2014. "Counter-mapping and Globalism." In *Design in the Borderlands*, edited by Eleni Kalantidou and Tony Fry, 132–50. London: Routledge.

Hanson, Robin. 2008. "Catastrophe, Social Collapse and Human Extinction." In *Global Catastrophic Risks*, edited by Nick Bostrom and Milan M. Cirkovic, 363–77. Oxford: Oxford University Press.

Hanson, Thor, Thomas M. Brooks, Gustavo A. B. Da Fonseca, Michael Hoffmann, John F. Lamoreux, Gary Machlis, Cristina G. Mittermeier, Russell A. Mittermeir, and John D. Pilgrim. 2009. "Warfare in Biodiversity Hotspots." *Conservation Geography* 23, no. 3: 578–87.

Haraway, Donna. 2008. *When Species Meet*. Minneapolis: University of Minnesota Press.

Haraway, Donna. 2015. *Staying with the Trouble*. Minneapolis: University of Minnesota Press.

Harris, Cheryl I. 1993. "Whiteness as Property." *Harvard Law Review* 106, no. 8: 1707–91.

Hatley, James. 2012. "The Virtue of Temporal Discernment: Rethinking the Extent and Coherence of the Good in a Time of Mass Species Extinction." *Environmental Philosophy* 9, no. 1: 1–22.

Head, John W. 2017. *International Law and Agroecological Husbandry: Building Legal Foundations for a New Agriculture*. London: Routledge.

Hegel, G. W. F. 2019. *The Phenomenology of Spirit*. Notre Dame, Ind.: University of Notre Dame Press.

Heise, Ursula K. 2010. "Lost Dogs, Last Birds and Listed Species: Cultures of Extinction." *Configurations* 18, nos. 1–2: 49–72.

Heise, Ursula K. 2016. *Imagining Extinction: The Cultural Meanings of Endangered Species*. Chicago: University of Chicago Press.

Helmreich, Stefan. 2009. *Alien Ocean: Anthropological Voyages in Microbial Seas*. Berkeley: University of California Press.

Higgins, Polly. 2010. *Eradicating Ecocide: Laws and Governance to Prevent the Destruction of Our Planet*. London: Shepheard-Walwyn.

Higgins, Polly, Damien Short, and Nigel South. 2013. "Protecting the Planet: Proposal for a New Law of Ecocide." *Crime, Law and Social Change* 59, no. 1: 1–18.

Homer-Dixon, Thomas. 2007. *The Upside of Down: Catastrophe, Creativity and the Renewal of Civilization*. Toronto: Vintage Canada.

Hubbard, Tasha. 2014. "Buffalo Genocide in Nineteenth-Century North America: 'Kill, Skin and Sell.'" In *Colonial Genocide in Indigenous North America*, edited by Alexander Laban Hinton, Andrew Woolford, and Jeff Benvenuto, 292–305. Durham, N.C.: Duke University Press.

Hunt, Elle. 2016. "Tasmanian Tiger Sightings: 'I Represent 3,000 People Who Have Been Told They're Nuts." *The Guardian*, November 30.

Hutching, Gerard. 2015. "Possums." *Te Ara: Encyclopedia of New Zealand*, July 1. https://teara.govt.nz.

Igoe, Jim, Katja Neves, and Dan Brockington. 2010. "A Spectacular Eco-Tour around the Historic Bloc: Theorising the Convergence of Biodiversity Conservation and Capitalist Expansion." *Antipode* 42, no. 3: 486–512.

Ingold, Tim. 2002. *The Perception of the Environment: Essays on Livelihood, Dwelling and Skill.* London: Routledge.

Inoue, Cristina, and Arlene Beth Tickner. 2016. "Many Worlds, Many Theories?" *Revista Brasileiro de Política International* 59, no. 2: 1–4.

Ipellie, Alootook. 1993. *Arctic Dreams and Nightmares.* Penticton, B.C.: Theytus.

Irigaray, Luce. 2008. *Sharing the World.* London: Continuum.

IUCN (International Union for Conservation of Nature). 2015. *No Net Loss and Net Positive Impact Approaches for Biodiversity.* Gland, Switzerland: IUCN.

IUCN (International Union for Conservation of Nature). 2020. "The IUCN Red List of Threatened Species. Version 2020–2." Accessed June 21, 2023. https://www.iucn redlist.org.

Jackson, Patrick Thaddeus. 2011. *The Conduct of Inquiry in International Relations: Philosophy of Science and Its Implications for the Study of World Politics.* London: Routledge.

Jaquette Ray, Sarah, and Jay Sibara, eds. 2017. *Disability Studies and the Environmental Humanities: Toward an Eco-Crip Theory.* Lincoln: University of Nebraska Press.

Johnston, Basil H. 2010. *The Gift of the Stars.* Neyaashiinigmiing Reserve No. 27: Kegedonce Press.

Jones, Megan S., and Jennifer Solomon. 2019. "Challenges and Supports for Women Conservation Leaders." *Conservation Science and Practice* 1, no. 6: e36.

Jørgensen, Dolly. 2017. "Endling, the Power of the Last in an Extinction-Prone World." *Environmental Philosophy* 14, no. 1: 119–38.

Judge, Sarah. 2017. "Languages of Sensing: Bringing Neurodiversity into More-than-Human Geography." *Environment and Planning D: Society and Space* 36, no. 6: 1101–19.

Kafer, Alison. 2013. *Feminist, Queer, Crip.* Indianapolis: Indiana University Press.

Kafer, Alison. 2017. "Bodies of Nature: The Environmental Politics of Disability." In *Disability Studies and the Environmental Humanities: Toward an Eco-Crip Theory,* edited by Sarah Jaquette Ray and Jay Sibara, 201–41. Lincoln: University of Nebraska Press.

Kameʻeleihiwa, Lilikalā. 1992. *Native Land and Foreign Desires: Pehea LA E Pono Ai? How Shall We Live in Harmony?* Honolulu: Bishop Museum Press. e-book.

Kaplan, Sarah. 2015. "'De-extinction' of the Woolly Mammoth: A Step Closer." *Washington Post,* April 24.

Kareiva, Peter, and Michelle Marvier. 2012. "What Is Conservation Science?" *BioScience* 62, no. 11: 962–69.

Kareiva, Peter, Michelle Marvier, and Robert Lalasz. 2012. "Conservation in the Anthropocene: Beyond Solitude and Fragility." The Breakthrough Institute, February 1. https://thebreakthrough.org.

Kaufmann, Eric. 2019. *Whiteshift: Populism, Immigration, and the Future of White Majorities.* Woodstock: Harry N. Abrams.

Kay, Kelly. 2018. "A Hostile Takeover of Nature? Placing Value in Conservation Finance." *Antipode* 50, no. 1: 164–83.

Kichwa of Sarayaku. 2018. "Declaration." *Kawshak Sacha: The Living Forest* (blog), June. https://kawsaksacha.org/.

Kickett, Everett. 1995. *The Trails of the Rainbow Serpent.* Midland, W.A., Australia: Chatham Road Publications.

Kimmerer, Robin Wall. 2013. *Braiding Sweetgrass: Indigenous Wisdom, Scientific Knowledge, and the Teachings of Plants*. Minneapolis: Milkweed.

King, Tiffany Lethabo. 2018. *The Black Shoals*. Durham, N.C.: Duke University Press.

Kirksey, Eben. 2015. *Emergent Ecologies*. Durham, N.C.: Duke University Press.

Klein, Naomi. 2014. *This Changes Everything: Capitalism vs. the Climate*. New York: Simon & Schuster.

Kohn, Eduardo. 2013. *How Forests Think*. Berkeley: University of California Press.

Kolbert, Elizabeth. 2014. *The Sixth Extinction: An Unnatural History*. London: Bloomsbury.

Koot, Stasja, Bram Büscher, and Lerato Thakholi. 2022. "The New Green Apartheid? Race, Capital and Logics of Enclosure in South Africa's Wildlife Economy." *Environment and Planning E: Nature and Space*. First published online, June 28.

Kosoy, Nicolás, and Esteve Corbera. 2010. "Payments for Ecosystem Services as Commodity Fetishism." *Ecological Economics* 69, no. 6: 1228–36.

Kovach, Margaret. 2009. *Indigenous Methodologies: Characteristics, Conversations, and Contexts*. Toronto: University of Toronto Press.

Kuokkanen, Rauna. 2007. *Reshaping the University: Responsibility, Indigenous Epistemes, and the Logic of the Gift*. Vancouver: University of British Columbia Press.

Kurki, Milja. 2020. *International Relations in a Relational Universe*. Oxford: Oxford University Press.

Kymlicka, Will. 1992. "Two Models of Pluralism and Tolerance." *Analyse & Kritik* 14, no. 1: 33–56.

Laboucan-Massimo, Melina. 2014. "Awaiting Justice: The Ceaseless Struggle of the Lubicon Cree." In *A Line in the Tar Sands: Struggles for Environmental Justice,* edited by Stephen D'Arcy, Toban Black, Tony Weis, and Joshua Kahn Russell, 113–18. Toronto: Between the Lines Books.

Ladner, Kiera K. 2014. "Political Genocide: Killing Nations through Legislation and Slow-Moving Poison." In *Colonial Genocide in Indigenous North America,* edited by Alexander Laban Hinton, Andrew Woolford, and Jeff Benvenuto, 226–45. Durham, N.C.: Duke University Press.

LaDuke, Winona. 1994. *All Our Relations: Native Struggles for Land and Life*. Boston: South End Press.

Lambertini, Marco. 2018. "A New Global Deal for Nature and People Urgently Needed." In *Living Planet Report 2018: Aiming Higher,* edited by Monique Grooten and Rosamunde Almond, 4–5. Gland, Switzerland: World Wildlife Fund.

Lamemam, Crystal. 2014. "Kihci Pikiskwewin: Speaking the Truth." In *A Line in the Tar Sands: Struggles for Environmental Justice,* edited by Stephen D'Arcy, Toban Black, Tony Weis, and Joshua Kahn Russell, 118–27. Toronto: Between the Lines Books.

Lamkin, Megan, and Arnold I. Miller. 2016. "On the Challenge of Comparing Contemporary and Deep-Time Biological-Extinction Rates." *BioScience* 66, no. 9: 785–89.

Landry, Alysa. 2017. "The Real Story of That Giant Squash: Separating Myth from Reality." *Indian Country Today,* April 21. https://ictnews.org/.

Latour, Bruno. 2016. "*Onus Orbis Terrarum*: About a Possible Shift in the Definition of Sovereignty." *Millennium Journal of International Studies* 44, no. 3: 305–20.

Leduc, Timothy B. 2010. *Climate, Culture, Change: Inuit and Western Dialogues on a Warming North*. Ottawa: University of Ottawa Press.

Leduc, Timothy B. 2016. *A Canadian Climate of Mind: Passages from Fur to Energy and Beyond*. Montreal: McGill-Queen's University Press.

Leigh, Julia. 2001. *The Hunter*. London: Faber & Faber.

Lentz, Cheyenne. 2015. "A Really Cool Squash Makes a Comeback in Wisconsin after 800 Years." Wisconsin Public Radio, October 30. https://www.wpr.org/.

Leslie, John. 1996. *The End of the World: The Science and Ethics of Human Extinction*. New York: Routledge.

Lewis, Paul. 2006. "Irwin's Death Sparks Bout of Stingray Mutilations." *The Guardian*, September 13.

Lewis, Simon L., and Mark A. Maslin. 2015. "Defining the Anthropocene." *Nature* 519:171–80.

Liboiron, Max. 2020. *Pollution Is Colonialism*. Durham, N.C.: Duke University Press.

Linnaeus, Carl. 1758. *Systema Naturae per regna tria naturae, secundum classes, ordines, genera, species, cum characteribus, differentiis, synonymis, locis*. 10th rev. ed. Holmiae [Stockholm]: Laurentius Salvius.

Linton, Jamie. 2009. *What Is Water? The History of Modern Abstraction*. Chicago: University of Chicago Press.

Locke, John. 1980. *Second Treatise of Government*. Edited by C. B. Macpherson. Cambridge, Mass.: Hackett.

Lovelock, James, and Lynn Margulis. (1974) 2010. "Atmospheric Homeostasis by and for the Biosphere: The Gaia Hypothesis." *Tellus* 26, no. 2: 2–10.

Low, Tim. 2002. *Feral Future: The Untold Story of Australia's Exotic Invaders*. Chicago: University of Chicago Press.

Madley, Benjamin. 2016. *An American Genocide: The United States and the California Indian Catastrophe, 1846–1873*. New Haven, Conn.: Yale University Press.

Malm, Andreas, and Alf Hornberg. 2014. "The Geology of Mankind? A Critique of the Anthropocene Narrative." *Anthropocene Review* 1, no. 1: 62–69.

Mandel, James T., C. Josh Donlan, and Jonathan Armstrong. 2010. "A Derivative Approach to Endangered Species Conservation." *Frontiers in Ecology and the Environment* 8, no. 1: 44–49.

Manuel, Arthur. 2017. *The Reconciliation Manifesto: Recovering the Land, Rebuilding the Economy*. Toronto: Lorimer.

Mao, Frances. 2019. "How One Heatwave Killed 'a Third' of a Bat Species in Australia." BBC, January 15. https://www.bbc.com/.

Martin, Keavy. 2011. "Rescuing Sedna: Doorslamming, Fingerslicing, and the Moral of the Story." *Canadian Review of Comparative Literature* 38, no. 2: 186–200.

Max-Planck-Gesellschaft. 2008. "Decision-Making May Be Surprisingly Unconscious Activity." *Science Daily*, April 15. https://www.sciencedaily.com.

Mazis, Glen. 2008. "The World of Wolves: Lessons about the Sacredness of the Surround, Belonging, the Silent Dialogue of Interdependence and Death, and Speciocide." *Environmental Philosophy* 5, no. 2: 69–92.

Mazzoni, Alana. 2020. "Prepare for a Bat INVASION: 250,000 Flying Foxes Are Expected to Cause Chaos in the City as They Escape Bushfire-Ravaged Areas." *Daily Mail*, January 30.

Mbembe, Achille. 2003. "Necropolitics." Translated by Libby Meintjes. *Public Culture* 15, no. 1: 11–40.

Mbembe, Achille. 2017. *Critique of Black Reason*. Durham, N.C.: Duke University Press.

McAfee, Kathleen. 1998. "Selling Nature to Save It? Biodiversity and Green Developmentalism." *Environment and Planning D: Society and Space* 17, no. 2: 133–54.

McCauley, Douglas J., Malin L. Pinsky, Stephen R. Palumbi, James A. Estes, Francis H. Joyce, and Robert R. Warner. 2015. "Marine Defaunation: Animal Loss in the Global Ocean." *Science* 347, no. 6219.

McConnell, R. G. 1910. *Geological Survey of Canada, 1891–1910*. Ottawa: Geological Survey of Canada.

McGregor, Davianna Pōmaikaiʻi. 2007. *Nā Kuaʻāina: Living Hawaiian Culture*. Honolulu: University of Hawaiʻi Press.

McGregor, Davianna Pōmaikaʻi, Paula T. Morelli, Jon K. Matsuoka, Rona Rodenhurst, Noella Kong, and Michael S. Spencer. 2003. "An Ecological Model of Native Hawaiian Well-Being." *Pacific Health Dialog* 10, no. 2: 106–28.

McGregor, Deborah. 2005. "Traditional Ecological Knowledge: An Anishnabe Woman's Perspective." *Atlantis* 29, no. 2: 103–9.

McGuire, Anne. 2016. *War on Autism: On the Cultural Logic of Normative Violence*. Ann Arbor: University of Michigan Press.

McGuire, Tess. 2022. "New Zealand Denies Entry to Autistic Daughter of Immigrant Couple." *The Guardian*, April 25.

MCH (Ministry for Culture and Heritage). n.d. "Plant and Animal Quarantine." Accessed June 17, 2023. https://nzhistory.govt.nz.

McHugh, Susan. 2013. "'A Flash Point in Inuit Memories': Endangered Knowledges in the Mountie Sled Dog Massacre." *English Studies in Canada* 39, no. 1: 149–75.

McNeely, Jeffrey A. 2003. "Conserving Forest Biodiversity in Times of Violent Conflict." *Oryx* 37, no. 2: 142–52.

MEA (Millennium Ecosystem Assessment). n.d. "Guide to the Millennium Assessment Reports." United Nations. Accessed June 21, 2023. https://www.millenniumassessment.org/.

Meillassoux, Quentin. 2008. *After Finitude: An Essay on the Necessity of Contingency*. London: Continuum.

Merchant, Carolyn. 1983. *The Death of Nature: Women, Ecology, and the Scientific*. New York: Harper.

Milam, Erika Lorraine. 2018. "The Hunt for Human Nature: We Still Live in the Long Shadow of Man-the-Hunter: A Midcentury Theory of Human Origins Soaked in Strife and Violence." *Aeon*, November 28. https://aeon.co/.

Milburn, Richard. 2015. "Gorillas and Guerrillas: Environment and Conflict in the Democratic Republic of Congo." In *Environmental Crime and Social Conflict: Contemporary and Emerging Issues*, edited by Avi Brisman, Nigel South, and Rob White, 57–74. London: Routledge.

Million, Dian. 2014. "There Is a River in Me: Theory from Life." In *Theorizing Native*

Studies, edited by Audra Simpson and Andrea Smith, 31–42. Durham, N.C.: Duke University Press.

Mining Watch. 2017. Report to the UN Committee on the Elimination of Racial Discrimination. Toronto: Mining Watch.

Mitchell, Audra. 2010. "Peace beyond Process." *Millennium* 38, no. 3: 641–64.

Mitchell, Audra. 2014a. *International Intervention in a Secular Age: Re-enchanting Humanity?* London: Routledge.

Mitchell, Audra. 2014b. "Only Human? A Worldly Approach to Security." *Security Dialogue* 45, no. 1: 5–21.

Mitchell, Audra. 2016. "Beyond Biodiversity and Species: Problematizing." *Theory, Culture & Society* 33, no. 5: 23–42.

Mitchell, Audra. 2017a. "Decolonizing against Extinction, Part III: White Tears and Mourning." *Worldly* (blog), December 14. https://worldlyir.wordpress.com.

Mitchell, Audra. 2017b. "Is IR Going Extinct?" *European Journal of International Relations* 23, no. 1: 3–25.

Mitchell, Audra. 2018. "Sister." *Worldly* (blog), September 3. https://worldlyir.word press.com.

Mitchell, Audra. 2019a. "Congratulations, Dr. Judy Da Silva!" *Worldly* (blog), November 15. https://worldlyir.wordpress.com.

Mitchell, Audra. 2019b. "Flying Foxes, Moving Futures." *Worldly* (blog), January 31. https://worldlyir.wordpress.com.

Mitchell, Audra. 2022. "Resonant Relations: Eco-lalia, Political Ec(h)ology and Autistic Ways of Worlding." *Environment and Planning E: Nature and Space* 6, no. 2: 1229–51. https://doi.org/10.1177/25148486221108177.

Mitchell, Audra, and Aadita Chaudhury. 2020. "Worlding beyond 'the' 'End' of 'the World': White Apocalyptic Visions and BIPOC Futurisms." *International Relations* 34, no. 3, 309–32.

Mitchell, Audra, and Noah Theriault. 2020. "Extinction." In *Anthropocene Unseen: A Lexicon,* edited by Cymene Howe and Anand Pandian, 177–82. Brooklyn: Punctum Books.

Mitchell, Audra, and Zoe Todd. 2016. "Spiked: Violence, Coloniality and the Anthropocene." *Worldly* (blog), January 31. https://worldlyir.wordpress.com.

Mitzen, Jennifer. 2006. "Ontological Security in World Politics: State Identity and the Security Dilemma." *European Journal of International Relations* 12, no. 3: 341–70.

Montgomery, Cal. 2012. "Critic of the Dawn." In *Loud Hands: Autistic People, Speaking,* edited by Julia Bascom, 22–86. Washington, D.C.: Autistic Press.

Mooallem, Jon. 2013. "Who Would Kill a Monk Seal?" *New York Times,* May 8.

Moore, Jason W. 2015. *Capitalism in the Web of Life: Ecology and the Accumulation of Capital.* London: Verso.

Moore, Tony. 2016. "Vanished Bat Colonies Show Up in Brisbane." *Brisbane Times,* July 14. https://www.brisbanetimes.com.

Morelli, Steve, Gary Williams, and Dallas Walker. 2016. *Gumbaynggirr Yluldarla Jandaygam: Gumbayngirr Dreaming Story Collection.* Nambucca Heads, Australia: Muurrbay Aboriginal Language and Cultural Co-operative.

Moreton-Robinson, Aileen. 2015. *The White Possessive: Property, Power, and Indigenous Sovereignty.* Minneapolis: University of Minnesota Press. e-book.

Morton, Timothy. 2013. *Hyper-Objects.* Minneapolis: University of Minnesota Press.

MPI (Ministry for Primary Industries). 2016. "Biosecurity 2025: Direction Statement for New Zealand's Biosecurity System." https://www.mpi.govt.nz.

MPI (Ministry for Primary Industries). 2019. "Biosecurity Act Overhaul: Frequently Asked Questions." July 19. https://www.mpi.govt.nz.

Murphy, Michelle. 2017. "Alterlife and Decolonial Chemical Relations." *Cultural Anthropology* 32, no. 4: 494–503.

Nagy, Kelsi, and Phillip David Johnson, eds. 2013. *Trash Animals: How We Live with Nature's Filthy, Feral, Invasive, and Unwanted Species.* Minneapolis: University of Minnesota Press.

Nancy, Jean-Luc. 2000. *Being Singular Plural.* Stanford, Calif.: Stanford University Press.

Nelson, Melissa K. 2013. "The Hydromythology of the Anishinaabeg: Will Mishipizhu Survive Climate Change, or Is He Creating It?" In *Centering Anishinaabeg Studies: Understanding the World through Stories,* edited by Jill Doerfler, Niigaanwewidam James Sinclair, and Heidi Kiiwetinepinesiik Stark, 213–33. Lansing: Michigan State University Press.

Nelson, Melissa K. 2017. "Getting Dirty: The Eco-Eroticism of Women in Indigenous Oral Literatures." In *Critically Sovereign,* edited by Joanne Barker, 229–60. Durham, N.C.: Duke University Press.

Newitz, Annalee. 2013. *Scatter, Adapt, and Remember: How Humans Will Survive a Mass Extinction.* New York: Penguin Books.

Nicholls, Christine Judith. 2014. "'Dreamtime' and 'the Dreaming': An Introduction." *The Conversation,* January 22. https://theconversation.com.

Nixon, Rob. 2011. *Slow Violence and the Environmentalism of the Poor.* Cambridge, Mass.: Harvard University Press.

Norberg, Jon, James Wilson, Brian Walker, and Elinor Ostrom. 2008. "Diversity and Resilience of Social-Ecological Systems." In *Complexity Theory for a Sustainable Future,* edited by Jon Norberg and Graeme S. Cumming, 46–79. New York: Columbia University Press.

Northern Land Council. 2018. "The Rainbow Serpent." December 13. https://www.nlc.org.au.

Noss, Reed F. 1990. "Indicators for Monitoring Biodiversity: A Hierarchical Approach." *Conservation Biology* 4, no. 4: 355–65.

Nuwer, Rachel. 2017. "How Western Civilization Could Collapse." BBC, April 18. https://www.bbc.com/.

NWLC (National Women's Law Center) / AWAN (Autistic Women's and Nonbinary Network). 2021. *Forced Sterilization of Disabled People in the United States.* Washington, D.C.: NWLC/AWAN.

NYSHN (Native Youth Sexual Health Network). 2016. "Violence on the Land, Violence on Our Bodies: Building an Indigenous Response to Environmental Violence." http://landbodydefense.org.

Oliveira, Katrina-Ann R. Kapāʻanaokalāokeola Nākoa. 2014. *Ancestral Places: Understanding Kanaka Geographies*. Corvallis: Oregon State University Press.

Oliveira, Katrina-Ann R. Kapāʻanaokalāokeola Nākoa, and Erin Kahunawaikaʻala Wright, eds. 2015. *Kanaka ʻŌiwi Methodologies: MoʻOlelo and Metaphor*. Honolulu: University of Hawaiʻi Press.

Oreskes, Naomi, and Erik M. Conway. 2014. *The Collapse of Western Civilization: A View from the Future*. New York: Columbia University Press.

Parker, Wendy Jane. 2015. "How a Silly Old Man's Squash Can Reawaken Taste for Traditional Indigenous Foods." CBC News. Accessed November 5, 2023. https://www.cbc.ca/news/canada/manitoba/how-a-silly-old-man-s-squash-can-reawaken-taste-for-traditional-indigenous-foods-1.4835556.

Parks Canada. n.d. "Guiding Principles." Parks Canada Guiding Principles and Operational Policies. Accessed May 2, 2023. https://parks.canada.ca.

Pawliczek, J., and S. Sullivan. 2011. "Conservation and Concealment in SpeciesBanking.com, USA: An Analysis of Neoliberal Performance in the Species Offsetting Industry." *Environmental Conservation* 38, no. 4: 435–44.

Pellow, David N. 2016. "Toward a Critical Environmental Justice Studies: Black Lives Matter as an Environmental Justice Challenge." *Dubois Review* 13, no. 2: 221–36.

Piepzna-Samarasinha, Leah Lakshmi. 2018. *Care Work: Dreaming Disability Justice*. Vancouver: Arsenal Pulp Press.

Piepzna-Samarasinha, Leah Lakshmi. 2023. *The Future Is Disabled*. Vancouver: Arsenal Pulp Press.

Plotnick, Roy, Felisa A. Smith, and S. Kathleen Lyons. 2016. "The Fossil Record of the Sixth Extinction." *Ecology Letters* 19, no. 5: 546–53.

Plumwood, Val. 2001. *Environmental Culture: The Ecological Crisis of Reason*. London: Routledge.

Povinelli, Elizabeth A. 1995. "Do Rocks Listen? The Cultural Politics of Apprehending Australian Aboriginal Labor." *American Anthropologist* 97, no. 3: 505–18.

Povinelli, Elizabeth A. 2016. *Geontologies: A Requiem to Late Liberalism*. Durham, N.C.: Duke University Press.

Powell, Christopher. 2007. "What Do Genocides Kill? A Relational Conception of Genocide." *Journal of Genocide Research* 9, no. 4: 227–47.

Pulido, Laura. 2000. "Re-thinking Environmental Racism: White Privilege and Urban Development in Southern California." *Annals of the Association of American Geographers* 90, no. 1: 12–40.

Pulido, Laura. 2017. "Geographies of Race and Ethnicity II: Environmental Racism, Racial Capitalism and State-Sanctioned Violence." *Progress in Human Geography* 41, no. 4: 524–33.

Puniwai, Noelani. 2020. "Pua ka Wiliwili, Nanahu ka Manō: Understanding Sharks in Hawaiian Culture." *Human Biology Open Access Pre-Prints*, 11–17.

Puniwai, Noelani, Steven A. Gray, Christopher A. Lepczyk, and Craig Severance. 2016. "Mapping Ocean Currents through Human Observations: Insights from Hilo Bay, Hawaiʻi." *Human Ecology* 44, no. 3: 365–74.

Purvis, Andy, Kate E. Jones, and Georgina M. Mace. 2000. "Extinction." *BioEssays* 22, no. 12: 1123–33.

QTC (Qikiqtani Truth Commission). 2013a. *Analysis of the RCMP Sled Dog Report.* Toronto: Inhabit Media.

QTC (Qikiqtani Truth Commission). 2013b. *Nuutauniq: Moves in Inuit Life.* Toronto: Inhabit Media.

QTC (Qikiqtani Truth Commission). 2013c. *QTC Final Report: Achieving Saimaqatigiingniq.* Toronto: Inhabit Media.

Quinn, Sandra C., and Michele P. Andrasik. 2021. "Addressing Vaccine Hesitancy in BIPOC Communities—Toward Trustworthiness, Partnership and Reciprocity." *New England Journal of Medicine* 385, no. 2: 97–100.

Real People's Media. 2020. "Letter to the Queen from the Sha'tekarihwate Family of the Mohawk Nation, Turtle Clan." February 16. https://realpeoples.media/.

Rees, Martin. 2003. *Our Final Hour: A Scientist's Warning.* New York: Basic Books.

Régnier, Claire, Guillaume Achas, Amaury Lambert, Robert H. Cowei, Philippe Couchet, and Benoit Fontaine. 2015. "Mass Extinction in Poorly Known Taxa." *PNAS* 112, no. 25: 7761–66.

Reo, Nicholas James, and Angela K. Parker. 2013. "Re-thinking Colonialism to Prepare for the Impacts of Rapid Environmental Change." *Climatic Change* 120, no. 3: 671–82.

Republic of Ecuador. 2008. *Constitución Política de la República del Ecuador.*

Revive & Restore. n.d. "Woolly Mammoth Revival." Accessed June 21, 2023. https://reviverestore.org.

Ricciardi, Anthony, and Jill Cohen. 2007. "The Invasiveness of an Introduced Species Does Not Predict Its Impact." *Biological Invasions* 9:309–15.

Richmond, Oliver P., and Audra Mitchell. 2011. *Hybrid Forms of Peace: From Everyday Agency to Post-Liberalism.* Basingstoke, UK: Palgrave.

Rifkin, Mark. 2017. *Beyond Settler Time: Temporal Sovereignty and Indigenous Self-Determination.* Durham, N.C.: Duke University Press.

Rincon, Paul. 2014. "Why Did Copenhagen Zoo Kill Its Giraffe?" BBC, February 10. https://www.bbc.com.

Risling-Baldy, Cutcha. 2015. "Coyote Is Not a Metaphor: On Decolonizing, (Re)claiming and (Re)naming 'Coyote.'" *Decolonization: Indigeneity, Education & Society* 4, no. 1: 1–20.

Robinson, Eden. 2017. *Son of a Trickster.* New York: Penguin Random House.

Robinson, Eden. 2018. *Trickster Drift.* Toronto: Knopf.

Rodas, Julia Miele. 2018. *Autistic Disturbances: Theorizing Autism Poetics from the DSM to Robinson Crusoe.* Ann Arbor: University of Michigan Press.

Roe, Dilys, Pavan Sukhdev, David Thoms, and Robert Munroe. 2010. *Banking on Biodiversity: A Natural Way Out of Poverty.* London: International Institute for Environment and Development.

Rolston, Holmes, III. 1985. "Duties to Endangered Species." *BioScience* 35, no. 11: 718–26.

Rose, Deborah Bird. 1992. *Dingo Make Us Human.* Cambridge: Cambridge University Press.

Rose, Deborah Bird. 2011a. "Flying Fox: Kin, Keystone, Kontaminant." In "Unloved

Others—Death of the Disregarded in the Time of Extinction," special issue, *Australian Humanities Review,* no. 50, 119–36.

Rose, Deborah Bird. 2011b. *Wild Dog Dreaming: Love and Extinction.* Charlottesville: University of Virginia Press. e-book.

Rose, Deborah Bird, Nancy Daiyi, Kathy Devereaux, Margaret Daiyi, Linda Ford, April Bright, and Sharon D'Amico. 2011. *Country of the Heart: An Australian Indigenous Homeland.* Chicago: Aboriginal Studies Press.

Rose, Deborah Bird, and Yumiko Tsumura. 2010. "Flying Fox: Kin, Keystone, Kontaminant." *Manoa* 22, no. 2: 175–90.

Salazar Parreñas, Juno. 2018. *Decolonizing Extinction: The Work of Care in Orangutan Rehabilitation.* Durham, N.C.: Duke University Press.

Sarchet, Penny, and Press Association. 2017. "Can We Grow Woolly Mammoths in the Lab? George Church Hopes So." *New Scientist,* February 16.

Secwepemc Assembly. 2017. "Women's Declaration against Kinder Morgan Man Camps." Accessed July 20, 2023. https://indigenouspeoples-sdg.org/.

SEF (Stop Ecocide Foundation). 2021. "Independent Expert Panel for the Legal Definition of Ecocide: Commentary and Core Text." June. https://www.stopecocide.earth/legal-definition.

Serres, Michel. 2011. *Malfeasance: Appropriation through Pollution.* Stanford, Calif.: Stanford University Press.

Shafaieh, Charles. 2022. "Shahidul Alam on the Majority World." *Harvard Design Magazine,* no. 50.

Shakespeare, Tom. 2010. "The Social Model of Disability." In *The Disability Studies Reader,* edited by Lennard J. Davis, 266–73. New York: Routledge.

Sharpe, Christina. 2016. *In the Wake.* Durham, N.C.: Duke University Press.

Sheridan, Joe, and Roronhiakewen "He Clears the Sky" Dan Longboat. 2006. "The Haudenosaunee Imagination and the Ecology of the Sacred." *Space and Culture* 9, no. 4: 365–81.

Shiva, Vandana. 1993. *Monocultures of the Mind: Perspectives on Biodiversity and Biotechnology.* London: Zed.

Shiva, Vandana. 2002. *Biopiracy: The Plunder of Nature and Knowledge.* Boston: South End Press.

Short, Damien. 2010. "Australia: A Continuing Genocide?" *Journal of Genocide Research* 12, nos. 1–2: 45–68.

Shotwell, Alexis. 2016. *Against Purity: Living Ethically in Compromised Times.* Minneapolis: University of Minnesota Press.

Silberman, Steve. 2015. *Neurotribes.* New York: Avery.

Silko, Leslie Marmon. 1992. *Almanac of the Dead.* New York: Penguin.

Simberloff, Daniel. 2003. "Confronting Introduced Species: A Form of Xenophobia?" *Biological Invasion* 5:179–92.

Simberloff, Daniel, and Betsy Von Holle. 1999. "Positive Interactions of Nonindigenous Species: Invasional Meltdown?" *Biological Invasions* 1:21–32.

Simmons, Kristen. 2017. "Settler Atmospherics." Society for Cultural Anthropology, November 20. https://culanth.org.

Bibliography

Simpson, Audra. 2014. *Mohawk Interruptus: Political Life across the Borders of Settler States.* Durham, N.C.: Duke University Press.

Simpson, Audra. 2016. "The State Is a Man: Theresa Spence, Loretta Saunders and the Gender of Settler Sovereignty." *Theory & Event* 19, no. 4.

Simpson, Leanne Betasamosake. 2011. *Dancing on Our Turtle's Back: Stories of Nishnaabeg Re-creation, Resurgence and New Emergence.* Winnipeg: ARP Books.

Simpson, Leanne Betasamosake. 2013. *The Gift is In the Making.* Winnipeg: Highwater Press.

Simpson, Leanne Betasamosake. 2017. *As We Have Always Done: Indigenous Freedom through Radical Resistance.* Minneapolis: University of Minnesota Press.

Simpson, Leanne Betasamosake. 2020. *Noopiming: The Cure for White Ladies.* Toronto: House of Anansi Press.

Simpson, Leanne Betasamosake, and Edna Manitowabi. 2013. "Theorizing Resurgence from within Nishnaabeg Thought." In *Centering Anishinaabeg Studies: Understanding the World through Stories,* edited by Jill Doerfler, Niigaanwewidam James Sinclair, and Heidi Kiiwetinepinesiik Stark, 279–93. Lansing: Michigan State University Press.

Singer, Peter. 1979. *Practical Ethics.* Cambridge: Cambridge University Press.

Singh, Julietta. 2018. *Unthinking Mastery: Dehumanism and Decolonial Entanglements.* Durham, N.C.: Duke University Press.

Sins Invalid. 2019. "An Unshamed Claim to Beauty in the Face of Invisibility." https://www.sinsinvalid.org.

Skjonnemand, Ursula. 2011. "The Bat Dilemma." ABC News, August 10. https://www.abc.net.au.

Skoglund, P., S. Mallick, M. C. Bortolini, N. Chennagiri, T. Hünemeier, M. L. Petzl-Erler, F. M. Salzano, N. Patterson, and D. Reich. 2015. "Genetic Evidence for Two Founding Populations of the Americas." *Nature* 525, no. 7567: 104–8.

Sloterdijk, Peter. 2016. *Spheres.* Vol. 3, *Foams: Plural Spherology.* South Pasadena, Calif.: Semiotext(e).

Smith, Linda Tuhiwai. 2008. *Decolonizing Methodologies: Research and Indigenous Peoples.* London: Zed Books.

Smith, Mick. 2011. *Against Ecological Sovereignty: Ethics, Biopolitics and Saving the Natural World.* Minneapolis: University of Minnesota Press.

Sodikoff, Genese Marie, ed. 2012. *The Anthropology of Extinction: Essays on Culture and Species Death.* Bloomington: University of Indiana Press.

Somerville, Margaret, and Tony Perkins. 2011. *Singing the Coast: Place and Identity in Australia.* Chicago: Aboriginal Studies Press.

Soulé, Michael. 1985. "What Is Conservation Biology?" *BioScience* 35, no. 11: 727–34.

Spencer, Baldwin, and F. J. Gillen. (1899) 1968. *The Native Tribes of Central Australia.* New York: Dover.

Spivak, Gayatri Chakravorty. 2003. *Death of a Discipline.* New York: Columbia University Press.

Stannard, David E. 1994. *American Holocaust: The Conquest of the New World.* Oxford: Oxford University Press.

Stanton, Gregory H. 2016. "The Ten Stages of Genocide." Genocide Watch, December 1. http://genocidewatch.net.

Steele, Brent J. 2007. *Ontological Security in International Relations: Self-Identity and the IR State.* London: Routledge.

Steffen, Will, Jacques Grinevald, Paul Crutzen, and John McNeill. 2011. "The Anthropocene: Conceptual and Historical Perspectives." *Philosophical Transactions of the Royal Society A* 369, no. 1938: 842–67.

Steffen, Will, Katherine Richardson, Johan Rockström, Hans Joachim Schellnhuber, Opha Pauline Dube, Sébastien Dutreuil, Timothy M. Lenton, and Jane Lubchenco. 2020. "The Emergence and Evolution of Earth System Science." *Nature Reviews Earth and Environment* 1:54–63.

Stengers, Isabelle. 2005. "A Cosmopolitical Proposal." In *Making Things Public: Atmospheres of Democracy,* edited by Bruno Latour and Peter Weibel, 994–1003. Cambridge, Mass.: MIT Press.

Subramaniam, Banu. 2001. "The Aliens Have Landed! Reflections on the Rhetoric of Biological Invasions." *Meridians* 2, no. 1: 26–40.

Sukhdev, Pavan, Heidi Wittmer, Christoph Schröter-Schlaack, Carsten Nesshöver, Joshua Bishop, Patrick ten Brink, Haripriya Gundimeda, Pushpam Kumar, and Ben Simmons. 2010. *The Economics of Ecosystems and Biodiversity: Mainstreaming the Economics of Nature: A Synthesis of the Approach, Conclusions and Recommendations of TEEB.* Geneva: TEEB.

Sullivan, Shannon. 2019. *White Privilege.* Cambridge, UK: Polity.

Sullivan, Sian. 2013. "Banking Nature? The Spectacular Financialisation of Environmental Conservation." *Antipode* 45, no. 1: 198–217.

Swingland, Ian R. 2001. "Biodiversity: Definition of." In *Encyclopedia of Biodiversity,* vol. 1, 377–91. San Diego: Academic Press.

Szerszynski, Bronislaw. 2012. "The End of the End of Nature: The Anthropocene and the Fate of the Human." *Oxford Literary Review* 34, no. 2: 165–84.

Tagaq, Tanya. 2018. *Split Tooth.* Toronto: Penguin Books.

Takacs, David. 1996. *The Idea of Biodiversity: Philosophies of Paradise.* Baltimore: Johns Hopkins University Press.

Tallbear, Kim. 2013. *Native American DNA: Tribal Belonging and the False Promise of Genetic Science.* Minneapolis: University of Minnesota Press.

TallBear, Kim. 2015. "Disrupting Life/Not-life: A Feminist-Indigenous Take on New Materialism and Inter-species Thinking." Dimensions of Political Ecology Keynote Address, University of Kentucky, Lexington, February 27–28. https://www.youtube.com.

TallBear, Kim. 2016. "Failed Settler Kinship, Truth and Reconciliation, and Science." Indigenous STS, University of Alberta, Edmonton, March 14. https://indigenoussts.com.

Taylor, Charles. 2007. *A Secular Age.* Cambridge, Mass.: Belknap Press of Harvard University Press.

Taylor, Dorceta. 2014. *Toxic Communities: Environmental Racism, Industrial Pollution, and Residential Mobility.* New York: New York University Press.

Taylor, Dorceta. 2016. *The Rise of the American Conservation Movement: Power, Privilege, and Environmental Protection*. Durham, N.C.: Duke University Press.

Taylor, Sunaura. 2017. *Beasts of Burden*. New York: New Press.

Tester, A. L. 1960. "Notes: Fatal Shark Attack, Oahu, Hawaii, December 13, 1958." *Pacific Science* 14, no. 2: 181–84.

Theriault, Henry C. 2010. "Genocidal Mutation and the Challenge of Definition." *Metaphilosophy* 41, no. 4: 484–524.

Thorbecke, Catherine. 2016. "Why a Previously Proposed Route for the Dakota Access Pipeline Was Rejected." ABC News, November 3. https://abcnews.go.com/.

Todd, Zoe. 2016. "An Indigenous Feminist's Take on the Ontological Turn: 'Ontology' Is Just Another Word for Colonialism." *Journal of Historical Sociology* 29, no. 1: 4–22.

Todd, Zoe. 2022. "Fossil Fuels and Fossil Kin: An Environmental Kin Study of Weaponised Fossil Kin and Alberta's So-Called 'Energy Resources Heritage.'" *Antipode*. First published online, November 8.

Tomuschat, Christian. 1996. "Draft Code of Crimes against the Peace and Security of Mankind (Part II)—Including the Draft Statute for an International Criminal Court." Extract from the *Yearbook of the International Law Commission*, vol. II. Geneva: International Law Commission.

Torres, Émile P. 2021. "Against Longtermism." Aeon, October 19. https://aeon.co.

Torres, Émile P. 2023. "AI and the Threat of 'Human Extinction': What Are the Tech-Bros Worried About? It's Not You and Me." *Salon*, June 29. https://www.salon.com.

Tsing, Anna Lowenhaupt. 1995. "Empowering Nature, or: Some Gleanings in Bee Culture." In *Naturalizing Power: Essays in Feminist Cultural Analysis*, edited by Sylvia Junko Yanagisako and Carol Lowery Delaney, 113–43. London: Routledge.

Tsing, Anna Lowenhaupt. 2005. *Friction: An Ethnography of Global Connection*. Princeton, N.J.: Princeton University Press.

Tsing, Anna Lowenhaupt. 2015. *The Mushroom at the End of the World: On the Possibility of Life in Capitalist Ruins*. Princeton, N.J.: Princeton University Press.

Tuana, Nancy. 2008. "Viscous Porosity: Witnessing Katrina." In *Material Feminisms*, edited by Stacy Alaimo and Susan Hekman, 188–213. Bloomington: University of Indiana Press.

Tuck, Eve, and K. Wayne Yang. 2012. "Decolonization Is Not a Metaphor." *Decolonization: Indigeneity, Education and Society* 1, no. 1: 1–40.

Tulloch, Ayesha I. 2020. "Improving Sex and Gender Identity Equity and Inclusion at Conservation and Ecology Conferences." *Nature Ecology and Evolution* 4:1311–20.

Tully, James, ed. 1994. *Philosophy in an Age of Pluralism: The Philosophy of Charles Taylor in Question*. Cambridge: Cambridge University Press.

Umeek [E. Richard Atleo]. 2012. *Principles of Tsawalk: An Indigenous Approach to Global Crisis*. Vancouver: University of British Columbia Press.

UN (United Nations). 1948. *Convention on the Prevention and Punishment of the Crime of Genocide*. New York: United Nations.

UN (United Nations). 1992. *Convention on Biological Diversity*. New York: United Nations.

UN (United Nations). 2003. *Millennium Ecosystem Assessment: Ecosystems and Human Well-Being.* Washington, D.C.: Island Press.

UN (United Nations). 2015. *Transforming Our World: The 2030 Agenda for Sustainable Development.* New York: United Nations.

UN (United Nations). 2019. *World Population Prospects 2019.* New York: United Nations.

UNDP (United Nations Development Program). 1994. *Human Development Report.* New York: United Nations.

UNDRIP (United Nations Declaration on the Rights of Indigenous Peoples). 2007. *United Nations Declaration on the Rights of Indigenous Peoples.* New York: United Nations.

University of Guelph. 2017. "Ontario's Chestnut Trees 'Frozen in Time,' Study Finds." August 22. https://news.uoguelph.ca.

US Water Alliance. 2019. *Closing the Water Access Gap in the United States: A National Action Plan.* Washington, D.C.: US Water Alliance.

van der Kolk, Bessel. 2015. *The Body Keeps the Score: Brain, Mind, and Body in the Healing of Trauma.* New York: Penguin Books.

van Dooren, Thom. 2014. *Flightways: Life and Loss at the Edge of Extinction.* New York: Columbia University Press.

van Dooren, Thom, and Deborah Bird Rose. 2016. "Lively Ethnography: Storying Animist Worlds." *Environmental Humanities* 8, no. 1: 77–94.

Veracini, Lorenzo. 2010. *Settler Colonialism: A Theoretical Overview.* London: Palgrave Macmillan.

Viveiros de Castro, Eduardo. 2012. *Cosmologial Perspectivism in Amazonia and Elsewhere.* Manchester: HAU Network of Ethnographic Theory.

Vizenor, Gerald. 1994. *Manifest Manners: Narratives on Postindian Survivance.* Lincoln: University of Nebraska Press.

Vizenor, Gerald. 1998. *Fugitive Poses: Native American Scenes of Absence and Presence.* Lincoln: University of Nebraska Press.

Vizenor, Gerald. 2015. "The Unmissable: Transmotion in Native Stories and Literature." *Transmotion* 1, no. 1.

Voyles, Traci Brynne. 2015. *Wastelanding: Legacies of Uranium Mining in Navajo Country.* Minneapolis: University of Minnesota Press.

Waldau, Paul. 2001. *The Specter of Speciesism: Buddhist and Christian Views of Animals.* Oxford: Oxford University Press.

Walia, Harsha. 2014. "Migrant Justice and the Tar Sands Industry." In *A Line in the Tar Sands: Struggles for Environmental Justice,* edited by Stephen D'Arcy, Toban Black, Tony Weis, and Joshua Kahn Russell, 84–91. Toronto: Between the Lines Books.

Walker, Nick. 2021. *Neuroqueer Heresies: Notes on the Neurodiversity Paradigm, Autistic Empowerment and Postnormal Possibilities.* Fort Worth: Autonomous Press.

Wallace-Wells, David. 2019. *The Uninhabitable Earth: Life after Warming.* New York: Random House.

Ward, Peter. 2009. *The Medea Hypothesis: Is Life on Earth Ultimately Self-Destructive?* Princeton, N.J.: Princeton University Press.

Watt-Cloutier, Sheila. 2015. *The Right to Be Cold.* New York: Allen Lane.

Watts, Vanessa. 2013. "Indigenous Place-Thought and Agency amongst Humans and Nonhumans (First Woman and Sky Woman Go on a European World Tour!)." *Decolonization: Indigeneity, Education and Society* 2, no. 1: 20–34.

Watts, Vanessa. 2016. "Smudge This: Assimilation, State-Favoured Communities and the Denial of Indigenous Spiritual Lives." *Journal of Child, Youth and Family Studies* 7, no. 1: 148–70.

Weber, Bob. 2019. "Increase Wolf Cull, Pen Pregnant Cows to Save Endangered Caribou: Study." CBC News, August 5. https://www.cbc.ca.

Weisman, Alan. 2008. *The World without Us.* London: Virgin Books.

Weisman, Alan, 2013. *Countdown: Our Last, Best Hope for a Future on Earth?* New York: Little, Brown.

West, Paige. 2004. *Conservation Is Our Government Now: The Politics of Ecology in Papua New Guinea.* Durham, N.C.: Duke University Press.

West, Paige. 2016. *Dispossession and the Environment: Rhetoric and Inequality in Papua New Guinea.* New York: Columbia University Press.

Wetherbee, B. M., C. G. Lowe, and G. L. Crow. 1994. "A Review of Shark Control in Hawaii with Recommendations for Future Research." *Pacific Science* 48, no. 2: 95–115.

Whyte, Kyle Powys. 2016. "Our Ancestors' Dystopia Now: Indigenous Conservation and the Anthropocene." In *The Routledge Companion to the Environmental Humanities,* edited by Ursula K. Heise, Jon Christensen, and Michelle Nieman, 206–15. New York: Routledge.

Whyte, Kyle Powys. 2017a. "Indigenous Climate Change Studies: Indigenizing Futures, Decolonizing the Anthropocene." *English Language Notes* 55, nos. 1–2: 153–62.

Whyte, Kyle Powys. 2017b. "The Roles for Indigenous Peoples in Anthropocene Dialogues: Some Critical Notes and a Question." *Inhabiting the Anthropocene* (blog), January 25. https://inhabitingtheanthropocene.com.

Whyte, Kyle Powys. 2019. Lecture delivered at the Balsillie School of International Affairs, Waterloo, Ontario, Canada, February 10.

Wiebe, Sarah Marie. 2016. *Everyday Exposure.* Vancouver: University of British Columbia Press.

Wildcat, Matthew. 2015. "Fearing Social and Cultural Death: Genocide and Elimination in Settler Colonial Canada—an Indigenous Perspective." *Journal of Genocide Research* 17, no. 4: 391–409.

Wilkins, John S. 2009. *Species: A History of the Idea.* Berkeley: University of California Press.

Wilson, Edward O., ed. 1989. *Biodiversity.* Washington, D.C.: National Academy of Sciences.

Wilson, Edward O. 2002. *The Future of Life.* London: Abacus.

Wilson, Edward O. 2004. *On Human Nature.* Cambridge, Mass.: Harvard University Press.

Wilson, Edward O. 2016. *Half-Earth: Our Planet's Fight for Life.* New York: Liveright.

Wolfe, Patrick. 1999. *Settler Colonialism and the Transformation of Anthropology.* London: Bloomsbury.

Wolfe, Patrick. 2006. "Settler Colonialism and the Elimination of the Native." *Journal of Genocide Research* 8, no. 4: 387–409.

Woolford, Andrew. 2009. "Ontological Destruction: Genocide and Canadian Aboriginal Peoples." *Genocide Studies and Prevention: An International Journal* 4, no. 1: 81–97.

Wright, Alexis. 2015. *The Swan Book.* London: Constable and Robinson.

Wright, Melissa. 2006. *Disposable Women and Other Myths of Global Capitalism.* New York: Routledge.

WWF (Worldwide Fund for Nature). 2016. *Living Planet Report 2016.* London: WWF.

Wynter, Sylvia. 2003. "Unsettling the Coloniality of Being/Power/Truth/Freedom: Towards the Human, after Man, Its Overrepresentation—An Argument." *New Centennial Review* 3, no. 3: 257–337.

Yergeau, Melanie Remy. 2017. *Authoring Autism: On Rhetoric and Neurological Queerness.* Durham, N.C.: Duke University Press.

Yusoff, Kathryn. 2011. "Aesthetics of Loss: Biodiversity, Banal Violence and Biotic Subjects." *Transactions of the Institute of British Geographers* 37, no. 4: 578–92.

Yusoff, Kathryn. 2018. *A Billion Black Anthropocenes.* Minneapolis: University of Minnesota Press.

Zalasiewicz, Jan. 2008. *The Earth after Us.* Oxford: Oxford University Press.

Index

abiotic, 62–63, 74, 80, 83–85, 89, 291

ableism, 2, 19, 28, 46, 52, 97, 102, 105–8, 117, 136, 198–200, 204, 207, 277, 280, 292–93, 297

Aboriginal and Torres Strait Islander communities, 78, 81, 127, 195, 221, 244, 249–50

abstraction, in the measurement of biodiversity, 64, 73, 77, 142, 291

agency, 31, 44, 85, 135, 168, 203, 226, 242, 244, 257, 260, 266–67, 274, 276, 290; nonhuman, 13, 17, 23, 41, 73, 291

Akule, story of, 14–17, 81

Almanac of the Dead, 245, 250, 257, 261, 263, 268, 273

Anishinaabe law, 12–13, 18, 88, 114, 118, 169

Anthropocene, discourses of the, 11, 49–51, 212, 226, 264

Aotearoa/New Zealand, and biosecurity laws, 120, 136–39, 141, 235

apocalyptic narratives, 3, 5–6, 18, 242, 245, 247, 249, 255, 257, 260–61, 263–66, 268–69, 275, 279; in conservation, 30, 167, 193, 197–200, 212, 221, 224–25, 230, 235, 237–39, 242, 245, 285–87, 289, 292, 300, 302. *See also* existential risk

Australia, 21, 56, 69, 77–81, 91–92, 103–4, 109, 127, 138, 140–41, 152, 158–59,

161–62, 184, 194, 207, 221–22, 245–46, 250–52, 267, 269

Arctic, the, 14, 53, 107, 118, 176, 178

background rate of extinction, 42

Barnosky, Anthony, 5–6, 36, 200–201, 208, 221, 225

Bawaka Country, 59–60, 73

being. *See* ontology

beings, definition of, 23

billionaires, 68; conservation and, 30–31, 61, 299, 302

biodiversity, 1–2, 5, 8–11, 22, 27–29, 46, 54, 58, 60–76, 85, 90, 93–94, 95, 97, 116, 132–33, 138, 142, 164, 170, 214, 218, 220–25, 228–30, 235, 237, 286, 288–91, 298, 301; and capital, 2, 9–10, 29–30, 69–70, 75–76, 142, 144, 150, 154, 214, 297–98, 303; definitions of, 8–11, 60; and homogeneity, 48, 60–69, 94, 142, 28

biodiversity banking, 70

(bio)plurality, 27, 29–31, 61, 76–77, 82–83, 93–97, 99, 101, 108, 112, 115–16, 118–19, 122–24, 133, 142, 144, 155, 160–61, 164–65, 172–74, 187, 190, 192–93, 198, 206, 224, 239, 242–43, 245, 280, 286, 288, 290–94, 296–98, 301, 303–4; definition of, 29, 61, 76–77, 83

362 *Index*

(bio)pluralization, 29, 31, 100–101, 108, 129, 152, 154, 164, 198, 239, 243, 267, 293, 295, 297

biopolitics, 37, 246. *See also* life, management of

bioprospecting, 8

biosecurity, 29, 122, 133–41, 150, 235, 304

biotic, 40, 62, 74, 83–84, 291

BIPOC futurisms, 243

Black Oak savanna, 41, 46, 55, 65

breeding programs, 38–39, 62, 111, 143–44, 155. See also *ex situ* conservation

buffalo, as subjects of genocide, 128, 160, 187–91, 264; as revenants, 58, 264, 273–74, 276

Canada, 132, 222, 281; and colonization, 72, 104, 121, 149, 178–79; and conflicts with Indigenous peoples, 121, 178

climate change, 11, 14, 25, 62, 97, 102, 107, 117, 128, 139, 154, 203, 224, 245, 259, 260, 284, 302

co-constitution, 2, 29, 76–77, 81, 84, 95, 100–02, 115, 134, 164, 174, 185, 191

cohabitats and cohabitation, 29, 96–97, 102, 104–5, 107–8, 112–13, 115–18, 129, 131, 133, 141–43, 148–49, 151–52, 164, 167, 169, 172, 176, 193, 216, 242, 251–52, 263–64, 269–70, 274–76, 278, 285–86, 288, 291–92, 294–97, 301, 303–4

co-intelligence, 86

colonization, 19, 41, 43, 46, 87, 103, 107, 170, 257, 264, 280; and academic research, 16–22; and biosecurity, 124, 130–31, 154; and conservation, 198–200, 211, 235, 237

conservation, 14–15, 46, 60, 69, 91, 286, 308; apocalyptic, 197–239, 242, 250, 268, 285–86, 300, 324–28; and biodiversity for, 46, 60, 62–63, 69–71, 74, 93–94, 97, 133–34, 139, 141–42, 154, 218, 221, 223, 288–305; and colonization, 7, 170, 186–87, 198–200, 211, 232, 235, 237, 250, 289; criticism, critiques of, 2–12,

87, 93–94, 97–98, 110–11, 122, 143, 242–43, 245, 288–305; and extinction, 41, 48; and financial models of, 69–70, 75, 139, 144, 149–51, 153–55, 169, 214, 289, 292, 301–3, 313, 321; history of, 1–5, 7–12, 71–72, 136; idea of redundancy and substitution in, 66–67, 69–70; role of zoos in, 38

continuity, 24, 36, 38, 40, 53, 73–74, 84–85, 91–92, 95, 100, 104, 112, 116, 118, 128, 131, 155, 203, 264–65, 285, 287, 296, 301

Convention on Biological Diversity (UN CBD), 8, 72, 167

corporations, 10, 69, 105–6, 112–15, 117, 146, 166, 233, 299

cosmology, 37, 44, 58; cosmologies, 56–57

cosmovision and cosmovisions, 15, 17, 22, 54–56, 58, 71, 83, 85, 93, 125, 164, 172–73, 228, 244, 273; Indigenous, 76, 84, 125, 184, 263–64

Country, in Aboriginal and Torres Strait Islander cultures, 36, 56–57, 59–60, 76–77, 79–82, 88, 94, 152–53, 160, 253, 255, 265, 269–70, 272–73, 277, 279

death, as extinction, 23, 28, 35–38, 40–42, 54–55, 58, 91, 288. *See also* extinction

de-extinction, 18, 39–40. *See also* extinction

difference, production of, 7, 29, 59–66, 72, 76–78, 82–83, 90, 93–94, 100, 116, 142, 164, 288, 290

dingos, 81, 162, 175

disability, 6–7, 29, 46, 51, 99, 101–2, 105–6, 117, 164, 201, 203, 205, 244, 274, 295, 297

dissimilarity, 60, 64, 66, 94

Dreamings, 44, 76–79, 81–82, 99, 152–53

Earth / earth, 1–6, 8, 11, 25–27, 29, 33–34, 43–44, 48–49, 55, 57, 62–63, 68–69, 72, 75, 79, 82–84, 91, 96, 100, 101, 108, 115, 137, 153, 172–73, 197–99, 202–3, 205, 211, 216, 218–19, 222, 224–25, 228–30, 233,

235, 237–38, 245–46, 250, 257, 259, 262–66, 273–75, 277–80, 281, 287–90, 294–95, 299, 302, 305

earth/body violence, 27, 29, 96–113, 116–18, 123, 131, 143, 295–96

ecocide, 30, 98, 160–61, 193, 323; critique of, 160–61, 169–73, 193; theories of, 165–67

ecosystem services, 48, 68, 73–75, 90

eliminative violence, 27–28, 30, 44–45, 47, 155, 159–60, 162, 165, 174–76, 182–83, 187–88, 191–93, 224, 243, 303–5

endling, 35–36, 38, 42, 91, 279

environmental ableism, 97, 102, 105–7, 117. *See also* ableism

environmental racism, 97, 102–5, 200. *See also* racism

eroticism, 24, 29, 100, 108, 112, 287, 295–96

ethics, 20, 25–26, 58, 169, 204, 227, 270, 279, 287, 294

eugenics and eugenicists, 28, 51, 162, 193, 204, 210, 226, 228, 245, 249, 264, 280, 288, 296

euthanasia and euthanize, 38–39, 64

Eurocentric and Eurocentrism, 8, 19, 22, 28, 37, 48, 55, 71, 79, 100, 108, 114, 125–26, 129, 134, 136, 160, 169, 171, 173, 184–85, 191–92, 198–99, 207, 213–14, 216, 221, 226, 230, 233, 252, 261, 286, 293, 296, 303

evental logics, 35, 53, 58

evolution, 24, 91, 241, 247, 252, 261; normative accounts of, 71–74, 208, 226–28; as an object of protection, 7, 60, 69, 71–74, 90, 226–28

existential risk, 7, 30, 197–98, 204, 214

ex situ conservation, 8, 38, 155. *See also* conservation

extant state, 29, 41–43, 49, 53–57, 91–92, 226, 253, 262, 269, 276, 285, 291. *See also* ontology

external difference, 29, 60, 63, 76–77, 82, 94, 164, 288

extinction: alternative, non-Western, non-nihilistic, refusal narratives of,

12–18, 19, 50–53, 260–66, 275–76, 279–80; biodiversity and, 2, 9–10, 62–76; (bio)plurality and, 76–82, 93–97; conservation and, 2–3, 7–12; contesting mainstream/theories of, 1–19, 40–41, 87–88, 288–90; de-, 18, 39–44; earth/body violence and, 295–96, 315; environmental humanities and, 308–10; environmental violence and, 102–5; extirpation and, 69, 307; extractive relations and, 153–55; the fight against, 3, 50–53, 297–303, 304–5; functional, 41; genocide and, 44–48, 161–65, 174–93, 303; human, 2, 6, 7, 50–53, 197–239, 325–26; invasive states (colonialism) and, 122–23, 126, 128, 137, 155; love in the face of, 304–5; mass extinction, 5, 33–58, 311; mass extinction events, 48–54; mass extinction thresholds, 42–48; mega-death and, 35–41; near-, 205–6; non-human, 174–90; Gete Okosomin and, 281–88; ontology and, 54–58; pluralizations and, 88–93; reframing as violence, earth/body violence, eliminative violence, patterns of violence and, 3, 44–48, 50–53, 97–99, 95–119, 174–90, 290–94, 303, 304, 307; revenant ecologies and, 241–80; theories of, two stories of, 1–18; Western scientific definition of, 2, 4–12, 33–35, 264, 275; E. O. Wilson's *Half-Earth* and, 224–38

extirpation, 5, 15, 18, 55, 69, 141, 291. *See also* extinction

extraction, 1, 10, 30, 61, 122–23, 127, 142–47, 149–55, 219, 222, 251, 297, 299; earth/body violence and, 103, 106, 110, 134; extinction and, 30, 123, 155, 304. *See also* extinction

flying foxes, 158–62, 193–94

fossil record, 5, 42–43, 56, 261

Four Horsemen, the, 4

Fruit Bats (Lin Onus), 194

364   *Index*

function, in ecology, 1, 37, 41, 66–67, 69, 216, 286

future generations, 12, 56, 84, 203, 244, 260, 278, 284

gender, 6, 14, 16, 19, 26, 28–30, 49–50, 81, 91, 97, 99, 101–2, 108–12, 115–18, 126, 135, 143, 148, 198, 207, 229, 237, 244, 249, 252, 274, 280, 285, 287, 289, 295–97

genetics, 8, 38–40, 52, 63–64, 72, 74, 82, 85, 91–92, 106, 117, 129, 164, 167, 176, 203–5, 210, 227, 249, 286; gene banks and, 8, 39; seed banks, 39

genocide, 28, 40, 47, 52, 101, 156, 157–95, 198, 199, 231, 268, 282, 319, 322, 323, 324, 325, 330; critical theories of, 40, 45–46, 160–64, 182–83, 311, 322; extinction and, 19, 27, 30, 40, 47, 97, 160–65, 191–95, 303–4; law and, 40, 45, 97, 160–63, 165, 168, 303–4, 311, 323; non-human, 157, 160, 163, 164, 165, 166, 168, 174–90, 258, 264, 303–4, 322

Genocide Convention, UN (United Nations Convention on the Prevention of Genocide), 161, 311

geological, 3–5, 83; conditions, 131; discourses, 311; disruption, 246; epochs, 34, 53; event(s), 5, 227; force, 80; layer, 49; nonliving, 313; periods, 311; phenomena, 311; strata, 53; temporal/time/timespan, 5, 34, 42, 44, 48, 130, 311; Western geological thought/time, 44, 48–49

geontology, frameworks, 63; geonto-power, 63, 313

Gete Okosomin, 281–87, 305

Gimi (people), 15

habitat destruction, 96–97, 101, 118, 220–21

Half-Earth (Wilson), theory in, 213, 224–26, 232–34, 298

Haudenosaunee (people), 41, 86–87, 283–84

heteronormativity, 2, 19, 28, 85, 100, 108, 115–16, 135, 267, 297

Hoof Clan, story of, 12–18, 169, 254

homogenization, 48, 61, 66, 93–94, 123, 155, 160, 243, 288, 293, 298

humanity, alternative non-universal norms of/future of, 264, 279–80, 304–5, 323; devolution of, 247–48; dominant norms of universalism, universality, 16, 22, 26, 30, 51–52, 71–72, 163–65, 198, 225–28, 248–52, 292–94, 312; erasure of inequality and, 7; "fifth crime against humanity" (ecocide), 165, 167; as protagonist of extinction/conservation narratives, 4, 6, 16, 30, 49, 50, 74, 197–213, 216, 219–24, 230–39, 288–90, 292–94, 323; as the subject of extinction, 2, 6, 30, 49, 50, 197–213, 219–24

human extinction, 2, 6–7, 30, 49, 198–200, 202, 204–10, 212–13, 218–19, 221–22, 224–26, 230, 236, 238–39, 241–42, 245, 289. *See also* existential risk; extinction

human security, 9–10, 167

Indigenous futurisms, 27, 243

Indigenous knowledge, 18–19, 21, 127, 243; research methods, 20; systems, 11, 20, 85, 87, 161, 173, 217

Indigenous legal orders, political systems, 3, 8, 122, 134–35, 160–61, 164, 174–93, 324; attempts to undermine, 126–27, 152–53

in situ conservation, 8

interchangeability, logics of, 63–64

internal difference, plurality, 76, 82, 94, 164, 172, 288, 293

International Union for Conservation of Nature (IUCN), 8–9, 69–70, 252, 313

Inuit, knowledge systems, 86, 160; and Qimmit, 175–83, 191–92, 324; stories about extinction, 13–14

Index

invasive species, 4, 97, 122–24, 320; invasive state(s) and, 133–42
irreversibility, of extinction, 18, 46, 190, 219, 238, 260–66

Kānaka Maoli (people); cosmos/ cosmovisions of, 57–58, 84–85, 309
killing, direct, 4, 97, 183
Kumulipo, 57, 84

land return, 231, 244; global, 297–303
land-sparing conservation, 216, 224, 298, 333
law, 158, 272, 287, 315; ancestral, 278; Anishinaabe, 324; Canadian, 179, 320; community, 157; Country, 277; Dreamings and, 78; enforcement, 110; Eurocentric, 8, 169, 191–92, 303; federal, 121; Indigenous, 8; international, 97, 112, 121, 124, 160, 167, 169, 171–72, 174, 303, 315, 324; Inuit, 179; national, 324; Nêhiyaw, 191; provincial, 121; rule of, 121; Secwepemc, 115; stories, 270; tribal, 324; Westphalian, 160, 187
life-form(s), 7, 16–18, 23–25, 30, 37–40, 44, 54–55, 60, 65, 67, 81–82, 92, 97, 128–29, 131, 135, 141–43, 150, 153, 161, 163, 165, 174–75, 179, 186–88, 208, 268, 272, 275, 278, 282, 285–86, 292, 295–97, 301, 303, 311, 322
life, management of, 4, 8, 10, 48, 140, 158, 220
Living Planet Report(s) (LPR(s)), 154, 197, 213–24, 237. *See also* Worldwide Fund for Nature (WWF)
Lonesome George, 35, 38

māno, 160, 184–87, 189, 191. *See also* shark, culls in Hawai'i
Marius the Giraffe, 38–39, 63, 310
mass extinction, 5, 33–58, 311; events, 48–54; thresholds, 42–48. *See also* extinction

massification, political theory of, 47–48, 68, 292
Marrow Thieves, The (Dimaline), 212, 244–47, 251, 254, 256–58, 265, 268, 270, 274, 276
modeling, mathematical, 34, 154, 223–24, 291
military, 110, 138, 147, 165–66, 171, 179, 188–89, 221, 231, 249, 258, 272, 294, 297, 327, 333; *Convention on the Prohibition of Military or Any Other Hostile Use of Environmental Modification Techniques (ENMOD)*, 173

"net positive impact" (NPI), 69–70. *See also* "no net loss"
non-being, 54–58
"no net loss" (NNL), 69, 288, 321. *See also* "net positive impact"
nongovernmental organizations (NGOs), and conservation, 1, 61, 69, 150–51, 213, 299, 302, 321
nonlife, 29, 37, 62–63, 83

offsetting, biodiversity, 70
ontology, 54–58, 312–13
orangutans, 111, 155
organisms, definitions of, 23–24, 39–40, 62–63, 83

park(s), 7–8, 98, 232; national, 2, 7, 9, 35, 72, 110, 231–32, 238, 273, 302, 316; Parks Canada, 72; U.S. National Park Service, 110, 316
plesiosaurus/pliosaurus, 56–57
possum(s), 79, 140–41
private conservation, 8, 10, 39, 61, 151–52, 198, 223, 231, 288–89, 302, 333. *See also* billionaires
processes, in the context of biodiversity, 71–76
productivity, in the context of biodiversity, 71, 73, 75, 224

366   *Index*

Qimmit, 160, 175–84, 324. *See also* Qikiktani Truth Commission (QTC); sled dog massacre

Qikiktani Truth Commission (QTC), 175–83, 324. *See also* Qimmit; sled dog massacre

queer relationality, 27, 85, 100, 117–18, 243, 276, 294–96, 332

racism, 280, 292–93, 297, 309, 312, 323, 326, 329; anti-, 3; biosecurity and, 136–37; in conservation, 2; ecological, environmental, 97, 102–6, 200, 316; extractive processes and, 107; structural, 207–8, 325; and targeting for elimination, extinction, 52, 102–6, 193; in Western academia, 18–20

Rainbow Serpent, 79–82, 88, 314

redundancy, in ecology, 60, 66–70, 82, 288

refusal, refusing, 2, 14, 17, 31, 53, 92, 94, 97, 241–42, 248, 250, 260–67, 270, 272, 280, 285–86, 292, 294

relationality, 34, 76, 93, 100, 116, 154

repetition(s), 36, 66, 77, 88

reproduction, 131, 141, 278, 286; in apocalyptic conservation narratives, 235; biological, 24, 40, 85, 155, 159, 186, 189, 205, 295–96, 319; in conservation, 14; in dehumanizing and/or violent terms, 209–10, 212, 250, 295, 319; and extractive processes, 123; heteronormative ideals of, 100, 116, 296, 327–28; and the land, 84; mass, 124, 130; nonsexual, 24, 226; pluralizations and, 91, 112, 287; sexual, 38; social, 155, 159, 189; in zoos, 38–39

resources, 1–2, 8, 17, 26, 49, 74–75, 83, 85, 96, 100, 107, 116, 127, 129, 134–35, 139, 145, 152–53, 162, 173–75, 182, 192, 204, 212, 215, 219, 221, 223, 226, 259, 280, 292, 294, 296, 299–300, 302

responsibility, vii, 82, 84, 115, 124, 152, 173, 202, 255; distributed, 62, 166;

inequality and, 6, 17; reparations and, 301; Responsibility to Protect, 45, 168; as a white settler scholar, 16–22

restoration, 44, 69, 118, 148–50, 169, 185, 191–92, 218, 232, 264, 296, 299

resurgence, Indigenous, 3, 20, 190, 245, 268–69, 286, 309

revenance, ix, 3, 18, 31, 40, 190, 239, 241–80, 285, 291–92, 299, 301, 305, 328–29

revenant ecologies, 30–31, 241–80, 286

reversal, fear of, 30, 219, 247

Robinson, Eden, 33, 56, 258, 275

Rose, Deborah Bird, 11, 36, 43, 79, 81–82, 129, 132, 141, 160–63, 309–10, 315

Royal Canadian Mounted Police (RCMP) (formerly North West Mounted Police), 121–22, 176, 178–79, 182, 317, 324

Sedna, story of, 13–14, 16–17, 81, 118, 308, 309

seedkeepers, seed libraries, 281–82, 285

settler colonialism, 51, 105, 108–9, 122–27, 129, 134, 136, 141–42, 147, 151, 155, 217, 231, 297, 307, 318–19, 332; theories of, 99

sexual violence, 14, 28, 47, 102, 106, 109–13, 116, 118, 143, 193, 237, 296; land-based gendered, 102, 108–11; sexual earth / body violence, 97

shark, culls in Hawai'i, 183–87. *See also* māno

singular-plural, 82

"sixth mass extinction," 1–7, 42, 49, 225, 325. *See also* mass extinction

sled dog massacre, 175–83. *See also* Qimmit; Qikiktani Truth Commission (QTC)

sovereignty, colonial/settler, 123, 127, 140, 172, 178, 182, 184–87, 189, 213, 222–23, 290, 294, 297; ecological, 169; extractive, 109, 156, 223, 233, 294, 297; Indigenous, more-than-human,

182, 184–86, 189, 251, 272; over possible futures, 203, 233; state-based, state-centric, state, 8, 167, 172, 288, 297, 308

speciation, 74, 91

species, 2, 5, 9, 11, 14, 172, 183; critiques of Western conservation, scientific definition of, 6, 23, 81, 89, 91–92, 96, 114, 175, 244, 246, 268, 274–76, 291; endangered, 48, 134, 144, 166, 186; extinction of, 75, 98, 128, 137, 153, 161–62, 166, 168, 281, 291, 307, 311, 315, 321; invasive/native, 4, 97, 122–24, 133, 135–37, 141, 150, 260, 320; as measure of mass extinction, 33–36, 38–43, 45–46, 49–50, 54–55, 69; survival plans, 8, 52, 205, 211; value, future values, 154, 204; Western conservation, scientific definition of, 1, 22, 60, 63–72, 85, 87, 96, 146, 164, 166, 180, 213, 216–17, 228–29, 235–36, 238, 313, 318, 327

stories/theories, 1–18, 20, 22, 24, 27–28, 30, 80, 83, 88, 92, 118, 184, 197, 242–45, 250, 254, 262, 265, 267–68, 271, 274–76, 285, 288–90, 300, 308, 331

structural violence, 29, 31, 46, 47, 48, 52, 53, 93, 98, 99–102, 104, 105, 108, 159, 224, 236–37, 239, 242, 245, 291–92, 304

subsistence, practices of, 9, 109, 129, 132, 181, 186, 212, 308, 318, 327

substitution, logics of, 60, 66–70, 148, 153, 174

survival, 4, 7, 8, 37, 41, 86, 91–92, 95, 131, 134, 136, 149, 152, 154, 167, 184, 200, 202–3, 210, 212, 227, 233, 236–37, 244, 250–51, 254, 261, 266, 274–75, 284, 286, 296, 304, 312, 319; human, of humanity, 2, 4, 6, 200, 202, 209, 221, 225, 238, 279, 304; rates of, 209–10, 236

survivance, 52, 190, 268, 272, 285, 312

Swan Book, The (Wright), 244–46, 249, 250–56, 265, 267, 268–69, 272, 275–79

Tar Sands, Alberta, 103, 121, 146, 148–49, 169, 321

taxonomy, 60, 64–65, 82, 145

temporalities: climate change, 154, 203; deep future, 238; deep history, 49, 70, 299; deep time, 26, 79, 204, 244–45, 257, 263, 266; Eurocentric, 42–44, 50–51, 53, 73, 78–79, 89, 252, 261; of extraction, 151, 153–54; Kānaka, 184; plural, multiplicity, simultaneous, 25, 31, 46, 61, 78, 99, 175, 242, 244, 261; revenant, 260

TESCREAL, 203–06, 219, 224, 226–27, 229, 238, 32–26

time, Western, 6, 34–35, 37, 42–44, 48–54, 73, 260, 273. *See also* temporalities

threshold, definitions of extinction/thinking, 28, 34, 35, 42–47, 53, 58, 311. *See also* extinction

"total economic value" (TEV), theory of, 9–10, 66–68, 73–76, 107, 129, 134, 136, 142, 144–45, 148–51, 153, 154, 155, 169, 193, 214, 218–19, 223, 286, 288, 291, 303, 313, 321

toxic, toxicity, toxins, and toxification, 107, 116, 118, 148, 154, 246, 272, 278, 325

trauma, 29, 116, 131, 132, 143, 183, 251, 255; and bodyminds, 149; and earth/body violence, 116, 294–96; and extinction, 31; generational/intergenerational, 101, 107; and healing, 118, 264, 294–96; and land, 106; and land/body relationships, 108, 116; retraumatizing, 256; sexual, 118

Two-Spirit, 9, 126, 282; and land/body relationships, 108, 116

value, in discourses of biodiversity, 9, 10, 65–70, 73–76, 107, 123, 144, 150–51, 153–54, 214, 223, 233, 288, 291, 303, 312, 313, 321. *See also* conservation: and financial models of

variation, in ecology, 1, 64–66

water, in Indigenous knowledge systems, vii, 13–15, 21, 73–74, 80–82, 89–91, 100–101, 115, 128–29, 246, 247, 259–60, 265, 273, 276, 282–83, 317

Wet'suwet'en (peoples), the Canadian state and, 121–22, 172, 317

whiteness, 19, 125, 198–99, 212–13, 309, 316

white supremacy, 2, 162, 287

Whyte, Kyle Powys, 10, 51, 67, 154, 212, 218, 264, 331

Wilson, Edward O., 4, 18, 98, 213, 224–39, 298, 327–28

worlds, definition of, 23–27

Worldwide Fund for Nature (WWF), 5, 8, 154, 197–98, 213, 218, 224, 302, 327. See also *Living Planet Report(s) (LPR(s))*

Yolŋu, 153

zoos, 38–40, 64, 91

AUDRA MITCHELL is professor and Canada Research Chair in Global Political Ecology at the Balsillie School of International Affairs, Wilfrid Laurier University, Canada. She is author of *International Intervention in a Secular Age: Re-enchanting Humanity?* and *Lost in Transformation: Violent Peace and Peaceful Conflict in Northern Ireland* and coeditor of *Hybrid Forms of Peace: From Everyday Agency to Post-Liberalism.*

Printed and bound by CPI Group (UK) Ltd, Croydon, CR0 4YY
02/02/2025

14636610-0001